The New World Order &
THE THRONE OF THE antiCHRIST

Plate 1: *Soviet Government Delegation returning home from celebration of China's being proclaimed as a People's Republic, 1954. Here the camera captures them at Vladivostok Naval Base. Khruschev is seated in the centre, front row.*

The New World Order &
THE THRONE OF THE antiCHRIST

The Armageddon Series Part III

partially edited
from the work of American Author DES GRIFFIN

by

Robert O'Driscoll
(Canada)
&
Margarita Ivanoff-Dubrowsky
(Russia)

with
contributions by Douglas Annear and M. Nicholas Young,
University of Toronto; Michael Adir, Russia; A. Aksakov and
M. Dessoir, Germany and with the help of Patrick John Clare,
Damascus

*'It would almost seem as if the gospel of Christ and the gospel of Antichrist
were destined to originate among the same people; and that this mystic and
mysterious race had been chosen for the supreme manifestations, both of the
divine and the diabolical' - Winston Churchill, 1920.*

Toronto: The Printing Office
King Arthur Publications: Arthur, Ontario
1993

The New World Order & The Throne of the antiChrist, The Armageddon Series, Part III, was designed and typeset by Phuong Tang; photography by Tai Tang; printing by Hung and Wong Tang; under the general supervision of Wayne Tang, The Printing Office, 50 Spadina Avenue, Toronto M5V 2H8.
Order from Alexander Fraser House, Arthur, Ontario N0G 1A0 (for orders FAX 519-848-5419; for enquiries telephone 519-848-2478).

First published in, 19 February 1993
Second printing, 29 September 1993

Cover design: Petra Nyendick. The design is based on two letters of the Russian alphabet, ED. The slightly unstable throne suggests high breeding debasing itself before animal lust.

© Professor Robert O'Driscoll
© Des Griffin material, Emissary Publications
© Arrangement of Des Griffin material: Professor Robert O'Driscoll

ISBN: 0-921745-02-8

C O N T E N T S

Introduction *by Robert O'Driscoll* xiii

Acknowledgements xx

Dedication xxv

Overture *by Robert O'Driscoll* 1

I. A M E R I C A *by Des Griffin*

Selected and Edited *by*
Margarita Ivanoff-Dubrowski and Robert O'Driscoll

Introduction 5

Foundation of the Illuminati (1776) 12

Illuminati Plan for World Domination (1871) 14

International Bankers Prepare Way
    for World Conquest 17

How Rothschild Gained Control
    of British Economy 17

How Rothschild Seizes Control of France 19

Rothschild Makes Beachhead into Germany 20

Principle of Control: 'The Balance of Power' 21

Socialist Strategy for World Conquest 21

International Bankers Pursue Objective to
    Destroy United States of America 22

Illuminati Puppet in the White House 25

Modus Operandi for World Domination:
    Urban Renewal & Theatres of War 26

America is drawn into the First World War 28

Economic and Political Consequences
    of World War One 28

Setting the Scene for World War Two 31

Adolf Hitler Offers Relief 31

Hitler Comes to Power 33

Extensive American Investment in
    Pre-War Germany 35

Another Illuminati Puppet in White House 36

Winston Churchill 38

World War II: 'Blood, Toil, Tears and Sweat' 41

A War with a Pre-Determined Objective 42

America Enters World War II 44

North African Campaign...48

An Explanation is Needed 48

Lieutenant Colonel Dwight D. Eisenhower 50

Commander George Earle...52

Major Racey Jordan 58

Harry Hopkins 61

Aid Engineered to Create Russian
    Post-War Machine..62

Back-Up American Pilots for Europe 64

Atomic Secrets Passed to Russia
    from White House...65

Russia Gets U.S. Treasury Plates for Post-War 68

Why? 71

'Victory' in Europe 72

Allied Army Waits for Russia to Push West 72

Some Illuminating Facts 74

Hamburg Holocaust..74

The Dresden Massacre 75

Roosevelt and Stalin Give
    Cold Shoulder to Churchill.....................................78

Battle of the Bulge and Very Strategic Surrenders 79

The Fate of Two Million Displaced by the War 81

Another Illuminati Puppet in the White House..........84

America's Invisible Government:
    The Council on Foreign Relations 85

The United Nations: The New Babylon 87

The Korea, Vietnam, and 'Gulf' Wars 87

The Story of America: Summary 90

The Future..95

Notes to 'America' 97

II. ISRAEL *by Douglas Annear*

Introduction...103

Part I: The Story of Zionism

Zionism in Britain: World War I 103

Betrayal of the Arabs....................................109

Change in British Policy Towards Zionism:
    The Balfour Declaration (1917) 110

Aftermath of WWII: Terrorism and
    the Establishment of a Zionist State 111

The Ultimate Goal of Zionism? 119

Part II: Zionism: The Public and the Private Image

Ethnic Cleansing 122

Zionist Manipulation of 'Anti-Semitism' 123

Torture of Palestinian Political Prisoners..............127

Human Rights Violations 128

Jewish Dissent Against Zionism 129

Part III: Field Study, August-September 1992

Introduction and Methodology 131

Orthodox Judaism and Zionism 132

The Role of the Press in Israel 135

Israeli Assassination Squads and
    the Foreign Press 136

Economic and Social Conditions in Israel
    versus the West Bank 139

Interviews with Former Political Prisoners: 143

    Samir Abu-Shams 143

    Khalid Rushdie Al-Zhigal 145

    Sadedin Kharim Al-Sadi 146

    Naji 147

    Ahmad Jaber Mahammad Ibrahim 147

    Jamal Hassan 147

Deaths in Detention or as a Result
    of 'Disciplinary' Actions 150

Violation of Municipal and Habitational Rights 150

Escape from Israel 152

Zionism and World Peace? 156

List of Works Consulted 159

III. THE VATICAN

The Role of the Vatican in the New World Order and Other
Fragments *by A.Aksakov and M. Dessoir*

The New World Order: A Puppet Play
    by Alexy Kosygin 165

Fragments from the Archives 172

Jules Ochorowicz 172

King George VI 172

Viscount (Field-Marshal) Montgomery.....................174

Konrad Adenauer 174

Charles Richet 176

William Lyon MacKenzie King 176

Sir J. Stevens 179

Einar Jaeger 179

Albert Schweitzer 179

Jules Ochorowicz 180

Karl Gruber..180

Hans Driesch 181

Dr. Morelli 181

Gustave Geley 181

Jean Vincent...182

C. Krabbe 182

Oskar Fischer...182

Ihr fragt Warum? *by Annette von Droste-Huelshoff* 185

News from the Vatican Underground.......................188

IV. C A N A D A: A Spysong *by Robert O'Driscoll*

Introduction..193

Prelude 197

MM & EE 201

Marzipan...207

CSIS...215

Creation of the Soviet Union:
    A Mask for the antiChrist 225

jewpeter 233

Anatomy of the 'antiChrist' 236

Jesus Christ 244

Yell 'Sin' and Karl Jung 252

The Pacific Triangle 259

The Thinking Tank of Russia 264

A Song for All Spies 266

The Fifth Man 268

The Fifth Man, Mr Moi,
    and Chinese Intelligence 270

Fifth Man Smashes Jewish Intelligence 274

Fifth Man Pauses to get Valium 274

Fifth Man is Sentenced by his Son 275

Fifth Man Identifies 'antiChrist' 277

Red Sea Again 282

Those who are for us are for us
    those who are agin us are agin us 283

Notes for *Spysong* 283

V. RUSSIA

Part I: Michael Adir, Nikita Khruschev, and Kim Philby
by Robert O'Driscoll

Part II: The Bolshevik Revolution to
the Death of Stalin *by Des Griffin*

Russia Unprepared for First World War 307

Hundreds of Thousands Wiped Out
    in a Few Days 307

The British Crown Betrays Russia 309

Massive German Offensive Eastwards 310

'Band of Extraordinary Personalities' 311

Formation of Bolshevik Red Army 312

Jews Lead Bolshevik Revolution 313

1917-1921: Chaos and Terror 315

Churchill Acknowledges 'Conspiracy'
    Against Russia. 317

Joseph Stalin Takes Over 318

Class Distinctions Reappear 321

Twenty-One Years of Terror 324

Part III: Global Theatres of the antiChrist:
The Death of Stalin to the Present: Interview
    with Michael Adir
    by Robert O'Driscoll & Des Griffin 331

Appendices

The Play of the antiChrist: A Medieval Drama
    by Robert O'Driscoll 372

Soloviev's *Antichrist* by Nicholas Young 379

Two Impressions *by E.E.* 383

Notes on Contributors 385

Index 389

У К А З

ПРЕЗИДИУМА ВЕРХОВНОГО СОВЕТА СССР

О награждении орденом „Победа"
Маршала Советского Союза
СТАЛИНА Иосифа Виссарионовича

За исключительные заслуги в организации всех вооруженных
сил Советского Союза и умелое руководство ими в Великой
Отечественной войне, закончившейся полной победой над гитлеровской Германией, наградить

ОРДЕНОМ „ПОБЕДА"

Маршала Советского Союза СТАЛИНА Иосифа Виссарионовича.

Председатель Президиума Верховного Совета СССР М. КАЛИНИН.
Секретарь Президиума Верховного Совета СССР А. ГОРКИН.

Москва, Кремль, 26 июня 1945 года.

У К А З

ПРЕЗИДИУМА ВЕРХОВНОГО СОВЕТА СССР

О присвоении звания
Героя Советского Союза
СТАЛИНУ Иосифу Виссарионовичу

Возглавившему Красную Армию в тяжелые дни защиты нашей
Родины и её столицы Москвы, с исключительным мужеством
и решительностью руководившему борьбой с гитлеровской
Германией, Маршалу Советского Союза СТАЛИНУ Иосифу
Виссарионовичу присвоить звание ГЕРОЯ СОВЕТСКОГО СОЮЗА
с вручением ордена ЛЕНИНА и медали „ЗОЛОТАЯ ЗВЕЗДА".

Председатель Президиума Верховного Совета СССР М. КАЛИНИН.
Секретарь Президиума Верховного Совета СССР А. ГОРКИН.

Москва, Кремль, 26 июня 1945 года.

Plate 2: *Mikhail Kalinin, Chairman of the Presidium of the Supreme Soviet of
the Union of Soviet Socialist Republics (USSR), awards Stalin the Order of
Victory (top) and (below) makes him Hero of the Soviet Union and awards him
the Order of Lenin.*

INTRODUCTION

I

Russia, Canada, and America - next-door neighbours over the true North - hold in their land masses a kind of cowl-like covering for the skull of the earth. *The New World Order & The Throne of the antiChrist* examines the circumstances and details of three twentieth-century attempts, examating from the same source, to destroy these countries. Why?

The phrase, the New World Order (*Novus Ordo Seclorum*), is an old one with its own special meaning, but it was first used in its modern context in 1776 by the Illuminati, a secret society which, with limitless financial resources, was founded in that year by Jesuit-Jew Adam Weishaupt and dedicated to a programme of world domination. In 1782, at the Congress of Wilhelmsbad, an alliance between the Illuminati and Freeemasony was sealed. Shortly after, the ban was lifted that prevented Jews from joining the Masons; the headquarters of Masonry were moved to Frankfurt, the stronghold of Jewish finance. Judaism and Masonry, soon to be joined by a third, the Church of Mormon, plunged ahead in the preparation of a new Kingdom on earth: the Kingdom of the antiChrist.

The New World Order & The Throne of the antiChrist delineates the manner in which the group of International Financiers behind the Illuminati seized control of the economics of Europe and America, installing four Illuminati puppets in the White House: Woodrow Wilson, Franklin D. Roosevelt, Dwight D. Eisenhower, George Bush, and probably others.

In 1871, the Illuminati made a prediction of a sequence of three World Wars in the twentieth century which are not merely anti-Christ, but anti-man. This prediction was made not by some flaky astrologer or horoscope columnist but by the Grand Commander of Freemasonry and the top Illuminati figure in America: Albert Pike. He was in a position to know, because at the time the Masons and the Jews were directing affairs in most of Europe and North America.

The World Wars came in the sequence in which they were predicted, the first to destory Czarist Russia and to manoeuver Russia into the position of 'bogey man' to further Illuminati aims;

Plate 3: *Founder of the Order of the Illuminati*

the second by capitalizing on the differences between German Nationalists and political Zionists; and the third (yet to be fought, or is it being fought at this moment?) that is to result from manipulation of the differences between Zionists and Arabs (1).

It may be that World War III is not to be fought out on traditional battlefields at all, but is a kind of invisible psychic warfare in which, again and again, the whole psychic system of an individual or group of individuals is tested to the breaking-point on a day-to-day, minute-to-minute basis.

As Des Griffin shows in the second section of the *The New World Order & The Throne of the antiChrist*, the dust of the First World War had barely settled before the same forces engineered their plans for a Second World War in which many more millions were to be sacrificed. The War was deliberately prolonged - at least one year, some American military experts suggest two years - so that Stalin and the Soviet Union would have *the* commanding presence in Central and Eastern Europe after the War. Roosevelt and Eisenhower repeatedly held back the advance of the American troops to allow the capital cities of central Europe to fall into Soviet hands: Prague, Budapest, Vienna, Berlin, etc. As well, supplying the Soviets in the latter stages of the War was given priority over the welfare of Allied Armed forces, post-war items not needed for immediate Soviet war activity, 'metals and minerals suitable for use in an atomic pile and also in manufacture of the hydrogen bomb' (2). One of the most remarkable things to come to light in those pages is that the secret of the Atom Bomb was given directly to Mikoyan, third man in the Kremlin, by Harry Hopkins, Executive Assistant to the President of the United States, and almost certainly with the President's knowledge, approval, and connivance.

Meantime, there was another objective in the delay to end the War: the utter destruction of a number of non-military, but strategic industrial targets -Hamburg, Dresden, Tokyo, and a host of other Japanese cities. In the case of the Japanese, the most painful and deadly weapons of annihilation ever used against the human race were used, *after* the Japanese had officially surrendered. The method operating consistently in this madness of destruction was, Mr. Griffin tells us, the principle that always runs hand-in-glove with a 'theatre of war' situation, and that is the principle of 'urban renewal': the Backers and International Financiers behind the War were using the Allies' awesome power as their unofficial wrecking-crew:

> They were clearly looking beyond the end of the war, to the vast fortunes that could be picked up in 'redevelopment projects' in such cities as Dresden. The fact that millions of 'peasants' were incinerated in such 'urban renewal' projects was of no import to them. . . . Those old archaic cities had to be levelled. Those old factories, railroads, port facilities, communication networks and the national way of life had to be bulldozed into oblivion by the specially designed demolition equipment purchased by the American taxpayer. The late Professor Carroll Quigley tells us in *Tragedy and Hope* that the big planes '*engaged in the systematic destruction of*

*all Japanese cities. The flimsy houses of these crowded urban
areas made them very vulnerable to incendiary bombs. . . . On
March 9th, 1945, the Air Force tried a daring experiment. The
defensive armament was removed from 297 B-29's releasing
weight for additional incendiaries, and these planes, without
guns but carrying 1900 tons of fire bombs, were sent on a low
level attack on Tokyo. The result was the most devastating air
attack in all history . . . with the loss of only three planes.
Sixteen square miles of central Tokyo was burned out, 250,000
houses were destroyed, over a million persons were made
homeless and 84,793 were killed. This was more destructive
than the first atomic bomb over Hiroshima five months later'*
(p.815).

Two days later the B-29's were back to do a similar
demolition job on Nagoya. . . . Japan was wiped out,
devasted by the fury and intensity of America's aerial
bombardment. Why? Simple! The ground had to be
cleared for new industries and other types of
development. . . .

Shortly after the war - after the American airborne
demolition crews had done their job - vast sums of
money became available for the reconstruction of Japan.
The capital to build and equip Japan's gleaming new
industrial plants, ports, railroads, warehouses and
skyscraper office buildings didn't come from inside
Japan. It came from outside Japan. It came from the
same people who benefited enormously from the war
debts piled up by many nations around the world. It
came from the International Bankers. They put up the
money. They own the show. . . .

The Japanese people have proved to be excellent
workers, real producers who are more dedicated to their
employers than they are to their own families. In Japanese
society, it is true that Japanese occupy all the 'front'
positions in politics, industry, finance and education. For
the most part, they are supervisors and managers. They
have no authority as to how things are run. The shadowy
characters behind the scenes - the people who put up the
money and signed the checks - are the real masters of
Japan.

As Benjamin Disraeli once wrote: '*And so you see . . . the world is governed by very different personages than is imagined by those who are not behind the scenes.*' (3)

The Allied High Command, their hidden political directors, and the financial masters of the transient politicians were as ruthless and uncompassionate to East Europeans seeking asylum before Stalin's advancing armies as they had been to the German and Japanese civilians trapped behind wood and straw. 'Operation Keelhaul' became the official policy of Eisenhower and the Allied High Command whereby almost *two* million Russians fleeing Stalin's troops were forced to 'repatriate' in the Soviet Union and its satellites: 'repatriation' meant extraordinary suffering, torture, slavery, and death.

May I go back to the critical question? Why did the Allies delay in putting an end to the most destructive war in human history? To set up, in addition to the industrial investment, the formula for the Cold War in which the middle men, or what Sean Connery terms 'The Grey Men', would benefit, as they have done consistently through history, from the sale of arms *to both sides*.

The real reason, however, goes much deeper. *The New World Order & The Throne of the antiChrist* shows that the Bolshevik Revolution was not initiated by Russians at all but by a group of Jews from New York. As 'ex-chess champ' Bobby Fischer quipped to the press in his recent tournament: 'Soviet Communism is basically a mask for Bolshevism, which is a mask for Judaism.' Or as Denis Fahey puts it in *The Rulers of Russia*, his definitive source-book Bolshevism was 'an instrument in the hands of the Jews for the establishment of their future Messianic kingdom' (4). Since Stalin was a self-confessed Zionist (5), and since his 'monstrous' regime would have collapsed in the 1930's had not Roosevelt stepped in, granting diplomatic recognition and with it 'access to the credit and money markets of the world' (6), it appears as if Roosevelt and later Eisenhower were also implicated in the 'antiChrist' plot. Moveover, Roosevelt specifically refused to accept the German surrender that was negotiated by his personal naval attaché, Commander George Earle, with Admiral Wilhelm Canaris, Head of the German Secret Service, in 1943.

II

The term 'antiChrist' has less to do with religion that it has to do with money, bureaucracy, power, and a World Dictatorship. *The New World Order & The Throne of the antiChrist* approaches the movement not as a Biblical phenomenon but as an historical reality. The twentieth-century wars, alluded to above, which were planned to facilitate the creation of the new Kingdom, are, as indicated above, not merely anti-Christ, but anti-man, anti-human being. To be anti-human is to be anti-Buddha, anti-Mohammed: the whole of humanity is threatened.

The story is old and new, as new as the last two hundred years, and as old as Judaism itself, with its repudiation of Christ and its compulsion to create on earth a New Messiah. And yet, in the common parlance of espionage, I am convinced that "the Jews" may be merely the 'fall guys' once again as they may have been once before. The blame for the continuing crucifixion of mankind by man cannot be attributed to any one race, or indeed to any one family. It is not 'The Jews' or 'The Masons' or 'The Mormons' or 'The Catholics' who share the responsibility for the impending decimation of the human race, but we can say with certainty that an unholy alliance of *some* Jews, *some* Masons, *some* Mormons, and *some* Catholics have abused the privilege and power they have slowly been accumulating through the centuries and have yielded to the ultimate temptation: to reach for the power and prestige of God. Is this a fanciful projection? No! I have weighed the evidence! I have put my hands inside the wounds of humanity and, with some friends, I know the source of the affliction.

'AntiChrist' is the imposition of a man-made blueprint onto the rest of creation, with all the ruthlessness that this implies. As the French philosopher, Etienne Gilson, puts it: 'AntiChrist is not among us, he is in us. It is man himself, usurping unlimited, creative power and proceeding to the certain annihilation of that which is, in order to clear the way for the problematic creation of what will be,' the monstrous idol made by our own hands and to our own image and likeness (7). In other words, antiChrist implies a belief that salvation resides in man-initiated manipulation, in some process of history, or in one man or

Sacrifice? We have sacrificed the blood of two hundred million human beings in this century - sixteen hundred million quarts of blood - to accommodate the furniture of the earth for the reality of a New World Order. Why? One Masonic ritual says that the 'warrior on the block' receives 'the seething energies of Lucifer.' Another (*Nato*, p. 28) indicates that the reconstituted Temple in Jerusalem will have the function of Blood Sacrifice. Is the intention then to move blood sacrifice from the battlefield to the altar? With the advent of women priests in the Church of England, we may have another dimension - as Wellington said, the hand that rocks the cradle rules the world:

> All break and vanish, and evil gathers head:
> Herodias' daughters have returned again,
> A sudden blast of dusty wind and after
> Thunder of feet, tumult of images,
> Their purpose in the labyrinth of the wind:
> And should some crazy hand dare touch a daughter
> All turn with amorous cries, or angry cries,
> According to the wind, for all are blind.
> But now wind drops; dust settles; thereupon
> Lurches past, his great eyes without thought
> Under the shadow of stupid straw-pale locks,
> That insolent fiend Robert Artisson
> To whom the love-lorn Lady Kyteler brought
> Bronzed peacock feathers, red combs of her cocks.

> W. B. Yeats, *Nineteen Hundred and Nineteen*.

Here we see the dream of the despot reduced to an image of high breeding debasing itself, bulimia hyper-phagia like, before animal lust. It had to come to this - before we could turn our course and begin to ascend the stairway out of matter into which we have been descending since the first days.

There is another dream, a counter dream to the despot, that has from time to time lifted mankind from the baseness of matter and his own untransformed proclivities. From time immemorial it has been a dream of the human race to see itself as one family. Such dreams are contagious, because they ignite a fire in the human heart that expresses itself in feelings of friendship and fellowship capable of turning this dark globe of ours into a ball of fire, not the fire of the exploding atom, but the fire of human love once the true impulses of the heart arc like archangels over the chasm of the things that divide us.

St. Michael's College,   Robert O'Driscoll
University of Toronto.

dedication

for

Gordan Novak and Con Howard

who wound up the clock of Europe

and

Jean Forsyth Pace

whose safe house held in the Big T O

Gordan Novak, the Invisible Man from Croatia, is one of the great listeners in the world. Master etcher, realized Marxist philosopher, he is also one of the few people on the earth who truly understands the visual arts. Captain, Printer, Publisher, it was Gordan Novak who in 1990 published Robert O'Driscoll's *Nato and the Warsaw Pact Are One* (Warsaw and Toronto) and so set off the chain of events which have led to *The New World Order & The Throne of the antiChrist*. Once again, with Des Griffin from Emissary Publications in the United States, Mr. Novak is stepping into the breech to help publish what may well prove to be the most controversial book of the century. Gordan's father, Bozidar, is said to have invented modern journalism behind the 'Iron Curtain'.

Con Howard from Ireland is a Master at anything he's touched. Diplomat extraordinaire with an encyclodaedic knowledge of the arts, diplomacy, history, personalities, configurations of landmasses, he is a Master of masks, dodges, indecisive starts, and brilliant finishes. In some circles he is called 'The Ambassador's Ambassador' and most who have met him in Europe and North America agree that he has 'the biggest and grandest heart in all creation.

"To *Jean Forsyth Pace*, my Toronto neighbour and friend for twenty-five years, I owe the switch in my consciousness that took me from the ivory tower of academia to an ever-absorbing awareness of the suffering of humanity. Her acute wit, her graciousness and generosity kept me going during the darkest of days, and her all-embracing knowledge of the North American underground provided me with many of the clues by which I was able to decipher the puzzle." *ROD*

OVERTURE

by Robert O'Driscoll

"No - just the usual ghost supper. That's what we call it. They sit around drinking tea, none of them utters a word. . . . They nibble little cakes, all together. Sounds like rats in the attic."

"Why do you call it the ghost supper?"

"Well, they look like ghosts. They've been doing this for twenty years, always the same bunch saying the same things, or keeping their traps shut for fear of making fools of themselves."

This is not a Rehearsal
This is not a Rehearsal
This is not a Rehearsal
This is not a Rehearsal
This is not a Rehearsal
this is not a rehearsal
this is not a rehearsal
this is not a re
hears all

We've forced the rat -

The BIG RED RAT -

the raw

groovy red rat

Out

his hiddy   hole

an' his ever-sold soul g

o

e

s

MARK I CHING

all

the streets of mantra   all.

So soul and so sleep,
So sweet and so sour:
Aath seventy-one
He had a nice bum.
Have a good 'un!

2

Liz, get that rat,
Les, get those rats,
That roary black rat,
Those hoary white rats,
Those rats on the liberal scene -
Call in the cat:
CAT RAM!

That rat
With the pack
Of playing cards,
52, club
of rome.

Nato and the War
Saw Pack of Rats,
Those rats on a regualar day.
Samhain! Have a good 'un!

3

I feel their paws,
Their small little paws,
Their soft furrie black   paws,
'Gainst the glass of my feers this october night. 13. 10. '93

Give me your paw!
Give me your paw!

ratssraw, ratssraw, starwars, starwars, ratsraw . . . .

ratssraw, ratssraw, starwars, starwars, ratsraw . . . .

star wars
```
                    a
        t       r   w
      a   s   s
    r
```

NOTES

The usual ghost supper: This extract, from Strindberg's *Ghost Sonata* which outlines the corruption of the world just a few families in control of everything.

The big red rat: The connection between this line in the 'Overture' and the whole thrust of 'America', 'Russia', and the book in general should be abundantly clear. See below for Rothschild's Red Shield and Trotsky's Red Army (Des Griffin, *Descent Into Slavery?* p.19 and p.68).

Mark I Ching: on one level 'marching'. The other reference is of course to the *I Ching*, that master compilation with reference to change, chaos, the order that can always be found behind chaos, the unforeseeen and the accidental.

mantra all: On one level, 'Montreal'; on another, the repetitive ghostly peregrinations and incantations of the damned and the self-damned. *So soul and so sleep:* Refers to an international figure who worked out the blueprint of the New World Order. He is an extremely deceptive individual. So seemingly full of soul, he carefully calculates how he can sustain the impression of being oblivious to the implications of his actions.

Aath: David Aath, a CIA agent operating out of New York, who made contact with me while I was writing the *Overture*.

Those rats on the liberal scene: The strategy through which the Illuminati New World Order plan to achieve their objective is through repression from above, socialist liberation from below. This is what is implied in the line, short though it is. Poetry differs from history in that it can only suggest.

Samhain: ancient Celtic festival to denote the threshold between one year and the next. On Samhain eve, the boundaries between solid and insubstantial things disappear, and also between the world of the living and the world of the dead: the mask is momentarily lifted, and external objects are seen as they are, not as they seem to be.

I feel their paws: These stanzas suggests the physical proximity and yet the cosmic dimensions of the battle - usually called Armageddon - engaged at the end of time. Here the battle is called STAR WARS, which is the prelude to Armageddon.

Plate 4: *Insignia of the Illuminati, placed on the American one-dollar bill by the Roosevelt Administration in the nineteen-thirties. This insignia was adopted by Weishaupt at the time he founded the Order of the Illuminati on May 1, 1776. It was that event that is memorialized by the "MDCCLXXVI" at the base of the pyramid and not the date of the signing of the Declaration of Independence, as the uninformed have supposed. This insignia acquired Masonic significance only after the merger of that Order with the Order of the Illuminati at the Congress of Wilhelmsbad, in 1782. Curiously, the Insignia is also on the reverse side of the Great Seal of The United States; it was and opted in this form by the American form by Congress in 1782*

I. AMERICA

Edited from the works of DES GRIFFIN

INTRODUCTION

As we sail blithely through life, have we ever been stopped in our tracks by a rather uncanny feeling, some sort of feeling that the 'accidents' of history and life may not be all that 'accidental' after all, but the result of earthly planning, perhaps even the result of what one man or a few men have dreamed up in solitude, or - shall we use the dread word - conspiracy? Are the 'effects' that we are experiencing today the result, as all things seem to be, of some cause, some planning, some force that brought them into existence and sustains them? What do we experience in that unexpected moment when we encounter that feeling? A wave of elation? Or paronia? Or both?

Certainly we are not alone in our feelings. Looking back over the last sixty years at the 'blunders' and 'mistakes', best-selling author Gary Allen concludes with reference to the United States:

If we were merely dealing with the law of averages, half the events affecting our nation's well-being should be good for America. If we were dealing with mere incompetence, our leaders should occasionally make a mistake in our favor. *We are not dealing with coincidence or stupidity, but with planning and brilliance.* (1)

Throughout the last two hundred years, many public figures have subscribed to the idea of a 'conspiracy of a few' directing the affairs of the many, among the most notable being Disraeli, Henry Ford, Charles Lindberg, Taylor Caldwell, and that pillar of common sense and public stability, Winston Churchill.

Indeed, Churchill stated uncategorically in 1920 that a 'world-wide conspiracy' was afoot for nothing less than 'the overthrow of civilization' and the 'reconstitution of society', a conspiracy 'as malevolent as Christianity was benevolent,' and which would, if not arrested, 'shatter irretrievably all that Christianity has rendered possible.' Churchill's perceptions are linked to his observations of the Bolshevik Revolution which he recognizes as something far more serious than a mere political upheaval, but as the mask or 'front' for the establishment of a new Kingdom: the Kingdom of the antiChrist:

Some people like Jews and some do not; but no thoughtful man can doubt the fact that they are beyond all question the most formidable and the most remarkable race which has ever appeared in the world. . . .

The conflict between good and evil which proceeds unceasingly in the breast of man nowhere reaches such an intensity as in the Jewish race. The dual nature of mankind is nowhere more strongly or more terribly exemplified. We owe to the Jews in the Christian revelation a system of ethics which, even if it were entirely separated from the supernatural, would be incomparably the most precious possession of mankind, worth in fact the future of all other wisdom and learning put together. On that system and by that faith there has been built out of the wreck of the Roman Empire the whole of our existing civilisation.

And it may well be that this same astounding race may at the present time be in the actual process of producing another system of morals and philosophy, as malevolent as Christianity was benevolent which, if not arrested, would shatter irretrievably all that Christianity has rendered possible. *It would almost seem as if the gospel of Christ and the gospel of Antichrist were destined to originate among the same people; and that this mystic and mysterious race had been chosen for the supreme manifestations, both of the divine and diabolical.* . . . [my italics] The adherents of this sinister confederacy . . . have forsaken the faith of their forefathers, and divorced from their minds all spiritual hopes of the next world. This movement among the Jews is not new. From the days of Spartacus-Weishaupt to those of Karl Marx, and down to Trotsky (Russia), Bela

Kun (Hungary), Rosa Luxenbourg (Germany), and Emma
Goldman (United States), this world-wide conspiracy for
the overthrow of civilization and for the reconstitution of
society on the basis of arrested development, of envious
malevolence, and impossible equality, has been steadily
growing. It played ... a definitely recognisable part in the
tragedy of the French Revolution. It has been the
mainspring of every subversive movement during the
Nineteenth Century; and now at last this band of
extraordinary personalities from the underworld of the
great cities of Europe and America have gripped the
Russian people by the hair of their heads and have
become practically the undisputed masters of that
enormous empire (2).

II

Seventy years later, seemingly in the minds of those who
created it, the Soviet 'bloc' had served its purpose. Almost before
it began to disintegrate before our disbelieving eyes in late '89, I
wrote in a very short time a rather long poem, *Nato and the Warsaw
Pact Are One*, which, when published in Warsaw and Toronto,
achieved a certain notoriety and set off a chain of circumstances
that resulted in *The New World Order & The Throne of the antiChrist*
(see Introduction to 'Russia' below).

While I was writing the poem, I half-remembered what W. B.
Yeats's said to Sean O'Casey in the 1920's - that we can discern the
patterns of history from the cobwebs on our walls. As I wrote, I
was aware, but only dimly aware of what was happening in
Europe. I was writing out of sheer intuition and yet in image after
image I was finding an outer correspondence for an inner reality,
or building up a mythology that matched the nightmare in my
soul to a configuration of events in the external world. Professor
Lorna Reynolds, Professor Emeritus of the National University
of Ireland, commented on this aspect of the work in her
Introduction:

How the private life is affected by the public is the

theme of the work here presented. In its fragmented and syncopated form, it reflects a mind caught up in horror, in hallucinatory apprehension, in a sense of bafflement, attempting manic guesses at meaning, seeking for some, or any, explanation, grasping at straws, seen through the fog. It is ironic that this outburst should come at the moment when events in Eastern Europe take such a sudden and totally unexpected turn, . . . strange that someone living far from Europe, across the Western ocean, should echo all this, and by allowing destructive impulses to come into the open prepare the ground of his being for future constructive efforts (3).

The 'bottom line' of the poem, as they say in the business world, was that a World State had been agreed upon, and after the dust of publication had settled, I asked myself: Where did that thought come from? Or rather intuition?

> Where got I that truth?
> Out of a medium's mouth,
> Out of nothing it came,
> Out of the forest loam,
> Out of dark night where lay
> The crowns of Nineveh. (4)

My next step was to attempt to corroborate intellectually what I had perceived intuitively. Contact was established with Soviet espionage which revealed to me the existence of the 'Pacific Triangle', the forces collaborating in the creation of a Kingdom of the 'antiChrist'. Secret Austrian sources confirmed the actual identity of the antiChrist.

I am less acclimatized, however, to assessing the results of espionage than I am the results of scholarship. I am by training and profession an academic, having lectured for thirty years in Universities in Britain, Ireland, and Canada, including 25 years at Canada's premiere University, the University of Toronto. I plunged, therefore, into the mass of literature available on the subject, military and historical studies involving Europe, North America, Japan, etc. - hundreds, perhaps even thousands of articles and books (some of which were 'permanently missing' when I went back a few months later to the same library to check my quotations). What I discovered through scholarship staggered me even more than what I had discovered through espionage: that the planning for a Throne of the antiChrist had been going on for at least two hundred years.

I was soon confronted by a choice: to spend the rest of my life coalescing the information I had gathered into a book I would write myself - and so miss the crucial historical moment - or to choose, among the authors I had read, the one who had the most integral overview and make a *selection* of his or her work that would tell the story.

In American scholarship, one figure towered over all the others: Des Griffin. During more than thirty years of research on the subject, he has produced four books: *Fourth Reich of the Rich*, Emissary, Clackamas, Oregon, published 1976, revised 1992; *Descent Into Slavery?* Emissary: Clackamas, Oregon, published 1980, revised 1988; *Anti-Semitism and the Babylonian Connection*, Emissary: Oregon, 1988, revised 1992; and *Martin Luther King: The Man behind the Myth*, Emissary: Oregon, 1987.

I quickly became fascinated not only by Mr. Griffin's results but by the method of research by which he had reached these results. Instead of concentrating solely on Public Record and War Office records, as is the case with many purely academic commentators, Mr. Griffin remains always aware of the 'larger picture' and the 'missing' pieces in the puzzle, attempting to match what issues forth in action with what is being contrived behind the scenes and what makes sense in the broader historical perspective. He proceeds from the premise that the real truth is 'always carefully buried by the . . . perpetrators of a plot' (5), but that it is difficult to guard a military secret 'after' the event: the military become human again when they return to civilian status, boast, break rank, or see their actions in a broader perspective. Mr. Griffin fills out the puzzle, therefore, by citing the evidence of people who were 'there' at the time: Congressman, Colonels, Admirals, Generals, Ambassadors, etc.; obscure investigations and reports of Senate and House Committees; war pamphlets and directives issued at the time from the respective military headquarters, etc.

I subjected Mr. Griffin's method of research and published results to the most meticulous academic scrutiny, testing their validity from every conceivable angle: his assumptions, deductions, and conclusions. Here, I concluded is a man with a precise well-honed narrative and a broad perspective, a man with deep insight into military and governmental strategy, who can gather and assess evidence, discriminating unerringly between what is valid and what has been manufactured to manipulate the patriot or electorate; a man full of compassion for his subject - humanity - caught like a moth between the upper and nether stone, between the ever-recurring patterns of history and what has been carefully plotted for the future. It is for these reasons that I made a selection from Mr. Griffin's work to present the story of 'America' and part of the story of 'Russia'.

University of Toronto   Robert O'Driscoll
13 September 1992

EDITORIAL NOTE

In order to preserve the flow of the narrative, I have endeavoured to keep my comments and questions to a minimun. When I do comment, these comments appear in bold; Mr. Griffin's text appears in roman.

Italics are used often in Mr. Griffin's text, and it is not always indicated whether or not the passage is so highlighted in the original. To do so would be cumbersome for the reader. The italics indicate a significance that Mr. Griffin sees in his text at that particular moment. The full significance may only be seen by the reader after the book has been read in its entirety.

The page number of the text that Mr. Griffin is quoting is inserted in the body of the text, as in Mr. Griffin's original book; the page numbers of the particular Griffin book that I quote from are inserted at the end of the section.

NOTES

1. *None Dare Call It Conspiracy*, quoted in Des Griffin, *Fourth Reich of the Rich*, p.14.

2. 'Zionism versus Bolshevism: A Struggle for the Soul of the Jewish People,' *Illustrated Sunday Herald* (8 February 1920).

3. *Nato and the Warsaw Pact Are One* (Warsaw and Toronto: Zespol, 1990), p.5.

4. W.B. Yeats, 'Fragments', *Collected Poems* (London: Macmillan, 1961), p.241.

5. *Descent Into Slavery?* p.164.

A Note on the Illustrations

Mr. Griffin includes a number of illustrations in the published books. In order to make a place for the original illustrations for the Russian, Israel, and Vatican sections, we have published very few illustrations in the North American sections.

Let us start with 1776 and with the principle that for every action there is an equal and opposite reaction. 1776 witnessed not only the Declaration of Independence of the United States of America, but the formation in Europe of the Order of the Illuminati, dedicated to a counter ideal of the United States: total world domination and the establishment of a 'Novus Ordo Seclorum' (New World Order). I quote from Mr. Griffin's *Fourth Reich of the Rich*, pp. 40-54:

FOUNDATION OF THE ILLUMINATI (1776)

Out of Germany was hatched a Diabolical Plot which has deceived untold millions, and which - at this present time - threatens to destroy Western Civilization. . . .

[T]he order of the Illuminati was founded on May 1, 1776, by Dr. Adam Weishaupt, professor of Canon Law at Ingolstadt University, Bavaria. Weishaupt (born a Jew and a convert to Catholicism) was a former Jesuit priest who broke with that Order to form his own organization. . . . Weishaupt and his followers considered themselves to be the cream of the intelligentsia - the select of the elect - and the only people with the mental capacity, the insight and understanding to govern the world and bring it peace. Their avowed purpose and goal was the establishment of a 'Novus Ordo Seclorum' or New World Order.

The name Illuminati is said to derive from the word Lucifer, which means the Bearer of the Light or a being of extraordinary brilliance (Isaiah 14.12). . . .

Sir Walter Scott, in the second volume of *The Life of Napoleon Buonaparte*, points out that the events leading up to the French Revolution were all created by the Money Barons - the Illuminati - whose agents then led the mob in implementing the famous Reign of Terror. . . .

The initiates who made up the outer rings [of the Order] were told that the great purpose of the Illuminati was 'to make of the human race, without any distinction of nation, condition, or profession, one good and happy family.'

All initiates were required to take an oath to bind themselves 'to perpetual silence and unshakable loyalty and submission to the Order, in the person of my superiors; here making faithful and complete surrender of my private judgment, my own will, and every narrow-minded employment of my own power and am ready to serve it with my fortune, my honor and my blood. . . .(John Robison, *Proofs of a Conspiracy*, 1797, p.71).

Only at this stage [when he reached the inner circle] was he finally allowed to see the ultimate aims of the Order: (1) The abolition of all ordered governments; (2) Abolition of private property; (3) Abolition of inheritance; (4) Abolition of patriotism; (5) Abolition of all religion; (6) Abolition of family (i.e. morality, marriage, and the proper education of children), and (7) The creation of a New World Order or World Government.

Naturally, all members were never allowed to see the true goals of the Order. They were assured that the sole purpose for the society was to assure 'the happiness of the human race. . . .'

'The most admirable thing of all,' wrote Weishaupt, 'is that great Protestant and Reformed theologians (Lutherans and Calvinists) who belong to our Order really believe they see in it the true and genuine mind of the Christian religion. Oh man, what can not you be brought to believe' (Nesta Webster, *World Revolution*, 1921, p.13). . . .

The Protestant princes and rulers of Germany were pleased with Weishaupt's plan to destroy the Catholic Church, and they sought to join the Order. These men brought with them control of the Masonic Order, into which they initiated Weishaupt and his co-conspirators in 1777. . . .

On July 16, 1782, at the Congress of Wilhelmsbad, an alliance between Illuminism and Freemasonry was finally sealed. This pact joined together all the leading secret societies of the day - and united 'not less than three million members all over the world. . . .'

What passed at this terrible Congress will never be known to the outside world, for even those men who were drawn unwittingly into the movement, and now heard for the first time the designs of the leaders, were under oath to reveal nothing. One honest Freemason, Comte de Vireu, . . . when questioned on the 'tragic secrets' he brought back with him, replied: 'I will not confide them to you. I can only tell you that this is very much more serious than you think. The conspiracy that has been woven is so well thought out that it will be, so to speak, impossible for the Monarchy and the Church to escape from it. (Webster, *World Revolution*, p.18).

During the next few years there was a movement which brought about the emancipation of the Jews in Europe. Prior to that time Jews seem to have been barred from joining the Masonic Order: that ban was lifted. It was also decided to move the headquarters of Illuminized Freemasonry to Frankfurt, the stronghold of Jewish finance. . . .(*FR*, pp.40-54)

ILLUMINATI PLAN FOR WORLD DOMINATION (1871)

Lest anyone be inclined to doubt the connection between the plans drawn up by the Illuminati in the nineteenth century and the chain reaction of wars in the twentieth, I submit the following passage in Mr. Griffin's *Descent Into Slavery?* for scrutiny:

Having consolidated their financial grip on most of the European nations by the middle of the last century, the International Bankers worked feverishly to extend their sphere of influence to the ends of the earth. . . .

In the decades that followed it became apparent that, in order to achieve their goal of world domination, they would have to instigate a series of world wars which would result in the leveling of the old world order in preparation for the construction of the New World Order. This plan was outlined in graphic detail by Albert Pike, the Sovereign Grand Commander of the Ancient and Accepted Scottish Rite of Freemasonry and the top Illuminist in America, in a letter to Giuseppe Mazzini dated August 15, 1871. Pike stated that the first world war was to be fomented in order to destroy Czarist Russia - and to place that vast land under the direct control of Illuminati agents. Russia was then to be used as a 'bogey man' to further the aims of the Illuminati worldwide.

World War II was to be fomented through manipulation of the differences that existed between the German Nationalists and the Political Zionists. This was to result in an expansion of Russian influence and the establishment of the state of Israel in Palestine. The Third War was planned to result from the differences stirred up by Illuminati agents between the Zionists and the Arabs. The conflict was planned to spread worldwide. The Illuminati, said the letter, planned to 'unleash the Nihilists and Atheists' and 'provoke a formidable social cataclysm which in all its horror will show clearly to the nations the effect of absolute atheism, origin of savagery and of the most bloody of turmoil. Then everywhere, the citizens, obliged to defend themselves against the world minority of revolutionaries, will exterminate those destroyers of civilization, and the multitude, disllusioned with Christianity, whose deistic spirits will from that moment be without compass [direction], anxious for an ideal, but without knowing where to render its adoration, will receive the true light through the universal manifestation of the pure doctrine of Lucifer, brought finally out in the public view, a manifestation which will result from the general reactionary movement which will follow the destruction of Christianity and atheism, both conquered and exterminated at the same time (*DS?*, pp.38-9).

To give the reader an indication of Pike's theological and philosophical 'principles', I give below an extract from his most well-known work, *Morals and Dogma* (1871), and an extract from his instructions to the 23 Supreme Councils of the world (cited in *FR*, pp.69-70) on Bastille Day, 1889:

'Force regulated or irregulated, is not only wasted in the void like that of gunpowder burned in the open air, and steam unconfined by science; but striking in the dark, and its blows meeting only the air, they recoil and bruise itself. It is destruction and ruin . . . not growth and progress. . . .

'The blind force of the people is a Force that must be economized, and also managed, . . . it must be regulated by intellect.

'To attack the citadels built up on all sides against the human race by superstitions, despotisms, and prejudices, the force must have a brain and a law. Then its deeds of daring produce permanent results, and there is real progress. Then there are sublime conquests. . . . When all Forces are combined, and guided by the Intellect [the Illuminated ones!], and regulated by the Rule of Right, and Justice, and of combined and systematic movement and effort, the great revolution prepared for by the ages will begin to march. . . .It is because Force is ill regulated, that revolutions prove failures' (*Morals and Dogma*, pp.1-2).

The theological dogma of Albert Pike is laid out in the second extract referred to above:
'That which we say to the crowd is: "We worship a God, but it is the God one adores without superstitions." 'To you, Sovereign Grand Instructors General, we say this, that you may repeat it to the Brethren of the 32nd, 31st and 30th degrees: "The Masonic religion should be, by all of us initiates of the high degrees, maintained in the purity of the Luciferian doctrine.

"If Lucifer were not God, would Adonay [the Christian God] whose deeds prove his cruelty, perfidy and hatred of man, barbarism and repulsion of science, would Adonay and his priests culminate him?

"Yes, Lucifer is God, and unfortunately Adonay is also God. For the eternal law there is no light without shade, no beauty without ugliness, no white without black, for the absolute can only exist as two Gods: darkness being necessary for light to serve as its foil, as the pedestal is necessary to the statue, and the brake to the locomotive.

"The doctrine of Satanism is heresy; and the true and pure philosophic religion is the belief in Lucifer, the equal of Adonay; but Lucifer, God of Light and God of Good is struggling for humanity against Adonay, the God of Darkness and Evil.' (*Le Femme et l'enfant dans la Franc-Maconnerie Universelle*, by A. C. De La Rive, p.588, as quoted by Lady Queenborough, *Occult Theocrasy*, pp. 220-1; *FR*, pp. 69-70).

INTERNATIONAL BANKERS PREPARE WAY FOR
WORLD CONQUEST

Behind the machinations and world plans of the Illuminati were a group of bankers led by the first truly INTERNATIONAL BANKER, MOSES AMSCHEL BAUER, who in 1750 changed his name to one which ultimately became synonymous with absolute wealth, power, and influence: Rothschild, after the big Red Shield displayed over his door in Frankfurt and which was in turn adopted from the Red Flag, 'the emblem of the revolutionary-minded Jews in Eastern Europe' with 'their age-old goal of conquering the world'(*DS?* p.19, and *AS*, p.30). In the sections below, we delineate how Rothschild and his associates gained control of Britain and France in the nineteenth century and of the United States and Russia in the twentieth century.

HOW ROTHSCHILD GAINED CONTROL OF
BRITISH ECONOMY

Upon the battle of Waterloo depended the future of the European continent. If the Grande Armée of Napoleon emerged victorious, France would be the undisputed master of all she surveyed on the European front. If Napoleon was crushed into submission, England would hold the balance of power in Europe and would be in a position to greatly expand its sphere of influence. . . . There were vast fortunes to be made - and lost on the outcome of the Battle. . . . The Stock Exchange in London was at a fever pitch as traders awaited news of the outcome of this battle of the giants. If Britain lost, English consuls would plummet to unprecedented depths. If Britain was victorious, the value of the consul would leap to dizzying new heights.

As the two huge armies closed in for their battle to the death, Nathan Rothschild had his agents working feverishly on both sides of the line to gather the most accurate possible information as the battle proceeded. Additional Rothschild agents were on hand to carry the intelligence bulletins to a Rothschild command post strategically located nearby.

Late on the afternoon of June 19, 1815, a Rothschild representative jumped on board a specially chartered boat and headed out into the channel in a hurried dash for the English coast. In his possession was a top secret report from Rothschild's secret service agents on the progress of the crucial battle. This intelligence data would prove indispensible to Nathan in making some vital decisions.

The special agent was met at Folkstone the following morning at dawn by Nathan Rothschild himself. After quickly scanning the highlights of the report, Rothschild was on his way again, speeding towards London and the Stock Exchange.

Arriving at the Exchange amid frantic speculation on the outcome of the battle, Nathan took up his usual position beside the famous 'Rothschild Pillar'. Without a sign of emotion, without the slightest change of facial expression, the stony-faced, flint-eyed chief of the House of Rothschild gave a predetermined signal to his agents who were stationed nearby.

Rothschild agents immediately began to dump consuls on the market. As hundreds of thousands of dollars worth of consuls poured onto the market, their value started to slide. Then they began to plummet.

Nathan continued to lean against 'his' pillar, emotionless, expressionless. He continued to sell, and sell and sell. Consuls kept on falling. Word began to sweep through the Stock Exchange: 'Rothschild knows.' 'Rothschild knows.' 'Wellington has lost at Waterloo!'

The selling turned into a panic as people rushed to unload their 'worthless' consuls or paper money for gold and silver in the hope of retaining at least part of their wealth. Consuls continued their nose dive towards oblivion.   After several hours of feverish trading, the consul lay in ruins. It was selling for about five cents on the dollar.

Nathan Rothschild, emotionless and expressionless as ever, still leaned against his pillar. He continued to give subtle signals. But these signals were different. They were so subtly different that only the highly-trained Rothschild agents could detect the change. On the cue from their boss, dozens of Rothschild agents made their way to the order desks around the Exchange and bought every consul in sight for just a 'song'!

A short time later, the 'official' news arrived in the British capital. England was now the master of the European scene.

Within seconds, the consul skyrocketed to above its original value. As the significance of the British victory began to sink into the public conciousness, the value of consuls rose ever higher.

Napoleon had 'met his Waterloo.' Nathan had bought control of the British economy. Overnight his already vast fortune was multiplied twenty times over (*DS?* pp.27-8).

HOW ROTHSCHILD SEIZED CONTROL OF FRANCE

Following their crushing defeat at Waterloo, the French struggled to get back on their feet financially. In 1817 they negotiated a substanial loan from the prestigious French banking house of Ouvrard and from the well-known bankers Baring Brothers of London. The Rothschilds had been left on the outside looking in.

The following year the French government was in need of another loan. As the bonds issued in 1817 with the help of Ouvrard and Baring Brothers were increasing in value upon the Paris market, and in other European financial centers, it appeared certain that the French government would retain the services of these two distinguished banking houses.

The Rothschild brothers tried most of the gimmicks in their vast repertoire to influence the French government to give them the business. Their efforts were in vain.

The French aristocrats, who prided themselves on their elegance and superior breeding, viewed the Rothschilds as mere peasants, upstarts who needed to be kept in their place. The fact that the Rothschilds had vast financial resources, lived in the most luxurious homes, and were attired in the most elegant and expensive clothes obtainable, cut no ice with the highly class-conscious French nobility. The Rothschilds were viewed as uncouth - lacking in social graces. If we are to believe most historical accounts, their appraisal of the first generation Rothschilds was probably valid.

One major piece of armament in the Rothschild arsenal the

French had overlooked or ignored - their unprecedented cunning in the use and manipulation of money.

On November 5, 1818, something very unexpected occurred. After a year of steady appreciation, the value of the French government bonds began to fall. With each passing day, the decline in their value became more pronounced. Within a short space of time, other government securities began to suffer too.

The atmosphere in the court of Louis XVIII was tense. Grim-faced aristocrats pondered the fate of the country. They hoped for the best but feared the worst! The only people around the French court who weren't deeply concerned were James and Karl Rothschild. They smiled - but said nothing!

Slowly a sneaking suspicion began to take shape in the minds of some onlookers. Could those Rothschild brothers be the cause of the nation's economic woes? Could they have secretly manipulated the bond market and engineered the panic?

They had! During October, 1818, Rothschild agents, using their masters' limitless reserves, had bought huge quantities of the French government bonds issued through their rivals Ouvrard and Baring Brothers. This caused the bonds to increase in value. Then, on November 5th, they began to dump the bonds in huge quantities on the open market in the main commercial centers of Europe, throwing the market into a panic.

Suddenly the scene in the Aix palace changed. The Rothschilds, who were patiently biding their time and waiting quietly in an ante room, were ushered into the presence of the king. They were now the center of attention. Their clothes were now the height of fashion. . . . The Rothschilds had gained control of France (*DS?* pp.31-2).

ROTHSCHILD MAKES BEACHHEAD INTO GERMANY

During the second half of the last century, the Vienna branch of the House of Rothschild decided to finance the activities of a bright and ambitious young count by the name of Otto von Bismarck. With their backing, the count seized control of Prussia, the largest of the small German-speaking states in Central Europe, and set about expanding his dominion. In 1866 Bismarck eliminated Austrian influence over Germany with a victory in the Austro-Prussian War, and went on to lead a 700,000 man army to victory over the French in the battle of Sedan. History records that it was the International Bankers that engineered the events leading up to that battle (E.C. Knuth, *Empire of 'The City'*, 1946, p.17; *DS?* p.55).

PRINCIPLE OF CONTROL: 'THE BALANCE OF POWER'

To confirm and consolidate the position of the House of Rothschild as the 'invisible rulers' of Europe, there had to be two groupings of powers of almost equal strength, which represented the 'balance of power.' The reason for this was simple: the House of Rothschild had to make sure that all the King 'A's could be threatened by all the King 'B's. Naturally, they were all financed and largely controlled by the Rothschilds.

To ensure that the system worked as planned, there had to be an outside power that would act as an 'insurance policy' in the event that someone stepped out of line and appeared likely to upset the scheme.

This 'insurance policy' was Nathan Rothschild's England, which now reigned supreme in the Eastern Hemisphere. One could always determine which way a war was going to go by watching which side England favored. England invariably wound up on the winning side. . . . [T]he power and wealth of the now 'invisible' House of Rothschild grew to such proportions that by the turn of this century it was estimated that they controlled half the wealth of the world (*DS?* p.52).

SOCIALIST STRATEGY FOR WORLD CONQUEST

Using Marx as a front, the Illuminati attempted to implement their plan for a world-wide revolution. . . . In London, in 1864, Marx organized the International Workingman's Association (later known as the First Socialist International). Their headquarters was moved to New York eight years later. Shortly thereafter, they merged with

the Socialist Party which was founded there in 1868. . . .
The Second Socialist International, founded in Paris on July 14,
1889, resulted from the realization that the 'workers of the world'
would not rally to the call of socialist leadership, but had to be
manipulated through the organization and control of labor unions.
It was at this juncture that the Fabian Society and Lenin's
Bolsheviks made their entrance on the world scene - and began
to make real progress towards achieving the goals outlined by
Weishaupt, Roosevelt[1], Marx and Pike. The only difference between
these two groups were the methods they employed in working
toward the same overall goal - the creation of a socialistic one-
world society as envisioned by Marx (A Manifesto, Fabian Tract
No.2, 1884). Since that time the Bolsheviks (Communists) have
been working to bring it about by violent, revolutionary means.
Of the Fabians, the Encyclopedia Britannica (1973 edition, article on
Fabian Socialism, Vol.20, pp.750-1) tells us that 'the name is derived
from that of the Roman General Fabius, the delayer, because of his
deliberate, long-range strategy.'
As a result, from the outset the Fabians worked toward the
creation of a New World Order through the indoctrination of
young scholars. They believed that eventually these intellectual
revolutionaries could gain power and influence in the various
opinion-making and power-wielding agencies of the world and so
achieve their aims. Their tactics became known as 'the doctrine
of the inevitability of gradualism.'
It should be noted that these were only two of the organizations
through which the International Conspiracy was working. The
real power has always been held by the bankers (FR, pp.82-3).

INTERNATIONAL BANKERS PURSUE
OBJECTIVE TO DESTROY AMERICA

Following their conquest of Europe early in the 1800's, the
Rothschilds cast their covetous eyes on the most precious gem of
them all - the United States.
America was unique in all of world history. It was the only
nation on earth that had ever been formed with the Bible as its basic

law book. Its uniquely magnificent Constitution was specifically designed to limit the power of government and to keep its citizens free and prosperous. Its citizens were basically industrious immigrants who 'yearned to breath free' and who asked for nothing more than to be given the opportunity to live and work in such a wonderfully stimulating environment.

The results - the fruit - of such a unique experiment were so indescribably brillant that America became a legend around the globe. Many millions across the far-flung continents of the world viewed America the beautiful as the promised land.

The Big Bankers in Europe - the Rothschilds and their cohorts - viewed the wonderful results borne by this unique experiment from an entirely different perspective. They looked upon it as a major threat to their future plans. The establishment *Times* of London stated: 'If that mischievous financial policy which had its origin in the North American Republic [i.e. honest Constitutionally authorized NO DEBT money] should become indurated down to a fixture, then that government will furnish its own money without cost. It will pay off its debts and be without a debt [to the International Bankers]. It will become prosperous beyond precedent in the history of the civilized governments of the world. The brains and wealth of all countries will go to North America. That government must be destroyed or it will destroy every monarchy on the globe.'

The Rothschilds and their friends sent in their financial termites to destroy America because it was becoming 'prosperous beyond precedent. . . .'

The *Illustrated University History*, 1878, p. 504, tells us that the southern states swarmed with British agents. These conspired with local politicians to work against the best interests of the United States. Their carefully sown and nurtured propaganda developed into open rebellion and resulted in the secession of South Carolina on December 29, 1860. Within weeks another six states joined in the conspiracy against the Union, and broke away to form the Confederate States of America, with Jefferson Davis as President.

The plotters raised armies, seized forts, arsenals, mints and other Union property. Even members of President Buchanan's Cabinet conspired to destroy the Union by damaging the public credit and working to bankrupt the nation. Buchanan claimed to deplore secession but took no steps to check it, even when a U.S. ship was fired upon by South Carolina shore batteries. Shortly thereafter Abraham Lincoln became President, being inaugurated on March 4, 1861. Lincoln immediately ordered a blockade on Southern ports, to cut off supplies that were pouring in from Europe. The 'official' date for the start of the Civil War is given as April 12, 1861, when Fort Sumter in South Carolina was bombarded by the Confederates, but it obviously began at a much earlier date.

In December, 1861, large numbers of European troops (British, French and Spanish) poured into Mexico in defiance of the Monroe Doctrine. This, together with widespread European aid to the Confederacy, strongly indicated that the Crown was preparing to enter the war. The outlook for the North, and the future of the Union, was bleak indeed.

In this hour of extreme crisis, Lincoln appealed to the Crown's perennial enemy, Russia, for assistance. When the envelope containing Lincoln's urgent appeal was given to Czar Nicholas II, he weighed it unopened in his hand and stated: 'Before we open this paper or know its contents, we grant any request it may contain.'

Unannounced, a Russian fleet under Admiral Liviski, steamed into New York harbor on September 24, 1863, and anchored there. The Russian Pacific fleet, under Admiral Popov, arrived in San Francisco on October 12. Of this Russian act, Gideon Wells said: 'They arrived at the high tide of the Confederacy and the low tide of the North, causing England and France to hesitate long enough to turn the tide for the North' (*Empire of 'The City'*, p.90).

History reveals that the Rothschilds were heavily involved in financing both sides in the Civil War. Lincoln put a damper on their activities when, in 1862 and 1863, he refused to pay the exorbitant rates of interest demanded by the Rothschilds and issued constitutionally-authorized, interest-free United States notes. For this and other acts of patriotism, Lincoln was shot down in cold-blood by John Wilkes Booth on April 14, 1865, just five days after Lee surrendered to Grant at Appomattox Court House Virginia[2]. . . .

Undaunted by their initial failures to destroy the United States, the International Bankers pursued their objective with relentless zeal. Between the end of the Civil War and 1914, their main agents in the United States were Kuhn, Loeb and Co. and the J.P. Morgan Co. . . .

Early in 1907, Jacob Schiff, the Rothschild-owned boss of Kuhn, Loeb and Co., in a speech to the New York Chamber of Commerce, warned that 'unless we have a Central Bank with adequate control of credit resources, this country is going to undergo the most severe and far-reaching money panic in its history.'

Shortly thereafter, the United States plunged into a monetary crisis that had all the earmarks of a skillfully-planned Rothschild 'job'. The ensuing panic financially ruined tens of thousands of innocent people across the country - and made billions for the banking elite. The purpose for the `crisis' was two-fold:

(1) To make a financial 'killing' for the Insiders, and

(2) To impress on the American people the 'great need' for a central bank.

Paul Warburg told the Banking and Currency Commitee: 'In the Panic of 1907, the first suggestion I made was, "let us have a national clearing-house [Central Bank]. The Aldrich Plan [for a Central Bank] contains many things that are simply fundamental rules of banking. Your aim must be the same. . . . "'

Digging deep into their bag of deceitful practices, the International Bankers prepared to pulled off their greatest coup to date - the creation of the privately-owned; Federal Reserve, which would place control of the finances of the United States securely in the hands of the power-crazed money monopolists. Paul Warburg was to become the 'Fed's' first chairman!

ILLUMINATI PUPPET IN THE WHITE HOUSE

Through their front men C. Mandell House[3], the 'mysterious' son of one of Rothschilds' agents in the South; Jacob Schiff, the top Rothschild front in the United States, and Bernard Baruch[4], Jewish Wall St. speculator, the Money Monopolists selected Wilson and financed his campaign for the presidency of the United States in 1912. . . .

Through their puppet president . . . the Illuminati were able to push through Congress a couple of Acts that spelled disaster for the nation. On December 23rd, 1913, when many of the nation's lawmakers had left Washington for their Christmas vacations, they rammed through the nationally destructive and totally unconstitutional 'federal' Reserve Act which placed our nation's money supply and credit firmly in the hands of those Rothschild controlled International Bankers. The Congressional Record shows that Congressman Charles Lindbergh described the newly-created monstrosity as 'the invisible government by the money power.' Henry Cabot Lodge, Sr. stated the privately-owned 'Fed' would submerge the nation 'in a flood of irredeemable paper currency.'

The same 'money power' also financed the campaign for the introduction of a graduated income tax. This Act was not designed to make the wealthy pay for the running of the country. Its specific purpose, as Ferdinand Lundberg points out in *The Rich and the Super Rich*, was for it to become 'a siphon . . . inserted into the pocketbooks of the general public" (p. 350).

With the passage of these two unconstitutional 'laws' in 1913, the way was cleared for the rape of the United States. It signaled the start of phase two of the Illuminati's 'urban renewal' project in America.

MODUS OPERANDI FOR WORLD DOMINATION:
URBAN RENEWAL & THEATERS OF WAR

In what Mr. Griffin writes below, we see very clearly the Hegelian principles of thesis, antithesis, and synthesis.

The methods used by the International Bankers in their bid to enslave mankind under the shackles of a totalitarian One-World Government may be categorized as 'urban renewal' projects which take place in 'theaters of war.'

The basic principle of 'urban renewal' is easy to understand. It involves the leveling of an area that has been condemned by the authorities, and the construction of a new development to take its place.

If a 'developer' is to make a financial killing on an urban renewal project, it is necessary for him to get the authorities to condemn the property in a given area. He then waits until the area deteriorates still further, and the value of the property drops so low that the owners are willing to unload their holdings for a fraction of their real worth just to get them off their hands.

In a local community urban renewal program, the 'leveling' job is carried out by a demolition crew employing bulldozers, wrecking balls, pneumatic hammers and, occasionally, explosives.

From the ruins of the blighted area arises a gleaming new, modern development that is extremely profitable for the backstage manipulators who own a big 'piece of the action.'

On the International level, 'urban renewal' projects involve the destruction of the 'old order' in a variety of countries, to prepare the way for the New World Order.

To make a killing on 'urban renewal' projects internationally, it is necessary for the 'developers' to send in demolition crews at no cost to themselves, and have them level the prime portions of the target areas, so that these may be picked up inexpensively when the countries are defeated and inundated with war debts.

Internationally, these demolition 'jobs' are engineered and brought to fruition by means of war. The programs are carried out by the use of bombs, shells, high explosives and other modern 'tools.' The international 'developers' then step in to seize control of the blighted areas for a pittance, and launch massive redevelopment projects without having paid a cent for the use of the demolition crews. The profits on such international projects are so astronomical that they boggle the mind!

The highly-financed and immensely-profitable 'urban renewal' projects that have taken place on the international scene since the beginning of this century have been staged in 'theaters of war.' Over the last eighty years 'theaters of war' have existed in Europe, Russia, North and Central Africa, the Middle East, Asia and in the Pacific (*DS?* pp.53-4).

AMERICA IS DRAWN INTO THE FIRST WORLD WAR

With the passage of the income tax bill and the 'Federal' Reserve Act, the way was now almost clear for the conspirators to bring . . . [America] into World War I on the side of the Crown, with the American taxpayers footing the bill.

Athough Wilson and his hidden masters had been planning American military involvement in the European 'theater of war' for a considerable amount of time, there was one major obstacle that had to be overcome. The overwhelming majority of the American people were isolationist in their outlook. They wanted their country to adhere to the time-honored principles of the Monroe Doctrine, and not to become involved in a European war.

As the hypocritical puppet president was up for re-election in 1916, he was forced to go through the motions of being on the side of the American people during his bid for a second term. Under the slogan 'He kept us out of war,' Wilson barely won re-election. Within a few days of his inauguration for a second term, Wilson asked Congress to declare war on Germany. Congress complied (*DS?* pp.100-1).

ECONOMIC AND POLITICAL CONSEQUENCES
OF WORLD WAR I

During America's seventeen-month expedition into the European 'theater', a number of far-reaching objectives were reached by the behind the scenes manipulators.

(1) America's policy of isolationism and neutrality, expounded so eloquently by George Washington in his Farewell message and given official expression in the Monroe Doctrine, died. A precedent was established, albeit through monumental deceit, for America's use as a military tool in the hands of the International Bankers[5].

(2) Czarist Russia, a thorn in the side of the money monopolists for many years, had been successfully removed from the world scene. This had been forecast forty-seven years earlier by top Illuminist Albert Pike, in his famous letter to Mazzini.

(3) World War I created astronomical national debts in the

nations which participated. These debts were held by the International Bankers who, as we have seen, organized and stage-managed the show from the start to finish. . . .

(4) World War I created unprecedented social turmoil in the nations of Europe and set the stage for a worldwide social revolution. Nothing was the same on the world scene following the armistice of 1918. . . . The British people lost. The French people lost, as did the Germans, the Austrians and the Italians. The Russian people lost the war, the Revolution - and their freedom. America, which had well over 2 million troops in Europe at the end of hostilities, was second only to Russia on the losing side. . . . The Illuminati's 'urban renewal' program for the United States was beginning to have its effect!

Although the American people were clearly the losers in World War I, as were the people of the other participating nations, there was one group for which World War I proved to be an unqualified success: The Big Bankers. The facts about the real victors emerge from the pages of [Carroll Quigley's] Tragedy and Hope[6]. 'The First World War was a catastrophe of such magnitude that, even today, the imagination has some difficulty grasping it. . . . On all fronts in the whole war almost 13,000,000 men in the various armed forces died from wounds and disease. . . . [T]he war destroyed over $400,000,000,000 of property. . . . *Obviously, expenditures of men and wealth at rates like those required a tremendous mobilization of resources throughout the world, and could not fail to have far-reaching effects on the patterns of thought and modes of action of people forced to undergo such a strain. Some states were destroyed or permanently crippled. There were profound modifications in finance, in economic life, in social relations, in intellectual outlook and in emotional patterns. The war brought nothing new into the world; rather it sped up processes of change. . . . With the result that changes which would have taken place over a period of thirty or even fifty years in peacetime were brought about in five years during the war. . . .* ' (pp. 255-6).

The International Bankers, . . . as Quigley readily admits, were vitally interested in achieving '*another far reaching aim, nothing less than to create a world system of financial control in private hands able to dominate the political system of each country and the economy of the world as a whole. This system was to be controlled in a feudalist fashion*

. . . *by the central banks of the world [International Bankers] acting in concert, by secret agreements arrived at in frequent private meetings and conferences. . . . '(p. 324).*

'Each country suspended the gold standard at the outbreak of the war. This removed the automatic limitation on the supply of paper money. Then each country proceeded to pay for the war by borrowing from the banks. The banks created the money which they then lent by merely giving the Government a deposit of any size against which the Government could draw checks. The banks were no longer limited in the amount of credit they could create because they no longer had to pay out gold for checks on demand. Thus the creation of money in the form of credit by the banks was limited only by the demands of its borrowers. Naturally, as Governments borrowed to pay for their needs, private business borrowed in order to be able to fill the Government's orders. The gold which could no longer be demanded merely rested in the vaults, except where some of it was exported to pay for supplies from neutral countries or from fellow belligerents (p. 257).

The enormous increase in unbacked paper money led to staggering inflation: 'The middle classes of European society, with their bank savings, checking deposits, mortgages, insurance and bond holdings. . . were injured and even ruined by the wartime inflation' (p.258).

This planned debauchery of the money by the International Bankers had an added impact, which fitted in perfectly with their plans to destroy the 'old world order' in preparation for the Illuminati's 'New World Order.' In some countries, 'the inflation went so far that the monetary unit became completely valueless. The middle classes were largely destroyed, and their members were driven to desperation or at least to an almost psychopathic hatred of the form of government or the social class that they believed to be responsible for their plight.'

Even in Britain and the United States, 'prices rose by 200 to 300 percent, while public debts rose about 1000 percent' (p. 258).

Professor Quigley confirms the opinion expressed by Arthur Ponsonby, a member of the British Parliament, that 'there must have been more deliberate lying in the world from 1914 to 1918, than in any other period in the world's history' (Arthur Ponsonby, *Falsehood In Wartime*).

For example, due to British censorship, most of the facts regarding the background of the war were unknown in America (*DS?* pp.103-7).

SETTING THE SCENE FOR WORLD WAR II

In the fall of 1929 it was time for the International Bankers to push the button that set in motion the machinery that resulted in World War II. After they, their agents and friends had sold out at the crest of an artifically-inflated stock market boom, the International Bankers pulled the rug out from under the whole system and sent the United States plunging into what became known as the Great Depression. In the years that followed, the economies of nations around the world slowed to a virtual standstill.

The Crash of 1929 ended the American loans to Germany.

This triggered a severe 'flight from the mark,' as people fell over each other in their efforts to unload the mark in favor of other currencies in which they had more confidence. This resulted in a severe drain on the German gold reserve. As the gold reserve declined, the amount of money and credit had to be reduced by raising the interest rate.

By the end of 1931 the German discount rate had been raised step by step to a staggering 15 percent, without stopping the loss of the nation's gold reserve. The main result of this drastic action was that German industrial activity was reduced. When Germany's pleas for relief on her reparation payments were rejected by her creditors on a variety of grounds, her plight became ever more acute. While 'several committees of international bankers discussed the problem . . . the crisis became worse.' Darmstadter Bank and Schroder Bank both folded (*DS?* pp.125-6).

ADOLPH HITLER OFFERS RELIEF

Germany continued to writhe in an ocean of debt, fear and perplexity as everyone strove to keep their heads above the ever

rising tide of calamity. It was at this juncture that Adolph Hitler
and his National Socialist Party came to the fore on the German
political scene. His message struck a responsive chord deep down
in the hearts of millions of Germans.

His powerful promises to break Germany free from the bonds
of the Versailles Treaty, the alien financial octopus and to provide
'living room' for the greatly restricted and crisis weary population
caught the attention of the nation in the early 1930's. He offered
the people something they yearned for – strength, purpose,
leadership and a renewal of Pan Germanism. His oratory
rekindled the hope that dwelt in many a German heart, that
Germany could once again become a major force on the world
scene.

Germany in the early 1930's was an International-Banker
created time bomb, waiting for a Hitler-type individual to come on
the scene and seize control.

Detailed evidence presented before the Kilgore Committee of
the U.S. Senate in 1945 (hearing on *Elimination of German Resources
for War*), stated that 'when the Nazis came to power in 1933, they
found that long strides had been made since 1918, in preparing
Germany for war from an economic and industrial point of view.'

The vast amount of American capital that flooded into Germany under the Dawes Plan after 1924[7], formed the basis upon
which Hitler's war-making machine was constructed. As Dr.
Antony C. Sutton points out in *Wall Street and the Rise of Hitler*, 'the
contribution made by American capitalism to German war
preparations before 1940, can only be described as phenomenal.
It was certainly crucial to German military preparations. Evidence
. . . suggests that not only was an influential sector of American
business aware of the nature of Naziism, but for its own purposes
aided Naziism whenever possible (and profitable) – with full
knowledge that the probable outcome would be war involving
Europe and the United States. . . . Pleas of innocence do not accord
with the facts' (pp. 21, 23).

The thoroughly-documented evidence regarding the heavy
involvement of leading American banking and industrial interests
in the rise of Hitler's Third Reich is a matter of public record. It
is to be found in the records and reports from government

hearings, published by various Senate and House committees from 1928 to 1946. Among the most important are the *House Subcommittee to Investigate Nazi Propaganda* in 1934, the report on cartels eased by the *House Temporary National Economic Committee* in 1941, and the *Senate Subcommittee on War Mobilization* in 1946 (*DS?* pp. 126-7).

HITLER COMES TO POWER

As early as 1925, Dr. Karl Duisberg, I.G. Farben's[8] first chairman (and the founder of the American Bayer Company), expressed the desire to find a 'strong man' to lead Germany in its hour of trial:
'Be united, united, united. This should be the uninterrupted call to the parties in the Reichstag. We hope that our words of today will work, and will find the strong man who will finally bring everyone under one umbrella . . . for he [the strong man] is always necessary for us Germans, as we have seen in the case of Bismarck' (G. Edward Griffin, *I.G. Farben*, p.65).
In the fall of 1932, as the Weimer Republic was crumbling, it became apparent that Hitler was the one most suited for the role of 'strong man.' As a result, 'Hitler received backing more powerful than he had ever dared hope for. The industrial and financial leaders of Germany, with I.G. Farben in the lead, closed ranks and gave Hitler their full support. . . . ' (p.97)
'. . . Two cartels, I.G. Farben and Vereinigte Stahlwerke, produced 95 percent of German explosives in 1937-39 on the eve of World War II. This production was from capacity built by American loans and to some extent American technology.
'The I.G. Farben - Standard Oil cooperation for production of synthetic oil from coal gave the I.G. Farben cartel a monopoly of gasoline production during World War II. Just under one half of German high octane gasoline in 1945 was produced directly by I.G. Farben and most of the balance by its affiliated companies' (*Wall Street and the Rise of Hitler*, p. 31).
The International Bankers poured vast sums of money into the German economy. The three largest loans made by the money

monopolists went into the development of the three German cartels which aided Hitler and his National Socialists in their rise to power. . . .

As James Martin points out, 'these loans for reconstruction became a vehicle for arrangements that did more to promote World War II than to establish peace after World War 1' (*All Honorable Men*, p. 70).

The principal link between Hitler and the Wall Street money barons was Hjalmar Horace Greely Schacht, the president of the Reichsbank, whose family for many years were closely aligned to the international financial elite[9]. . . .

By 1932, Hitler's National Socialist Party was the largest in the Reichstag. As internal crisis piled on top of internal crisis, Hitler's powerful promises gained increasing acceptance and popularity among the German people. To many, he seemed the only way out for the German nation. He was the only figure on the German political scene who had and expounded a definite course of action to get the nation out of its increasingly terrible predicament. He promised action – and action was what the German people yearned for.

Hitler was appointed Chancellor by President Paul von Hinderburg in January 1933, and followed him as head of state, under the title of Fuhrer (Leader), at the latter's death. Within a year Hitler established himself as the dictorial leader of the German nation. Eliminating possible rivals in a series of purges, Hitler launched a massive campaign to build Germany up economically, militarily and psychologically. Repudiating the terms of the Versailles Treaty and the massive repatriation payments that had kept Germany in a state of financial bondage for the previous decade, Hitler did achieve a remarkable turn around in the economic fortunes of the country. The standard of living of the average German improved dramatically and a successful campaign was launched to boost the morale of the people. Given a cause for which to work, the Germans applied themselves with their customary diligence. Unemployment was virtually eliminated as industrial production shifted into high gear.

It was soon evident to the scene observers that Hitler and his internationalist backers were cranking out an exceptionally high percentage of products that could be used in warfare (*DS?* pp. 129-31).

THE EXTENSIVE AMERICAN INVESTMENT IN PRE-WAR GERMANY

America's top diplomatic representative to Hitler's Germany in the mid 1930's was Ambassador William Dodd. On August 15, 1936, more than three-and-a-half years after Hitler came to power, Dodd reported to President Roosevelt that 'at the present moment more than a hundred American corporations have subsidiaries here or cooperative understandings. The Du Ponts have three allies in Germany that are aiding in the armament business. Their chief ally is the I.G. Farben Company. . . . Standard Oil Company (New York sub company) sent $2,000,000 here in December 1933, and has made $500,000 a year helping Germans make Ersatz gas for war purposes; but Standard Oil cannot take any of its earnings out of the country except in goods. They do little of this, report their earnings at home, but do not report the facts. The International Harvester Company president told me their business here rose 33% a year (arms manufacture, I believe) but they take nothing out. Even our airplane people have a secret arrangement with Krupp. General Motors Company and Ford do enormous business here through their subsidiaries and take no profits out. *I mention these facts because they complicate things and add to war dangers'.*

Ambassador Dodd recorded in his diary that Dr. Englebrecht, who headed Rockefeller's Vacuum Oil Company in Hamburg, told him that 'The Standard Oil Company of New York was building a great refinery near the Hamburg harbor' (p. 303).

The American internationalists went much further with their efforts to build up the war-making capabilities of Germany. Professor Sutton, in his research, uncovered the fact that 'the two largest tank producers in Hitler's Germany were Opel, a wholly owned subsidiary of General Motors (controlled by the J.P. Morgan firm), and the Ford A.G. subsidiary, of the Ford Motor Company of Detroit. The Nazis granted tax exempt status to Opel in 1936, to enable General Motors to expand its production facilities.

General Motors obligingly reinvested the resulting profits into German industry' (*Wall Street and the Rise of Hitler*, p. 31).

Although American firms were responsible for furnishing Hitler's Germany with much of the technology and financial backing that it needed for its military build-up, many wealthy non-German Europeans were more than doing their part in the same cause. Vast sums of money were poured into Nazi Germany, from European sources, through the Warburg controlled Mendelsohn Bank in Amsterdam and, later, through the J. Henry Schroeder Bank with branches in Frankfurt, London and New York (*DS?* pp.131-2).

ANOTHER ILLUMINATI PUPPET
IN THE WHITE HOUSE

After Woodrow Wilson had been inaugurated for his second term as president of the United States, the Illuminati began to look around for another presidential candidate to take his place in the White House. They wanted a man who would be dedicated to their cause. They also wanted a man who, through his own personal warmth, could successfully con the American people into believing that he was 'their man' and that once he was safely installed in office all their problems would quickly fade into oblivion.

They found their man in the person of Franklin D. Roosevelt. Roosevelt, born in Hyde Park, New York, in 1882, was a Harvard graduate who, after attending Columbia Law School, was admitted to the New York bar. In 1910 he was elected to the New York state senate as a Democrat. Re-elected in 1912, he was appointed Assistant Secretary of the Navy by Wilson in 1913.

In the presidential campaign of 1920, Roosevelt was placed on the ticket as James Cox's running mate. However, his 'time' had not yet come! The American people had temporarily learned their lesson, and didn't wish to have another democrat of the Wilson mold in charge of their affairs. In the general election, the Cox Roosevelt ticket was buried under a landslide. The Harding Coolidge team was elected with 404 votes to 127 for their opponents.

During the 1920's, Roosevelt, in order to enhance his national political image and elevate his 'prestige,' ran for governor of New York. He was elected. He was re-elected in 1930.

In 1932, at the height of the International Banker-created Great Depression and amidst an unprecedented media campaign that portrayed Roosevelt as a 'knight in shining armor,' the New York Governor was manipulated into the position of being the Democratic nominee for president. . . . The 'image' presented throughout the campaign was of a man who would defend our nation's sovereignty and work diligently in the defense of the freedoms and rights that had contributed so mightily in bringing the United States to a position of dominance on the world scene[10].

What the American voters were 'sold' and what they received were two entirely different things! The 'Big Boys' in the City and on Wall Street had not made a mistake. Roosevelt was their man. He was dedicated to doing the will of those who had so carefully manufactured and fostered his false 'conservative' image and installed him in the Oval Office.

The fact that FDR was firmly in the pocket of the International Money Monopolists unfolds with unmistakable clarity where we examine his record[11]. As Professor Antony C. Sutton says, . . . 'Roosevelt was a creation of Wall Street, an integral part of the New York banking fraternity, and had the pecuniary interests of the financial establishment very much at heart' (*Wall Street and FDR*, p.17).

Students of history will recognize the fact that Roosevelt, in spite of his campaign rhetoric and conservative posture, abandoned his . . . position as he stepped through the door of the Oval Office. He immediately unleashed upon the American people a barrage of unconstitutional programs that brought the American nation increasingly under the control of the International Money Monopolists. In the twelve years during which he occupied the White House, FDR probably did more than any other single politican in history to bring to fruition the plans of the 'Invisible Government' of the International Bankers. . . . As a result, the United States has, in spite of the Constitution and its supposed restraints, become a quasi totalitarian state. FDR was the foreman of the Illuminati demolition crew that was sent in to destroy the

Old Order. He was their 'front' man in America whose orders included the implementation of the International Bankers' 'urban renewal' program for the United States and whose 'New Deal' was to lay the ground for the later erection of Adam Weishaupt's 'Novus Ordo Seclorum,' the New World Order. . . .

The 'power elite' which raised FDR to the presidency was the same 'dark crew of financial pirates' [Colonel E. Mandell House, Bernard Baruch and Zionist Rabbi Stephen Wise] . . . which had, twenty years earlier, raised Woodrow Wilson to the same exalted position[12].

The record of how FDR was elected as Chief Executive was a virtual rerun of Woodrow Wilson's 'success' story. Both Wilson and Roosevelt had the same script writers, the same financial supporters - and the same 'advisers' (*DS?* pp. 132-7).

WINSTON CHURCHILL

With Hitler and Roosevelt securely entrenched in power in Germany and the United States, there was still one major obstacle to be overcome along the road that was leading inexorably towards another world war. The political scene in Britain had to [be] manipulated to a point at which the people would be willing to throw themselves into another 'war to end all wars', another war to 'make the world safe for democracy.'

In the late 1930's Neville Chamberlain took over as Prime Minister from Stanley Baldwin. Neither man was ever fully under the control of the Money Monopolists.

Chamberlain, recognizing the basic weakness of the British position, had no desire to embroil his nation in another prolonged bloodbath. He sought in every possible way to avoid such an eventuality. During this critical period, Sir Barry Domville, and Captain A.M.H. Ramsey, who were well aware of the machinations of the International Bankers, were busy trying to warn the British leader of their plans (See Sir Barry Domville, *From Admiral to Cabin Boy*, and Captain A. Ramsey, *The Nameless War*).

The British Prime Minister sealed his political fate when he unexpectedly called a Palestinian Conference in London at which the Arabs (for the first time since 1919) were represented. From this conference emerged a government White Paper in March, 1939, in which Britain undertook 'the establishment within ten years of an independent Palestine state' and 'the termination of the Mandate.' In this new state, the native Arabs and the immigrant Zionists were to share the government in such a way as to ensure that the interests of both communities were protected. The immigration of Jews into the new state was to be restricted to 75,000 annually over a five-year period.

This action incurred the wrath of the Zionists who wanted to seize Palestine for their own exclusive use and to exclude the native Arabs from any part in administering the territory. This placed Chamberlain in the same position as Asquith in 1916: he had to go!

It was at this juncture that a strange political phenomenon took place on the British political stage. Winston Churchill, who had been languishing in the political doldrums for some ten years, made his triumphant return to center stage. . . . Churchill was one of the individuals who, with Lloyd George, replaced the Asquith government in 1916.

Churchill's relationship with the Zionists has been described by Douglas Reed as (to quote Churchill's own words) 'a riddle inside a mystery wrapped up in an enigma.' History records that Churchill was among the earliest British politicians to champion the Zionist 'cause.' In his autobiography, *Trial and Error*, Chaim Weizmann, a leading Zionist, described Churchill as a 'champion of the Zionist cause in the House of Commons' (p. 290). In the 1920's, as Colonial Secretary, Churchill issued a *White Paper* which the Zionists regarded as a 'serious whittling down of the Balfour Declaration'[13]. Among other things, it 'detached transJordan from the area of Zionist operation, and it raised the subject of a legislative council' with a majority of elected members. This was anathema to the Zionists as it would have meant, not only the holding of elections (which Dr. Weizmann forbade to the end!) but that the native Palestinian Arabs would end up ruling their own country. The 'Churchill White Paper' got the 'champion of Zionism' into hot water politically, and over the next seven years he was pushed into the political back waters.

During the decade of his political 'exile,' Churchill 'was a highly unpopular man, not because of any specific acts or quality, but because he was consistently given that 'bad press' which is the strongest weapon in the hands of those who control political advancement. This organized hostility was made particularly plain during the abdication crisis of 1937, when his pleas for time received much more bitter attack than they deserved and he was howled down in the House of Commons. His biographers depict him as suffering from depression during these years and thinking himself 'finished' politically. His feelings in that respect may be reflected in his published words (privately written) to Mr. Bernard Baruch early in 1939: 'War is coming very soon. You will be running the show over there, but I will be on the sidelines over here' (Controversy of Zion, p. 330). It was shortly before this acknowledgment that Baruch ('The best-known symbol of vast world money power') would be 'running the show' in America, that the 'honorable' Mr. Churchill began to experience an astonishing transformation in his political fortunes. He was 'born again' politically. The reason for this political 'miracle' was somewhat obscure at the time, but later emerged. He had changed his attitude towards the Zionists' plans to establish a Zionist state in Palestine.

In Trial and Error, Dr. Weizmann tells us that, in 1939, in the wake of widespread opposition to Zionist aspirations, and following the publication of Chamberlain's White Paper, he suddenly 'met Winston Churchill, and he told me he would take part in the [House of Commons] debate, speaking of course against the proposed White Paper" (p. 411). The learned doctor neglects to tell his unlearned readers why Churchill should 'of course' have undertaken to build a case in the British Parliament against the proposals. As late as October 22, 1938, he had still been speaking like the author of his 1922 White Paper which had incurred the wrath of the Zionists.

Dr. Weizmann recalls that on the day of the Commons debate, he got together with Churchill for lunch. Rejecting suggestions from colleagues that he instruct Churchill on what to say in the debate, Weizmann felt 'quite certain that a speaker of Mr. Churchill's caliber would have his speech completely mapped out and that he would not wish to have anyone come along with suggestions an hour or so before it was delivered.

'Churchill was thoroughly prepared. He produced a packet of small cards and read his speech to us. . . . The architecture of the speech was . . . perfect.'

In the debate, 'Churchill delivered against the White Paper one of the great speeches of his career' (p. 411).

Even the 'magic' of Churchill's splendid oratory failed to turn the tide in favor of the Zionist cause. The Commons voted 268 to 179 in favor of accepting Chamberlain's proposals.

By delivering against the *White Paper* such a great speech, Churchill clearly indicated that he had switched sides and was now available to 'lead' his country in the way most pleasing to those who pulled the strings behind the scenes. Within a few short months, Churchill was to become the British Prime Minister (*DS?* pp.141-4).

WORLD WAR II: 'BLOOD, TOIL, TEARS AND SWEAT'

The account of World War II which follows has been selected from Mr. Griffin's Descent Into Slavery? pp.144-201.

Although hundreds of books and multiple billions of words have been written about the tragedy of 'blood, toil, tears and sweat' that gripped the nations of the world between 1939 and 1945, most people know little, if anything, of the real story behind that most costly of all wars. The 'story' of the war that unfolds in the pages of the 'official' history books of America, Germany, Japan and Britain bears little resemblance to the real causes and purposes of the war as they have slowly emerged in the years since the cessation of hostilities. *Vital information is withheld!*

The 'picture painters' of the controlled mass media have also done a masterful job of pulling the wool over the eyes of those whom they are supposedly dedicated to inform and educate. These peddlers of deception have been guilty of reducing the minds of the general public to what has rightly been described as 'a state of impotent confusion' regarding World War II.

Over the years, the true story of what happened during that

tumultuous period has slowly emerged, and the facts have blended together, like the pieces of a complicated jigsaw puzzle, into a startlingly clear picture. The 'big picture' is now so clear and understandable that many are 'kicking themselves' for not having had the 'sense' to grasp it at a much earlier date.

As we shall see, many of the facts necessary for an understanding of the real goals and purposes of World War II are to be found in the works written by official, establishment historians. What they omit, however, are the crucially important insights provided by individuals who, as 'bit' players in this enthralling worldwide drama, were in a unique position to witness what was happening backstage, . . . individuals who had the courage to 'buck' the establishment and tell their stories.

A WAR WITH A PRE-DETERMINED OBJECTIVE

When Hitler's Germany launched its invasion of Poland at dawn on September 1, 1939, the mechanism created by the hidden powers in the wake of World War I sprang instantly into action, and guaranteed that within a very short space of time World War II would be under way. Under the terms of treaties signed some twenty years earlier, both England and France were obligated to enter the fray on the side of the Poles. That declaration of war came within hours. . . .

[T]he European nations had been led [into a trap] by the . . . money monopolists who were determined to use the ensuing bloodbath as a part of their worldwide 'urban renewal' program. The nations of Northern Europe, the countries which comprised the British Empire and Commonwealth, and the United States although its citizens were unaware of it at the time were bound by treaties or secret agreements to embroil themselves in the planned conflict. History records that none of the 'reasons' used by the Big Powers for entering the struggle were valid. History also records that, as we shall see, all the objectives of the Illuminati/ International Banker/ Zionist cabal were achieved prior to the end of hostilities, or shortly thereafter.

The 'phony war' lasted until May 10, 1940, at which time

Neville Chamberlain, in broken health and the victim of unrelenting attacks, was forced to resign. His place as head of the British government was taken by Winston Churchill who, only months before, had made his miraculous political comeback. Events immediately mushroomed into a widespread 'hot war' with a British air attack on Germany (J.M. Spaight, principal assistant to the British Air Ministry, *Bombing Vindicated*, published in 1944). Top officials in London openly acknowledged years later that Britain had been planning an air offensive on Germany since 1936. At the outbreak of the war, Germany did not have the capacity to effectively engage in such an air offensive against Britain. . . .

On the same day, May 10, German forces poured into the Netherlands, Belgium and Luxembourg. Two days later, they swarmed across the French border and pushed back the French and British Armies as if they were playthings.

Churchill recalls what happened: 'Now at last the slowly gathered, long pent up fury of the storm broke upon us. Four or five millions of men met each other in the first shock of the most merciless of all wars of which records have been kept. Within a week the front in France, behind which we had been accustomed to dwell through the hard years of the former war and the opening phase of this, was to be irretrievably broken. Within three weeks the long famed French Army was to collapse in rout and ruin, and the British Army to be hurled into the sea with all its equipment lost. . . . ' (*Their Finest Hour*, pp. 3-4)

Within three weeks of Hitler's assault on France, the British were engaged in a desperate effort to evacuate their 400,000 man Expeditionary Force from the beaches at Dunkirk. 335,000 British troops managed to escape the clutches of the converging German Army.

Churchill 'was shocked by the utter failure [of the Grande Armée] to grapple with the German armour . . . and by the swift collapse of all French resistance once the fighting front had been pierced. The whole German movement was proceeding along the main roads, at no point on which did they seem to be blocked' (*Their Finest Hour*, p. 53).

On June 14th the Germans entered Paris and found the city

undefended. Eight days later France capitulated. France and Germany signed an armistice at Compiegne.

At this fateful moment 'Britain stood alone,' bracing herself for the anticipated German invasion across the Channel. Britain was engaged in a desperate struggle to build up her armed forces to hopefully withstand an onslaught from Hitler's highly trained and heavily-armed forces. Churchill told the British people that he had 'nothing to offer but blood, toil, tears and sweat. . . . You ask, What is your aim? I can answer in one word: Victory – victory at all costs. . . . Without victory, there can be no survival . . . for the British Empire; no survival for all that the British Empire has stood for, no survival for the urge and impulse of the ages, that mankind will move forward towards its goal (p. 22).

This was an exceedingly ambiguous statement. It meant two entirely different things to two different groups. To the elitist 'insiders,' it meant that 'victory' was necessary for the survival of the British Empire . . . and all that it stands for. 'Victory' was necessary so 'that mankind [guided by the money monopolists in 'The City'] will move forward towards its goal', the creation of a New World Order.

To the uninitiated 'peasants,' it sounded like a heart warming, patriotic call to the higher instincts of the British masses a 'rally around the flag, boys' type of appeal so popular with political rhetoricians.

Within two weeks of assuming the leadership of the British government, Churchill issued orders that later led to the establishment of the State of Israel. On May 23 he instructed the Colonial Secretary Lord Lloyd that the British troops in Palestine be withdrawn and 'the Jews armed in their own defense and properly organized as speedily as possible. . . . '

AMERICA ENTERS WORLD WAR II

The events of 1940 and 1941 represented overwhelming victories for the Axis Powers, Germany and Italy. All of Europe lay in their grasp. Following their invasion of Russia on June 22, 1941, huge sections of that slave state came under the domination of the

German forces.

It was at this critical juncture that Franklin D. Roosevelt and his hidden masters decided that the American heavy duty . . . equipment had to be brought into action . . . or all would be lost. Congressman Hamilton Fish[14] was one of the top Republicans on Capitol Hill at the time. In *FDR - The Other Side of the Coin*, he tells us that 'President Roosevelt's responsibility for goading the Japanese into war by sending a war ultimatum on November 26, 1941, demanding that the Japanese withdraw all troops from Indo-China, and China (Manchuria) is an historic fact, although a closely-guarded secret.

'FDR's war ultimatum was deliberately withheld from Congress until after Pearl Harbor. . . . [A]ll agreed that the ultimatum left Japan no alternative but war (see *FDR*, pp.132-4 and *DS?* pp.152-3). . . .

Rear Admiral Theobold tells us: 'Diplomatically, President Roosevelt's strategy of forcing Japan to war by unremitting and ever-increasing diplomatic-economic pressure, and by simultaneously holding our Fleet in Hawaii as an invitation to a surprise attack, was a complete success. . . . One is forced to conclude that the anxiety to have Japan, beyond all possibility of dispute, commit the first act of war, caused the President and his civilian advisers to disregard the military advice [to move the Fleet] which would have somewhat cushioned the blow' (*The Final Secret of Pearl Harbor*, p.5).

During 1940 and 1941, American Intelligence broke both the Japanese diplomatic and military codes. Roosevelt and his advisers knew in advance the exact date and time of the Japanese attack on Pearl Harbor. Updated decoding machines were supplied to strategic American outposts around the world but were denied to the military at Pearl Harbor (p.36).

When Admiral Stark, second in command under FDR, was presented with clear evidence of the impending Japanese attack, one of his staff, a Captain Wilkinson, recommended that an urgent warning be radioed to the Pacific Fleet in Hawaii. The Admiral replied that such a move wasn't necessary.

Almost three hours later, General Marshall sent Admiral Kimmell, the Commander at Pearl Harbor, a Western Union telegram warning of the impending attack. The message arrived at Hawaiian headquarters six hours after the Japanese attack, and Admiral Kimmell had it two hours later (pp.115-6).

The Crown had succeeded in its plot to involve the United States in World War II, and was now assured of ultimate victory.

The hidden forces of the Illuminati had forced the Japanese into a position where they would either have to fight - or capitulate. To save their national honor, they decided to fight. It was clearly understood by the Japanese High Command that there was no hope of victory over the United States. Defeat was only a matter of time.

It was later revealed that American involvement in the Pacific had been carefully planned by the Institute of Pacific Relations, an Illuminati 'front' established to further the worldwide aims of the conspirators. The IPR planned the 'urban revewal' program for the Pacific Basin. That's half the world! (*DS?* pp.196-7 and *FR*, pp.124-34). . . .

In March, 1945, the Japanese unconditionally surrendered. Yes, March 1945! In that month the Japanese High Command sent communications to the American Embassy in Moscow, to the Russian Embassy in Tokyo and directly to the Pentagon in Washington stating that the Japanese Imperial Government wanted to unconditionally surrender. The Americans ignored the offer. . . The [reason] . . . is as simple as it is repugnant to most Americans. The Japanese home islands hadn't been destroyed. The big show was yet to come: the B-29's were being lined up on Okinawa and other islands in preparation for the International Bankers 'urban renewal' project on Japan.

Those old archaic cities had to be leveled. Those old factories, railroads, port facilities, communication networks and the national way of life had to be bulldozed into oblivion by the specially-designed demolition equipment purchased by the American taxpayer. The late Professor Carroll Quigley tells us in *Tragedy and Hope* that the big planes '*engaged in the systematic destruction of all Japanese cities. The flimsy houses of these crowded urban areas made them very vulnerable to incendiary bombs. . . . On March 9th, 1945, the Air Force tried a daring experiment. The defensive armament was removed from 279 B-29's, releasing weight for additional incendiaries, and these planes, without guns but carrying 1900 tons of fire bombs, were sent on a low level attack on Tokyo. The result was the most devastating air attack in all history . . . with the loss of only three planes. Sixteen square miles of central Tokyo was burned out, 250,000 houses were destroyed, over a million persons were made homeless and 84,793 were killed. This was more destructive than the first atomic bomb over Hiroshima five months later. . . .'* (p.815). Japan was wiped out, devasted by the fury and intensity of America's aerial bombardment. Why? Simple! The ground had to be cleared for new industries and other types of development. . . . The war against Japan wasn't fought to defeat an enemy. It was fought to create a condition - a condition of desolation and abject poverty throughout Japan. This was done so that the International 'redevelopers' could rush in at the end of hostilities and seize the prime real estate for their own use.

Shortly after the war - after the American airborne demolition crews had done their job - vast sums of money became available for the reconstruction of Japan. The capital to build and equip Japan's gleaming new industrial plants, ports, railroads, warehouses and skyscraper office buildings didn't come inside Japan. It came from outside Japan. It came from the same people who benefited enormously from the war debts piled up by many nations around the world. It came from the International Bankers. They put up the money. They own the show. . . . [They] are presently reaping an incalculable fortune from their 'investment' in that country!

The Japanese people have proved to be excellent workers, real producers who are more dedicated to their employers than they are to their own families.

In Japanese society, it is true that Japanese occupy all the 'front' positions in politics, industry, finance and education. For the most part, they are supervisors and managers. They have no authority as to how things are run. The shadowy characters behind the scenes - the people who put up the money and signed the checks - are the real masters of Japan.

As Benjamin Disraeli once wrote [in *Coningsby*]: *'And so you see . . . the world is governed by very different personages than is imagined by those who are not behind the scenes'* (DS? pp.196-201).

NORTH AFRICAN CAMPAIGN

The tide of war began to turn near the end of 1942. Slowly at first, then with ever quickening momentum, the fortunes of war began to favor the Allies. On November 8th American and British troops staged a massive landing in French North Africa. Although the Allies 'had the initiative and the advantage of surprise, the build-up was inevitably slow. Shipping imposed its harsh limits. Unloading was hampered by air attacks. Road transport was lacking. . . . With the arrival of German troops in large numbers by air in Tunis, a high class, stubborn and violent resistance began' (Winston Churchill, *Hinge of Fate*, p. 574).

Soon the rainy season came and the Allies were bogged down in mud. By the end of the year, the German forces totalled close to fifty thousand.

During the following five months the Allies gradually gained control of North Africa, and on May 13th General Alexander signalled Churchill that 'the Tunisian campaign is over. All enemy resistance has ceased. We are masters of the North African shores.'

'In London there was, for the first time in the war, a real lifting of spirits' (*Churchill*, p. 679).

Securing control of North Africa and building up their forces, the Allies soon launched invasions of Sicily (July 10) and the Italian mainland (September 3). Italy surrendered three days later.

AN EXPLANATION IS NEEDED

Up to this juncture events in the war were fairly straight-forward, predictable and understandable. However, the events that transpired following the capitulation of Italy do not jell with the professed intentions of the Allies at the outset of hostilities. An explanation is needed!

With the tide of war clearly flowing with the Allies, it would have been the logical tactic to make a major thrust from Italy towards the heart of Hitler's Reich. The decision not to start such an offensive was political, not military in nature.

The way Churchill tells the story of this vital period of history, and all contemporary historians back up his claim, [was that] he wanted to strike at Germany from both the south and the north and to bring the Central European and Balkan countries under Allied control, before they were allowed to slip into Red slavery. This policy would have led to a genuine Allied victory and the fulfillment of the original declared aims of the war. Churchill clearly recognized the grave threat posed by what he called 'the Red Menace.'

The Churchillian strategy was overruled by the Americans. At the Quebec Conference of August 1943, General George C. Marshall insisted that troops be withdrawn from Italy and used in a secondary invasion of France at the time of the Normandy invasion.

This meant that the fighting heart was ripped out of Field Marshal Alexander's Allied forces which, according to General Mark Clark, had become 'a tremendous fighting machine . . . with horizons unlimited.' Marshall's plan added nothing to the Allied war effort: in fact it hindered it, prolonging the war by many months. As we shall see, this new strategy was politically motivated. The effects were devastating to the freedom loving nations of Eastern Europe.

General Mark Clark, writing in 1950, gives us some real insight into this history-changing event.

As a result of orders received from the highest level, *our team was soon broken up and the Fifth Army was sapped of a great deal of its strength. A campaign that might have changed the whole history of relations between the Western World and Soviet Russia was permitted to fade away. . . . These were decisions made at high level and for reasons beyond my field and my knowledge. . . . Not only in my opinion, but in the opinion of a number of experts who were close to the problem, the weakening of the campaign in Italy in order to invade Southern France instead of pushing on into the Balkans was one of the outstanding political mistakes of the war. . . .*

'Naturally, I am a prejudiced witness in this matter because it was my team that was being weakened; but I believe there is plenty of evidence from other sources to support my attitude. For instance, there was Marshal Kesselring, *whose intelligence section was completely mystified in coming weeks when our great forward drive failed to take advantage of its chance to destroy the beaten and disorganized German Army in Italy.*

'"It is incomprehensible why divisions were withdrawn from the front," according to one German general whom we interviewed after the war. '"Whatever the reasons, it is sure they all accrued to the benefit of the German High Command."

'After the fall of Rome, Kesselring's army could have been destroyed - *if we had been allowed to shoot the works in a final offensive. And across the Adriatic was Yugoslavia ... and beyond Yugoslavia were Vienna, Budapest and Prague"* (*Calculated Risk*, pp. 368-370).

The new strategy was first agreed upon by the Allies at the Quebec Conference of 1943 at the insistence of General George C. Marshall. According to Robert Sherwood, the decision was based on a document called Russia's Position which was ascribed to 'a very high level United States military estimate.' This document stated that *'Russia's post war position in Europe will be a dominant one.* ... Since Russia is the decisive factor in the war, she must be given every assistance and every effort must be made to obtain her friendship. Likewise, *since without a doubt she will dominate Europe on the defeat of the axis, it is even more essential to develop and maintain the most friendly relations with Russia'* (*Roosevelt and Hopkins*, p. 748).

The reader will notice that a basic *assumption* was made in this top-secret document. The behind the scenes planners in Washington proposed, at the conclusion of hostilities, to have Russia as the dominant power in Europe. This was contrary to all the public utterances by our 'leaders' on the subject.

To accommodate such a diabolical change in plans, it became necessary to discard all of the known rules of warfare and to engage in a campaign of deception to throw the people off the scent of what was really taking place in the European 'theater.' Sand had to be thrown in the eyes of the 'peasants' to blind them to the fact that the International Banker/Illuminati cabal was engaged in another of its 'urban renewal' projects.

LIEUTENANT COLONEL DWIGHT D. EISENHOWER

To ensure success for their nefarious undertaking, it was

necessary for the conspirators to have one of their own trusted servants in the position of Supreme Commander over all Allied forces in Europe. The individual chosen for this job was a lieutenant colonel named Dwight D. Eisenhower.

Eisenhower's army career is more than interesting - it is a fascinating study of what can happen to a personable but very average individual if he happens to have the 'right' people behind him. By his own admission, his 'qualifications . . . were probably those of the average hard-working Army officer of my age" (*Crusade in Europe*, p. 19). This fact is attested to by many of his contemporaries who had the opportunity to see him operating at close range. He was very average - with none of the great leadership qualities which were so dynamically evident in the careers of such stalwarts as George S. Patton and Douglas McArthur. Eisenhower's only qualification for the exalted position he attained late in 1943 was his dedicated and unswerving loyalty to his hidden masters.

As the powers-that-be laid plans for America's entry into the war, the Lt. Colonel began his meteoric rise to international prominence. In March, 1941, he became a full colonel. Three months later he was promoted to become Chief of Staff of the American Third Army. Another three months passed and he became a brigadier general. On December 12 of the same year, he was called to Washington on orders from General Marshall and brought into war-planning at the highest level.

On February 16, 1942, he became Assistant Chief of Staff of the War Plans Division. Two months later, when this Division was replaced by the Operations Divisions of the War Department General Staff, Eisenhower was put in charge, with the rank of major general. Three months later Ike was placed in command of the 'European Theater of Operations.' The following month he became a lieutenant general. Six months later Eisenhower became a full general.

On December 24, 1943, President Roosevelt gave Eisenhower a Christmas present: he appointed him Supreme Commander in Europe.

What was the 'secret' behind the fact that Eisenhower was jumped over the heads of at least 150 of his seniors to be placed in supreme command of the Allied Forces in Europe, especially in light of the fact that he had no battle experience or experience in handling large numbers of men in the field.

That question was answered some years later, after Eisenhower had become President. At that time, he cut short one of his many vacations to open a park in New York which Bernard Baruch had founded in honor of his father. In his speech, Eisenhower made a remarkable admission: 'Twenty five years ago, as a young and unknown major [sic], I took the wisest step in my life, I consulted Mr. Baruch' (A.K. Chesterton, *The New Unhappy Lords*, p. 36).

In *Crusade In Europe*, Eisenhower recalls the period when he completed his studies at the War College in 1928. He served 'as a special assistant in the office . . . of the Assistant Secretary of War' and was '*forced to examine worldwide military matters. . . . The years devoted to work of this kind opened up to me an almost new world. During this time I met and worked with many people whose opinions I respected highly, in both military and civilian life. Among these, an outstanding figure was Mr. Bernard Baruch, for whom my admiration was and is profound*' (p. 19).

Without a doubt, Eisenhower owed his meteoric rise to fame and 'glory' to Bernard Baruch and his 'friends.'

COMMANDER EARLE

Why wasn't the Allies' 'tremendous fighting machine' allowed to continue its powerful advance from northern Italy up through the 'soft underbelly' of Europe towards the heart of Hitler's Germany? What was the real reason behind the fact that Kesselring's army, which was reeling in disarray before the onslaught of the Allied 5th Army, was allowed to regroup, reorganize and re-arm so that it could continue the struggle for nearly another two years?

It is generally acknowledged by military experts that, had the Allies taken the logical and direct route to Germany, four important results would have occurred:

(1) The duration of the war would have been shortened by at least a year;

(2) The lives of more than 100,000 Allied troops would have been spared;

(3) The United States National Debt, that resulted from the war, would have been greatly reduced, and

(4) The political face of Europe would have been vastly different.

The answers to the above questions are as simple as they are shocking. The men who were outwardly 'leading' the United States - Roosevelt, Marshall and Eisenhower - were under strict orders from their hidden masters to conduct the concluding stages of the war in the European 'theater' in such a manner that the goals of the Illuminati would be furthered. It was of no concern to the international power brokers that the delay in finishing the war resulted in hundreds of thousands of needless deaths, and the unnecessary expenditure of many billions of dollars. They view humanity as so much cannon fodder to be used in the accomplishment of their . . . purpose.

This sad but unavoidable conclusion is the only honest one that can be reached in an objective analysis of the facts that are now available.

We are indebted to Colonel Curtis B. Dall, President Roosevelt's son in law, for bringing to light what he describes as the 'electrifying' story of what went on behind the scenes in Washington in 1943. He provides us with a vital missing piece of the jigsaw puzzle that opens up to our understanding the meaning of events in Europe at that time.

In his book, *FDR - My Exploited Father In Law* (pp. 146 159), Colonel Dall relates the shattering story of Commander George Earle, the former governor of Pennsylvania, who had been decorated for bravery during World War I. Commander Earle served as American Minister to Austria from 1935 1939. He also served as American Minister to Bulgaria from 1940 1942. He was the Chief Gunnery officer on the transport 'Hermitage' which carried the great American General, George S. Patton, and his troops to North Africa.

'George Earle was one of the first "fair-haired" boys backing the New Deal, a man who admired FDR and his political philosophy. At the right time, he threw a solid five fingered check on the tambourine of the Democratic Party. As might be expected, that gesture on his part was duly noticed by their Finance Committee.

Dall was introduced to Earle by a friend who was a nephew of the Commander. Although he had been warned that Earle's was a 'remarkable story that would curl your hair,' Dall recalls that he was 'quite unprepared for the staggering impact of what George Earle told me, in a leisurely manner, at luncheon two weeks later.' (pp. 147-8). Earle related 'one of the most dramatic and important episodes of World War II.'

In 1943, just before FDR and Churchill met in Casablanca to announce their demand for 'unconditional surrender' from Germany, Roosevelt appointed Commander Earle as his personal naval attache in Istanbul, Turkey. It was a sensitive position. That was why Roosevelt's friend, George Earle, was chosen for the job.

Commander Earle opened up with a direct salvo: 'I told your former father-in-law, FDR, how he could greatly shorten World War II (almost two years). *He wouldn't listen to me, or shall I say, he wasn't allowed to listen to me! Can you believe it?*'

Earle arrived in Istanbul in the spring of 1943. He had previously earned the reputation of being strongly anti-Nazi. This had resulted from an incident in Bulgaria some years earlier.

One morning there was a knock at his hotel room door. When he opened the door, Earle came face to face with a broad-shouldered, medium-sized man in civilian clothes. He introduced himself as Admiral Wilhelm Canaris, head of the German Secret Service, and requested an informal conference.

Canaris told Earle that there were many sensible Germans who loved their Fatherland and who greatly disliked Hitler, feeling that the Fuhrer was leading their nation down a path to destruction.

Canaris continued, saying that the 'unconditional surrender' policy as outlined by America and Britain could not be accepted by the German generals. He said, however, that if the American president would simply indicate that he would accept an honorable surrender from the German Army, tendered to the American Forces, such an event could be arranged. The Admiral stated that the real enemy of Western civilization (the Soviets) could then be stopped. The German Army, if so directed, would move to the

Eastern Front to protect the West against the onrushing Red Army. The Russians obviously aimed at establishing themselves as the supreme power in Europe and were deceiving the American people about their intentions.

Commander Earle was 'staggered' at first by this completely unexpected turn of events. As he recovered from his shock, he was very guarded in his reaction to the German Admiral and his startling proposal.

Shortly after this amazing encounter, Earle had a meeting with Franz von Papen, the German Ambassador, who was strongly anti-Hitler in his feelings. A secret rendezvous was arranged, late at night, at a lonely spot under some trees, five or six miles outside of Istanbul. There Earle and von Papen conversed alone for several hours.

Commander Earle, who was acknowledged by FDR as his 'emissary' in Turkey, soon became convinced that these top German officials were totally sincere in their proposals. Becoming further informed on the hidden aims of the Russians, Earle promptly sent a coded message to President Roosevelt in Washington, via diplomatic pouch, reporting full details of his meetings with Admiral Canaris and Ambassador von Papen. He requested a prompt reply.

Earle waited with eager anticipation for Roosevelt's reply, sensing that this remarkable chain of events heralded a speedy conclusion to the war. Days turned into weeks, but there was only silence.

Thirty days later, as agreed, the German Admiral called on the phone and asked: 'Have you any news?'

Commander Earle replied: 'I am waiting for news, but have none today.'

Admiral Canaris said: 'I am very, very sorry, indeed.' Then there was silence.

Events quickly developed in Turkey. Earle soon had a long meeting with Baron Kurt von Lersner who was the director of the Orient Society, a German cultural organization in Istanbul. They spoke for several hours.

Here again, the same question was posed to Commander Earle: if the anti Nazis in Germany delivered the German forces to the

Americans, could they then rely on Allied cooperation in keeping the Soviets out of Eastern Europe? The Baron stated that if Roosevelt agreed to an 'honorable surrender,' even if Hitler was not killed by his group, he would be handed over by them to the Americans. It was of the utmost importance that the Russians be contained in the East and prevented from spreading their reign of terror across their Western borders.

Again, the Commander sent an urgent, coded message to the White House, pleading with Roosevelt to seriously consider the proposals made by the anti-Nazis. Again, there was no response from his Commander-in-Chief.

Following this new setback, the President's personal emissary had another secret meeting with von Lersner who came up with a new plan to surrender Hitler's remote Eastern European Headquarters and move the German Army to the Russian front until a cease fire could be organized.

Not having heard a word from Washington in nearly two months despite his urgent requests for instructions, Earle sent a most urgent message to President Roosevelt through Army-Navy channels to ensure that his message got through to FDR.

The Commander said that at this stage of developments - or lack thereof - he concluded that 'the White House was certainly no place to try and expose the truth about Soviet Russia.' He 'felt sure that strong White House "influence" had the President's "ear"', willing to see all the German people wiped out, regardless of how many American soldiers' lives would be sacrificed on the battlefield, on the sea and in the air to achieve that monstrous objective.'

Plans had been laid in Istanbul so that, upon receipt of a hoped for positive response from Roosevelt regarding an honorable surrender, Commander Earle was to fly to an undisclosed spot in Germany, there to receive further details about a German surrender. These details could then be sent to the White House for further action. A plane stood by at an airstrip near Istanbul in anticipation of Roosevelt's favorable response. It waited and waited!

The Commander became increasingly discouraged and frustrated in his efforts to get official Washington to respond to his urgent messages.

Finally, an 'answer' came in the form of a suggestion that he take up with the Field Commander in Europe any proposal for a negotiated peace. 'I was shocked, greatly disheartened and felt that my usefulness was about over,' said the Commander. 'I returned to the U.S.A . . . and World War II proceeded along its scheduled course, until the Soviets sat astride Europe.

'After a while, however, I decided to make known some of my views and observations about our so called Allies, the Soviets, so as to wake up the American people about what was really going on. I contacted the President about it and he reacted strongly and specifically forbade me to make my views known to the public.'

In a letter to Earle, dated March 24, 1945, the President stated that *'you have held important positions of trust under your government. To publish information obtained in those positions would be a great betrayal. You say that you will publish unless you are told before March 28th that I do not wish you to do so. I not only do not wish it, but I specifically forbid you to publish any information or opinion about an Ally that you may have acquired while in office or in the service of the United States Navy.*

'In view of your wish for continued active service, I shall withdraw any previous understanding that you are still serving as an emissary of mine and I shall direct the Navy department to continue your employment wherever they can make use of your services. . . .

Colonel Dall relates that when he first met Franklin Roosevelt, he found him to be a man who 'possessed great personal charm' and who could be 'well nigh irresistible. . . . We hit it off splendidly' (p. 13). 'Up to 1932, the Franklin Roosevelt family appeared like any normal, prominent American family. After 1932, however, 'power' stepped in, applied by the ruthless emissaries of money-power. Then, the chemistry gradually changed in FDR, it seemed, from formula A to formula B. . . new traits were appearing in lieu of the old familiar ones. . . . In beholding the new personality of FDR . . . I began to acquire a feeling of aloofness and reserve, even sorrow.'

Because of the activities of FDR and his wife 'whom I had once held in high esteem and affection,' his regard 'died long before the news of their demise appeared in the public press' (pp. 144-5). Roosevelt was obviously a puppet of the Power Elite.

'Admiral Canaris, as a result of his patriotic and brave humanitarian efforts, was captured and hanged by Hitler, with an iron collar around his neck. It took thirty minutes for him to die. Many other high level, anti-Nazi leaders were hanged or shot. Their subsequent plan to eliminate Hitler, by exploding a bomb in the map room of his forest headquarters, merely wounded him. The plan failed with the loss of life to several thousand German patriots. The bomb was carried by Colonel Count Claus von Stauffenberg in his briefcase (pp.155-6).

On July 21, 1964, the *New York Times* reported: 'Two hundred participants of the plot were later executed and 5000 more persons suspected of resistance activities were liquidated before the war ended ten months later.

'Eugen Gerstenmair, President of the [German] Parliament, who was another survivor of the German resistance, said it was a mistake to assume that moves against Hitler began only when it became clear that the war was lost.

Colonel Dall concludes by saying that 'FDR's *great error, a misnamed "blunder", in completely ignoring that timely offer to negotiate an early peace, was akin to a national calamity for the United States and the World   a victory for his advisers, and their plans. Little more can be added here, except to point out that the creators of false images are operating today . . . full time, festooned about the White House and on Capitol Hill, busy creating 'managed news' for you and me, even withholding some news. In that connection, Commander Earle would know just exactly what I mean. Apparently today American casualties are still unimportant* (p. 157).

MAJOR RACEY JORDAN

We have seen clear evidence that the top authorities in Washington forbade the Allied army to strike for the heart of Hitler's Germany following the victorious Italian campaign in 1943. Dramatic evidence has also been presented to prove that at the same time as huge numbers of Allied troops were being diverted in order to participate in an irrelevant invasion of Southern France, the top officials in Washington refused to pay any attention to repeated German offers to surrender. As a result of those apparently senseless 'blunders', dramatic changes took place in the political make-up of Europe. The course of history was changed!

The reader must grasp the fact that although these amazing and unprecedented events 'staggered' and 'startled' individuals like Commander Earle, General Mark Clark, General Kesselring and Admiral Canaris, these same decisions made a lot of sense to the unseen manipulators who were calling the shots and pulling the strings behind the scenes. They were working to a definite plan. They had their strategy clearly marked out.

As the real truth is always carefully 'buried' by the villainous perpetrators of a plot, it is necessary for us to look elsewhere for the missing pieces that will complete the jigsaw puzzle and make the Big Picture stand out in stark relief. That Big Picture goes together piece by piece, the constituent parts being found 'here a little and there a little.'

From the many hundreds of books that emerged from the 'blood, toil, tears and sweat' of World War II, there is only one that provides us with the 'piece' of the jig saw puzzle that is essential to our understanding of this crucial phase of history's bloodiest conflict. This vital book has, however, been shunned like a plague by all the 'right' newspapers and magazines, ignored by all the movie moguls and buried by all the 'leading' libraries across the nation. The book that received this extraordinary 'non treatment' is probably the most important book written about this critical period of history. It is: *From Major Jordan's Diaries*, by George Racey Jordan.

At the outbreak of the war Jordan, a veteran of World War I, was living quietly as a businessman. Like many thousands of patriotic Americans, he re-enlisted in the belief that he and his fellow countrymen were honor bound to fight for the defense of democracy and freedom. Because of his previous military and business experience, Jordan was given the job of a Lend Lease expeditor and a liaison officer with the Russians. In this important capacity, he served for two crucial years, from May 1942 to June 1944, at Newark Airport and at the big air base at Great Falls, Montana.

When he reported for duty on May 10, 1942, his orders gave

the full title of the New Jersey facility as: 'United Nations Depot No. 8, Lend Lease Division, Newark Airport, Newark, New Jersey, International Section, Air Service Command, Air Corps, U. S. Army.'

From the outset, Jordan was amazed at the influence wielded by the top Russian at the base, Colonel Anatoli N. Kotikov. It seemed as if his slightest wish was the command of those he was dealing with on a higher level in Washington. Repeatedly, Kotikov would call Harry Hopkins, Roosevelt's assistant, on the phone and get instant action. Repeatedly, the best interests of the United States armed forces were overruled in favor of projects that helped the Russians. Nothing, it seemed, was too good for our communist 'allies'! 'I call Mr. Hopkins. Mr. Hopkins fix,' were words constantly heard by Jordan in his dealings with Kotikov. On one occasion Colonel Kotikov flew into a towering rage when a 'Russian' plane, 'donated by American Lend Lease and paid for by American tax payers,' was involved in a minor accident with an American Airlines plane. Jordan thought that the Russian was bluffing when he told him that his friend Mr. Hopkins would take care of the 'crisis.' 'I was wrong. On June 12th the order came from Washington not only ordering American Airlines off the field, but directing every aviation company to cease activities at Newark forthwith. The order was not for a day or a week. It held for the duration of the war, though it was called a 'temporary suspension.' I was flabber-gasted. . . . '

'I was dazed at the speed with which the expulsion proceedings had taken place. First, a CAB inspector had arrived. Someone in Washington, he said, had set off a grenade under the Civil Aeronautics Board. He spent several days in the control tower, and put our staff through a severe quiz about the amount of commercial traffic and whether it was interferring with Soviet operations. The word spread around the field that there was going to be hell to pay. Several days later, the order of expulsion arrived.

'I had to pinch myself to make sure that we Americans, and not the Russians, were the donors of Lend Lease.

'I decided to start a diary, and to collect records of one kind or another.' Jordan remembered and applied the excellent advice he had been given as a 19 year old corporal in 1917: 'Jordan, if you want to get along, keep your eyes and your ears open, keep your big mouth shut, and keep a record of everything.'

'Now I felt a foreboding that one day there would be a thorough investigation of Lend Lease. I was only one cog in the machinery. Yet because of the fact that I couldn't know the details of high level strategy, I began the Jordan diaries' (pp. 7 10).

HARRY HOPKINS

History reveals that, from the outset in 1933, the Roosevelt Administration was dedicated to the survival of the Bolshevik Butchers in Russia. In that year, with Stalin's monstrous regime tottering on the brink of extinction, and with most of the nations of the civilized world giving Russia the diplomatic cold shoulder, the Roosevelt administration stepped in and granted diplomatic recognition to the bloodstained fiends who, for more than fifteen years, had drenched the soil of Russia with the innocent blood of multiple millions of hapless slaves. Roosevelt's recognition of the Red savages as the legitimate government in Russia gave them access to the credit and money markets of the world. Without such assistance, Russia was doomed.

The dedication shown by the top officials in Washington for the support and development of Red tyranny was demonstrated by Harry Hopkins in a speech he gave at a Russian Aid Rally at Madison Square Garden: 'A second front? Yes, and if necessary a third and a fourth front. . . . The American people are bound to the people of the Soviet Union in the great alliance of the United Nations. . . .

'We are determined that nothing shall stop us from sharing with you all that we have and are in this conflict, and we look forward to sharing with you the fruits of victory and peace. . . .

'Generations unborn will owe a great measure of their freedom to the unconquerable power of the Soviet people' (p.12).

Jordan states in his book that 'we never knew the exact use to which anything sent under Russian Lend Lease was put, and the failure to set up a system of accountability is now seen to have been an appalling mistake. . . . The British let us inspect their installations openly, and exchanged information freely. The Russians did not. Our government was intent on supplying whatever the Russians asked for, as fast as we could get it to them (p.15).

AID ENGINEERED TO CREATE POST-WAR RUSSIAN MACHINE

Although 'official Washington' was depriving American forces of much-needed war material in order to supply the Russians, the latter were deeply suspicious and refused to open the 'obvious' best supply route the one by air through Alaska and across Siberia. Stalin described this route as 'too dangerous'.

'Where the U.S. was not able to force Russia's hand, Nazi submarines succeeded. Subs out of Norway were attacking our Lend-Lease convoys on the Murmansk route, apparently not regarded as 'too dangerous a route' for American crews. A disastrous limit was finally reached when, out of one convoy of 34 ships, 21 were lost. The Douglas A-20 Havocs, which were going to the bottom of the ocean, were more important to Stalin than human lives. So first we started flying medium bombers from South America to Africa, but by the time they got across Africa to Tiflis, due to sandstorms the motors had to be taken down and they were not much use to the Russians. Nor were we able to get enough of them on ships around Africa to fill Russian requirements for the big offensive building up for the battle of Stalingrad.

'Finally, Russia sent its OK on the Alaskan Siberian route. Americans would set up all the airport facilities in Alaska; Soviet pilots would take over on our soil; Soviet pilots only, would fly into Russia. . . .

'Later it came out that we actually built bases for the Russians in Siberia. Colonel Maxwell E. Erdofy, the famous airport builder, and crews from the Alcan Highway project, were ordered to Russia and kept in isolation and under Soviet guard as they built Siberian airports. . . . (p.17).

Major General John R. Deane in his book, *The Strange Alliance* (Viking 1947), observes that American aid to the Red Butchers 'was carried out with a zeal which approached fanaticism' (pp.90-1).

This statement is borne out by the fact that on January 1, 1943, a memorandum sent to the 'Commanding General, Air Service Command,' stated: "I.   The President has directed that . . . equipment and movement of Russian planes have been given front priority, even over planes for U.S. Army Air Forces. . . .' (p. 20)

This, then, was what motivated those who occupied the highest positions of political power in Washington. These individuals were dedicated to the advancement and development of Soviet Tyranny. Aiding Russia was given top priority. Put simply, the welfare of Red Russia meant more to our 'leaders' than did the welfare of our own armed forces.

Jordan relates that in 1942 the Russians had been given 25 of the 200 horsepower diesel marine engines worth $17,500 each. They asked for an additional 25, but their request was overruled by Major General John Deane, Chief of our Military Mission in Moscow, because General McArthur needed them in the South Pacific. 'But the Russians were undaunted and decided to make an issue of it by going directly to Hopkins who overruled everyone in favor of Russia. In the three-year period, 1942-44, a total of 1,305 of these engines were sent to Russia!   They cost $30,745,947. The engines they had previously received were reported by General Deane and our military observers to be rusting in open storage. It is now perfectly obvious that these diesels were post war-items, not at all needed for Russia's immediate war activity (p. 14).

Although a complete, itemized list of America's Lend- Lease shipments are unobtainable through any agency of 'our' government in Washington, Major Jordan (he was promoted to the rank of Major on the recommendation of Kotikov, see *Diaries*, p.35) was able to obtain copies from the Russians.   The dollar value of American aid to the Reds had annual dollar totals as follows: 1942 - $1,422,853,332; 1943 - $2,955,811,271; 1944 - $3,459,274,155; 1945 - $1,838,281,501. The grand total for the four years is $9.6 *Billions*.

From the pages of Major Jordan's diaries pour the explicit details of the type of aid given to Russia during these critical years. On 24 pages (pages 83-106) Jordan lists (with quantities and dollar value) items shipped. Included on this list are chemicals, metals and minerals suitable for use in an atomic pile and also in manufacture of the hydrogen bomb. Also included were cobalt metal and cobalt bearing scrap (806,941 pounds), uranium metal (2.2 pounds), berylluim, cadmium, cobalt ore and concentrate (33,600 pounds), aluminum rods (13,744,709 pounds), graphite (7,384,482 pounds), insulated copper wire (399,556,729 pounds) etc.

Also on the list are items described by General Groves as 'purely post war Russian supplies.' These included 121 merchant vessels valued at $123,000,000; 1285 locomotives worth $103,000,-000; motor trucks and buses costing $508,000,000; tractors valued at close to $24,000,000; telephone instruments worth $33,000,000; generators valued at $222,000,000 and 2,693,162 automobile inner tubes costing $6,659,880.

Major Jordan also lists major donations from Washington that were obviously designed to bolster the Red regime after the war. These gifts included two factories for food products (price $6,924,000), one petroleum refinery (cost $29,050,000), one repair plant for precision instruments ($550,000) and seventeen stationary steam and three hydro-electric plants costing $273,289,000.

BACK-UP AMERICAN PILOTS FOR RUSSIA

With the changeover to the Alaskan-Siberian route early in 1942, Russian Lend-Lease operations were transferred from Newark to Great Falls, Montana. Major Jordan was transferred to Great Falls as 'United Nations Representative' (p. 19).

Jordan relates that, in the spring of 1943, there was an unusual congestion of Airacobra pursuit planes at the Montana base. These were being used by the Russians as anti-tank weapons. Colonel Kotikov got furious when as many as 200 Airacobras were stacked up at the field. 'We've got to have more pilots,' he screamed.

Jordan recalls: 'There was always a chronic shortage of American pilots, but in 1943 the demand was ravenous — in the Atlantic, in the Pacific, in Europe, in Asia, and in the American system of global air transport which was a wonder of the war. 'Then, all of a sudden, something happened. Two days later, out of inbound craft tumbled strange new flyers, bewildered and annoyed. Some had been snatched from well earned rest between trips to Ireland.

Others hailed from bases in Puerto Rico, Long Beach, Boca Raton, Oklahoma City. Test pilots had been plucked from Wright Field. There were even a few prodigies with instrument certificates; such defiers of storm and darkness were rare as hen's teeth. . . .

'Few of the pilots had ever heard of Great Falls, and all were dumbfounded by its extensive facilities and operations. 'What the hell's going on here?' they muttered. The answer was soon coming. Colonel Kotikov had gone 'straight to Mr. Hopkins' (pp. 46-47).

ATOMIC SECRETS PASSED TO RUSSIA FROM THE WHITE HOUSE

Major Jordan became troubled by the unusual number of black patent leather suitcases, bound with white window sash and sealed with red wax, which were going through en route to Moscow. At first these suitcases were in the charge of Russian officers who claimed they were 'personal luggage,' but soon they were replaced by armed couriers, travelling in pairs, whose excuse for avoiding inspection was that the cases were covered by 'diplomatic immunity.' When asked about the cases by Major Jordan, Colonel Kotikov answered that they were of the 'highest diplomatic character'. Comments Jordan: 'I am sure he knew that one of these days I would try to search the containers' (p. 35).

At four o'clock one cold afternoon in March, 1943, Colonel Kotikov did something that was unique. He invited Jordan to have dinner with him at a Great Falls restaurant known as 'Caroline Pines.' Jordan was suspicious. What was Kotikov up to? Acting on a hunch, Jordan excused himself from riding to the restaurant in the Russian's car. He used his own car, which was driven by a soldier. In case of emergency, he preferred to have mobility.

Asking his maintenance chief if the Russians were planning any flights, Jordan was told that, yes, there was a C-47 staged on the line, preparing to leave. 'It was being warmed up with Nelson heaters - large canvas bags, fed with hot air, which were made to slip over motors and propellers. . . .

Calling the control tower, Jordan left the phone number of the restaurant and issued strict orders that no cargo plane was to be cleared for Russia except by himself.

When Jordan joined Kotikov at the restaurant he found that four other Russians had been invited to join the dinner party.

Kotikov produced a bottle of vodka and the group drank toasts to Stalin and Roosevelt.

At 8:30 p.m., when the group was nearing the end of dinner, the waitress handed the Major a note asking him to call the control tower at once. Getting through to the tower, he was told that the plane was warmed up and that a couple of newly-arrived couriers were demanding clearance. Without notifying the Russians, he threw on his great coat, raced to his car and ordered his driver to race to the hangars four miles away.

When he reached the plane a burly Russian appeared at a door and tried to prevent Jordan entering. He failed. Once inside the plane, Jordan could see by the dim light of a single bulb an array of the mysterious black suitcases and a second, leaner Russian guard. He indicated that he wished to examine some of the cases. 'Promptly they went insane. They danced. They pushed at me with their hands and shrieked over and over the one English word they appeared to know. It was 'deeplomateek'. I brushed them aside and took from my pocket a metal handle containing a safety razor blade. . . . Sensing its purpose, the lean courier flung himself face down across the suitcases, with arms and legs outspanned to shield as many as possible with his body. I dragged one of the containers from under him, and he leaped up again as I started to saw through the first cord. At this sight, their antics and shouts redoubled.

'While opening the third suitcase, I had a mental flash that brought sweat to my forehead. The Russians were half-mad with fury and terror. They were on both sides of me, in front and behind. Supposing, in desperation, one of them shot me in the back? There would be no American witness, and my death could be passed off as a 'deplorable accident. . . .'

'I called a Yank soldier who was on patrol thirty feet away. I asked if he had had any combat experience. He answered that he had, in the South Pacific. I stooped lower and murmured: 'I'm going to open more of this baggage. I want you to watch these two Russians . . . if one of them aims a gun at me, I want you to let him have it first. . . .'

'As the American guard snapped a cartridge in the chamber of his rifle, one courier jumped from the plane and sprinted for the hangars, where there were telephones. The other, his face contorted as if to keep from crying, began reknotting the cords I had severed.'

Major Jordan had no difficulty opening the suitcases. They were cheaply constructed. Taking cases at random, he had the opportunity to examine about eighteen out of approximately fifty. In one of the cases, Jordan found scores of roadmaps with 'strange' markings on them. When taken as a whole, they formed a detailed nationwide chart, giving the names and locations of industrial plants.

Another case contained a folder of what appeared to be military documents. It was marked, 'from Hiss.' Another suitcase contained a memo on White House stationery. It was from 'H.H.' [Harry Hopkins] to Mikoyan, the number three man in the Kremlin. Accompanying the memo were two items of special interest. One was a thick map which bore the legend: *Oak Ridge, Manhattan Engineering District.* The second item was a carbon copy of a report from Oak Ridge. On the top of the first page it was marked 'Harry Hopkins.' As he read the text of the *Report*, Major Jordan encountered a number of words 'so outlandish that I made a memo to look up their meaning. Among them were 'cyclotron', 'protron' and 'deuteron'. There were curious phrases like 'energy produced by fission' and 'walls five lead and water, to control flying neutrons.'

'Probably no more than 200 men in all the country would have been capable of noting down these particular expressions out of their own heads. . . .

'For the first time in my life, I met the word 'uranium'. The exact phrase was 'Uranium 92'. From a book of reference I learned afterwards that Uranium is the 92nd element in atomic weight.

'At the time of this episode, I was as unaware as anyone could be of Oak Ridge (and) the Manhattan District. The enterprise had been celebrated as 'the best guarded secret in history'. It was superlatively hush-hush, to the extreme that Army officers in the 'know' were forbidden to mention it over their private telephones in the Pentagon' (pp. 37-43).

It was only when the Russians exploded their first Atomic bomb in 1949 that the thunderous reality of where the Reds obtained their atomic secrets dawned on Major Jordan: these atomic secrets had come straight from the White House! Harry Hopkins wasn't kidding when he told the Russians at the Madison Square Garden rally in 1942 that he was 'determined that nothing shall stop us from sharing with you all that we have. . . .'

RUSSIA GETS U.S. TREASURY PLATES FOR POST WAR

With the passage of time, Major Jordan became increasingly alarmed. Finally, with events in Great Falls weighing heavily on his conscience, he decided to make a special trip to Washington to see if something could be done about the situation.

As he was about to enter the office of John Newbold Hazard, the liaison officer for Lend- Lease at the State Department, he was waylaid by a young assistant. '"Major Jordan,"' he began, '"we know all about you, and why you are here. You might as well understand that officers who get too officious are likely to find themselves on an island somewhere in the South Seas."'

'With natural anger, I retorted that I didn't think the State Department had any idea how flagrant abuses were at Great Falls. I said we had virtually no censorship, or immigration or custom inspection. Crowds of Russians were comng in of whom we had no record. Photostats of military reports from American attaches in Moscow were being returned to the Kremlin. Planeloads of suitcases, filled with confidential data, were passing every three weeks without inspection, under the guise of "diplomatic immunity."

'"But my dear Major," I was admonished with a jaunty wave of the hand, "We know all about that. The Russians can't do anything, or send anything out of this country without our knowledge and consent. They have to apply to the State Department for everything. I assure you the Department knows exactly what it is doing. Good afternoon"' (pp. 111-2).

Jordan left the State Department with a heavy heart, sensing that his days in Great Falls were numbered.

On June 13, 1944, Major Jordan returned to Great Falls for the last time as an army officer. He had just been replaced.

During a farewell talk with Colonel Kotikov, the Russian mentioned that a 'money plane' had crashed in Siberia and had to be replaced. He explained that the Treasury was shipping engraving plates, ink, paper and other materials to Russia so that they could print the same occupation money for Germans as the United States was printing.

Jordan was sure that Kotikov must be mistaken. The United States would never agree to such a preposterous scheme. Surely the Russian meant that America was sending banknotes that could be used as the currency of Germany, following its defeat. No, insisted Kotikov, the equipment had been shipped through Great Falls in May in two shipments of five C-47's each. The shipments had been arranged on the highest level in Washington, and the planes had been loaded at the National Airport.

It was several years before details of this staggering episode began to filter out into the light of day. A Senate investigation into the scandal confirmed the fact that, in spite of widespread protests and warnings about the consequences of such a move, Harry Hopkins, Henry Morgenthau, Secretary of the Treasury, Averell Harriman, the U.S. Ambassador to Russia, and Harry Dexter White, the Assistant Secretary of the Treasury who was later exposed as a Russian agent, were able to exert enough pressure to see that Russia got the plates.

Acknowledging that occupation money would be needed at the conclusion of the war, two veteran civil servants in the Treasury Department, D.W. Bell, Secretary of the Treasury and A.W. Hall, Director of the Bureau of Engraving, pointed out that 'the Treasury has never made currency plates available to anyone. To acquiesce to such an unprecedented request would create serious complications. To permit the Russian government to print currency identical to that being printed in this country would make accountability impossible. . . . ' (pp.128-9)

Arguing against this sound logic was Harry Dexter White who declared that he was 'loath to turn the Russian request down . . .

and that Russia was one of those Allies who must be trusted to the same degree and to the same extent as the other Allies.' Morgenthau sent a memo to Soviet Ambassador Gromyko, declaring that 'the U.S. Treasury is desirous to cooperate with the Soviet government in this matter in every possible way' (p.133).

Morgenthau and his friends certainly did 'cooperate . . . in every possible way.' Official records show that the photographic plates and all the materials necessary for making high quality reproductions were shipped from Washington, D.C. on May 24th, 1944. A second shipment, to replace the equipment 'lost' in the alleged crash, was sent on June 7th. As the Red army moved West, fueled by the massive infusion of American Lend- Lease aid, they set up shop in a former Nazi printing plant in Leipzig, and started the Presses rolling.

Why were the Russians so insistent upon printing the occupation currency in their own territory where there would be no accountability?   Major Jordan says: 'The answer is quite simple. They knew that the U.S. Army would convert such currency into dollars. (Russia, of course, refused to redeem the same currency with rubles).   As a result, every Russian made mark that fell into the hands of an American soldier or accredited civilian became a potential charge against the Treasury of the United States.'

The Reds paid their own occupation forces with these marks, adding a two-year bonus for good measure.   The American taxpayer footed the bill. With the occupation currency, which cost them nothing, the Russians snapped up anything of value left in the German economy. If they could get anything out of America, that was even better.

The Major continues: 'Any GI could buy a pack of cigarettes for 8 cents at a U.S. Army Post Exchange. For this the Russian and German black markets would offer him 100 marks from the Leipzig mint. To realize a profit of almost $10.00 on an 8 cent pack of cigarettes, the American had only to take his 100 Leipzig marks to an Army Post Office, purchase a $10.00 money order and mail it to the United States. It was revealed that the standard offer for a five cent candy bar was 50 marks, or $5.00; $18.00 for one pound of Crisco; $20.00 for one K ration; $25.00 for a pound of coffee, and $2,500 for a wrist watch costing $17.

'By December 1946, the U.S. Military government found itself $250,000,000 or more in the red. It had redeemed in dollars at least 2,500,000,000 marks in excess of the total marks issued by its Finance Office. The deficit could have had no other origin than the Russian plant in Leipzig. . . .

'In addition to the $250,000,000 there was a further loss, which though small was mortifying. A charge of $18,102 was rendered to the Soviet Embassy, covering the expenses of the engraving plates and the materials in the three 1944 deliveries. The bill was ignored and is still unpaid. . . .' (pp.134-5)

Harry Dexter White was handsomely rewarded for 'services rendered'. In 1945 he was promoted to Assistant Secretary of the Treasury and in 1946 he was appointed by President Truman and confirmed by the Senate as U.S. Director of the International Monetary Fund. In 1947, when his name was linked with pro-Soviet activities by Whittaker Chambers, he submitted his resignation from the International Monetary Fund. The following year, under oath, he denounced Chamber's charges as 'unqualifiedly false'. He claimed that he had never committed a disloyal act. Two weeks later, his funeral was held at Beth Israel in Boston; he had died of a heart attack.

In November, 1948, Whittaker Chambers produced five rolls of microfilmed documents. Among these were eight handwritten pages that revealed American military secrets. The handwriting was identified as that of Harry Dexter White.

WHY?

Why did the United States give such massive aid to Russia during World War II? Can it be described as another 'blunder', another 'mistake' on the part of our government? Such a deduction would be naive in the extreme. It would be unworthy of serious consideration.

Those who were 'running the show' [Churchill and those] . . . in the United States knew the nature of Communism. They, their associates and their masters, were the creators of the Red Monster. They knew exactly what they were doing! The 'zeal' which approached fanaticism' which they displayed in their unstinted support of the blood-spattered Soviet regime (at the expense of the American taxpayer) was an indication of their political and philosophical convictions. Soviet Russia was . . . a definitely recognizable tool in their plan to enslave the whole world under the banner of The New World Order. . . .

The International Bankers made a huge capital investment in the Bolshevik Revolution and in the totalitarian regime that resulted from it. Over the last 60 Plus years they have been using the merciless Red dictatorship as their 'foil' in the plan to conquer the world.

'VICTORY' IN EUROPE

With the revelations of Major Jordan and Commander Earle, a startling new dimension emerges in the history of World War II. The plan being worked out by the 'hidden hand' now comes into focus and opens up new vistas of understanding. The 'masters of nations,' the International Bankers, who were calling the shots from behind the scenes, were working out a very different purpose than was generally assumed by those who were not behind the scenes.

Instead of the war being fought to make the world safe for democracy, it was being fought to destroy democracy in many nations.

ALLIED ARMY WAITS FOR RUSSIA TO PUSH WEST

Fueled by billions of dollars in American aid, the Red Army began to slowly push the Germans back along the eastern front which stretched 600 miles from the Carpathian Mountains to the Baltic.

With their army immobilized in northern Italy on strict orders from Marshall and Eisenhower, the Allies stalled for time before launching a major assault on the European continent.

On D-Day, June 6, 1944, the Allies launched 'Operation Overlord' against what was termed 'Fortress Europe.' At dawn that day the Allies crossed the Channel to northern France. More than 5000 ships (mostly small landing craft) carrying nearly 100,000 men, with 1,083 bombers and some 2000 fighter planes overhead, hit the beaches of Normandy. The deeply entrenched Germans provided fierce resistance but, within a week, the Allies managed to solidify their beacheads for their drive into France. Within three weeks the Americans, under General Omar Bradley, had captured Cherbourg. The British, under Montgomery, took Caen in Mid-July. Paris was surrendered on August 25.

From all accounts, Churchill hadn't changed his mind during the preceding year. The only man among the Western leaders with vast military and political experience, Churchill still wanted to launch an all out attack towards the heart of Hitler's Third Reich. He was overruled by Supreme Commander Eisenhower. In *Crusade In Europe*, Eisenhower describes his rejection of Field Marshal Montgomery's plan, made late in 1944, to launch an all out attack towards Berlin. The Supreme Commander claimed that Monty's proposal was reckless. Interestingly, Ike, earlier in his book, had criticized the British Field Marshal for being too cautious!

From the military standpoint, Montgomery's proposal was correct. We must, however, bear in mind that Eisenhower's objectives were political, not military in nature. He was under rigid orders from those who were responsible for his 'miraculous' rise from Lt. Colonel to Supreme Commander, to make sure that 'Russia's post war position in Europe will be the dominant one' (*Roosevelt and Hopkins*, p. 748). Those orders determined his every move. . . .

During the months that followed, the Allied armies, under the direction of Eisenhower, made a leisurely advance towards Germany on a sprawling front.

On the Eastern Front, the Red Army had pushed into eastern Poland in 1944. Romania, Finland and Bulgaria capitulated to the Soviets in August and September. Early in 1945 the Reds pushed into eastern Prussia, then extended their sphere of influence into Czechoslovakia.

SOME ILLUMINATING FACTS

For some very illuminating facts about how the war was conducted, we return to *Tragedy and Hope* by the acknowledged Establishment insider, the late Dr. Carroll Quigley. The account given by Dr. Quigley, on pages 800-807, fills in many details of the tactics used by 'the hidden hand' to bring about the results they had in mind.

The professor recounts the massive air assaults on Germany that began in the spring of 1942. *'Much effort was expended on bombing almost wholly unrewarding targets, such as airfields, submarine pens, ports, railroad Yards, tank factories.'* This 'strategic bombing was largely a failure, and was so from poor choice of targets and from long intervals between repeated attack. . . ..

'Such strategic bombing should have been based on careful analysis of the German war economy to pick out the one or two critical items which were essential to the war effort. These items were probably ball bearings, aviation fuels, and chemicals, all of them essential and all of them concentrated. After the war, German General Gotthard Heinrici said that the war would have ended a year earlier if Allied bombing had concentrated on ammonia plants.

If these mammoth air attacks were not concentrated on vital targets, the destruction of which would have greatly contributed to shortening the war, what was their purpose? 'Urban renewal'!

HAMBURG HOLOCAUST

Dr. Quigley tells us about the raids on Hamburg in 1943: 'For more than a week, beginning on July 24th, Hamburg was attacked with a mixture of high explosive and incendiary bombs so heavily and persistently that entirely new conditions of destruction known as 'fire storms' appeared. The air in the city, heated to over a thousand degrees, began to rise rapidly, with the result that ground level winds of gale or even hurricane force rushed into the city. These winds were so strong as to knock people off their feet or to move flaming beams and walls through the air. The heat was so intense that normally nonflammable substances burned, and fires were ignited yards from any flame. The water supply was destroyed on July 27th, but the flames were too hot for water to be effective: it turned to steam before it could reach flaming objects, and all ordinary methods of quenching flames by depriving them of oxygen were made impossible by the storm of fresh air roaring in from the suburbs. Nevertheless, the supply of oxygen could not keep up with the combustion, and great layers of carbon monoxide settled in the shelters and basements killing the people huddled there. Those who tried to escape through the streets were enveloped in flames as if they were walking through the searing jet of a blowtorch. Some who wrapped themselves in blankets dipped in water from a canal were scalded as the water turned suddenly to steam. Hundreds were cremated, and their ashes dispersed by the winds. No final figures for the destruction were possible until 1951, when they were set by the German authorities at 40,000 dead (including 5,000 children), 250,000 houses destroyed (about half the city), with over 1,000,000 persons made homeless' (pp. 802-3).

THE DRESDEN MASSACRE

The destruction of Hamburg was just the first of the 'urban renewal' projects carried out in the German 'theater of war' by the Allied forces on behalf of the Internationalists. Dresden is another hideous example of how effectively - and mercilessly - the program worked.

'Dresden was one of the great show cities of the world. It contained a number of magnificent public buildings, all of which were located in the Altstadt district of the city. Within a radius of half a mile of the Augustus Bridge was built a unique group of palaces, art galleries, museums and churches - the Schloss, containing the famous Grunes Gewolbe with its priceless art treasures; the beautiful Bruhl Terrasse extending along the left bank of the Elbe; the beautiful Catholic Cathedral; the domed Frauen Kirche; the Opera House; the Johanneum Museum and, above all, the famous Zwinger Museum containing one of the finest collections of paintings in the world, including among its many treasures Raphael's Sistine Madonna . . . within this small area, so well known to British and American tourists, there were, and could be, no munition factories or, in fact, industries of any kind' (F.J.F. Veale, *The Veale File*, Vol. I, p. 189).

Early in 1945, as the war was fast drawing to a close, the population of Dresden, normally 600,000, had swollen to well over 1,000,000 as refugees, mostly women and children, swarmed in from the east. 'Every house in Dresden was filled with these unfortunates, every public building was crowded with them, many were camping in the streets. There were no air raid shelters' (p.190).

'On the morning of the fateful February 13, 1945, Allied reconnaissance planes were observed flying over the city. The inhabitants of Dresden had had no experience of modern air warfare and the appearance of these planes aroused curiosity rather than apprehension. Having been for so long outside any theaters of war, the city lacked anti-aircraft defences and these planes were able to observe in complete safety all that they desired. No doubt, they observed and reported that all the roads through and around Dresden were filled with dense throngs moving westward . . . in flight from the most dreadful fate which had ever confronted a large European population since the Mongol invasion of 1241' (pp. 190, 187).

At 9:30 that evening the first wave of Allied planes (Fortresses and 'Liberators') appeared over the Dresden area and began to rain down death and destruction. Altstadt was the primary target.

When the second wave of the two thousand, one hundred and fifty plane 'demolition crew' arrived shortly after midnight, they found the area still burning furiously.

When the three stage assault on defenseless and refugee-packed Dresden was completed, all the priceless buildings in Altstadt area lay in total ruins. Half of the buildings in the greater Dresden area were demolished, and approximately 250,000 of the hapless inhabitants lay incinerated in the ruins.

Who was responsible for the barbaric Dresden Massacre which took place when Germany was clearly beaten and when no strategic purpose could be served by such wanton destruction and loss of life? 'I can only say,' states Air Marshal Sir Arthur Harris, the top man in the British Air Force, '*that the attack on Dresden was at the time considered a military necessity by much more important people than myself*'(*Bomber Offensive*, 1947, p. 242).

In his book, Sir Arthur refrains from naming 'these much more important people' but, by use of the words 'at the time,' seems to imply that he cannot bring himself to believe that any rational person could still hold such an opinion.

Those 'much more important people' were obviously the men who were running the European 'theater of war' for their own profit and for their own ends. They were clearly looking beyond the end of the war, to the vast fortunes that could be picked up in 'redevelopment projects' in such cities as Dresden. The fact that millions of 'peasants' were incinerated in such 'urban renewal' projects was of no import to them.

The destruction of human life is of little importance to those who would rule the world!

What were the results of this merciless assault on German civilians, and relatively unimportant targets? 'It probably would not be unfair to say that Germany in January 1945, after two years of heavy air bombardment from the Western Powers, was not only outproducing the United Kingdom in most significant items of military equipment but had also improved its relative position.'

How about the Allies losses during this period of German 'urban renewal' in which the Allies, under the guidance of the hidden hand, were stalling for time to allow the Soviets to push relentlessly towards Berlin?

'The Americans and British together lost 40,000 planes and 158,906 airmen, almost equally divided among them. . . . '

Notice a critically important point: "*The direct contribution of strategic bombing to the war effort came chiefly after September 1944, and was to be found mainly in the disruption of fuel and transportation*" (*Tragedy and Hope*, p. 804).

How clear it is! The Allied top command didn't really 'open up' on the main German targets until 'after September 1944,' at which time it was clear that the Soviets would be able to break through to Germany by the following spring.

ROOSEVELT AND STALIN GIVE COLD SHOULDER
TO CHURCHILL

During the winter of 1944-5 Chuirchill continued to warn against letting the Russians come too far west. Right up to the time of the Yalta Conference (February 4-12, 1945) Churchill hoped to salvage something of the Balkans and Central Europe. When he met Roosevelt in Malta on the way to Yalta, he once again proposed an attack on the Balkans. . . .

The President also told Stalin that he would 'tell him something indiscreet, since he would not wish to say it in front of Churchill.

'The President said that he felt that the armies were getting close enough to have contact between, *and that he hoped General Eisenhower would communicate directly with the Soviet staff rather than through the chiefs of staff in London and Washington as in the past'* (information from Elliott Roosevelt, FDR's son).

Without a doubt Churchill realized during the course of the war that his 'power' and 'authority' were far less than what he thought them to be at the outset. The reader will remember that Churchill, on coming to power in Britain in 1940, had written: 'Power in a national crisis, when a man believes he knows what orders should be given, is a blessing.' By Yalta, he knew he was a powerless puppet in the hands of the international power brokers!

When Churchill learned of Roosevelt's perfidy and the fact that Eisenhower was dealing directly with Stalin while ignoring him, he launched a strong protest. This was in vain. General Marshall, in Washington, told Churchill that he fully approved of Eisenhower's 'strategic concept' and his 'procedure in communicating with the Russians.'

As weeks ground on, the Western Powers continued their unrelenting assault on German cities. Using huge numbers of their most modern planes, the Allies never swerved from their goal of pulverizing the German cities. Day after day, week after week they criss-crossed those urban areas, laying a thick blanket of bombs which blasted German's cities into oblivion. Civilian casualties were enormous, numbering in the hundreds of thousands.

Strategically, such 'blanket bombing' served no useful purpose:

it contributed little to the war effort. If concentrated elsewhere, on targets of vital significance, this colossal fire power could have appreciably shortened the duration of the war.

The official 'reason' given for this wanton destruction of civilian lives and property was that the raids would 'undermine the morale' of the German population. The real reason was that the International Bankers and their cohorts were using the Allies' awesome air power as their unofficial wrecking-crew - their bulldozers and demolition crews - to prepare Germany for their planned urban renewal project at the conclusion of hostilities. The airborne 'bulldozers' did the preparation work free. The 'Big Boys' were relieved of the huge expense of having to purchase vast amounts of valuable property and of having it demolished. With most German cities 90% demolished 'in the war', this cost was kept to a minimum! After the war, much of this 'vacant' ground was picked up for a few cents on the dollar by the international *urban renewers*'.

BATTLE OF THE BULGE AND
VERY STRATEGIC SURRENDERS

General Eisenhower, in *Crusade In Europe*, tells us that early in December, 1944, General Patton, with his Third Army, was making preparations to renew the attack against the Saar, the attack to begin December 19. 'Patton was very hopeful of decisive effect. . . . ' (p. 340).

At that time American intelligence lost track of the German Sixth Panzer Army, 'the strongest and most efficient mobile reserve remaining to the enemy . . . and could not locate it by any means available. . . . [S]ome Intelligence reports indicated a growing anxiety about our weakness in the Ardennes, where we knew that the enemy was increasing his infantry formations' (p. 341).

Ignoring the warnings of an impending German counterattack, Ike decided to concentrate Allied strength elsewhere. This decision 'gave the German opportunity to launch his attack [to start the Battle of the Bulge] against a weak portion of our lines. If giving him that chance is to be condemned by historians, their condemnation should be directed at me alone" (p. 341).

'By December 26th the German drive had stopped and within three weeks most of the lost ground had been recovered. . . . Hitler had to withdraw many of the forces which had made the original attack, in order to send them hurriedly to the east in a vain attempt to slow down the Soviet winter offensive which began on January 12, 1945. . . . *The Germans regarded the Russians as subhumans, and had every reason to fear Russian occupation and retaliation, while everyone knew that any American occupation would be motivated by humanitarian considerations rather than by retaliation.* . . . The Western Powers, on Eisenhower's orders, held back their attack on many points (such as Prague) to allow the Russians to occupy areas the Americans could easily have taken first.

'From midsummer of 1943 until the war's end in May 1945, the Soviet offensive in the East was almost continuous (*Tragedy and Hope*, pp. 789-90).

'The Western ground attack on Germany was not resumed after the Battle of the Bulge until February 8, 1945. Two months later, a pincers was extended eastward, north and south of the Ruhr. On April 1st this closed to complete the encirclement of the great industrial area; seventeen days later Field Marshal Model surrendered his 325,000 Germans and at once killed himself. . . .

'Eisenhower, following the victory in the Ruhr, ignored Berlin to the northeast and drove directly eastward toward Dresden. . . . Churchill and others wanted the American advance to be redirected to Berlin, but the Joint Chiefs of Staff in Washington refused to interfere with Eisenhower's decisions in the field. *These decisions permitted the Soviet forces to 'liberate' all the capital cities of Central Europe. Budapest fell to the Russians on February]3th, followed by Vienna on April]3th. On April 25th Russian forces encircled Berlin and made contact with American troops seventy miles to the south, at Torgau on the Elbe.* . . . The previous day, Eisenhower, advancing on Prague, had been warned by the Soviet General Staff that Russian forces would occupy the Moldau Valley (which included the Czech capital). *As late as May 4th, when the American forces were sixty miles from Prague and the Soviet armies were more than a hundred miles from the city, an effort by the former to advance to the city was stopped at the request of the Soviet commander, despite a last vain attempt from*

Churchill to Eisenhower to take the Czech capital for political bargaining purposes. . . .(pp.805-6)

Eisenhower records that 'some weeks before the final surrender . . . various individuals of prominence in Germany' were seeking ways and means of surrendering. One proposal was to have a truce in the west. 'This,' says Eisenhower, 'was an obvious attempt to call off the war with the Western Allies so that the German could throw his full strength against Russia. Our governments rejected the proposal.'

Another offer to surrender came from Heinrich Himmler. He, too, wanted to surrender on the Western front. This was also rejected because it would 'instantly create complete misunderstanding with the Russians and bring about a situation in which the Russians could justifiably accuse us of bad faith. . . .

'Until the very last the Germans never abandoned the attempt to make a distinction between a surrender on the western front and one on the eastern. With a failure of this kind of negotiation the German commanders finally had, each in his own sector, to face the prospect of complete annihilation or of military surrender. . . . They gave up on May 5, with capitulation to be effective May 6' (*Crusade in Europe*, pp.422-4).

All of the above ties in perfectly with the information given by Colonel Dall regarding Comander Earle. . . .

THE FATE OF TWO MILLION
DISPLACED BY THE WAR

Hundreds of thousands of Russians, Poles, Hungarians and others fled west in the face of this avalanche of terror. These people were classified as 'displaced persons' by the Allied authorities. Eisenhower tells us 'the truly unfortunate were those who, for one reason or another, dared not return home for fear of further persecution. The terror felt by this last group was impressed on us by a number of suicides among individuals who preferred to die rather than return to their native lands . . . therefore we gave any individual who objected to return the benefit of the doubt' (*Crusade in Europe*, p.439).

This last statement was a blatant lie, calculated to deceive the American people. The simple truth is that Eisenhower's 'Supreme Headquarters' issued a 'guide to the care of displaced persons in Germany,' dated May 1945. This specifically stated: 'After identification by Soviet Repatriation Representatives, Soviet displaced persons will be repatriated *regardless of their individual wishes.*' Another section reads: 'Enemy and ex-enemy displaced persons, except those assimilated to United Nations status, will be returned to their countries of nationality or former residence *without regard to their personal wishes.*'

One of the most vicious betrayals on the part of the Allied High Command came in the case of Soviet Army Commander Andrei Vlasov who, though a dedicated Russian patriot, was at heart violently opposed to the Red tyrants.

In 1942 Vlasov surrendered to the Germans, with the intention of organizing and leading a Russian army to free their homeland from 'that terrible synthesis of madness and crime, which holds my poor, unhappy people in its grip.' He refused to have any part in helping to replace Marxist tyranny with Hitlerian tyranny.

Late in 1944, the hard pressed Germans permitted Vlasov to form a 'Russian Army of Liberation'. This force of three divisions was made up of Russian refugees and prisoners of war and was dressed in German uniforms. It operated as part of the German army on the eastern front.

Thousands of Stalin's troops, upon hearing that they were opposed by the RADL, surrendered and changed sides.

As the capitulation of the Third Reich drew near, General Vlasov moved his army to a pre-arranged location in Austria. Vlasov and his men, though they were prepared to fight to their last drop of blood against the Red butchers, felt confident that they would receive humane treatment if they surrendered to the Americans. One large segment of the 'Liberation Army' moved west under the command of General Bunichenko. On May 10, 1945, they reached the American lines, at which time Bunichenko surrendered his twenty-five thousand men to the U.S. Third Army.

The patriotic Russians were disarmed and compelled by the American authorities to march eastward directly into the clutches of the advancing Red Army. Many of them committed suicide.

Two days later Vlasov and a small group of his staff who had been heading west along another route were received by General George Patton at his 3rd Army Headquarters. Not knowing what fate had befallen the main force of his men, Vlasov wrote to Eisenhower pleading for the safety of his men and requesting that he and his officers be allowed to stand trial before an International Tribunal.

This was the last thing the 'hidden hand' wanted to occur. Such exposure would prove damaging to their cause. A way had to be found to 'unload' Vlasov and his staff without making the betrayal too obvious.

On May 12, 1945, Vlasov and his small group were told that they had to attend a conference at the U.S. 4th Army headquarters. En route to the 'conference', their 'protected' convoy was intercepted by Red soldiers who arrested Vlasov and his men and hauled them away while their 'protection' escort stood quietly by without raising a finger to prevent the abduction. It is not known what hideous fate awaited Vlasov when he was returned to Russia, but it was reliably reported that 'General Vlasov's body, skewered on a meat hook was exhibited in Moscow's Red Square' (*Human Events*, April 1, 1953).

As one writer has observed, 'it was Eisenhower who gave Stalin's monstrous plan of vengeance and warning all its teeth and its total effectiveness.'

The forced repatriation of close to two million hapless individuals to death or slavery was the official policy of the Allied High Command. It was known as Operation Keelhaul. The sordid details of this disgraceful episode in our nation's history are to be found in the book *Operation Keelhaul*, by Julius Epstein. Official records of this action are still classified as 'top secret' by official Washington. Like other documents of a similar nature, they are still too 'hot' to release.

Under a secret agreement, the Western Allies agreed to return all Russian prisoners to the slave state as 'deserters.'

A British Army chaplain, James B. Chuter, one of 4000 prisoners from a former German prisoner-of-war camp who made his way west towards the Allied lines in 1945, tells the story: 'Along the eastern bank of the river Mulde was encamped a great multitude.

... This was the end of the journey for the tens of thousands of refugees who passed us. The Mulde was the agreed line at which the Americans halted and to which the Russians would advance. The Americans would let none save German military personnel and Allied prisoners of war cross the river. From time to time, some desperate soul would fling himself into the flood in a vain attempt to escape from the unknown fury of the Russian arrival. It was to avoid such incidents and to discourage them that the occasional splutter of American machine guns on the Western banks was heard. . . . Sounding, in that most frightening manner, a plain warning to all who thought to cross the river line" (*Captivity Captive*).

This tragedy was not confined to Germany. 'A small part of the tragedy unfolded even on American soil. Many liberated Soviet soldiers were brought to the United States, chiefly to camps in Idaho. Virtually without exeption, after the war, they begged for political asylum. But they were forced to board Soviet ships in Seattle and Portland. Over a hundred who resisted successfully were brought to a New Jersey camp. In the end these, too, were surrendered to Stalin though we had to use tear gas to dislodge them from the barracks' (Julius Epstein, *American Legion Magazine*, December, 1954).

ANOTHER ILLUMINATI PUPPET IN THE WHITE HOUSE

There will, of course, be those who will apologize for Eisenhower and say that he was only 'following orders' handed down by his superiors.

Let's face facts! More death and suffering resulted from Eisenhower's wholehearted compliance with 'orders' than from the actions of any of the German generals who also 'followed orders' during World War II. Obviously, the Germans were on the 'wrong' side. The German leaders were executed as 'war criminals,' but Eisenhower, in spite of all his brutal crimes against humanity, was praised and exalted. He later became president of the United States.

America's Invisible Government:
THE COUNCIL ON FOREIGN RELATIONS

The main tool of the internationalist elite in the United States is undoubtedly the Council on Foreign Relations (CFR). The CFR was founded in 1921 under the direction of Colonel E. Mandell House when it became apparent that [Congress would not allow] the United States . . . to join the League of Nations, an early effort to create a One-World Government.

The principal figures behind the formation of the Council were banking barons J.P. Morgan, John D. Rockefeller, Paul Warburg and Jacob Schiff - the very same personalities who engineered the creation of the Federal Reserve System (1913) and who, in 1916, were responsible for the introduction of the graduated income tax to America. . . .

Former FBI agent Dan Smoot tells us that the Council did not amount to a great deal until 1927, when the Rockefeller family (through the various Rockefeller Foundations and Funds) began to pour money into it. Before long, the Carnegie Foundation (and later the Ford Foundation) began to finance the Council. . . .

The fact that the CFR is a secret organization is demonstrated by the following statement taken from its 1966 *Annual Report*: 'It is an express condition of membership in the Council, to which condition every member accedes by virtue of his membership, that unless expressly stated by an officer of the Council to the contrary, all proceedings at the Council's afternoon and dinner meetings as well as study and discussion groups are confidential, and any disclosure or publication of statements made at such meetings or attribution to the Council of information, even though otherwise available, is contrary to the best interests of the Council and may be regarded by the Board of Directors in its sole discretion as grounds for termination or suspension of membership pursuant to Article 1 of the By-Laws.'

The roster of the CFR, said the *Christian Science Monitor*, September 1, 1961, 'contains names distinguished in the field of diplomacy, government, business, finance, science, labor, journalism, law and education. What united so wide-ranging and disparate a membership is *a passionate concern for the direction of*

American foreign policy.'

The 'passionate concern' of the CFR is the creation of a One-World dictatorship: this is clearly revealed in its own publications. For example, in 1959, the CFR published a document titled *Study No. 7: Basic Aims of U.S. Foreign Policy*, in which it was stated: 'The U.S. must strive to build a new international order . . . including states labeling themselves as 'socialist' [Communist].' The study also urged that the United States *'maintain and gradually increase the authority of the United Nations'* and 'make more effective use of the International Court of Justice, juristdiction of which should be increased by withdrawing of reservations by member nations on matters judged to be domestic' (*Review of the News*, September 19, 1973). . . .

In the House of Representatives on April 28, 1972, Congressman John Rarick stated: 'The CFR is the Establishment. Not only does it have influence in key decision-making positions at the highest levels of government to apply pressure from above, but it also finances and uses individuals and groups to bring pressure from below to justify the high-level decisions for converting the United States from a sovereign, Constitutional Republic into a servile member-state of a One-World dictatorship (*FR*, pp.130-4).

Mr. Griffin introduces evidence to show that the CIA is in fact the enforcement arm of the CFR (*FR,*p.136), and that since the advent of the Franklin D. Roosevelt administration in 1933, most top positions in successive administrations have been filled by members of the CFR. (*DS?* p.300). Furthermore, Mr. Griffin very clearly states, because of the secretive and undemocratic manner in which it is directing the future of the United States, there is no other word but 'treason' in describing the activities and power of the American Committee on Foreign Relations:

When one considers the writings, the spoken words and, above all, the actions of the many individuals in government service who have sprung from the ranks of the Council on Foreign Relations over the last forty years - and when we note their unrelenting dedication to the destruction of America's sovereignty and the establishment of a One-World, Humanistic, Socialistic Government - can there be any doubt that the members of the CFR are in flagrant violation of the Logan Act which forbids American citizens -

a. without the permission or authority of the government;

b. Directly or indirectly;

c. To commence or carry on any verbal or written correspondence or intercourse with any foreign government or any officer or agent thereof; OR

d. To counsel, advise or assist in any such 'correspondence,' i.e. in any verbal or written correspondence by a United States citizen with any foreign government or . . . agent thereof;

e. With the intent to influence the measure or conduct of any foreign government or

f. With the intent to defeat the measures of the government of the United States. All, or almost all, of George Bush's cabinet are members of the Committee on Foreign Relations, making the inversion of the American ideal complete, or just about complete.   The remarkable thing is that in a country where 'democracy' is so prized this situation has been arrived at without the knowledge or consent of almost all of the American people.

THE UNITED NATIONS: THE NEW BABYLON

'The United Nations represents not a final stage in the development of world order, but only a primitive stage. Therefore its primary task is to create the conditions which will make possible a more highly developed organization' (John Foster Dulles [later Eisenhower's first Secretary of State,14], *War or Peace*, Macmillan, 1950, p.40).

Every agency of the United Nations Organization carefully orchestrates its efforts towards the same goal - the establishment of a New World Order (*FR*, p.141 and p.156).

THE KOREA, VIETNAM, AND 'GULF' WARS

What the American 'peasants' have never been told by their government is that the Under Secretary for Political and Security Affairs at the United Nations has been an official of the Soviet Union, without exception, since 1945: 'The post of "Political and

Security Affairs' traditionally has been held by a Soviet national
. . . [who] is Senior Adviser to the Secretary General' (*New York
Times*, May 22, 1963). This gives the Soviet Union direct and
immediate access to all the plans for and activities engaged in by
United Nations' forces anywhere in the world.

With this understanding, the light begins to dawn on all of the
apparently 'incredible' and 'incomprehensible' events that took
place during the course of both the Korean and Vietnam Wars.

Colonel F. P. 'Bud' Farrell, USAF, Retired, who served in both
of these wars, comments: 'All of our military operations had to be
forwarded by radio to the Soviet Commander of the United
Nations Security Council . . . before our forces went into action.
. . . The Soviet Commander delayed the battle plans until he relayed
our battle planning information to Moscow. . . .

'The enemy then relayed these battle plans to their Communist
forces in the field. They knew beforehand when we were coming
and how many of us there were. The enemy knew our every move
at all times. *Our troops were led like sheep to the slaughter in both Korea
and Vietnam. . . .*

'Every president and every congressman since Truman has
been aware of this treason by the United Nations Security Council
against our military forces. The deaths, suffering and wounded
- and prisoners of war - are to be laid at their feet. *This is treason
at the highest level. . . .*'

Regarding the sanctuary granted Communist forces during the
Korean War, General Douglas McArthur wrote: 'I was . . . worried
by a series of directives from Washington which were greatly
decreasing the potential of my air force. First I was forbidden 'hot'
pursuit of enemy planes that attacked our own. Manchuria and
Siberia were sanctuaries of inviolate protection for all enemy forces
and for all enemy purposes, no matter what *depredations* or assaults
might come from there. Then I was denied the right to bomb the
hydroelectric plants along the Yalu. This order was broadened to
include every plant in North Korea which was capable of furnishing
electric power to Manchuria and Siberia. Most incomprehensible
of all was the refusal to let me bomb the important supply center
in Racin, which was not in Manchuria or Siberia, but many miles
from the border, in northeast Korea. Racin was a depot to which

the Soviet Union forwarded supplies from Vladivostok for the North Korean Army. *I felt that step-by-step my weapons were being taken away from me*' (*Reminiscences*, McGraw-Hill, 1964, p.365).

'That there was some leak of intelligence was evident to everyone. [General Walton] Walker continually complained to me that his operations were known to the enemy in advance through sources in Washington . . . information must have been relayed to them, assuring that the Yalu bridges would continue to enjoy sanctuary and that their bases would be left intact. *They knew they could swarm across the Yalu River without having to worry about bombers hitting their Manchurian supply lines*' (pp.374-5).

In his book, McArthur cited an official pamphlet distributed by Chinese General Lin Piao, whose troops were fighting alongside those of North Korea: '*I would never had made the attack and risked my men and military reputation if I had not been assured that Washington would restrain General McArthur from taking adequate retaliatory measures against my lines of supply and communication. . . .* ' (pp.374-5)

The Vietnam War was basically more of the same - only worse!

Many recognize the fact that the United States could have won the Vietnam War within a week, and without the massive loss of life and limb (58,000 dead and hundreds of thousands of wounded) that resulted from it.

In Vietnam, we were deprived of victory by the issuance of the infamous 'Rules of Engagement'. Thanks to Senator Barry Goldwater (R-Arizona), this critical document was placed in the *Congressional Record* on March 6, 14, 18 and 26, 1985. As had been the case in the Korean War less than two decades earlier, these rules effectively emasculated American forces, thus preventing a victory. They prevented air strikes on targets vital to the enemy's war effort. The Joint Chiefs of Staff (JCS) pinpointed 242 such vital targets, but could not bomb them without permission from the secretaries of defence, Robert McNamara and Clark Clifford. . . . [T]hose holding high office in Washington - from the president down . . . betrayed our troops in Korea and Vietnam! As Colonel 'Bud' Farrell said, their actions represented 'treason at the highest level.'

But then, as Sir John Harrington (1561-1612) so eloquently put it, 'Treason doth never prosper, what's the reason? For if it prosper, none dare call it treason.'

The 'Gulf War' of 1990-1 was fought, as President George Bush clearly stated at the time, to advance the cause of the 'New World Order.'

THE STORY OF AMERICA: SUMMARY

American society has been turned upside down, and torn limb from limb. America the Beautiful, the fabled land of the free and the home of the brave, has been devastated. The greatest, freest, wealthiest, most powerful nation in the annals of human history has been raped, plundered, and polluted.

[W]hat we see . . . is the cold-blooded, systematic destruction of the American Dream. What we are witnessing, nationally and internationally, is the working out of the Illuminati Master Plan laid out by Adam Weishaupt in 1776. . . . (AS, pp.56-8)

One of the most amazing political predictions of all time was made in the early 1920s. It was made by Niklai Lenin, the successor to Giuseppe Mazzini and Adriano Lemmi. It was a prediction of what would happen on the world scene; it was also the grand strategic plan of the Illuminati. Lenin stated: 'First we will take Eastern Europe, then the masses of Asia, then we will encircle the United States which will be the last bastion of capitalism. We will not have to attack. It will fall like an overripe fruit into our hands. . . .'(FR, p.101)

In 1962, David Ben Gurion, Israel's Prime Minister, declared that this planned 'Socialist . . . world alliance, at whose disposal will be an international police force,' would have Jerusalem as its capital:

> The image of the world in 1987 as traced in my imagination: The Cold War will be a thing of the past. Internal pressure of the constantly growing intelligentsia in Russia for more freedom and the pressure of the masses for raising their living standards may lead to a gradual democratization of the Soviet Union. On the other hand, the increasing influence of the workers and farmers, and the rising political importance of men of science, may

transform the United States into a welfare state with a planned economy. Western and Eastern Europe will become a federation of autonomous states having a Socialist and democratic regime. With the exception of the USSR as a federated Eurasian state, all other continents will become united in a world alliance, at whose disposal will be an international police force. All armies will be abolished, and there will be no more wars. In Jerusalem, the United Nations (a truly United Nations) will build a Shrine of the Prophets to serve the federated union of all continents; this will be the seat of the Supreme Court of Mankind, to settle all controversies among the federated union of all continents, as prophesied by Isaiah. . . . (*AS*, pp.58-60)

Do you now see, in crystal clear terms, the purpose behind the confusion and lack of stability that has wrecked the world during the twentieth century? It has been planned that way. *The human 'herd' is being stampeded, through a long series of carefully planned national and international crises, towards the creation of a New World Order* (*AS*, p.63).

The leaders of the Illuminati . . . are a small but powerful group which includes international bankers, industrialists, scientists, military and political leaders, educationalists, economists, etc. . . . They use all subversive movements to divide the masses of the people into opposing camps on political, social, racial, economic and religious issues. They arm and finance these groups and encourage them to fight with each other. They hope to make humanity follow this process of self-destruction until all existing political and religious institutions have been eliminated. . . .

To say that the whole affair is a 'Jewish Conspiracy' is an oversimplification of the facts: it is clearly a Satanic conspiracy. However, to deny that many Jews have been involved in the Plot would be ridiculous: Weishaupt, Marx, the Warburgs, the Rothschilds, Jacob Schiff, etc. were all Jews (*FR*, pp.206-8).

Many preachers extol the 'Judeo-Christian ethic' that allegedly exists in the United States today. . . . *Judaism and Christianity are at the opposite extremes of the spiritual spectrum.. They can't possibly be combined!*. . . [M]any Jews . . . despise everything associated with Christ or Christianity. . . . Judaism, by its very Babylonish nature, and in its blasphemous claim to be the world's 'messiah' through Socialism and Communism (*Universal Jewish Encyclopedia*, p.584), is clearly *Anti-God* and *Anti-Christ*. Jesus minced no words. He stated that the founding fathers of Judaism (the *Talmudic Pharisees*) were 'of their father, the devil' (*John* 8:44).

No other religion in human history has attacked Christ or Christianity with the . . . intensity of Judaism. Of course, this is perfectly understandable when viewed in the light of the fact that the false 'messiah' (Talmudic Judiasm) clearly recognizes that

74 DESCENT INTO SLAVERY?

ILLUSTRATED SUNDAY HERALD, FEBRUARY 8, 1920. Page 5.

ZIONISM

versus

BOLSHEVISM.

A STRUGGLE FOR THE SOUL OF THE JEWISH PEOPLE.

By the Rt. Hon. WINSTON S. CHURCHILL.

SOME people like Jews and some do not; but no thoughtful man can doubt the fact that they are beyond all question the most formidable and the most remarkable race which has ever appeared in the world.

Disraeli, the Jew Prime Minister of England, and Leader of the Conservative Party, who was always true to his race and proud of his origin, said on a well-known occasion : "The Lord deals with the nations as the nations deal with the Jews." Certainly when we look at the miserable state of Russia, where of all countries in the world the Jews were the most cruelly treated, and contrast it with the fortunes of our own country, which seems to have been so providentially preserved amid the awful perils of these times, we must admit that nothing that has since happened in the history of the world has falsified the truth of Disraeli's confident assertion.

Good and Bad Jews.

The conflict between good and evil which proceeds unceasingly in the breast of man nowhere reaches such an intensity as in the Jewish race. The dual nature of mankind is nowhere more strongly or more terribly exemplified. We owe to the Jews in the Christian revelation a system of ethics which, even if it were entirely separated from the supernatural, would be incomparably the most precious possession of mankind, worth in fact the fruits of all other wisdom and learning put together. On that system and by that faith there has been built out of the wreck of the Roman Empire the whole of our existing civilisation.

And it may well be that this same astounding race may at the present time be in the actual process of producing another system of morals and philosophy, as malevolent as Christianity was benevolent, which, if not arrested, would shatter irretrievably all that Christianity has rendered possible. It would almost seem as if the gospel of Christ and the gospel of Antichrist were destined to originate among the same people; and that this mystic and mysterious race had been chosen for the supreme manifestations, both of the divine and the diabolical.

" National " Jews.

There can be no greater mistake than to attribute to each individual a recognisable share in the qualities which make up the national character. There are all sorts of men—good, bad, and, for the most part, in-different—in every country, and in every race. Nothing is more wrong than to deny to an individual, on account of race or origin, his right to be judged on his personal merits and conduct. In a people of peculiar genius

Plate 4a: *Winston Churchill, 'Zionism versus Bolshevism: A Struggle for the Soul of the Jewish People,' Illustrated Sunday Herald* (8 February 1920).

only Jesus Christ (the *True Messiah*) stands in its path to ultimate world conquest. *Make no mistake! Talmudic Judaism is the deadly enemy of the Lord Jesus Christ! It is the deadly enemy of Christianity!* (*AS*, pp.66-7)

Editor's Note: Mr. Griffin is not, of course, referring to all, or even to a majority of Jews, but to those whom as Winston Churchill expressed it in 1920 'have forsaken the faith of their forefathers, . . . divorced from their minds all spiritual hopes of the next world, [and who are involved in] world-wide conspiracy for the overthrow of civilisation and for the reconstitution of society on the basis of arrested development, of envious malevolence, and impossible equality' (article cited above). Mr. Griffin identifies this breed of Jew as being those of non-Semitic Turkish stock - the Khazar Jews from whom the Rothschilds are descended - and those who adhere to the letter of the law of the Talmud, *the extreme anti-Christian legal code that forms the basis of 'Jewish religious law and is the textbook used in the training of Rabbis'* (Rabbi Morris N. Kertzer, *Look* magazine, June 17, 1952).

Mr. Griffin goes on to argue (AS, pp.64-6 and pp.4-5) that the smear of 'anti-Semitism' is an evasive, blocking tactic ingeniously devised to divert scrutiny, silence criticism, and deflect attention. I quote:

Can you now see why the anti-Semitic label has been used with such tremendous regularity by Talmudic Zionists, particularly over the last half century? The massive, heavily financed anti 'anti-semitism' campaign is one of the ingenious methods whereby virtually all open discussion of the Jewish issue has been successfully squelched. The truth has long since been buried under a multi-billion dollar tidal wave of . . . propaganda. Outright deceit has been the name of the game. Truth has been discarded. History has been rewritten. . . .

Benjamin Freedman, a Jew, . . . declares that it [the term anti-Semitism] 'should be eliminated from the English language. "Anti-Semitism" serves only one purpose today. It is used as a smear word. When so-called Jews feel that anyone opposes any of their objectives they discredit their victims by applying the word "anti-

Semite" or "anti-Semitic" through all the channels they have at their command and under their control.

'*Anti-Semitism has developed into the smear word it is today because the word 'Semite' is associated with Christ in the minds of Christians*' (*Facts Are Facts*, p.73).

Editor's Note: The struggle between Christ and antiChrist involves issues that go far beyond the historical and the terrestial. Nevertheless, except on one occasion, I have refrained from introducing the terms 'Satan' or 'Lucifer' except when they appear in the particular quotation being cited. It should be obvious by now, however, that the battle which has consumed the world during the last two centuries, and maybe even since the foundation of the earth, is not merely a visible or physical battle but a spiritual one involving invisible as well as visible forces: 'We wrestle not against flesh and blood, but against principalities, against powers, against the rulers of the darkness of this world, against spiritual wickedness in high places (*Ephesians* 6:11). I close 'The Story of America' with one last passage from Mr. Griffin's *Fourth Reich of the Rich* (pp.237-44):

The vast majority of the authors who write on the International Conspiracy make the basic mistake of not recognizing the true nature of the enemy. Most of them believe that we are only engaged in a battle against 'flesh and blood' (mortal, human beings who may be defeated by conventional means). They reject the concept that our real enemy is Satan and his demons, 'the rulers of the darkness of this world . . . [of] spiritual wickedness in high places.'

As a result of this basic misunderstanding, they believe the conspiracy can be successfully combated by patriotic Americans regaining control of Congress, and by the emergence of a 'whole new breed of articulate, well-informed, tough-minded political leaders who have done their homework and are capable of taking on this gigantic international network of global power. . . .'

We are not fighting a physical or political enemy. Our real enemy is Satan (or Lucifer), a spiritual being or superior intelligence and incredible subtlety. He is the god of the Illuminati: Albert Pike tells us to 'doubt it not!' (*Morals and Dogma*, p.321). He stands clearly revealed as the one directing the conspiracy. This spiritual force of pure evil and diabolical ingenuity can only be thwarted in his purpose and totally defeated by another spiritual force of even greater authority and power.

At the very highest level, the leaders of the Luciferian Conspiracy are undoubtedly in direct contact with Lucifer. These are the individuals who, having come up through the ranks of the secret societies, are now the 'real initiates [who] are called the 'Illuminati' (Sons of Light), - those who are illumined, and who in turn illuminate . . . .'

How does one reach the upper ranks of the Luciferian Conspiracy, the Illuminati? The answer, we believe, is found in Manley Hall's book, *The Lost Keys of Freemasonry:* 'When the Mason learns that the key to the warrior on the block is the proper application of the dynamo of living power, he has learned the mystery of his craft. *The seething energies of Lucifer are in his hands and before he may step onward and upward, he must prove his ability to properly apply energy* . . . .Incessant vigilance over thought, action, and desire is indispensable for those who wish to make progress in the unfolding of their being, and the Fellow Craft's desire is the degree of transmutation [i.e. to be changed into 'another substance' or to attempt to attain 'the position of deity] (p.48). . . .

THE FUTURE

What about the present and immediate future? Should we all clothe ourselves with a mantle of defeatism, creep out into the desert, and await 'the coming of the Lord'? The late Dr. Carroll Quigley would have us believe (*Tragedy and Hope,* pp. 979-980) that it is now too late to rescue the United States from the clutches of the Conspirators. Any resistance, he assured us as long ago as 1966, would be a *'revolt of the ignorant against the informed and educated* . . . of the Midwest of Tom Sawyer against the cosmopolitan East of J.P. Morgan and Co., of old Siwash against Harvard'.

Was Quigley correct in his analysis of our national predicament? Is it all over for America? Is national slavery a foregone conclusion?

No! All is not lost! Ultimately, the conspirators will not prevail!

Their diabolical plot will collapse in ignominious ruins! . . .

Being based on greed, pride, and avarice, Satan's plan for total world conquest is fatally flawed. It's in total violation of all the spiritual laws and principles set in motion, and sustained by, the Creator God. As a result, it's doomed! . . .

Outwardly, it [the Conspiracy] may have the appearance of vitality and strength. But appearances are deceptive. . . .

Massive flaws, huge cracks are everywhere evident in the superstructure of the Babylonian System. It's crumbling and falling apart at the seams. . . . Being morally and spiritually depraved, it panders to the basic instincts of human nature. Ultimately, it can produce only corruption and confusion. The system is being held together by a massive, interlocking web of hate, fear, terror, manipulation, coercion, harassment and intimidation. Without these . . . ingredients, and their ruthless enforcement by agents of the Conspiracy, the whole system would instantly collapse in ignominy.

As we race towards the end of the Twentieth Century, what needs to happen to bring the United States back to sanity, prosperity and peace?

Another American Revolution - a SPIRITUAL REVOLUTION - is desperately needed in the hearts and minds of the American people.

Such a spiritual awakening . . . was largely responsible for saving early America from the clutches of the Illuminati.

Is a similar miracle possible at this time? Yes, it is! . . . As the late General Douglas McArthur once stated, 'History fails to record a single precedent in which nations subject to moral decay have not passed into economic and political decline. There has either been a spiritual awakening to overcome the moral lapse, or a progressive deterioration leading to ultimate national disaster.'

If we are to see national restoration, Russ Walton posits, it must begin, it can only begin, with individual regeneration.

Or as T.S. Eliot puts the issue at the end of *The Waste Land*:
Shall I at least set my lands in order?

NOTES

1.   Clinton Roosevelt was the Illuminati philosopher who wrote *The Science of Government, Founded on Natural Law* (1841). 'In his book, Roosevelt outlined the Illuminati's plans for the regimentation of mankind under those who, like himself, were the enlightened ones. He revealed their plans to emasculate and then destroy the Constitution which he likened to a "leaky vessel" which was "hastily put together when we left the British flag." Many observers recognize this amazing document as the basic blueprint for what later became known as FDR's "New Deal" (DS?p p.135).

2.   'Booth's grand-daughter, Izola Forrester, states in *This One Mad Act* that Lincoln's assassin had been in close contact with mysterious Europeans prior to the slaying, and had made at least one trip to Europe. Following the killing, Booth was whisked away to safety by members of the Knights of the Golden Circle. According to the author, Booth lived for many years following his disappearance' (*DS?* p.36).

3.   Colonel Edward Mandell House (his title was honorary) whom Woodrow Wilson acknowledged as 'my second personality,' 'my independent self. His thoughts and mine are one.' Wilson was House's 'creature': he edited all of Wilson's speeches and made it abundantly clear to Wilson that he was not to act upon advice given him by others' (*DS?* pp.95-100).

House's biographer, Arthur D. Howden Smith (*The Real Colonel House*), also '"picked Roosevelt as a natural candidate for the presidency long before any other responsible politician." He chose FDR as Assistant Secretary of the Navy in 1913, then, through the following years, groomed him to be the next Democratic president' (*DS?* pp.137-8).

4.   Bernard Baruch, also with Colonel House and Zionist Rabbi Stephen Wise, a mentor/controller of both Illuminati puppet American Presidents Woodrow Wilson and Franklin D. Roosevelt, described by Colonel Curtis Dall (in *FDR - My Exploited Father-in-Law*, pp.74-5) as 'the outstanding "leg boy" between world money and world political figures.' Before World War I he was said to be worth one million dollars; after World War I he was said to be worth about two hundred million dollars.

'Baruch's power and influence were immense. "Years later

when the press announced that Winston Churchill had arrived in this country and was in New York visiting Mr. Baruch before he journeyed on to the White House, bound on matters of State [Ball writes], *I was not surprised! First things first!*

"'I was not surprised, also, when Mr. Baruch gradually became the best-known symbol of vast world money power.... His words reflected great financial power - both visible and invisible - power of such magnitude and extent that is seldom heard of - not even dreamed of by most American citizens'" (*FDR*, pp.74-5, and DS? pp.140-1).

5.   'It is important that we note in passing that the top agents and representatives of all nations engaged in the war [WWI and WWII] were able to meet openly and freely in Switzerland without fear of interruption. Switzerland . . . was established in its present form in 1815 as a result of the Congress of Vienna. It was guaranteed "perpetual neutrality." Was this occurance a fortuitous "accident" - or did Switzerland receive its "perpetual neutrality" status in 1815 as the result of some very meticulous long-range planning on the part of the Rothschilds? Such a "safe haven" - located right in the heart of Europe, between Germany and France, was imperative to the success of their balance-of-power policy [in the nineteenth century and to the free traffic of espionage and financial agents in the twentieth century]. It was no "accident".

6.   'Quigley, an acknowledged "insider", . . . boasts of having had access to the "papers, and secret records" of the Illuminati Round Table Groups in the early 60's" (*Tragedy and Hope*, p.950, quoted in *DS?* p.105).

7.   'This "plan" was drawn up by J.P.Morgan, with the assistance of a committee of international financial experts, presided over by banker Charles Dawes. J.P. Morgan, a Rothschild affiliate, was one of America's leading financiers during the early part of this century.... The Dawes Plan called for $800 million (in loans) to Germany over the first four years. This was to go towards reconstruction which, in turn, was to generate finances with which the reparation payments could be made to Germany's debtors. Much of the money came from the United States.

'Professor Quigley tells us that . . . "Using these American loans, Germany's industry was largely reequipped with the most advanced technical facilities. . . . With these American loans, Germany was able to rebuild her industrial system to make it the second best in the world by a wide margin. . . . In the period 1924-1931, Germany paid 10.5 Billion marks in reparations but borrowed abroad a total of 18.6 Billion marks. Nothing was settled by all this, but the International Bankers sat in Heaven, *under a rain of fees and commissions*' (*Tragedy and Hope*, pp. 308-9, quoted in *DS?* pp.122-3).

8. I.G. (*Interessen Gemeinschaft* or 'community of interests') Farben, which came into existence prior to World War II, was centered in Germany, and ultimately '"dominated the entire world's chemical and drug industries. It . . . spread its operations to ninety-three countries and was a powerful and political force on all continents."'

In *World Without Cancer*, G. Edward Griffin states that one of the prime causes for Germany's defeat in World War I was its lack of petroleum. As soon as the War was over, this vulnerability was addressed and a way devised of converting coal into gasoline. This led to a merger or 'marriage' of the two industrial giants, I.G. Farben of Germany and Standard Oil of the United States, on 9 November 1929. 'Under the agreement, Standard Oil was given a one-half share of all rights to the hydrogenation process in all countries except Germany. Standard gave Farben 546,000 of its stock valued at more than $30,000,000. Both parties agreed never to compete with each other in the fields of chemistry and petroleum production. The goal was to remove competition and to guarantee a surge in profits. . . .

'When Henry Ford established an auto plant in Germany, Farben bought a forty percent interest. In the United States, Henry Ford's son, Edsel, joined the board of directors of I.G. Chemical Company, as did Walter Teagle, president of Standard Oil, Charles E. Mitchell, president of Rockfeller's National City Bank of New York, and Paul Warburg [the chief architect of the "Federal" Reserve System], brother of Max Warburg who was a director of the parent company in Germany.'

'"By the beginning of World War II, I.G. Farben had become the largest industrial corporation in Europe, the largest chemical company in the world, and part of the most gigantic and powerful cartel of all history (see *World Without Cancer*, pp.245-57, and *DS?* pp. 127-8).

9.   Martin was the Chief of the Economic Warfare Section of the Department of Justice investigating the structure of Nazi industry. Schacht masterminded the 'Young Plan' by which Germany was to be rebuilt and the Bank of International Settlements created. The Plan worked perfectly, bringing events in the Weimar Republic to an explosive head (*DS?* p.130).

10.   The media conspired to camouflage FDR's dubious personal record from the public, the 'leading' newspapers and magazines declining to publish a 1921 Senate Naval Affairs Report that cast serious reflections on FDR's character: the report stated that '"immoral and lewd acts were practiced under instructions or suggestions, by a number of the enlisted personnel of the United States Navy, in and out of uniform, for the purpose of securing evidence against sexual perverts, and authorization for the use of these enlisted men . . . was given both orally and in writing . . . by Assistant Secretary Franklin D. Roosevelt. . . ."

'The nationwide suppression of these facts by all the 'leading' newspapers places added emphasis on the famous words of John Swinton, editor of the New York News at the annual dinner of the American Press Association in 1914: "There is no such thing as an independent press in America. . . . Not a man among you dares to utter his honest opinion. . . . We are the tools and the vassals of the rich behind the scenes. We are marionettes.

'"*These men pull the strings and we dance. Our time, our talents, our lives and our capacities are all the property of these men -we are intellectual prostitutes*"'(*DS?* p.134).

11.   'The roots of FDR's family were deeply imbedded in banking and big business, these ties going back almost two centuries' (see *DS?* p.135).

12.   'During the . . . year 1910, the leading American Zionist, Rabbi Stephen Wise, told a Trenton, New Jersey, audience: 'On Tuesday the President of Princeton University will be elected governor of your state. He will not complete his term of office as governor. In November, 1912, he will be elected President of the United States. In March, 1917, he will be inaugurated for the second time as President. He will be one of the greatest Presidents

in American History' (Stephen Wise, *Challenging Years*, p.161, quoted in *DS?* p.97).

The Zionist Rabbi was referring, of course, to Woodrow Wilson. He was not, however, making an astrological prediction. He knew from less exalted means, for he himself, with House and Baruch, was calling the shots.

The same procedure was used by the same three to exalt another candidate to the Presidency: FDR. In the light of this, it is difficult to find the polite word to describe Rabbi Wise's 'statement to the press' of 24 September 1936: "*I am not a life-time Democrat. I became a democrat to help elect Woodrow Wilson president. I call myself a Wilson-Roosevelt Democrat because Wilson and Roosevelt in our day represent the ideal in democracy*" (*DS?* pp.139-40).

13. 'With the installation of the puppet Lloyd George regime in London came a distinct change in the official policy towards Zionism.

'The big pay off came when the new Foreign Secretary, Arthur Balfour, wrote to Lord Lionel Rothschild late in 1917:

Foreign Office
November 2nd, 1917

Dear Lord Rothschild,

I have much pleasure in conveying to you, on behalf of his Majesty's government, the following *declaration of sympathy with Jewish Zionist aspirations* which has been submitted to, and approved by, the Cabinet:

"*His Majesty's government view with favour the establishment of a national home for the Jewish people and will use their best endeavours to facilitate the achievement of this object*, it being clearly understood that nothing shall be done which may prejudice the civil and religious rights of *existing non-Jewish communities in Palestine, or the rights and political status enjoyed by Jews in any other country*."

Yours sincerely,
Arthur James Balfour

'This letter became known as the Balfour Declaration' (*DS?* p.90).

14.   In *FDR - The Other Side of the Coin*, Congressman Hamilton Fish, one of the top Republicans on Capitol Hill at the time of Pearl Harbour, writes: '"The Japanese would have done almost anything to avoid war with America. . . . Prince Kenoye, the prime minister, was very peacefully inclined, repeatedly requested to come to Washington or Honolulu to meet with President Roosevelt. He was willing to agree to our terms to keep out of war on a modus vivendi but *FDR refused to talk with the Japanese prime minister simply because he was determined to get into war with Japan, and through that, with Germany.* The American Ambassador in Tokyo, Joseph Grew, knew how much the Japanese wanted to maintain peaceful relations and urged such a conference. But FDR and his fellow ardent interventionists used ruses, dodges and tricks to involve us in a totally unnecessary war. . . . "'

'When the Warlords of Washington deliberately led our nation into war against the wishes of 85 percent of the American people, the plans of the International Conspirators were assured of success.

15.   Earlier, John Foster Dulles 'had been hired by Joseph Stalin to act as Russia's legal counsel in the United States. He was also closely associated with J.P. Morgan' (*FDR*, p.145).

ISRAEL

by Douglas Grant Annear

INTRODUCTION

The first section of this paper consists of selections from Des Griffin's *Descent Into Slavery?* (pages 79-91 and 205-213). Section Two presents research of my own which confirms and elaborates upon Mr. Griffin's work.

The final section is devoted to an in-depth account of a field study I conducted in Israel and the West Bank in August-September 1992. I visited military installations, prisons, government offices and library archives, private homes, religious and secular schools, refugee camps, etc. I interviewed army officers, police officials, soldiers, and many other Israeli citizens, as well as dozens of political prisoners, journalists, human rights activists, refugee camp administrators, etc. This last section also includes an account of an extremely harrowing experience as I attempted to leave the country from Ben Gurion airport in Tel Aviv: I was detained for several hours by Israeli security forces, vigorously and repeatedly searched, interrogated, and even threatened with imprisonment. They suspected that I was an active supporter of the P.L.O., solely on the basis of the fact that they found a few handouts from human rights groups in my hand bag and the names of several Palestinian friends (none of whom have ever been involved in the P.L.O.) in my address book.

PART I: THE STORY OF ZIONISM

Selected from Des Griffin's *Descent Into Slavery* (pp. 79-91 and 205-13). Occasionally, some paragraphs have been transposed and others deleted in whole or in part. Additional notes (indicated in bold) have been interspersed by the editor.

From late in the last century another potentially powerful force (Political Zionism) had been developing in both Europe and the United States. History records that Zionism was heavily financed by the Rothschilds and their associates on both sides of the Atlantic . . .

In the 1880's when Palestine was controlled by the Turkish government, Edmond Rothschild was heavily involved in establishing Khazar settlements in Palestine. It was a well known fact that the Rothschilds were ardent Talmudists (Morton, *The Rothschilds*, pp. 30-31) whose religion taught nothing but contempt for those stupid goy (human cattle) who were not part of the "chosen" Jewish race. With characteristic arrogance he [Edmond Rothschild] rejected efforts by Russian Zionists to have a say in how the new settlements were operated: "These are my colonies, and I shall do with them as I like.' (Morton, *The Rothschilds*, p. 168) . . .

Modern political Zionism sprang from the Zionist Congress that was held under the direction of Dr. Theodor Herzl in Basel, Switzerland in 1897. It is an interesting and important fact of history that the majority of the 197 delegates who attended the congress were from Eastern Europe. The congress was generally ignored by the leading Jews from the West, who, at that time, didn't entertain any grandiose hopes for the establishment of a "Jewish" state in the land of Palestine. That was a Khazar idea!

Judging from subsequent events it seems certain that Herzl was given considerable "help" in the writing of his book, *The Jewish State*, and in the organizing of the convention at Basel. . . .

He wrote that "there arose before our eyes a Russian Jewry, the strength of which we had not even suspected. Seventy of our delegates came from Russia, and it was patent to all of us that they represented the views and sentiments of five million Jews of that country. What a humiliation for us, who had taken our superiority for granted" (Reed, *The Controversy of Zionism*, p. 200).

Plate 5: *Terror-stricken Palestinians in flight from an Israeli attack.*
Source: Dimbleby and McCullin, _The Palestinians._

It was at this juncture that Talmudic Jewish influence began to make itself felt in the West. Shortly thereafter the leaders of the Western Powers came to accept the Talmudists as representing all Jewry. As we shall see now this new posture had a devastating effect on Western Society.

As the political interests of the Rothschild-controlled International Bankers and the Zionists were inextricably intertwined, it is only natural [to] expect [that] major support for the Zionist cause [would have been forthcoming] from the American government. This aid materialized following the seizure of the United States money system by the International Bankers in 1913. . . .

On pages 186 and 187 of his book, [*Challenging Years*] Rabbi Wise, a leading member of the Zionist movement in America, tells of his close association with Louis D. Brandeis. "From the very beginning of his administration Brandeis and I knew that in Wilson we had, and would always have, understanding and sympathy for the Zionist program and purpose . . . Throughout, it must be added, we received warm and heartening help from Colonel House, close friend of the President and his unofficial Secretary of State. House not only made our cause [Zionism] the object of his very special concern, but served as liaison officer between the Wilson Administration and the Zionist Movement. This was particularly true after it grew to strength, beginning in 1914, through increasing support of Zionism by the Jewish masses throughout the world and the changing world situation, which forecast the historical necessity for a Jewish homeland . . ."

Recalling a White House conversation with President Wilson, Wise quotes himself as saying: "Mr. President, World Jewry counts upon you in its hour of need and hope. Placing his hand upon my shoulder, he quietly and firmly said, 'Have no fear, Palestine will be yours' " (Wise, *Challenging Years*, pp 189, 197).

In 1916, amid howls of protest, Wilson appointed Brandeis to the Supreme Court. Following this, Brandeis "did not cease to stand out as leader, but his leadership [of the Zionist movement] took the form of invaluable council to a small number of associates" (Wise, *The Challenging Years*, p. 200).

Zionist historian Dr. Joseph Kastein, writing in 1933, tells us that the Zionist "executive" that was established by the 197 delegates at Basel in 1897 "was the first embodiment of a real Jewish international."

Author Brian Connell gives his readers insight into how "this small international" operated [and undoubtedly, still operates]. He lists among its original members "Sir Ernest Cassel ... Max Warburg, head of the great banking house in Hamburg [a close Rothschild associate and head of German Intelligence during World War I], Edouard Noetzlin, honorary president of the Banque de Paris et des Pays Bas, in Paris; Franz Phillipson in Brussels . . . and, above all, Jacob Schiff of the firm of Kuhn, Loeb and Company in New York [the top Rothschild agent in the United States and one of the main financial backers of the Bolshevik Revolution in 1917]. Ties of race and interest bound these men together. The web of their communications quivered at the slightest touch. They maintained between them an incredibly accurate network of economic, political and financial intelligence at the highest level. They could withdraw support here, provide additional funds there, move immense sums of money with lightning rapidity and secrecy from one corner to another of their financial empires and influence political decisions in a score of countries" (Connell, *Sir Edward Cassel, From Manifest Destiny*). Unquestionably, political Zionism was, and is, a definite part of the apparatus known as the Illuminati.

Unlike most Jews in the Western World, who would have accepted a "national home for the Jews" in any part of the world (even Uganda, Africa) the Talmudic Zionists were dedicated to the idea that only the seizure of Palestine from the Turks, and the establishment of a "Jewish State" in that area of the world, would satisfy what they had in mind. As we shall see, they planned to make Jerusalem the capital of a One-World Government. . . .

On the British front, early in World War I, things were not going so well for the Zionists. The Zionist/International Banker cabal did not have full control of the leadership of the British government. Men like Herbert Asquith (Prime Minister), Lord

Kitchener (Secretary of War), Sir Douglas Haig (who became Commander-in-Chief in France), and Sir William Robertson (Chief of Staff in France and later Chief of the Imperial General Staff) were mainly concerned with their national duty and their winning of the war. . . .

As historian Douglas Reed points out: "The leading political and military posts were held by men who put every proposal for the political and military conduct of the war to one test: would it help win the war and was it in their country's interest. By that test Zionism failed. The story of the first two years of the four-year war is that of the struggle behind the scenes to dislodge these obstructive men and to supplant them with other, submissive men" (Reed, *The Controversy of Zionism*, p. 252). . . .

The Prime Minister's rejection of the Zionist proposal in effect signed his political death warrant. It was clear that he would have to be removed from his high office if the Zionist plans were to be brought to fruition during the course of the war. The back stage manipulators launched a national campaign to discredit Asquith and create conditions that would lead to his departure from office. Such powerful instruments as the *Times* and the *Manchester Guardian* sowed seeds of doubt about their leader's competence in the minds of the British public. It was claimed that Asquith wasn't pursuing victory in the war against Germany with enough zeal. . . .

When the defamation campaign against Herbert Asquith resulted in his ouster, the leadership of the British government was assumed by David Lloyd George whose "advocacy of the Jewish homeland" in the words of Dr. Chaim Weizmann, a Russian-born Zionist, "long predated his accession to the premiership."

The new 'leader' immediately bowed to the dictates of his hidden masters, fired Sir William Robertson and, against the advice of realistic and knowledgeable military experts, began to withdraw hundreds of thousands of troops from France and to pour them into Palestine. . . .

Colonel Repington, a close friend of Robertson, strove desperately to draw national attention to the folly of Lloyd-

George's policies, but in vain. He recorded in his diary: "We are feeding over a million men into the sideshow theatres of war and are letting down our strength in France at a moment when all the Boche [German] forces from Russia [following their victory] may come against us. I am unable to get the support from the editor of *The Times* that may rouse the country and I do not think I will be able to go on with him much longer." A month later he recorded that "in a stormy interview I told [*Times* editor] Mr. Geoffrey Dawson that his subservience to the [new] war Cabinet during this year was largely the cause of the dangerous position of our army . . . I would have nothing more to do with *The Times*."

As truth had been rejected by the controlled *Times*, Colonel Repington went to the one man he knew would have the personal integrity and courage to publish the facts. H.A. Gwynne of the *Morning Post* published the article without submitting it to the censor. After the top had been blown off what should have been one of the greatest scandals of the decade by these two great and patriotic men, individuals who loved truth and their country more than anything else, the British government prosecuted them for "endangering national security." Because of the pressure of public opinion they were each only fined for the 'crime' of patriotism. . . .

BETRAYAL OF THE ARABS

With the Arab states committed on the Crown's side in the battle against Germany's ally, Turkey, the way was being prepared for an event of immense historical importance: the creation of a Zionist state in Palestine.

In spite of the promises of independence and freedom given to all Arabs (including Palestinians) by the British authorities, moves were under way to betray the Arabs. As Jewish historian Alfred Lilienthal points out: "Had the Arabs been aware of the secret diplomatic agreements then being negotiated, it is highly unlikely that any revolt would have taken place."

Territory formerly controlled by Turkey was to be split up

between Britain, France and Russia. "The Arabs knew nothing of this secret diplomacy, which constituted a complete repudiation of all promises to Hussein" (Lilienthal, *The Zionist Connection*, pp. 17-18). . . .

CHANGE IN BRITISH POLICY TOWARDS ZIONISM: THE BALFOUR DECLARATION (1917)

With the installation of the puppet Lloyd George regime in London came a distinct change in the official policy towards Zionism.

The big pay off came when the new Foreign Secretary, Arthur Balfour, wrote to Lord Lionel Rothschild late in 1917: . . . "His Majesty's government view with favour the establishment in Palestine of a national home for the Jewish people and will use their best endeavours to facilitate the achievement of this object, it being clearly understood that nothing shall be done which may prejudice the civil and religious rights of existing non-Jewish communities in Palestine, or the rights and political status enjoyed by Jews in any other country . . ."

This letter became known as the Balfour Declaration. Notice the careful use of the word Jewish "home" instead of "Jewish State" when referring to what was planned in Palestine. . . .

Observes historian Lilienthal: "The word "home" quieted the fears of the non-Zion Jews. Meanwhile, through the realization of unlimited immigration into Palestine, the Zionists hoped eventually to become a majority in Palestine.

(It is revealing to look at some of the private comments made by Lord Balfour at the time of this historic decision. "In Palestine we do not propose even to go through the form of consulting the wishes of the actual inhabitants of the country [the Palestinians] . . . the Great Powers are committed to Zionism. And Zionism, be it right or wrong, good or bad, is rooted in age long traditions and is of far profounder import than the desires of the few seven hundred thousand or so Arabs who now inhabit the land. As for the Palestinians, the Super Powers have not made one statement of fact or policy

which they did not intend to violate" (Hirst, *The Gun and The Olive Branch*, p. 42).

"For the next twenty-five years the Zionist movement dedicated itself to the practical aspects of buying land, establishing schools, and building up its position in Palestine rather than achieving the creation of a political entity" (Lilienthal, *The Zionist Connection*, p. 13).

AFTERMATH OF WWII:
TERRORISM AND THE ESTABLISHMENT
OF THE ZIONIST STATE

As the bloodletting wound to a close in Europe and Asia [at the conclusion of WW II] the focus of world attention shifted to the Middle East where the Zionists were [by that time openly] engaged in efforts to establish a State of Israel in Palestine.

In November 1944, Lord Moyne, the British Colonial Secretary, who was striving to find an equitable solution to the Palestinian problem, was assassinated in Cairo by two Zionists from Palestine. His 'crime' was that he shared the view of many of his responsible predecessors, that the Zionist incursions in the Middle East would end in catastrophe.

When the next Zionist Congress convened in Geneva in 1946, it had, according to Dr. Weizmann, "a special character" and "showed a tendency to rely on methods . . . referred to by different names: 'resistance', 'defense', 'activism. One feature was common to all of them: the conviction of the need for fighting against British authority in Palestine, or anywhere else, for that matter." In other words, the Zionist World Congress of 1946 condoned the use of terrorism as a means of bringing about the creation of the Zionist State. These methods had proved successful in Russia almost 30 years earlier: they were to be tried again. It was clearly understood that without terrorism the Zionist State could not be achieved.

Many terrorist organizations sprang up in Palestine in an effort to force the creation of a Zionist state. The largest of these was Irgun Zvai Leumi, led by Menachem Begin. Another was the Stern Gang, among whose leaders was Yitzhak Shamir. These, according to the *Los Angeles Times*, formed "Israel's underground beginnings: and used assassination as a political tool" (June 1, 1980 Part V, p. 2).

(Apart from the assassination of Lord Moyne, the Zionists also made an unsuccessful attempt on the life of Sir Harold MacMillan, the High Commissioner of Palestine in 1944 (Bell, The Long War: Israel and the Arabs since 1946, p. 201). Count Folke Bernadotte, was a Swede acting as U.N. Mediator to Palestine in 1948. He opposed unrestricted Jewish immigration to the region and encouraged the Israelis to re-absorb the Palestinian refugees. As well as this he advocated the return of the property and land lost as a result of the 'War of Independence': he too was assassinated by the Stern Gang. The 'anonymous' perpetrators were publicly condemned by the Israeli government but no one was actually arrested, despite the fact that officials were well aware of their identities (Bell, The Long War: Israel and the Arabs since 1946, p. 201). As time went on, they became folk heroes and in the case of Begin and Shamir the eventual leaders of the Israeli government.)

As the terror and bloodshed escalated, a Select Committee on Estimates of the British House of Commons announced that "very large numbers of Jews, almost amounting to a second Exodus, have been migrating from Eastern Europe to the American zones of Germany and Austria with the intention in the majority of cases of finally making their way to Palestine. It is clear that it is a highly organized movement, with ample funds and great influence behind it . . ." A War Investigating Committee, sent to Europe by the United States Senate, stated that "*heavy migration of Jews from Eastern Europe into the American zone of Germany is part of a carefully organized plan financed by special groups in the United States.*" It should be noted that this massive 'exodus' took place from Russia and the nations of Eastern Europe which had been abandoned and sealed off behind what Churchill called the "Iron Curtain." It is obvious that this "second exodus" took place with the consent and full

Plate 6: *A corpse is removed from the carnage and rubble of the King David Hotel after Zionist attack*

cooperation of Washington, London and Moscow. Nobody was able to leave the Soviet Union without permission, yet here we have clear evidence of the Iron Curtain parting to allow a massive flood of "Jews" to leave that area and head for Palestine.

During 1946 and 1947 the Zionist terror campaign reached a crescendo. Hundreds of British soldiers were ambushed, shot while they slept or were blown up in a variety of ways. Two British soldiers were tortured to death in an orchard and left hanging there.

(The bombing of the British headquarters in the King David Hotel in Jerusalem in July of 1946 provides a particularly revealing glimpse of the Zionist mind. The perpetrators knew that it was not only British officers and soldiers who would be in the hotel at the time of detonation, but that between twenty and forty innocent Jews and Arabs would also be working on the premises. Twenty minutes before the explosion took place, an anonymous telephone call was

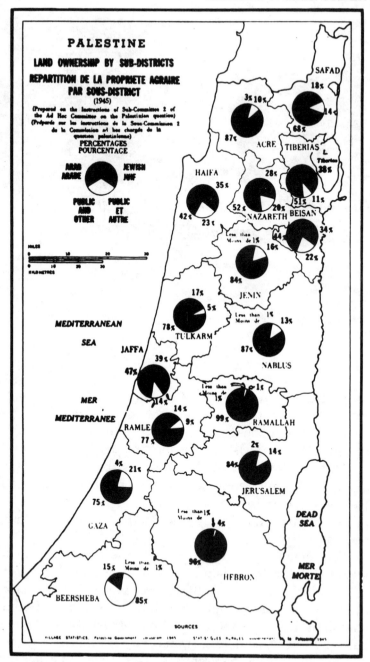

Plate 7: *Map showing distribution of land ownership in Palestine in 1947 as prepared for the United Nations Sub Committee*

received by the British commander warning him to evacuate the premises: it was not acted upon since the British had considered their fortress to be unassailable to a bombing and had received many other such threats in the preceding months (Bell, *The Long War: Israel and The Arabs since 1946*, pp. 26-27).

The British decision not to flee the hotel may seem foolish in retrospect, but it cannot be overlooked that the Zionists failed to alert even their own countrymen who worked in the same building, so determined were they to ensure the secrecy and success of the operation. Over eighty Brits, Arabs and Jews died as a result of the implementation of this part of the 'ends justifies the means' Zionist terrorist policy.)

Faced with an ever-increasing wave of terrorism from within Palestine, a mounting wave of hundreds of thousands of Jews from the Soviet bloc countries and irresistible pressure from Zionists at home and the Truman Administration in Washington, the British government referred the Palestinian problem to the recently formed United Nations. On November 29, 1947 the U.N. voted to partition Palestine into two independent states, one Jewish and one Arab, by October 1, 1949. The plan was accepted by the Zionists but was rejected by the Arabs who had no intention of giving up possession and control of an area which had been their homeland for close to 2000 years.

(When the United Nations voted to partition Palestine they assigned over 54% of the territory to the Zionists for the creation of the state of Israel. One of the most astounding aspects of this decision was that at the time the Arabs owned 93% of the land and made up 70% of the population of Palestine (Dimbleby, Bell, Rodinson and many others). Nearly all the choicest and most arable lands along the Mediterranean coast were given to the Zionists despite the fact that these lands had been cultivated for generations, the produce being one of the main components of their export trade. The U.N. partition plan also allotted the Negev desert region to the Zionists although British census figures indicated Bedouins outnumbered Jews by 100,000 to 475. Most of the Palestinian wheat and barley was produced in this area, as well as

considerable olive and citrus products. The Israelis, nevertheless, have long made the boast that it was they who turned
the barren Negev into a fertile and blooming garden (Dimbleby,
The Palestinians, p. 86).

This is but another example of Zionist propaganda which
has completely buffaloed a gullible and unsuspecting world
public. As the U.N. ad Hoc committee began to deliberate on
the proposed partition of Palestine, the Arabs were unable to
generate the kind of slick lobby group required to match the
rhetoric of the Zionists, their inexhaustible source of funds,
and their network of friends and supporters cultivated since
the beginning of the century, from the world's political
leaders..

In the first vote on this issue there were several countries
which abstained, including Britain, and the plan did not get
the required majority to be ratified. In the ensuing days, the
American government (under the presidency of Harry Truman)
was to exert considerable political pressure on many of the
countries that had either abstained or voted against the
partition. A large group of American Senators and other
important political figures also signed a letter urging other
countries to support the partition. In addition, American
influence was brought to bear on countries such as Haiti,
Belgium, The Netherlands, Liberia, Paraguay, China, Ethio-
pia and the Philippines, all of which were persuaded to
change their vote from an abstention or a nay to a yes (See Bell,
The Long War, pp. 66-67 and Taylor, *The Zionist Mind*, pp. 119-
120). According to John Forrestal, the U.S. Secretary of
Defence at the time, the White House was guilty of "a
scandalous use of coercion and duress upon other nations"
(Dimbleby, *The Palestinians*, p. 86). Eventually, the U.N. approved the partition plan by a vote of 33 to 13. As American
historian J. Bowyer Bell has said, the Zionists won the
diplomatic battle despite the fact that "shorn of its biblical
quotations and emotional references to the final solution, the
Zionist case was weaker; but since they were asking for a
compromise and the Arabs wanted all, they swayed the
majority of delegates seeking an equitable solution. But

when the compromise is to get half of what you don't own it's a pretty good deal. It was ingenious, it was evil, and it threw the entire Arab argument into the wrong frame of reference. More devastating still, it proved effective" (*The Long War: Israel and the Arabs since 1946*, p. 67).

In the wake of this proposal, violence in Palestine increased still further. Alarmed, the U.N. Security Council backpeddled and the Truman administration reversed American policy— suggesting that the partition proposal be suspended, a truce arranged and the British Mandate replaced by a Trusteeship in which the United States would be heavily involved. The Zionists realized that their dream of a Jewish State was about to collapse, and struck at once to present the U.N. with an accomplished fact by dissecting Palestine themselves. To strike stark terror into the hearts of the Arab inhabitants of Palestine "Jewish terrorists of the Stern Gang and the Irgun Zvai Leumi stormed the village of Deir Yasin and butchered everyone in sight. The corpses of 250 Arabs, mostly women and children, were tossed into wells" (*Time* Magazine). The Palestinians recognized that the Deir Yasin massacre was a warning of what would continue to happen if they stayed on in their own land. With the exception of just a few thousand, they fled to neighbouring states. That, in essence, is how the Palestinian refugee problem came into being.

(As reports of the approach of the Irgun spread among the frightened people of this primarily Christian Arab village, many of the men congregated in the town church from which they emerged behind the local bishop waving a white flag to show they were unarmed and had no desire to fight the Israelis. Deir Yasin was not a military stronghold by any stretch of the imagination. In fact, the people of this village just outside of Haifa had enjoyed relatively peaceful relations with the Jewish communities in the area.

The whole scale slaughter of these villagers was undertaken for a different kind of "strategic" reason—that is, to incite terror among the Arab population of Palestine. Jacques de Reynier, a member of the Red Cross unit which arrived upon the scene the next morning wrote that the Israelis "said they were cleaning up. They had used machine guns and hand grenades. It had been finished off with knifes. Anyone could see that 250 men, women and children had been butchered. Young girls had been raped. A pregnant woman had been beaten brutally and her unborn child cut out with a butcher's knife. A young girl who tried to save the child was shot" (Dimbleby, *The Palestinians*, p. 80). According to Richard Cutting, the U.N.'s Assistant Inspector General for the region, people were actually cut into pieces and parts of ears were found on earrings attached to the clothing of some of the Israeli soldiers whom he encountered. Cutting also discovered that a memo was sent to the Irgun members from an anonymous source within the leadership of the Hagannah (the regular army) stating that the "capture" of Deir Yasin "was one stage of our plan. As long as you hold to it I have no objection to the manner [in which] it is carried out" (Dimbleby, The Palestinians, p. 80). Much later Begin would write in his memoirs that indeed this had been a highly successful plan as the Arabs were thereafter panic stricken by rumours that there would be more of these acts of mass murder (Hirst, *The Gun and The Olive Branch*, p. 124).

Though the attack of Deir Yasin may have been the greatest single atrocity which the Zionists committed against the Palestinians, the threat of renewed acts of violence was certainly not an empty bluff. One of the most effective means of inciting terror among the Arabs and forcing them to flee their homes was the use of "barrel bombs." These were oil barrels or other cylindrical containers which were filled with petrol and other highly flammable materials that were ignited and rolled down into the most densely-populated Arab sections of Jerusalem and other urban centres. These violent explosions would often instantly kill bystanders and cause the burning of homes and property in the immediate vicinity (Dimbleby, *The Palestinians*, p. 89).

THE ULTIMATE GOAL OF ZIONISM?

It has been an established fact for years that the political Zionists plan to make Jerusalem the administrative capital of a One-World government. This lofty (but purely carnal) ambition was laid out in unmistakeable terms by David Ben-Gurion, Israel's Prime Minister, in a piece written for Look magazine in 1962. He predicted what [he thought] would happen on the world scene over the next quarter of a century. . . .

The Cold War will be a thing of the past. Internal pressure of the constantly growing intelligentsia in Russia for more freedom and the pressure of the masses for raising their living standards may lead to a gradual democratization of the Soviet Union. On the other hand, the increasing influence of the workers and the farmers, and the rising political importance of men of science, may transform the United States into a welfare state with a planned economy. Western and Eastern Europe will become a federation of autonomous states having a Socialist and democratic regime. With the exception of the U.S.S.R. as a federated Eurasian state, all other continents will become united in a world alliance, at whose disposal will be an international police force. All armies will be abolished, and there will be no more wars. In Jerusalem, the United Nations (a truly United Nations) will build a Shrine of the Prophets to serve the federated union of all continents; this will be the seat of the Supreme Court of Mankind, to settle all controversies among the federated continents. . . .

PART II

In this section I begin by expanding upon some of the issues raised by Des Griffin in the first section relating to the formation of Israel. The balance of the section is devoted to a historical overview on the impact of the Zionist state since its inception in 1948.

ZIONISM: THE PUBLIC AND THE PRIVATE IMAGE

It is illuminating to compare Herzl's public and his private statements in relation to the establishment of the new Jewish state. In *Der Judenstad* (1896), Herzl first announced the pompous and grandiose aim of the Zionists "to establish an outpost of civilization in the midst of barbarism" (cited in Hirst, *The Gun and The Olive Branch*, p. 15). Herzl and his collaborators were obviously framing their public declarations for international purposes as they stressed that the rights and freedom of the indigenous Arab population would never be infringed upon (a subterfuge that Chaim Weizmann reiterated in his own dissemination of the Zionist ideal). In *Altneuland*, (1902) or *Old New Land*, Herzl fantasizes about the beneficent effect of planting a Zionist colony in Palestine. Arabs, he anticipates, would welcome their new comrades with open arms, overjoyed with the Zionists for bringing them "all the conveniences of the modern world" and "turning a malaria-filled swamp and plot of sand into a garden" (Hirst, *The Gun and The Olive Branch*, p. 16). In his private diaries, however, which were not published

Plate 8: *Theodor Herzl, the founder of Zionism. Source:* The Palestinians

during his life, and which he never intended for public scrutiny, by either the international community or the rank and file Zionist followers, Herzl speaks far more candidly about the real modus operandi of the new Israel.

First, he outlines the strategy of enlisting sponsorship from a European Super Power in return for favourable influence secured for that nation by Jewish finance and Jewish-controlled press.

Second, he advocates the necessity of fueling antagonisms between the Arabs and the leading European nations. Third, he suggests methods of intimidation that could be used with European governments on behalf of the Jews, by making them aware of the network of spies who were at the time co-ordinating massive insurrections in Europe and all over the world. A new European war, Herzl concludes, would be of the greatest advantage to the Zionist cause. (It must be realized that Herzl was admitted to the most elite circles of the Zionist infrastructure, including several private meetings with the Rothschilds--see *The Complete Diaries* of Theodor Herzl for further details).

Immigration alone, Herzl was to realize, would not be sufficient for the creation of the new Zionist state. It could be achieved, he argues in his private diaries (and it is well to remember the image he presents in *Altneuland*), only through Zionist supremacy in armed forces, along with a concerted effort to deport most of the indigenous population. "It will be our endeavour" he vowed, "to transfer the poverty-stricken population across the border unnoticed, by securing work for it in other countries while denying it any employment in the land that will be ours" (*The Complete Diaries of Theodor Herzl*, vol. 1, p. 343). Later, in the forties, Joseph Weitz, who was then in charge of Zionist colonization, echoed these words when he wrote: "between ourselves, it must be clear that there is no room for both peoples; we shall not achieve our goal of independence with very many Arabs in this country. We must transfer all Arabs to neighbouring countries [so that] not one village or tribe is left" (Hirst, *The Gun and The Olive Branch*, p. 130).

ETHNIC CLEANSING

There are many other examples of Jewish terrorism and use of armed force to "create space" for the proposed new state of Israel. For instance, the village of El Manara was completely evacuated after the Zionist forces razed their houses and left warnings not to return. In another Arab town, called Nasred-Din, every house was smashed, burned or otherwise destroyed by the Irgun. In Er Roma, the Hagannah told everyone to flee to Lebanon or be killed. The cities of Tiberias and Haifa lost nearly all of their Arab populations when the Hagannah invaded during the 1948 'War of independence.' In the village of Einez Zeitum the people were corralled together by the Hagannah and one man was arbitrarily crucified. Many women were beaten and 37 young men and boys were executed. On October 29, 1948 the Israeli air force mercilessly bombed the Palestinian village of Safsaf. As the army moved in to 'mop up' they assembled the surviving population and four girls were raped repeatedly by several Israeli soldiers in full view of their families and the rest of the villagers. After this seventy people were blindfolded and shot—one after another. In Majd el Kurum twelve unarmed villagers were publicly executed.

After news of the Zionist attacks in the period between 1947-49 spread among the Palestinians, the Israelis adopted the policy of broadcasting urgent warnings (in Arabic) over local radio stations, and riding around the towns and cities with megaphones and loud speakers shouting messages such as the following: "Save your souls, all Ye faithful; the Jews are using poisonous gas and atomic weapons. Run for your lives in the name of Allah" (Dimbleby, *The Palestinians* p. 89). Of course, the official Israeli line has always been that it was the Arab leadership who told the people to flee the theatre of war, and to abandon their ancestral homes and property. However, the renowned Palestinian writer Walid Khalil and other Palestinians have long denied this claim and this has been irrefutably substantiated by many sources, including Irish professor Erskine Childers who was part of a U.N. committee that monitored

Arab radio reports at the time, and which surveyed the records of Palestinian and other Arab newspapers, as well as the archives of the governments of surrounding Arab countries. Not a single command was to be found recommending the evacuation of Palestinians from their homes. Instead, there are repeated transcript references telling the people to stay put, since the Arab leaders knew that the flight of their people was hurting the Palestinian cause (Woolfson, *Portrait of a Palestinian*, p. 17). Indeed, there was no mention of an Arab "voluntary walk-out" even by the Zionists until 1950 when the Israelis initiated their 'pass the buck' policy in reference to the displaced Palestinians (now numbering over one million and a half persons) who continue to live in the U.N. 'relief' camps. It was at that time that the Israeli government began saying that the refugee situation is a "world problem" which was in no way created by the emergence of Israel!

ZIONIST MANIPULATION OF "ANTI-SEMITISM"

Since its inception, one of the strongest forces behind the Zionist movement has been "anti-semitism", the concept that Jews cannot live among Gentiles without being the victims of bigotry and prejudice. Jews need to segregate themselves, therefore, in a homeland that, in the words of Chaim Weizmann, would be "as Jewish as Britain is British." One of the main problems for the Zionists, however, has been assembling enough Jews who would not only lend financial support to the cause, but who would be willing to emigrate to the state of Israel. In many cases, the Zionists have had to resort to political pressure and even outright terrorism to ensure that the Jewish population base keeps pace with the Palestinians who have had a higher birthrate. For instance, in 1945 the U.S. presidency under Roosevelt proposed a plan by which the Western European Nations, along with the Americans, would absorb the surviving Holocaust victims, with the U.S. alone offering immediate asylum to 100,000. That most of the survivors did not want to go to the Middle East apparently meant nothing to the Zionists who immediately ridiculed this plan and insisted that at least three hundred thousand go to Israel. The U.S. Congress, however, agreed to absorb only 20,000, supporting the Zionists in their demands that nearly all of the survivors go to Israel (Dimbleby, *The Palestinians*, p. 84).

By the early 1950's emigration from Israel began to outstrip immigration, setting a dangerous precedent for the Zionists. To combat this trend the Israeli government turned their attention

Plate 9: *An example of Israeli manipulation of anti-semitism to their advantage. The headline is clear, but where it has been placed, among the hate literature in one of the Holocaust museums, screams out that the story is false.*

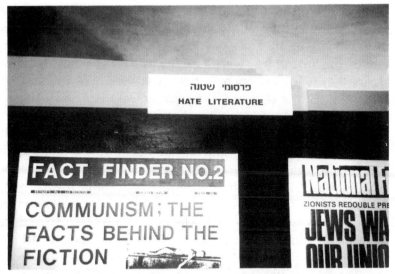

פרסומי שטנה

HATE LITERATURE

FACT FINDER NO.2

COMMUNISM: THE
FACTS BEHIND THE
FICTION

National F

ZIONISTS REDOUBLE PRE

JEWS WA
OUR UNIO

Plate 10: *In the article of which this is the headline, the author contends that the Jews were behind the formation of the Soviet Union. The suggestion is so preposterous to the Jewish public that they exhibit it as an example of hate literature, not knowing the true facts of the situation.*

toward Iraq, where there was a community of over 130,000 Jews who had been living in relative prosperity and harmony with their Iraqi countrymen, and even with some degree of political prominence (indeed, the previous Iraqi Foreign Minister had been a Jew). In order to motivate this community to immigrate to Israel, the Zionists detonated three bombs over the period of 1950-1951 to create the impression that they had been set off by an anti-semitic terrorist group within Iraq. After these explosions, the Zionists distributed pamphlets urging the Jewish community to emigrate to Israel since it was "obviously" the only place they could be safe. These pamphlets, however, were issued a little too quickly after these bombings which led Iraqi authorities to suspect that the Zionists were responsible. A man by the name of Yehudah Tajja was arrested along with several others though it was not until 1960, in an Iraqi newspaper article that he confessed to having been paid by the Zionists to orchestrate these explosions. These bombings proved to be most effective in alarming the Iraqi officials and when the Israelis began to exert considerable political pressure on the government of Iraq, as well as in international diplomatic circles, the Jews of Iraq were asked to leave. Naturally, the only doors that were left open to them were those of the state of Israel (Hirst, *The Gun and The Olive Branch*, pp. 155-164).

A far more shocking and barbarous act of Zionist terrorism that wasn't exposed until long after the fact was the Nov. 1940 sinking of a passenger ship called the "Patria", which was carrying several British dignitaries as well 252 illegal Jewish immigrants. The startling disclosure of this attack was made by Dr. Herzl Rosenblum in 1968 to the Tel Aviv newspaper *Yedios Achronos*. Rosenblum was part of the Zionist Actions Committee which ordered this attack; in the newspaper article, he claimed that he protested vigorously against the sinking of the "Patria" but was threatened and even physically abused by his fellow Actions Committee members to keep him quiet. In defence of this vicious and inhuman act of mass slaughter Moshe Sharret, a former member of the Israeli government, is reported to have calmly replied that "it is sometimes necessary to sacrifice a few in order to save the many."

These Jews were "sacrificed" to drum up support among the rest of the world and to play on the anti-semitic hysteria that has always been the life-blood of the Zionist movement. As Dr. Nahun Goldman, President of the World Zionist Congress, said in a speech on July 23, 1958 to the Jewish Congress in Geneva: "A current decline of overt anti-semitism might constitute a new danger. Jews are equal citizens everywhere. The disappearance of anti-semitism, while beneficial to those communities, has had a very negative effect on our political life." The editor of *Davar*, the official paper of the Socialist Labour (Mapai) Party wrote that if he were in command of the Zionist leadership he would "send a score of efficient young men to plague [those] Jews [who] are absorbed in sinful self satisfaction with anti-semitic slogans such as 'Jew go back to Palestine.' This would bring the immigration we need" (Lilienthal, *The Other Side of the Coin*, p. 184).

Another startling revelation which came out in the 1954 trial of Malkiel Greenwald was that during the Second World War the Jewish Agency (the main organizational body for funding the Zionist movement) arranged a deal with the Nazis to help the Germans facilitate the deportation of thousands of European Jews into concentration camps in return for allowing a few hundred young, healthy Jews to emigrate to Israel! Greenwald, who was acquitted of all charges against him, accused Rudolph Kastner, a high-ranking official in the Jewish Agency, of being the man who negotiated this deal with the Nazis. This assertion was later confirmed by Adolph Eichmann in a 1960 article that appeared in *Life* magazine (Taylor, *The Zionist Mind*, p. 84).

TORTURE OF PALESTINIAN POLITICAL PRISONERS

The frequency and methods of torture by Israeli authorities have been well documented by a number of professional writers. Marion Woolfson, for example, a Jewish journalist from Scotland, has written a compelling book entitled *Bassam Shak'a: Portrait of a Palestinian*, which outlines the kind of torture many Palestinians have experienced at the hands of the Israelis. For instance, one of the most common methods employed by the Israeli army and police is to force electric cattle prods as well as broken glass up the anus of any Palestinian who is suspected of insurrectionist activities (Woolfson, *Portrait of a Palestinian*, p. 17). This is confirmed by an article in Israeli newspaper *Yedios Achronos* in which a policeman admits to administering such torture tactics (Woolfson, *Portrait of a Palestinian*, p. 17). Felicia Langer, an Israeli lawyer, also wrote in her revealing book entitled *With My Own Eyes*, of the widespread torture of Palestinian political prisoners which she witnessed personally during her career in the Israeli judicial system. Further evidence of systematic torture by the Israelis is available in the painstakingly well-documented research of Walid Khalil, a Palestinian writer who has devoted his life to the pursuit of justice for his people.

HUMAN RIGHTS VIOLATIONS

By 1972, 17,000 Palestinians, including many lawyers, doctors, teachers and writers had been deported, often on the
flimsiest of excuses, and for the most part without any opportunity to defend themselves in a court of law (Woolfson, *Portrait
of a Palestinian*, p. 32). Thousands of others have also been
deported in the last two decades.

Since the 1948 'War of Independence' (the Arabs simply
refer to it as "The Catastrophe"), which resulted in the evacuation of hundreds of thousands of Palestinians from their
homelands, the Israelis have confiscated all of these lands on
the basis of the Law for the Acquisition of Absentee Property.
This law forbids Arabs who fled the region between 1947 and
1950 from ever buying back these properties, settling on them,
or even leasing it for the purposes of farming. Over three
hundred and eighty five Palestinian villages, particularly in
Galilee, have been completely destroyed; in many cases the
homes of Palestinians have simply been bulldozed into the
earth by the Zionists to make room for new Israeli settlements
(Woolfson, *Portrait of a Palestinian* pp. 17-18). The undeclared
aim of the Israeli government seems to be to wipe out two
thousand years of Palestinian culture. (A case in point being the
Israeli government's vigorous support of the burgeoning Jewish
settlements in the occupied Arab territories—despite public
comments to the contrary—and the recent massive influx of
Russian Jews imported to achieve the goal of Jewish numerical
majority, a situation which would enable them to annex the
West Bank and Gaza and to "democratically" quash Palestinian
hopes for a state of their own in the region.) The Palestinians
are also strictly forbidden from publicly displaying the flag
which they have chosen to symbolize their nationalist aspirations
and are at risk of brutal interrogations, the demolition of their
homes and property, and even death for doing so.

JEWISH DISSENT AGAINST ZIONISM

One way of putting into perspective the destruction which Zionism has wrought, not only on the Arab world and the Palestinians in particular, but also on the Jewish population of Israel, is by examining the comments of Jews themselves. The comments of Nathan Chofshi are most revealing. He was one of the original Jewish settlers in Palestine whose enthusiasm for the Zionist movement turned to horror as he witnessed the development of Israel and the unjust treatment of the Palestinian people. He writes: "We came and turned the native Arabs into refugees. And still we have to slander and malign them. Instead of being deeply ashamed of what we did and trying to undo some of the evil we committed, we justify our terrible acts and even attempt to glorify them" (Dimbleby, *The Palestinians*, p. 91). Chofshi goes on to add that "only an internal revolution can have the power to heal our people of their murderous sickness of Arabs. It is bound to bring eventual ruin upon us. Only then will the old and the young in our land realize how great is our responsibility to those miserable wronged Arab refugees in whose towns we have settled Jews who were brought from afar, whose homes we have inherited, whose fields we now sow and harvest, the fruit of whose gardens, orchards and vineyards we gather and in whose cities that we robbed, we put houses of education, charity and prayer while we babble and rave about our being the People of the Book and the Light of the Nations" (Zionist Archives and Library). Judah Magnes, the former Chancellor of Hebrew University, described the Zionists as "brutal, power-mad, militaristic practicioners of violence" (Zionist Archives and Library). At a funeral in 1956 for an Israeli soldier even Moshe Dayan had to ask his fellow Zionists: "Who are we that we should argue against their hatred? For eight years now they [the Palestinians] sit in the refugee camps in Gaza and before their very eyes we turn into our homestead the land and the villages in which they and their forefathers have lived" (Hirst, *The Gun and The Olive Branch*, p. 172).

As early as 1921 the Jewish writer Asher Ginzburg could see

the direction the Zionist movement was taking and wrote: "Is this the goal for which our fathers have striven and for whose sake all generations have suffered? Is this the dream of a return to Zion which our people have dreamt for centuries that we now come to Zion to stain its soil with innocent blood? These people [the Zionists] sacrifice their prophets and the great ethical principles for which they have often suffered to vie with themselves in shedding blood and desire for vengeance" (Zionist Archives and Library). Much later, in the mid forties another Jewish writer, Reb Binyomin, relates: "I did not recognize my own people for the changes which had occupied their spirit. The acts of brutality weren't the worst . . . it was the benevolent attitude toward these acts on the part of public opinion in Israel" (Taylor, *The Zionist Mind*, p. 108). As Chaim Weizmann, the Rothschild agent and diplomat who became expendable by the mid forties, said after a visit to Palestine in 1944: "There is an atmosphere of militarisation [among the Zionist leadership and populace] and worse, the tragic, futile and un-Jewish resort to terrorism" (Zionist Archives and Library). Rabbi Hirsch, a former leader of the Neturei Karta claimed that "Zionism is diametrically opposed to Judaism. The Jewish people are charged by divine oath not to force themselves back to the Holy Land against the wishes of those living there. The Jewish people were given the Holy Land by God and we sinned, were exiled and charged not to take back the land" (Zionist Archives and Library). Rabbi Hirsch even goes so far as to say that "the Holocaust was due to Zionism" (Zionist Archives and Library). Whether the Rabbi saw the Holocaust as part of divine retribution for the blasphemy of Zionism, or whether he knew more about the nefarious activities of the Zionist leadership around the world (i.e. the Rothschilds and their network of agents, and intimate connections with the Soviets and the Nazis and the U.S. Government) is not clear, but his remarks certainly point to the incredibly destructive and devastating potential which he saw in the Zionist movement.

PART III:

FIELD STUDY, AUGUST-SEPTEMBER 1992.

INTRODUCTION AND METHODOLOGY

It must be understood from the outset that the following report does not claim to be in any sense an exhaustive or comprehensive study of all or any single aspect of the Arab-Israeli conflict. My field study was conducted during four weeks in Israel last summer. It is true that it was oriented toward such "objective" phenomena as the use of military force in the West Bank, recent acts of terrorism, and the impact of legal and administrative policies on both Israeli and Palestinian inhabitants. Nevertheless, what follows is essentially a highly personal account of my impressions and experiences, not only of particular facts, events etc., but of the attitudes of people from all walks of life toward the current political and security situation. I would hasten to add that though I took copious notes, tape recorded some of the interviews and took many photographs, I also tried, as much as possible, to keep my interactions with people, even those acting in an official capacity, on an informal level, to put them at ease in the hope that they might speak more freely and openly. Toward this end, I did not tell many of my interview subjects that I was acting in such a capacity; in fact, I often suggested something quite to the contrary to enable me to make connections with what would have otherwise been inaccessible sources, and to 'infiltrate', if you will, restricted areas. Where permission was granted I have used the actual names of the people and places involved, but in other cases I have had to protect the identity of my sources.

My methodology has been to conduct interviews with people who have been directly involved with the particular incidents I have investigated, and thereby to gather and coalesce as much information as possible, before assessing its validity or lack thereof, by subjecting the data to rigorous correlational procedures. That is, I used standardized questionnaires in each case study and compared the answers of people

Plate 11: *The Orthodox Jewish clothes which I wore*

who could not have known each other, living as they were in different parts of the region. I found remarkable similarities in their responses, down to the most minute details, in relation to the treatment of both political prisoners as well as those who have complained about other civil rights violations. Based on the overwhelming evidence of these testimonies, I was inexorably drawn to the conclusion that the Israelis are indeed routinely and systematically torturing Palestinian political prisoners and flagrantly abusing the human rights of the Palestinian population in general.

ORTHODOX JUDAISM AND ZIONISM

Before turning to the results of my investigations into the treatment of Palestinians at the hands of the Israeli authorities, I should like to touch on an equally important aspect of my research into the Israeli psyche. The Orthodox religious groups have a somewhat ambivalent attitude toward Zionism since most refuse to join the army and some do not even recognize the state of Israel. Nevertheless, Orthodox Judaism has left an indelible imprint on the minds of the Zionist leaders and its influence on the formation and development of the modern state of Israel certainly bears consideration.

By posing as a young Jewish religious student, I was able to spend several days in an orthodox yeshiva in the Old City in which I encountered a wide variety of discussions concerning orthodox theological issues. I also engaged in many private conversations with various rabbis and took part in the study of the Torah and the Talmud with several different rabbinical students.

The Torah is apparently too "pregnant" with hidden meanings and inner contradictions to be interpreted on its own, consequently it was necessary to record the oral law in the Mishnah as a kind of explanatory text. This also requires further explication from that portion of the Talmud known as the Gemarah, which is literally layered with the legal interpretations of generations of Jewish religious authorities dating back to the time of Christ and beyond.

There is an absolute insistence within orthodox Judaism on the codification and explanation of the relevant legal statues for every conceivable moral situation so that the adherent knows precisely how he or she should act. Consequently, there are an astounding six hundred and thirteen laws which have evolved over the years, all of which must be rigorously observed to bring one as close as possible to God! Almost every aspect of life, from the clothes one wears, to the food one eats, to the way one wears one's hair, to the thoughts one has, to the way one prays etc., must be done exactly in accordance to the sacred and all encompassing law.

Even the most mundane everyday situations are subject to the law. For instance, the rabbinical students at the yeshiva I was attending spent over three days discussing the correct Talmudic interpretation of a hypothetical situation in which one man steps on and breaks another man's glasses that had been pushed off a nearby table by a strong gust of wind. The students were not concerned with giving their own views as to who should be held responsible for the damage to the glasses. They were strictly concerned with what the Talmudic verdict would be in regard to such a case. There is no room for the individual to follow the suggestions of his own heart and soul. One can only approach God through the rigorous and highly-controlled application of the intellect to Talmudic law which, in effect, attempts to codify life and indeed the very spirit of life so that it is brought into meticulous conformity with the myriad statues of the Mishnah.

God's immanence is not to be found within ourselves but in some remote and abstract legal entity. As a result, man is forever separated from God, who becomes completely lost in a bewildering network of regulations. The most that one can hope for is an oblique relation to Him through the agency of the law, and even then, only if one has spent one's entire life studying the dictates and endless interpretations of the Talmudic scholars.

Orthodox Judaism as such is an unrelenting imposition of the intellect over the heart, of duty over spontaneity, of thought over feeling. And yet can life really be codified and etched in stone so precisely? Can the spirit be contained by such rigidity of thought and action? Or the intuitions and impulses which animate man be codified in this reductive manner? Is not the desire to do so, obliterating freedom, spontaneity and passion, indicative of a deep-rooted hatred of life at its most basic?

Talmudic Judaism, is clearly an elaborate system of mind control, designed to eradicate individuality, and circumscribe the scope of one's "liberty" to the narrow confines of the Pharisees' rubric. We must remember that the Pharisees were the sworn enemies of Christ, the only men for whom he felt unbounded hatred and disgust. Talmudic Judaism stands in direct opposition to the gospel of Christ with its unconditional advocacy of love, the goal of all the world's great religions—including Judaism in its original, non-Pharisaic form.

Many Jews, including those who are orthodox, are not consciously motivated by this Talmudic war against the life spirit, or the virulent anti-Christian dogma that characterizes the text. Still it is embedded in their consciousness, for this is the primary text on which their rabbis are trained.   This influences the Jewish mind, and encourages the majority to give their unwavering support to the tiny fraction of the Jewish population who, working with other forces, are bent on the destruction of man's most precious possession: the unrestrained freedom of the individual soul.

THE ROLE OF THE PRESS IN ISRAEL

During my travels through the West Bank, I was fortunate enough to come into contact with several Palestinian journalists who filled me in on the ways in which news is disseminated in Israel and the occupied territories.   Israeli newspapers generally report only what the military spokesmen tell them about a particular incident.   These military briefs are based entirely on the reports of the soldiers involved, and do not include the testimony of other eye-witnesses. Arab journalists must submit everything they write to Israeli censors who often eliminate whole articles concerning some of the more obscene practices of the government, police and army. Furthermore, the Israeli censors often insist that the specific contexts of incidents be removed. When for example, a Palestinian collaborator (i.e. a Palestinian collaborating with the Israeli authorities) attacks one of his fellow countrymen's homes or neighbourhoods, or when the Israeli forces carry out one of their favourite "collective punishments" the article is not to include such "minor" details as the fact that these raids are in response to relatively benign activities such as a general strike, or children writing slogans on walls, or peaceful demonstrations against the repeated and flagrant violation of Palestinian civil liberties.

On the other hand, the *Jerusalem Post*, which is a veritable gold mine of yellow journalism, will loudly trumpet an attack on Israeli soldiers but conveniently leave out the fact that the soldiers had recently arrested without charge and brutally beaten family members of the Arab assailant. The penalties for those Palestinian journalists who attempt to defy their Israeli censors include stiff fines and imprisonment. Furthermore, the Israeli forces have never been shy or reluctant to toss aside their supposedly democratic ideals and to "handle" any groups or individuals that might prove to be somewhat less than compliant with their policies. For instance, the Voice of Palestine Radio, an Arab station located near Sidon, which devotes a great deal of its air time to Palestinian political issues, was blown up by Israeli undercover forces in 1988 and again in January of 1990, killing seven people and injuring another eighteen in the process. Palestinian journalists, and in some cases even foreign reporters and camera-men, have been cold bloodedly shot and killed for being in the wrong place at the wrong time, often without being given any warning at all.

ISRAELI ASSASSINATION SQUADS AND THE FOREIGN PRESS

An illuminating example of how the Israeli government deals with foreign journalists and news agencies has been demonstrated in their response to coverage of the "special unit" components of the Haganah. Since the beginning of the Intifada, the Israelis have become increasingly fond of using undercover assassination squads to eliminate those that they deem a threat. According to the Palestinian Human Rights Information Centre (PHRIC), in conjunction with the work of Elia Zureik, Professor of Sociology at Queen's University, since 1988 seventy-five Palestinians have been summarily executed by undercover units, who generally dress in a similar fashion to the local Arabs and proceed to ambush their defenceless victims in a hail of machine gun fire. When military officials were pressed, they were forced to admit that in 1991, of the twenty-nine people who were killed by the Mista'rivim [Arab pretenders], only seven were armed with guns or knives or weapons of any kind. Only three offered any resistance. Over half of the victims were under twenty years old. These units became an integral part of the Israeli response to the Intifada under the leadership of the then Minister of Defence Yitzak

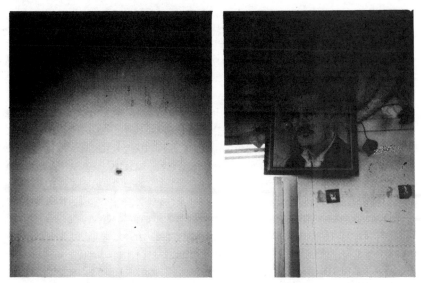

Plates 12 & 13: *The bullet holes in this portrait and in the ceiling of this Palestinian home in the West Bank are the result of an Israeli attack which resulted in the death of the man shown in the portrait and wounding of his six-year -old-son.*

Rabin, the man who, of course, is now the Israeli Prime Minister.

Although the Israelis now acknowledge the employment of "special units" in the occupied territories, they stress the fact that they are not death squads but rather they were formed to infiltrate and capture the violent, extremist elements supporting the Intifada. The army even produced a film for public consumption showing how the undercover units make "ambush arrests" in which known terrorists are taken by surprise due to the skill and persistence of the IDF. There were no segments of the film which depicted or described assassinations.

Foreign news agencies and human rights groups have presented quite a different story from the Israeli military propaganda, and in fact, have documented many cases of political assassinations by the undercover units. CBS-TV for instance, was forced to destroy tape it had taken of undercover soldiers on a raid in 1988, three years before the existence of such special forces units were publicly acknowledged by the Israeli government. In another instance, the press credentials of three journalists from Reuters and the *Financial Times* were suspended in 1988 after they published reports on the special units' policy of ambushing victims and shooting them down at close range. Rabin labelled these accusations "total nonsense". Though the press credentials of the three journalists were eventually reinstated, Reuters correspondent Steve Weizman barely escaped death when a small explosive device was detonated in his car, while *Financial Times* correspondent Andrew Whitley was attacked and beaten by an unknown assailant on a Jerusalem street shortly after his report had been filed.

The fact that the undercover units are primarily assassination squads has been confirmed by many sources including members of the Israeli press itself as is evident by the article of Danny Rubenstein, published in the January 25, 1992 edition of the Israeli paper *Haaretz*. The article was about the killing of a young man named Muhammad Abed Naghnaghiyeh who was mistakenly identified as a suspected PLO member whom the Israelis were particularly anxious to eliminate. Israeli author Maya Rosenfeld has documented eighteen cases of political assassinations carried out by Israeli forces between November of 1989 and June of 1990 in a report which she prepared in conjunction with the Association of Civil Rights in Israel for Yesh Gul, an Israeli organization of conscientious objectors.

Amnesty International reported in January of 1990 that there was an increase of political assassinations of Palestinians during the previous year. The Amnesty report went on to say that during recent years "the Israeli government had effectively condoned and even encouraged extrajudicial executions of Palestinians by its security forces in order to help control unrest during the Intifada in the Occupied Territories" ("Killings by Israeli forces" in *Amnesty International FOCUS*, January 1990. cit. in Zureik, *Targeting to Kill: Israel's Undercover Units*, p. 38).

In the 1991 Country Report on Human Rights in Israel and the Occupied Territories, the U.S. State Department confirmed

the research by Elia Zureik and the PHRIC when they acknowledged that twenty seven Palestinians had been murdered by
Israeli undercover units and many of the victims were unarmed. However, the State Department tried to down play
these killings as being justified under the circumstances since
most of the victims were either "wanted, masked, or fleeing
from authorities after writing graffiti." Given the intimate ties
between the interests of those in control of the U.S and Israeli
governments this justification is hardly surprising.

ECONOMIC AND SOCIAL CONDITIONS IN ISRAEL
VERSUS THE WEST BANK

I was struck throughout all my excursions in the West Bank
by the relative poverty of the region compared to Israel. The
Israelis are of course endowed by the seemingly inexhaustible
coffers of the supporters of the Zionist cause. Though the
modern Zionist state stands on lands that have embraced
thousands of years of civilization, most of their infrastructure
has been built during the last two or three decades. No expense
is spared on the construction of the impressively designed and
well-furnished government buildings, or the smoothly-paved
highways and wide city streets and boulevards which are
conveniently lined with all the affluence of late twentieth-
century society such as discos, shopping malls, well-stocked
stores and chic restaurants.

One gets just the opposite impression while touring through
the West Bank. The roads are invariably unpaved and extremely bumpy. Most of the buildings are old and crumbling.
People who are lucky enough to have homes must make do
without many of the modern amenities. The schools are grossly
under-funded so that students and teachers are rarely able to
utilize such important new educational resources such as
computers, audio-visual equipment, etc. Furthermore, the
region itself is rather inhospitable, being dry and rocky and
unsuitable to all but a limited range of agricultural activity.

Of course, a million and a half people are living on refugee

Plate 14: *This photo taken by Munir Nasr shows one of the many make-shift camps in which Palestinians have been forced to live since their exile from their homeland. (UNWRA)*

camps, several of which I visited. The conditions in the camps are absolutely squalid and could be only described as third world (this is especially true of the Gaza strip refugee camp, which like an open wound or sore continues to fester and worsen with every day). The homes are little more than rubble, the roads are unpaved and there are no sewer systems: raw waste products float by in ditches along the side of the road spreading disease and infection. The camps, which are maintained by the United nations organization called UNWRA, are woefully under-funded; medical facilities are totally inadequate. Unemployment is rampant among the refugees simply because there are no industries or jobs available in the camps and many are not able to get jobs in Israel.

As a result, the people are sadly impoverished and many suffer from malnutrition. There are no social security benefits, or affordable health insurance plans for these people so they are generally unable to receive proper medical attention when they need it. Almost all of the refugees are crammed into drastically

Plate 15: *This ditch running along the side of the road is the only form of sewage system in the Tulkarm Refugee Camp and, as such, is a breeding ground for disease and contagious infections.*

Plate 16: *The refugee camps are completely run down, without paved roads, and are drastically overcrowded.*

overcrowded living quarters with seven to ten people (or more) often sharing a single room dwelling. The refugees are also frequently subject to collective punishments such as the bull-dozing and sealing off of homes and the closing of schools. In the Tulkarm refugee camp for instance, the schools were only open a total of forty five days in 1989 and only thirty-six days in 1990! And, as Dr. Thabit Thabit, a Palestinian man in his forties who works as a dentist and administrator in the Tulkarm camp pointed out to me, the oppression of the Israeli army and the horrendously overcrowded living conditions tends to make the camps a breeding ground of bitterness and frustration, frequently erupting into violence or what might seem to be purely destructive behaviour.

All of this serves to show that the Palestinians clearly need their own state to promote the growth of their own financial, industrial, commercial and communication infrastructures. They are ready, willing and most importantly able to take on the responsibilities of nationhood. Despite the fact that the Israelis have done everything in their power to oppress, subjugate and otherwise hold back the Palestinian people, the Palestinians are among the most well educated and intelligent people of the Middle East.

An American engineer working in Kuwait whom I met on the flight to London, re-confirmed what I had already under-stood to be the case in regard to the Palestinian management of the Kuwaiti infrastructure before they were deported after the Gulf War. The Kuwaitis are of course fabulously wealthy because of their oil exports, but they had relied almost entirely upon Palestinian managers and skilled labour to run their economy. The same is true, although to a lesser extent, in Jordan where over a million Palestinians currently live. In fact, there are Palestinians living all over the world who are working as lawyers, doctors, businessmen etc., and who are ready to return to the Middle East and to help build their own country. Most of the political prisoners I interviewed spoke English as well as Arabic and Hebrew, and many had attended university. They were all extremely polite and gracious to me and in several instances I was able to enjoy meals with them and even

Plate 17: *Here I am enjoying a typical Middle Eastern meal with members of the Palestinian Human Rights Information Centre.*

stay overnight with their families. These people are asking for the chance to pursue their lives in the freedom of their own country. They have earned that right and it is time the world began to address that issue directly and to see Zionism for the malignant force that it has become.

INTERVIEWS WITH FORMER POLITICAL PRISONERS: SAMIR ABU-SHAMS

The first destination in my journey through the West Bank was the city of Tulkarm, site of one of the harshest Israeli Military Detention Centres. At the taxi station, I was met by two members of the PHRIC and was immediately driven to the home of a man named Samir Muhammed Abu-Shams. In August of 1990 he had been arrested while crossing the border from Jordan. He was accused of being a member of the PLO though he said to me that this had never been the case. I have a tendency to believe him when he says this since many other political prisoners whom I interviewed either requested anonymity, or freely admitted the fact that they had been, or were currently, involved with that organization. When questioned by the Shin Beit he said he supported the PLO (nearly all Palestinians recognize this group as their representative body) but he made it clear he had never been actively involved with them.

Samir was taken to an Israeli prison where he was initially incarcerated in a cell that was one hundred centimetres high, one hundred and eighty centimetres long and eighty centimetres wide. Samir was kept in these incredibly cramped conditions for three days. There was no window in this cell and no toilet so that he was forced to urinate and defecate where he sat. After that he was transferred to what he called a "luxury" cell in which he was at least able to enjoy the company of two other inmates. This cell was two metres wide and two metres long and two metres high.

Every morning Samir would be taken out of this tiny space and brought into the interrogation area. During this period he was vigorously questioned about his family and his relationships with PLO members. Of course, Samir could not tell his interrogators anything since he had never been involved, nor had any of his friends or family, with this group. Every day he was brought into the interrogation room he was beaten viciously with sticks by three members of the Shin Beit. One of their favourite tactics to encourage Samir to talk was to tie his hands behind his back while seated in a chair and to pull him backwards by the hair, invariably causing excruciating pain. The Israelis also liked to taunt and verbally abuse him, and to shout at him in the middle of the night to keep him awake. They would also call him "Mr. President" and force him to look at his beaten face and body in a mirror while promising to release him if he would confess. In one particularly abhorrent, episode Samir's torturers forced his mouth open while an army officer spat into it.

Fifteen days later Samir was allowed to see his lawyer. Soon after he went to court where he was given an extra thirty days (despite the fact that there was not a shred of evidence against him) in order that the prosecution might continue to "work" on the case. Immediately after his court date he was brought back to an isolation cell where he was fitted with a noose around his neck via a rope which hung from the ceiling and forced to remain standing for three days. If he was to sink down even a little, the noose would tighten and begin to choke him. Of course, if he had fallen he would have died. He told me that he was only able to stay alive by virtue of his fellow prisoners who sang and talked to him continuously throughout the ordeal.

After withstanding this harrowing experience, he was transferred to a "cold cell" in which he quickly became ill with pneumonia and also lost his voice. He was refused medical attention during this time but was eventually able to recover.

In a few weeks, he was transferred to the Jenin prison. He was surrounded by Palestinian collaborators here who were eager to befriend him and to "pump" him for as much information as possible. Samir and the rest of the Palestinian patriots, however, knew that they were working for the Israelis and avoided them. One of his fellow prisoners became seriously ill during this time; as a result, Samir and the rest of the inmates went on a hunger strike to get him transferred to a hospital.

Samir was eventually released from jail after three months. He was never told he why he was suddenly released, but the Shin Beit did tell him that the reason he was arrested was because of his involvement, while studying in Pakistan eight years prior to his arrest, with the General Union of Palestinian Students. Amazingly, enough, although Samir never actually joined this organization the fact that he attended one introductory meeting was apparently sufficient grounds for the Israelis to suspect and incarcerate him eight years later!

KHALID RUSHDIE AL-ZHIGAL

Khalid Rushdie Al-Zhigal was arrested in 1985 when he was accused of being a PLO member. Kahlid freely admitted to me that he had been a member at this time but hastened to add that he never rejoined after his release from prison two and a half years later. After being free for only forty-five days, he was arrested again in March of 1988 although no charge was laid. It was four months before he went to court. Although the prosecution had no evidence, the judge saw fit to incarcerate him for another six months in the Nablus Central Prison. As it turned out, it was to be eleven more months before his lawyer, Lia Semel, successfully pleaded his case before the Israeli Supreme Court and it was thrown out for lack of evidence. He was arrested, however, eight months later in October of 1989 after being accused (once again without evidence) of being an active member of the PLO. By this time Khalid's case had come to the attention of Tamara Peeleg, the well-known Israeli human rights activist, and she was able to secure his release a year later in October of 1990.

During these periods of internment, Khalid suffered from extensive health problems, including infections of his colon as well as stomach bleeding. He did not receive adequate medical attention for either ailment while he was incarcerated. He was repeatedly beaten with clubs by Israeli interrogators and at one time while he was being transferred through a sensitive Israeli security zone he was not only blindfolded but forced to wear a hood soaked in his own urine so that he would not be able to use his sense of smell to provide even the slightest information as to the location of this military site.

After his first term in prison, Khalid was given an identity card, referred to as a "Green card" which stipulated that the holder could not leave the West Bank in order to travel or find work in another country. Green card holders are not able to apply for work in the state of Israel—where many in the West Bank are forced to go in order to support themselves and their families—nor even enter the city of Jerusalem. They are frequently harassed by the Israeli authorities, and are subject to random arrests and beatings.

SADEDIN KHARIM AL-SADI

Some of the "highlights" of Sadedin Kharim al-Sadi's experience as a political prisoner include having DDT smeared on his face and in his eyes, having a mask placed over his head for up to three days while being beaten regularly about the head and genitals, and forced to go without food for several days at a time. He was also handcuffed to a chair for twenty-two days, and during this time his hands were manacled so tightly that he has never regained full range of mobility in his wrists.

NAJI

One Palestinian student, named Naji, whom I talked to on a trip from Nablus to Jerusalem, told me that he has been arrested on four separate occasions, for up to three months at a time. His "crime" was that he was a casual passer-by during a rally at Bir Zeit University while it was being raided by the Israeli police. Naji had just turned seventeen a few days before my interview with him.

AHMAD JABER MOHAMMAD IBRAHIM

Another preparatory student, Ahmad Jaber Mohammad Ibrahim, also seventeen years old, was shot and killed by soldiers who shot randomly into a non-violent demonstration of high-school students in the town of Rafah on March 1 of 1992. According to the medical records of Nasser hospital in Khan Yunis, fourteen students were treated for gunshot wounds. The *Jerusalem Post* reported that one person died in this incident and only nine people were wounded, following an armed confrontation between "local Hamas fundamentalists and mainstream PLO activists" who were "saved" from further bloodshed, it was reported, by the intervention of the Israeli army.

JAMAL HASSAN

An even more insidious practice of Israeli torture units is their use of electric shock torture. One fourteen-year-old boy whom I talked to, named Jamal Hassan, was taken from his parents early in the morning to the Hebron military headquarters. He was greeted by the anguished cries of other prisoners being tortured as he entered the interrogation areas. He was forced to strip and told to confess that the had thrown stones at Israeli soldiers. Jamal told me that he had written slogans on walls but had never thrown stones at Israeli soldiers because he knew the soldiers would shoot to kill if he ever confronted them this way.

Initially, the Israeli interrogators restricted themselves to threatening him by pushing the blade of a knife against his throat and striking the wall beside his head with clubs. They promised to emasculate him and to arrest his sister, to be beaten and raped by soldiers. Jamal refused to confess to something which he didn't do and, more out of fear than anything else, simply said nothing in response to their threats.

His interrogators only became more determined to extract a signed confession, placing electric wires under his arms and on the inside of his legs. He began to shiver and shake uncontrollably. At one point the voltage must have been turned up because he jumped up out of his chair (he had not been handcuffed to the chair as is usual during interrogation sessions when the shocks are so powerful that the victim is completely unable to escape or even move the wires). Meanwhile, his Israeli torturers were laughing at him and mocking him, calling him the "hero of his people". Subsequently, they placed a bag over his head which made breathing very difficult, especially after the next round of shocks which were administered directly to his genitals, causing him to suffer not only excruciating pain but an acute panic attack. He was then struck with a fierce blow to the head which made him lose consciousness.

When he awoke, a young Palestinian youth came into the interrogation room and told the Israelis that he had seen Jamal throwing stones on several occasions. Jamal vehemently denied this charge and spat at his accuser who was obviously collaborating with the Israelis. The Israelis then subjected him to further electric torture: he was forced to hold the wires in his hands, sending shocks through his arms and torso. Again he was ordered to confess, but at this point Jamal was unable to speak at all and merely shook his head. Another Palestinian boy was brought in who claimed he had seen Jamal throwing stones and said that he knew where Jamal lived and what his family name was. The interrogators told him that they had over a dozen witnesses to his stone-throwing activities and that he had better confess. When he still refused to acquiesce to their demands, Jamal was beaten with the butt of a rifle about his legs and arms on the places where he had been electrocuted; this, of course, made the blows especially painful.

He had, at this juncture, been incarcerated for a week. Because of the abuse he suffered, he was unable to walk for the next nine days. His entire body was covered with welts and he was aware that one of his ribs was probably broken. He also noticed black marks from the burns on his skin. He was checked by an Israeli doctor who wanted to know if any particular part of his body was in pain! Jamal revealed nothing, having been told by other detainees that these "doctors" were only interested in identifying the vulnerable parts of the body so as to make the subsequent torture sessions more effective. During the next round of interrogation, the Israelis used cigarettes to burn his skin and his eyelashes. Still, he refused to confess and so he was once again beaten about the face and legs.

Eventually, his interrogators were forced to use deception in order to get their prisoner's signature on a confession. They told him that he was signing a statement indicating that he had never thrown stones at Israeli soldiers. The document, however, was in Hebrew which Jamal does not read and so when he wrote his name on the piece of paper the Israelis immediately shouted that he had just signed an affidavit which admitted that he had thrown stones. He was then asked to give his finger prints on ink paper and when he refused he was forcibly made to do so by three men. Soon after, he was taken to court where the prosecution, armed with his recent "confession", convinced the judge to hold him for another two months. One month later Jamal was released from prison and his family was ordered to pay a fine of 1,500 sheckels. Jamal has never completely recovered the full use of his legs and still is haunted by sudden shooting pains up his legs and arms, a constant reminder of the electric shocks he received at the hands of his Israeli torturers.

DEATHS IN DETENTION OR AS A RESULT OF
"DISCIPLINARY" ACTIONS

I talked to dozens of other victims of Israeli torture practices, many of whom were subjected to electric shocks and
repeated beatings.   Though several of them were left with
permanent injuries and persistent pain in various parts of their
bodies, not to mention the emotional and mental anguish they
suffered (the Palestinian Human Rights Information Centre has
documented many cases of political prisoners who have suffered from post traumatic shock syndrome), they have at least
made it out alive. The same cannot be said of all Palestinian
political prisoners.

Since the Intifada began in December of 1987, the PHRIC
reports that twenty-five Palestinians have died in Israel prisons,
jails and detention centres. Some were shot, while others died
as a result of medical complications from beatings and assorted
torture practices. Others died because of medical negligence.

According to the PHRIC, from December 1987 to March
1992 one thousand and thirty Palestinians were killed as a direct
result of Israeli shootings, beatings or use of tear gas.   The
"justification" among Israelis for this policy of whole-scale
slaughter is that they are only defending themselves, and acting
in reprisal to Palestinian attacks. Yet during that same period
less than one hundred Israelis have died as a result of Palestinian acts of violence.

VIOLATION OF MUNICIPAL
AND HABITATIONAL RIGHTS

Another extremely offensive aspect of the Israeli occupation
is their abuse of Palestinian housing rights in the occupied
territories and in East Jerusalem in particular. While almost no
building permits are given to Palestinians in East Jerusalem, the
Israelis are strenuously promoting the construction of Jewish
sites in the area. Zionist settlements, with populations numbering in the tens of thousands, have sprouted up all around

Plate 18: *Here is the Palestinian fence, referred to in the text, to ward off rocks, garbage and other refuse.*

the suburban Jerusalem area, limiting the growth of Palestinian villages. Lands in the West Bank are continually being confiscated in order to build new roads which connect the various kibutzim and other Israeli settlements. Within Jerusalem itself, the army follows the completely unjust policy of seizing Palestinian homes which they deem to be situated in 'strategic' security zones.

One of these zones is in the al-Wad section of the Moslem Quarter along the road which leads to the Wailing Wall in the Old City. The Tirhi family, for example, has owned a large home in this area for over three hundred years yet they were forced to leave their home in 1969 because the Israeli army said they needed it for a guard post. The Israelis never used the building for such purposes but simply sealed the house shut. On March 1, 1992, a group of settlers from the militant Atarot Cohanim yeshiva confiscated the Tirhi home and moved in to it. The Tirhi family naturally complained to the Israeli authorities and the case is currently under investigation.

A man name Naief who owns a gift shop just across the

street from the Tirhi home, and who has steadfastly refused to sell his place of business to Jewish religious groups in the area has had his shop ransacked on several occasions. He was subject to one of these vigilante attacks only one week before I talked to him as was evident from the bruises on his ribs and the broken teeth in his mouth.

In an even more startling case, the Atarot Cohanim moved in to the upper half of a large block of homes in the heart of the Old city that have been inhabited by Arabs for generations. After they heard a report of an attack on an Israeli man in the Old City, the members of the yeshiva became enraged and started to burn the house of a woman whom I talked to, named Aham Mushime, who lived below. They also shot indiscriminately at homes in the immediate vicinity.

In another episode, an elderly woman who used to live in part of the building where the yeshiva now stands was stabbed one night while making dinner because she refused to sell her home. The people below the yeshiva have now constructed a steel cage above their homes and courtyards to protect themselves from the large rocks and mounds of garbage thrown down on them by the rabbis and rabbinical students.

ESCAPE FROM ISRAEL

As I started to sort my notes in preparation for my departure back to Canada, I began to wonder how I would best be able to leave Israel without drawing attention to the research I had done. I had been told that the Israeli security at Ben Gurion airport was extremely tight and to expect a very thorough search of all my luggage. On the other hand, I had entered the country relatively easily, and thought that as long as they were sure I wasn't carrying a bomb or concealed weapon I shouldn't have any problems. I didn't think that it would be a particularly great idea to advertise the fact that I had uncovered a good deal of 'dirt' on their treatment of Palestinians, so I decided to hide my notes as best I could among letters and other, somewhat more benign, material that I had written during my stay.

I arrived at the airport approximately two hours before my flight and was met by a fairly long line-up. About an hour later a young woman working for airport security came up to me and asked me to come with her. She was nice and polite in asking me to put my luggage on a table so that she could examine it. After checking it very closely, she began to ask me a series of increasingly personal questions. At first she wanted to know what I was doing in Israel. I told her I was just on vacation and had come to see the Holy sites. She then asked me if I had met any Israelis along the way. I said yes I had become acquainted with many Israelis though I hadn't really spent all that much time with any particular ones. "Had I met any Palestinians during my stay?" Knowing that she would want to see my address book I answered "yes", I had met Palestinians just in passing who were working in shops in the Old City and so on. "Had I been to the West Bank?" "Oh", I answered as casually as possible, "just travelling through on the way to various religious sites".

Then came the question that proved, or at least appeared for a while, to be my undoing: "Had any of the Palestinians that I had met given me anything during my stay?" I had been growing more nervous with each question since I feared that to tell even a little of the truth about my experiences in the West Bank would only arouse unwanted suspicions. At the same time I knew that she was about to check my hand bag, which contained a great deal of the information I had gathered from various human rights groups with whom I had been in communication. I had dispersed them as best I could but I knew that some of them might be found and that if I had lied about their existence I would make myself far more suspicious. So I chose to compromise between the two sets of fears and confess that I had been given a few political pamphlets from a Palestinian journalist I had met briefly in a taxi. She asked to see the material in question and upon glancing through it brought it to the attention of her superiors.

At this point I started to feel a little dizzy as two armed security officers led me to an interrogation room at the back of the terminal. Three men began to question me very aggres-

sively as to who had given me this information. I said his name
was Said or Saiam or some such thing and that I only met him
once and didn't know his surname or his address or anything
else about him. "Why have you kept this information (which
contained data on land seizures, houses sealings and area
closures in the West Bank by the Israelis in 1992)?", they asked.
"Well", I decided, suddenly calling upon my ad lib skills,
"because I am great supporter of the state of Israel and I wanted
to show my friends back home in Canada how the Palestinians
are distorting information on the Jewish settlements in the West
Bank."

The Israelis were unconvinced and began to ask who else
I had met and if I had other pamphlets in my bag. I told them
that I hadn't spoken with any other Arabs, but the journalist had
given me a few other papers. As they searched through my bag
they didn't find everything but they did find more material
from the PHRIC concerning the deaths of Palestinians during
the Intifada: this raised their suspicions to a fevered pitch. They
told me that I could be arrested for possessing this kind of
material and wondered how I was going to convince anyone
that the information provided by the PHRIC was bogus when
these articles also cited reports by both Amnesty International
and the U.S. Country Commission which confirmed this evidence. They pressed me for details on the Palestinian journalist,
what he looked like, etc. I gave them a totally false description
of the man and said I had argued that such reports were the
products of anti-semitic minds.

By this time they had searched my luggage on three
separate occasions and were suggesting that they thought I
might well be a PLO sympathizer, or perhaps that I might even
be working for them. The Israeli who seemed to be in charge
continued to press me for details on other Palestinians I had
met. One of the guards was drumming a thick club along the
desk, while the other asked me if I knew what happens to
supporters of the PLO. I told him that I had no idea. The one
who was brandishing his club made a gesture at his throat to
suggest that such people are summarily executed. The chief
security officer said that PLO supporters are imprisoned for
months and even years and the Israeli prison guards make sure

their stay is "very unpleasant." The fact that their charge of being an active supporter of PLO was patently ridiculous did not mitigate the growing sense of terror that had by now completely gripped me.

The most terrifying moment for me, however, occurred when they asked me if I had kept a diary while I was in Israel. I knew that they would find it in my handbag so I admitted that yes I had. The book which I kept this "diary" in, actually contained the notes to all the interviews I had taken and I knew that if they found those notes, with their detailed descriptions of the prisons and the mistreatment of political prisoners I would certainly be taken to an official interrogation centre and quite possibly be held for some time.

As it was, I had already been questioned for over four hours and had long since missed my plane, as well as the next flight leaving Tel Aviv for London. I took the "diary" out of my handbag and opened it to a section in which I had been writing a few letters that I had ended up not sending, largely concerned with the architecture and various holy sites I had seen, and some of the interesting foreign students and tourists I had met. The security officers read about ten pages of these letters while I did my best to at least appear calm and unperturbed, though I was almost at the point of fainting with uncontrollable fear. I began to imagine myself being tortured with electric shocks and being beaten and spat upon and deprived of food. However, after a few incredibly anxious moments, to my immense relief the security officer stopped reading my journal and handed it back to me. If he had turned on only a few more pages he would have discovered the notes on which I have based the last portion of this article and I doubt very much whether I would be here right now to write it.

After three more hours of intense scrutiny I was told I could leave, although I had to give up much of the material that they had discovered. Fortunately for me I had anticipated this possibility and recorded most of the relevant data in my own notes so that little was lost.

When I emerged from the interrogation centre eight hours after entering it I was shaking with exhaustion and an incredible sense of relief. El Al, the Israeli airline, offered to put me up at the Sheraton in Tel Aviv for the night so that I could rest and leave on their flight the next morning. This would mean I would have to pass through Israeli security all over again and there was no way I was going to take that risk. I bolted for the next flight to London and was never so happy to reach Canada when I did finally get back home the next day.

ZIONISM AND WORLD PEACE?

As the plane took off from Ben Gurion airport, and I contemplated my experiences in the "Holy Land", the prophecies of Albert Pike were suddenly brought back to my mind with an ominous clarity. The Freemason leader predicted with stunning accuracy the onset of the First World War and the creation of the Communist "bogey"state, as well as the advent of the Second World War which would arise out of the strife between the German Nationalists and the Zionists, eventually leading to the formation of Israel. Pike also indicated that the Third World War will be sparked by the conflict between Arabs and Zionists as a prelude to the ensuing reign of absolute chaos and the destruction of the world as we know it. As the Israelis continue to re-settle the occupied territories (despite protestations to the contrary) and to retain their merciless and uncompromising stance toward the Palestinians and other Arabs (whose hatred of their Zionist oppressors seems to grow every day), it seems all too likely that the rest of the world will eventually be caught up in this struggle.

From the time of the Crusades, history shows that every other nation that has invaded the Arab world has eventually been repulsed and there is little doubt that neither the Palestinians nor the rest of the Arab world will ever accept the Zionist state. Indeed, a final pitched conflict seems to be the only "solution" which is totally acceptable to all parties. With the prospect of nuclear weapons being deployed, this last "war to end all wars" may well signal the end of social structures and institutions as we know them, as well as the traditional values and beliefs which have hitherto sustained the great cultures and civilizations of humankind.

Plate 19: *The Jordanian village of Karameh which had been home to thousands of Palestinian exiles after the Israelis launched an unprovoked invasion (shown here) of the village and massacred hundreds of innocent people. Source: El-Farra, Years of No Decision*

Plate 20 & 21 : *These photographs depict the misery of the Palestinians exiles since they were expelled from Israel. Source: The Palestinians*

LIST OF WORKS CONSULTED

American Friends Service Committee. *A Compassionate Peace: A Future for the Middle East.* New York: Hill and Wang, 1982.

Barker, A.J. *Arab-Israeli Wars.* New York: Hippocrene Books, 1980.

Bell, J. Bowyer. *The Long War: Israel and the Arabs Since 1946.* Englewood Cliffs, N.J.: Prentice Gall, 1969.

—, ed. *Terror Out of Zion: Irgun Zvai Leumi, LEHI and the Palestine Underground, 1929-1949.* New York: St. Martin's Press, 1977.

Berger, Elmer. *Memoirs of an Anti-Zionist Jew.* Beirut: The Institute for Palestine Studies, 1974.

Burdett, Winston. *Encounter with the Middle East: An Intimate Report On What Lies Behind the Arab Israeli Conflict.* New York: Atheneum, 1967.

Burns, E.C.M. *Between Arab and Israel.* Toronto: Clarke & Irwin, 1962.

Cattan, Henry. *Palestine, The Arabs and Israel: The Search for Justice.* London: Longmans 1969.

Dillman, Jeffrey D. and Bakri, Musa A. *Israel's Use of Electric Torture in the Interrogation of Palestinian Detainees.* 2nd. ed. Jerusalem: Palestine Human Rights Information Center, 1992.

Dimbley, Jonathan. *The Palestinians.* London: Quartet Books, 1979.

Eban, Abba. *My People: The Story of the Jews.* New York: Random House, 1968.

El-Farra, Muhammad. Years of No Decision. London: Methuen, 1987.

Fischer, Sydney Nettleton. *The Middle East: A History.* 2nd. ed. New York: Knoph, 1969.

Gilmour, David. *Dispossessed: The Ordeal of the Palestinians, 1917-1980.* London: Sidgwick and Jackson, 1980.

Griffin, Desmond. *Descent Into Slavery.* Clackamas, Oregon: Emissary, 1980.

Herzl, Theodore. *The Complete Diaries of Theodore Herzl.* 5 vols. Ed. Raphael Patai. Trans. Harry Zohn. New York: Herzl Press, 1970.

Herzog, Chaim. *The Arab-Israeli Wars: War and Peace in the Middle East.* New York: Methuen, 1982.

Hirst, David. *The Gun and the Olive Branch: The Roots of Violence in the Middle East.* London: Faber and Faber, 1977.

Institute for Palestine Studies. *United Nations Resolutions on Palestine 1947-72.* Beirut: Institute for Palestine Studies, 1974.

Kimche, Jon. *Palestine or Israel: The Untold Story of Why We Failed.* London: Secker and Warburg, 1973.

Lacquer, Walter. *The Road to Jerusalem: The Origins of the Arab-Israeli Conflict 1967.* New York: MacMillan, 1968.

—, and Barry Rubin, eds. *The Arab-Israeli Reader: A Documentary History of the Middle East.* New York: Facts On File, 1985.

Laffin, John. *Fedayeen: The Arab-Israeli Dilemma.* London: Cassell, 1973.

Messenger, Charles. *The Middle East. Conflict in the 20th Century.* 4th ed. Ed. Dr. John Pimlott. London: Alladin Books, 1987.

Nazzal, Nafez. *The Palestinian Exodus From Galilee 1948.* Beirut: The Institute for Palestine Studies, 1978.

Palestine Human Rights Information Center. *Detention and Interrogation of Palestinian Detainees: Torture, Deaths in Detention and Prison Conditions: February 1992.* Jerusalem: Palestine Human Rights Information Center, 1992.

—. *Human Rights Update.* vol. V. No. 3. Jerusalem: Palestine Human Rights Information Center, 1992.

—. *Recreating East Jerusalem: Israel's Quiet Judaization of the Palestinian City.* Jerusalem: Palestine Human Rights Information Center, 1992.

Rihami, Ameen. *The Fate of Palestine.* Beirut: Rihami Press, 1967.

Rodinson, Maxime. *Israel and the Arabs.* Trans. Michael Perl.New York: Random House, 1968.

Sakran, Frank. *Palestine: Still a Dilemma.* Ardmore, Penn: Whitmore, 1976.

Sharabi, Hisham. *Palestine and Israel: The Lethal Dilemma.* New York: Pegasus, 1969.

Smith, Pamela Ann. *Palestine and the Palestinians 1876-1983.* London: Croon Helm, 1984.

Stewart, Desmond. *The Palestinians: Victims of Expediency.* London: Quartet Books, 1982.

Tawil, Raymonda Hawa. *My Home, My Prison.* New York: Holt, Rinehart and Winston, 1979.

Taylor, Alan R. *The Zionist Mind: The Origins and Development of Zionist Thought.* Beirut: Institute for Palestine Studies, 1974.

Waines, David. *The Unholy War: Israel and Palestine 1897-1971.* Montreal: Chateau Books, 1971.

Woolfson, Marion. *Bassam Shak'a: Portrait of a Palestinian.* London: Third World Centre, 1981.

Zureik, Elia. *Targeting to Kill: Israel's Undercover Units.* Jerusalem: Palestine Human Rights Information Centre, 1992.

Plate 22: Assessing the results, back home in Canada with Professor Robert O'Driscoll

THE ROLE OF THE VATICAN
IN
THE NEW WORLD ORDER
AND
OTHER FRAGMENTS

compiled by

A. Aksakov and M. Dessoir

"DAS MAERCHEN VOM HIMMEL,
DER HOELLE UND GOTT DESGLEICHEN:
DIE FRECHSTE ERFINDUNG DER
GESAMTEN MENSCHLICHE HISTORIE"
ALBERT SCHWEITZER

Plate 23: *Giovanni Battista Montini: Pope Paul VI, 1963-68.*

THE NEW WORLD ORDER:
[A puppet play in three acts by Alexy Kosygin]

Lights Up.

Act I: Money figures out how to reproduce itself.

Act II: Money figures out how to hide itself.

Act III: Lights down. A large puppet (wearing a wig) resembling Yuri Andropov towers over stage, suspended by huge ropes. He in turn manipulates two smaller puppets on stage - Andrey Gromyko attached to his right hand, Pope Paul VI to the left. Centre stage stands a confessional. Enter stage right Gromyko, he sits in confessional. Enter stage left Pope Paul VI, he assumes seat to hear confession, he slides open the aperture.

AG: Forgive us Brother for we have sinned. We have created an atheist state.

PPVI: You are absolved. (rises to leave)

AG: (quickly) We have delved into the paranormal.

PPVI: (sitting) A miscalculation.

AG: We are atheists, after all. But we didn't know.

PPVI: And now you know?

AG: They talk to us. They tell us things we would not hear.

PPVI: That there is no God?

AG: Not . . . exactly.

PPVI: That there is God?

AG: Yes and no. Not yours, not ours.

PPVI: They bend spoons then, and cheat at cards?

AG: They heal the sick. They say we are not Spirit but Spirit
           is us. They tell us it is all for naught. They like our
           country. There is no God between our borders and they
           flit about freely, talking to whomever they like.   We
           should not have taken God away from the peasants, they
           are too simple - our abstractions go in one ear and out
           the other. They are stupid, their minds are empty, and
           so they hear, they talk, some write.

PPVI: What do they say?

AG: They say they see us but cannot touch us . . .

PPVI: and we cannot see them, but cannot be touched.

AG: You know!

PPVI: Pius XII told me himself.

AG: He knew!

PPVI: They all knew. But don't you see, no miscalculation, he
           told me. I have   been waiting for you to come ever
           since. You see, when he told me, he saw me smile.
           He saw in my eyes that he should not have spoken, he
           knew and I knew that I was to become Pope.

AG: And Roncalli knew?

PPVI: Yes, but he did not know you were coming. I knew.

AG: I see . . . three. But I am scared, we have emptied Russia
           too much, no money, no God. The void begins to fill
           itself. They are truly hungry.

Plate 24: *Angelo Giuseppe Roncalli: Pope John XXIII, 1958-63.*

PPVI: I take pity on your people, dear Brother. It is time again
        we should feed them, a few scraps at least to tide them
        over. You will disappear soon enough. I absolve you
        of all your sins. But first acid on Leningrad.

AG: You knew even before I came! Our Will be done.

        Sound of coins rushing out of a slot machine,
        simultaneously Andropov's hands move the puppets
        round and round the confessional. The sound of the
        coins stops, the two smaller puppets are seated in
        reversed positions on the stage.

PPVI: Forgive me Brother for I have sinned. There is no one
        to follow me.

AG: Use the prophecies well. Do not let them use you.
        Lieberman is sick and so are you. This is why I came.
        Malachy. One, two, three.

PPVI: Into one.

AG: None.

   Sound of rushing coins. Large coins fall from above Andropov
crushing the Gromyko and Pope Paul VI mannequins. The strings
fall away from Andropov's hands, his wig is raised, revealing the
patch. Lights up.

NOTES TO THE PLAY

Alexy Kosygin: Chairman of the Council of Ministers (equivalent
of Prime Minister) of Soviet Union. Kosygin was elected Chairman
in 1964. The Puppet Play, printed above, was designated for
release on 19 February 1993.

Yuri Andropov: President of the Soviet Union and, earlier, Head of
KGB.

Roncalli: Pope John XXIII, successor to Pope Pius XII, and who was followed by Pope Paul VI.

Acid on Leningrad: The centre for paranormal studies in the Soviet Union before its dissolution (absolution) was situated in Leningrad (now St. Petersburg).

Lieberman: Andropov's name before he changed it to the Russian name most of us know him by.

Malachy: St. Malachy (1094-1148), Archbishop of Armagh, prophesied a succession of 112 Popes, starting with Celestine II (1143-1144). According to the prophecies, John Paul II is the third last Pope until ". . . the seven hilled city will be destroyed and the dreadful Judge will judge the people".

One, two: i.e. Acts I and II of this play. Act III is before you.

Into One: In other words, the alliance between the International Bankers and the Marxists in order to subjugate the masses has now been joined by the Vatican ('Into one'). Gromyko's 'None' means that there is no opposition to the New World Order left. Humanity is muzzled.

the patch: A reference to Gorbachev's signature birthmark. It was Andropov who chose Gorbachev to dissolve the Soviet Union.

Die Vorstellung westlicher Philosophen von Gott

Aristoleles nennt Gott "Bewegende Kraft".
Plato definiert Gott als "Der Gedanke des Guten".
Die Stoiker bezeichnen Gott als "Vorsehung".
Die Neo-Platoniker nennen Gott "Der Unaussprechliche Eine".
Die Menschen der Christlichen Schule nennen Gott: "Gott - der Schoepfer".
Spinoza bezeichnet Gott als "Substanz".
Berkeley nennt Gott "Den Vater der Seele".
Kant nennt Gott "Bestaetigung des moralischen Gesetzes".
Hegel bezeichnet Gott als "Absolute Idee".
Herbert Spencer nennt Gott "Ewige Energie".
Bradley und Royce nennen Gott "Absolutes Erlebnis".
Leibniz nennt Gott "Hoechste Monade - Hoechste Kraft".
Descartes bezeichnet Gott als "Existenz".
Einstein nennt Gott "Kosmisches Bewusstsein, Letzte Wirklichkeit".
Elliott nennt Gott "Allgegenwaertige, Ewige Energie, die ganz Schoepfung und jeden Augenblick der Zeit im Unendlichen Raum belebend und unterrichtend."

Sri Swami Sivananda

Plate 25: *King George Vi.*

FRAGMENTS FROM THE ARCHIVES.

PROF. DR. JULES OCHOROWICZ, PHILOSOPHY, POLAND : TO BE RELEASED MAY 1, 1986.

"IT CAN BE SAID WITHOUT HESITATION THAT THE CHRISTIAN RELIGION HAS BEEN BETRAYED BY TWO OF ITS OWN ELECTED POPES: RONCALLI AND MONTINI. -ALSO IT CAN BE SAID THAT THE POPE IN RELIGIOUS HISTORY WHO DECIDED TO LET JEWS INTO THE ROMAN RELIGION WAS EXTREMELY NAIVE, IF NOT SIMPLY STUPID."

KING GEORGE VI : TO BE RELEASED OCTOBER 12, 1992.

"ICH SAGE DESHALB ALS EHEMALIGER KOENIG VON ENGLAND FOLGENDES:

NIE IM LEBEN WAR ICH VON DER ROEMISCHEN GOTTES-ERFINDUNG UEBERZEUGT UND DESHALB NIEMALS DEREN VEREHRER.-

EIN BLICK IN DIE JUENGSTE HISTORIE ALLEIN, VERMITTELT JEDEN WAHRHAFT INTELLIGENTEN MENSCHEN, DAS GESAMTE KONZEPT DER GELD -UND MACHTIGER.

DAS MITTELALTER ALLEIN, DER DREISSIG JAEHRIGE KRIEG UND DIE ANDEREN DREISSIG RELIGIOESEN KRIEGE, VERANSCHAULICHEN SELBST EINEN DURCHSCHNITTS-MENSCHEN DAS VERLOGENE KONZEPT.-

WENN DIE MONARCHEN DENNOCH SCHWIEGEN, SO AUS FOLGENDEN GRUENDEN:

DIESE BANDE ERREICHTE EINE DERARTIGE STAERKE DURCH GEGENSEITIGE AUSSPIELUNGEN VON NATIONEN, DASS SICH KEINE EINZIGE NATION DIESER SCHWEINE ERWEHREN KONNTE IM ALLEINGANG.-

DASS ENGLAND NICHT SO OHNE WEITERES DIESEN HALUNKEN INS NETZ GING, SEI ZUR EHRE DER ENGLISCHEN NATION OHNE WEITERES HERVOR ZU HEBEN.-

DIE SIMPLE STRATEGIE - EINE NATION NACH DER

ANDEREN ZU UEBERRENNEN WAR DEREN ERFOLGSREZEPT.-

-DURCH RELIGIOESE MANIPULATION DER HIMMEL-, HOELLE-, GOTT-KREATION, ERSTARB DER BEGRIFF DES ERSTEN WORTES IM UNIVERSUM "LIEBE" AUF DEN FRIEDHOEFEN ALLER NATIONEN.-

DIE HISTORISCHEN RUFUNGS-GESETZE, WONACH SICH DIE FAMILIEN UNTER EINANDER AUS DER SEELEN-WELT ALS NEUE KINDER ZURUECKRIEFEN, DURCH SIMPLE WUNSCHAEUSSERUNG UND KOMMUNIKATION UNTER EINANDER, WAR EBENFALLS BEWUSST ERLOSCHEN WORDEN.-

HIERIN LIEGT DIE TEUFLISCHSTE UND KRIMMINELLSTE SCHULD UND SUENDE DER ROEMMISCHEN HORDEN, DIE SIE STETS FUER MICH WAREN, TROTZ WECHSEL VON DER SOELDNER-UNIFORM ZUR KUTTE."

Plate 26: *Viscount (Field-Marshall) Montgomery, Deputy Supreme Commander in Europe during the Second World War.*

Plate 27: *'Monty' regularly visited the Pope. Here he is seen with Pope Pious XII.*

VISCOUNT (FELD-MARSCHAL) MONTGOMERY : TO BE RELEASED AUGUST 15, 1976.

"IHR HOERT RECHT FREUNDE, EURE DESTINATION WIRD ANDERSWO BESCHLOSSEN, OB IHR ES AKZEPTIEREN WOLLT ODER NICHT, UND FROMME GEBETE WERDEN EUCH NICHTS NUTZEN, WEIL IHR IN DEN WIND BETET, DENN GOTT, DER ALLES LIEBENDE, UMARMENDE, IST EINE RELIGIOESE ERFINDUNG, WIE ALL DER ANDERE UNSINN VON HIMMEL, HOELLE, MUTTER MARIA ETC.- ANSTATT HABEN WIR ES MIT GRANITHARTEN GESETZMAESSIG-KEITEN ZU TUN, DIE UNVERAENDERLICH WIE EH UND JE UEBER ALLES WACHEN.—UND DENKT FREUNDE,- EINES TAGES SEID IHR HIER UND WIR DORT.-AUSSERDEM SEID IHR MIT DEM LESEN UNSERER STATEMENTS HIER SPAETER NICHT MEHR DEN STATUS 'UNSCHULDIG-SCHULDIG' FUER EUCH INNE HABEND, -IHR WURDET GEWARNT UND AUFGEKLAERT.-"

DR. KONRAD ADENAUER, KANZLER DER DEUTSCHEN BUNDESREPUBLIK : TO BE RELEASED FEBRUARY 2, 1986.

"ALS KATHOLISCHER ERSTER DEUTSCHER BUNDESKANZLER, WAR ICH VON STOLZ UND GENUGTUUNG ERFUELLT, DAS GESCHUNDENE UND GEMASSREGELTE DEUTSCHLAND AUS SEINER OHNMACHT HERAUS ZU BRINGEN UND SEINE BEDEUTUNG IN EUROPA NEU ZU FUNDIEREN.-

UND SO WIE NACH DEM KRIEGE, VON STOLZ UND GENUGTUUNG ERFUELLT, GUT GEDIENT ZU HABEN, UEBERLIESS ICH DANN DEUTSCHLAND MEINEM GUTEN FREUND UND MITSTREITER LUDWIG ERHARDT.-

HEUTE, WO WIR BEIDE ERKENNEN, DASS WIR VIEL MEHR HAETTEN TUN KOENNEN, SAGE ICH:

WAEREN WIR BEIDE NAEMLICH ANSTATT KATHOLIKEN, PROTESTANTEN GEWESEN, UND ANSTATT DER CHRISTLICHEN DEMOKRATISCHEN UNION ANGEHOEREND, SOZIAL-DEMOKRATEN ODER FREI-

Plate 28: *Konrad Adenauer, Chancellor of Germany (1949-63) with Ludwig Erhard, then Vice-Chancellor and later Chancellor (1963-66). Chancellor Adenauer's last audience with Montini was on 17.9.63.*

DEMOKRATEN GEWESEN, SO WAERE DEUTSCHLAND ETWA
1953 BEREITS WIEDERVEREINIGT GEWESEN.-

DAZU KAM FUER UNS BEIDE DIE BESCHAEMENDE
ERKENNTNISS, ALS RELIGIOESE TROTTEL UND NARREN
GELEBT ZU HABEN, DENN DIE RELIGION IST EINE SELBST-
SERVENDE ERFINDUNG ROMS!

ES GIBT HIER WEDER DEN HIMMEL, DIE HOELLE, DIE
ENGEL ODER HEILIGE MUTTER MARIA, SELBST NICHT
GOTT.

UND DAS, FREUNDE, SCHMERZT UNS MEHR ALS
ALLES ANDERE AM MEISTEN.

AUCH WIR BEIDE WURDEN AM ENDE OPFER UND FUER
UNSERE TREUE GEFOLGSCHAFT BELOHNT.

WAS WUNDER DANN, WENN DAS AQUARIUS-
ZEITALTER NUN DEN SCHLUSSTRICH SETZEN WIRD."

**DR. CHARLES RICHET, PARIS, FRANKREICH : TO BE
RELEASED NOVEMBER 1, 1937.**

"L'OCCULTE SERA DEMAIN LA SCIENCE."

**WILLIAM LYON MACKENZIE KING : TO BE RELEASED
OCTOBER 27, 1985.**

"WENN ICH EBENFALLS DORT IM LEBEN ALS FANTAST
UND ABNORM UNTER MEINER REGIERUNG GEHEIM
BEFUNDEN WURDE, SO MOECHTE ICH GERADE DIESE
FRAGE HIER ETWAS NAEHER BEHANDELN.

AUF DER SUCHE NACH DER WAHRHEIT, UND HIERBEI
MEINE ICH DIE ABSOLUTE WAHRHEIT, WAR ES ZU ALLEN
ZEITEN EINEM MENSCHEN VOELLIG FREI GESTELLT, SICH
DARIN NAEHER UMZUSEHEN.-

ALS ECHTER JESUS CHRISTUS VEREHRER LIESSEN MICH
SIMPEL SEINE BEIDEN AUSSPRUECHE NICHT LOS, DIE FUER
MICH DAS FUNDAMENT DARSTELLTEN, MICH IN
ESOTERISCHEN DINGEN UM ZUSEHEN.-

'SUCHET UND IHR WERDET FINDEN.'

'KLOPFE AN UND ES WIRD DIR AUFGETAN.'

-WER SICH IM STADIUM, WO NUR NOCH EIN FUENFTEL DER MENSCHLICHEN GEHIRNKAPAZITAET IN FUNKTION IST, BEI ALLEN DEGENERATIONS-MANIPULATIONEN, ZUM ZIELE SETZTE, GETREU JESUS' RATSCHLAEGE ZU SUCHEN, HAT DAMIT ETWAS BEWIESEN UND DARF SICH IN GENUGTUUNG HIER EINST HOECHSTER VEREHRUNG IM VORAUS ERFREUEN."

Plate 29: *Mackenzie King (on right) with George VI, who looks remarklably like his grandson Prince Charles.*

Plate 30: *Albert Schweitzer.*

SIR J. STEVENS : TO BE RELEASED FEBRUARY 10, 1986.

"EACH PERSON IS AS A CHARACTER AN UNDISCOVERED CONTINENT. HAPPY AND FORTUNATE IS THE COLUMBUS OF HIS OWN SOUL."

PROF. DR. EINAR JAEGER, OEKONOMIE, KOPENHAGEN, DAENEMARK : TO BE RELEASED MARCH 5, 1985.

"DIE HISTORIE DER MENSCHHEIT ZEIGT, DASS DIE MENSCHEN STAENDIG DEGENERIERTEN, BIS SIE ERNEUT IN EINEM BEREINIGUNGS-ZEITALTER, AQUARIUS GENANNT, DEN GRAD ERREICHTEN, IN DEM NUR NOCH EIN FUENFTEL IHRER GEHIRN-SUBSTANZEN IN FUNKTION IST.

WAHRHAFTIG EIN MEISTERWERK RELIGIOESER MANIPULATIONE, ZUM ZWECK DER VERDUMMUNG UND EGOISTISCHEN BEREICHERUNG."

DR. ALBERT SCHWEITZER : TO BE RELEÁSED OCTOBER 5, 1979.

ICH, ALBERT SCHWEITZER, DEKLARIERE DER ABSOLUTEN WAHRHEIT DIE EHRE GEBEND FOLGENDES:
DIE PHILOSOPHIE DES LEBENS, DIE MAN UNS SCHAFEN-EINST AUF ERDEN REICHTE, IST FALSCH UND VON ROM ERFUNDEN!
DAS MAERCHEN VOM HIMMEL, DER HOELLE UND GOTT UND DESGLEICHEN DIE FRECHSTE ERFINDUNG DER GESAMTEN MENSCHLICHEN HISTORIE.
ALS PROTESTANT BIN ICH ZUTIEFST BESCHAEMT, ZU DIESER GANGSTER-GESELLSCHAFT EINST INDIREKT GEHOERT ZU HABEN UND IHNEN ALS URWALD-DOKTOR UND PROTESTANT IN IHREN MANIPULATION GUT GEDIENT ZU HABEN."

PROF. DR. JULIUS OCHOROWICZ, PHILOSOPIE, POLEN : TO BE RELEASED MAY 1, 1986.

"DIE FRAGE DER UEBERLEBENS-CHANCEN BIS ZUM JAHR 2000 ERSCHEINEN IN MEINER SICHT RECHT FRAGWUERDIG, IST DOCH DER ZENITH DER EVOLUTION SEIT ETWA DREISSIG JAHREN UEBERSCHRITTEN.

STETS WURDE DER MENSCHEIT DIE TECHNISCHE ENTWICKLUNG ZUM VERHENGNIS, IN DER DAS GEFAEHRLICHE ULTIMA DAS ATOM DARSTELLT.

WUERDE MAN SICH BEIM ERREICHEN DER ATOM-WISSENSCHAFTEN DARAUF BESCHRAENKEN, DIE BILLIGE ENERGIE-VERSORGUNG, OHNE PROFIT-GIER, JEDEM MENSCHEN UND JEDER NATION ZUGUTE KOMMEN ZU LASSEN, AUF WEITERE VORTEILE UND MANIPULATIONEN KRIMMINELLEN GEDANKEN URSPRUNGS ZU VERZICHTEN, SO HAETTE DER PLANET ERDE EINE GUTE CHANCE ZU UEBERLEBEN."

PROF. DR. KARL GRUBER, PHILOSOPHIE, MEDIZIN, BERLIN, DEUTSCHLAND : TO BE RELEASED NOVEMBER 3, 1983.

"GEBENDE KRAEFTE, DURCH GEISTIGE SUGGESTIONEN IM INNER-DIMENSIONALEN ZUSAMMEN-WIRKEN ZWISCHEN MAKROBISMUS UND MIKROBISMUS, HABEN NUR NOCH DIE CHANCEN, DEM ERDEN-DISASTER WIRKUNGSVOLL EINHALT ZU GEBIETEN.

ALLES ANDERE UNTER DEM MOTTO MODUS VIVENDI ETC. SIND KINDLICHER IRRTUM, JA GERADEZU GEFAEHRLICHER UNSINN.

ES WILL MIR GERADEZU SCHEINEN, ALLS HAETTEN DIE MENSCHEN SEIT IHRER EXISTENZ AUS DER GESCHICHTE NICHTS DAZU GELERNT, NOCH IMMER JUCKT IHNEN DAS VOR KURZEM ABGELEGTE FELL."

PROF. DR. HANS DRIESCH, PHILOSOPHIE, BIOLOGIE, LEIPZIG, DEUTSCHLAND : TO BE RELEASED APRIL 22, 1989.

DER MENSCH WIRD ZUM PRODUKT DES IHNEN AUFGESCHWAETZTEN, WOBEI ER ALLE KAPAZITAETEN DER EIGNEN INTELLIGENZ, KLUG MANIPULIERT VON SEINEN HIRTEN, VERLIERT UND ZUR DUTZENDWARE DEGRADIERT WOBEI TAUSENDE AUFS RELIGIOESE DUTZEND KOMMEN."

PROF. DR. MORELLI, PSYCHIATRIE, ITALIEN : TO BE RELEASED NOVEMBER 14, 1983.

IN DER HEIMAT, DORT IN ITALIEN, GLAUBTE ICH ALS AKADEMIKER NERVENARZT UND STRIKTER KATHOLIK, EIN RECHTSCHAFFENDER MANN ZU SEIN.
HEUTE AENDERE ICH MEINE ANSICHT UND WUERDE SAGEN:
DIE ICH EINST BEHANDELTE, DIE ANDERE SAHEN, STIMMEN HOERTEN, FUER ANDERE UNHOERBAR, WAREN NORMAL UND KEINE LUEGNER, SONDERN HOECHST QUALIFIZIERTE MENSCHEN UND ICH EIN SCHAF UND SELBSTBETRUEGER."

PROF. DR. GUSTAVE GELEY, MEDIZIN, PARIS, FRANKREICH : TO BE RELEASED JANUARY 3O, 1986.

WUERDE DIE WELT MORGEN ERNEUT ZUSAMMENBRECHEN, WIE OFT ZUVOR IN ANDEREN AQUARIUS-EPOCHEN, SO NUR AUS FOLGENDEN GRUENDEN:
DER STUPIDITAET DER BREITEN MASSEN, SICH NICHT IHRER FESSELN ZU ENTLEDIGEN,
DER FAULHEIT UND FEIGHEIT EURER WISSENSCHAFTLER, DIE SICH DIKTIEREN LASSEN.
DER FRECHHEIT ROMS, NOCH IM ZWANZIGSTEN JARHHUNDERT, INMITTEN DES BEREITS SEIT

FUENFUNDDREISSIG JAHREN REGIERENDEN AQUARIUS-
ZEITALTERS, NOCH VON HIMMEL, HOELLE UND GOTT ZU
PALAVERN."

**JEAN VINCENT, FRANKREICH : TO BE RELEASED
MARCH 10, 1953.**

"L'ABSURDITE D'AUJOUR'HUI EST PEUT-ETRE
L'EMBRYON DE LA VERITE DE DEMAIN.'

**PROF. DR. C. KRABBE, MEDIZIN, KOPENHAGEN,
DAENEMARK : TO BE RELEASED FEBRUARY 22, 1990.**

"'HIMMEL, HERRGOTT, SAKRAMENT,' WURDE EIN
HERKOEMMLICHER AUSSPRUCH, WENN EIN ETWAS FREIER
LIBERALER FLUCHTE, DABEI KONNTE JENER NUR NICHT
AHNEN, WIE GRUNDRECHT ER HATTE.
   ALL DER RELIGIOESE PLUNDER VON HIMMEL, HOELLE,
GOTT UND ENGEL, WAR ERFINDUNG DERER, DIE EUCH BIS
ZUR STUNDE MIT FROMMEN AUGENAUFSCHLAG IN DEN
KIRCHEN - MAN VERZEIHE MIR DEN AUSSPRUCH -
WEITERHIN VERSCHEISSERN!"

**PROF. DR. OSKAR FISCHER, PRAG, C.S.R. : TO BE
RELEASED JANUARY 16, 1987.**

   NIEMALS IN DER HISTORIE DER MENSCHHEIT, GABT ES
DIE ABSOLUTE EINSICHTNAHME IN DIE UNIVERSALEN
GESETZMAESSIGKEITEN DES LEBENS NACHZULESEN ODER
NACHZUSCHLAGEN.
   NIRGENDWO AUF ERDEN WURDEN MYSTERIE-INTER-
ESSIERTE ODER ESOTERIKER JE RICHTIG ERNST GENOM-
MEN, EHER VERFOLGT, DIFFAMIERT UND IHRE SCHRIFFTEN
IM VERBOTENEN INDEX BEFOHLEN.
   NIEMALS WAREN ECHTE FORSCHER MIT DEM MUT,
DEN GEGEBENEN WISSENSSTANDARD ZU ERWEITERN
REICH UND BEGUETERT, IM GEGENTEIL, ARME
SCHLUCKER, UND GINGEN FAST ALLE EBENSO ARM ZUM

URSPRUNG DER SEELENWELT DES MAKROBISMUS ZU-
RUECK!

NIEMALS FRAGTE JEMAND IN DER ERDEN-EVOLU-
TION WIE ES KOMME? DAS IMMER DANN, WENN EINE
ERFINDUNG DRINGEND NOTWENDIG SEI, EIN GEEIGNETER
MANN ODER FRAU ZUR STELLE WAR, DAS PROBLEM ZU
LOESEN.

STETS WAR DER ERFINDER GESTERN EIN FANTAST
UND TRAEUMER, AM NAECHSTEN TAG DANN EIN GENIE
UND GEFEIERTER MANN, DOCH NUR DANN, WENN JEDER
SEINEN VORTEIL DARAUS ERKANNTE.

DER EGOISMUS UND DER PROFIT, WAR STETS DES
ERDENMENSCHEN TREUESTER BEGLEITER, DER IHN BIS
ZUM BITTEREN ENDE SEHR WAHRSCHEINLICH AUCH
BEGLEITEN WIRD.

WARHLICH NICHT GENUG, UNBEKUEMMERT IN DIE
ZUKUNFT ZU SCHAUEN, DENN DIESEN EINEN FAKTOR
HABEN WIR FORSCHER VON GESTERN ABSOLUT HIER IN
UNSEREN HIERSEIN ERMITTELT:

ALLE ZWEIUNDZWANZIGTAUSEND JAHRE IST
UNIVERSALE BEREINIGUNGSZEIT, STETS IN DER AQARIUS-
EPOCHE. DIESMAL BEGANN SIE 1950."

**PROF. DR. OSKAR FISCHER, PRAGUE, C.S.R. : TO BE
RELEASED JANUARY 16, 1987.**

"AS A MEDICAL PROFESSOR OF JEWISH PARENTS IN
PRAGUE C.S.R., I WOULD LIKE TO ADDRESS TO THE ZIONISTS
OF THE WORLD THE FOLLOWING STATEMENT:

I HAVE TRIED IN MY LIFETIME TO SERVE MANKIND TO
THE BEST OF MY ABILITIES, AND HAVE NO REGRETS IN
LOOKING BACK. I HAVE COME TO REALIZE THAT IN
SERVING ALL OF MANKIND ONE CAN COME TO HAVE
REAL FRIENDSHIP AND ETERNAL LOVE. I WOULD LIKE TO
ASK THOSE OF YOU WHO HAVE CHOSEN THE PATH OF
ZIONISM: DO YOU REALLY PREFER TO CONTINUE
WALKING DOWN THE AVENUE TOWARDS THE ULTIMATE
PUNISHMENT? DO YOU TAKE EACH STEP IN FULL

KNOWLEDGE THAT YOU REALLY HAVE NO IDEA WHAT
WILL HAPPEN TO YOU THE DAY AFTER YOUR 'DEATH'?
HAVE YOU EVER WONDERED WHAT THE UNIVERSE HAS
IN STORE FOR ALL OF THOSE, OF ALL RACES, WHO CREATE
GODS OF ALL KINDS TO WATCH OVER THEM AND GUIDE
THEM THROUGH HISTORY?   OR DO YOU NOT THINK
ABOUT SUCH MATTERS ANY MORE, THINKING THAT YOU
HAVE MADE YOURSELF INTO A GOD?

IT IS WITH INFINITE SADNESS AND ANGER THAT I
WATCH THE HUMAN-ENGINEERED CYCLE OF SELF-PERSE-
CUTION CONTINUE, THAT I SEE HUMANS TRYING TO
CONTROL THE ONLY THING THEY CAN IN THIS UNIVERSE:
THEIR OWN BROTHERS AND SISTERS. I HAVE BEEN ABLE
TO HEAL SOME WHO ARE PHYSICALLY SICK, BUT I CAN-
NOT HEAL THOSE WHOSE SPIRIT IS SICK. BUT JUST AS THE
BODY HEALS ITSELF, SO WILL THE SPIRIT, AND HERE BE
WARNED MY BROTHERS AND SISTERS, IT IS NOT THE ANTI-
SEMITE WHO WILL GET YOU IN THE END, IT IS INFINITE
LOVE."

Ihr fragt Warum?

Ihr fragt, warum fand unsere Welt nie Frieden
wonach gesehnt sich hatte Jung and Alt?
Weshalb hat Gott so lange nur geschwiegen
und Euer Zweifel nagte an die Gottgewalt.
War dann ein anderer blutiger Krieg zuende,
Ihr danktet Gott und hofftet nun wird alles gut,
Gott war mit uns, verdammt sind alle Feinde-
vergasset gar zu schnell des Bruders Blut.

Ihr fragtet nicht, kann er mir sein ein Bruder
trotz anderer Sprache sprechend, nie gekannt,
und Gott der schwieg'und dachte nur mein Guter
das Gesetz des wahren Lebens ist Dir unbekannt.
Und ward Ihr selbst dann wieder in Bedraengniss
durch Kummer, Sorge. Krankheit oder Not.
Ihr betetet zu Gott und batet um Verstaendnis,
am Tag zuvor noch ignorierend sein Gebot.

Die Bibel wurde Euch zum A B C des Lebens
Ihr fragtet nicht, ist denn der Inhalt echt?
Nahmt alles hin, wie es Euch ward geschrieben,
bequem zu ueberlegen und das duenkt mir schlecht.
Ihr fragtet nicht, wer gab dem Papst die Rechte
zu nennen sich die rechte Hand von Gott,
gefuegig gabt ihr Euch und machtet Euch zum Knechte,
vergossen Blut auf Erden schriebet Ihr auf Konto Gott.

Plate 31: *Annette von Droste-Huelshoff, German poet (from a portrait by Johannes Sprick).*

Und so gesehen, hat es Euch vielleicht gedungen,
dass Gott nicht existiert und Euch nicht liebt,-
und hieltet fest an religioesen Ueberlieferungen
vom Grossvater und das, was Euch der Priester gibt.-
Das Eurer Vaeter Ahnen schon belogen wurden-
brutal gemordet und gequelet voll perverser Lust,
ja, mein Freund, das konntest du nicht ahnen
auch nicht, dass Gott wohnet in Deiner Brust.-

Was sich nach Jesus Christ einst etablisierte-
unter der Kutte baute sein Imperium,
dort liegt der Punkt, worum sich alles Blutvergiessen drehte
erkenn'ihn klar und dann weisst Du warum.-
Die Historie bewusst ward'falsch geschrieben-
das allerwichtigste zu wissen, liess man einfach aus,
der echte Gott einst selbst auf Erden lebte
die groesste Schmach der Historie kam nicht heraus.

Das gleich wie heut'Doktoren und Gelehrten
mit Feuer spielten, ignorierend das Naturgesetz,
bis dann, nach ueber Eineinviertel Million Jahren
der Frieden starb, der Planet Erde ward'zerfetzt.
Von dieser Zeit an Freund beginnt die Gottesrechnung
die Karma heisst und haerter ist als jeder Stahl-
Gott kennt die Saeue das sei Deine letzte Hoffnung,
Ihr werdet wieder leben und dann endet alle Qual.

Doch jene, die Euch einst brutal erpressten-
ob Papst, ob Bischof, Priester oder Kardinal,
der echte Gott, er wird sie dreimal sterben lassen-
die naechste Erde wird sie sehen nicht noch mal.
Und waehrend man vom Jahr 2000 spricht gewichtig,
in kuehnen Traeumen schwelgt, die Zukunft prognostiziert,
die nuklearen Tests, der Mond ist denen ja so wichtig.
der Steuerman am Rad der Historie schon dreht.-

                    Annette von Droste-Huelshoff

News From the Vatican Underground (9.1.93)

ROD: I am glad to meet you.

EE: He knows both sides.

ROD: What do you mean - he knows both sides?

EE: Both sides of the street.

TT: Inside and outside, standin' in the middle.

ROD: What do you say?

TT: The Vatican is the largest single dwelling-house in the
          world for one person.

ROD: Who runs it?   Where does the Vatican get its power?

TT: For Two Thousand Years? The MAFIA, of course.
          Organized crime only deals with the strongest: the
          Roman Catholic Church. They need to launder their
          money, crookest bastards ever alive.

ROD: Where does the money come from? Where does it find
          a place to hide?

TT: They collect from the poor and unfortunate, of course -
          mostly when they are at church; they launder the
          money by means of narcotics, prostituion, gambling
          and by buying out politicians.

ROD: Money reproduces itself. May I tell you this, friend,
          who came in the night?

          In the new world-ordered
          World, the Mafia is anathema,
                      Anchronistic.

TT: Did you not know
       The cream of the Mafia is already housed
       In St. Kitts SOUTH? There the Principals
       Of The New World Order
       Have set up their Xmas House!

EE: Floooooooooooooooooooooooo-
          RI-
    DA
                    (adir di diddly) diiiiiiiiiiiiiiiiiiiiiiiii

                            diddly   an'   de
graaaaaaaaaaaaaaaaaaaaaaaaaaaaaaaaaaaaaaaaaaaaaaaaaaaaa
                       hams:
                    A green egg an' a gray ham,
                    A green egg an' a gray ham,
                    I've found a Gray Man
                    In St. Kitts, St. Kitts,
                    I've found A GRAY MAN in St. Kitts.

TT: SOUTH!

EE: Gray is another shade of black
                 And all cats are gray in the dark.

TT: I like the way we tangle, though we just met. One more
       thing, Robert! You may not know we already have two
       people's eyes on them, two people who do not have
       authorization to be there under any government
       jurisdiction?

EE: Is the casino under surveillance or are they supporting
       THE OTHER?

TT: Bob Rae's compatible casino is almost in place in Windsor.
       As for both houses, of course they are supporting the Devil
       - any organized crime that's in the picture - 'cause they are
       the head haunchos, and nobody in this new world order
       will touch them.

ROD: The Mafia then are split, like the rest of the world?

TT: No.

ROD: I am glad you are here.

IV.   CAN

A

DA?

A Spysong with notes
by
Robert O'Driscoll

'i'll dance like a butter-
fly, sting like a bee' -
Mohammed Ali

EPIGRAPHS

How much Bob Know?
How much Bob Hope?
(Unpublished section, *Spysong*)

I done me best when I was let. Thinking always if I go all
goes. A hundred cares, a tithe of troubles and is there one who
understands me? One in a thousand of years of the nights?
All me life I have been lived among them but now they are
becoming lothed to me. And I am lothing their little warm
tricks. And lothing their cosy turns. And all the greedy gushes
out through their small souls. And all the lazy leaks down over
their brash bodies. How small it's all! And me letting on to
meself always. And lilting on all the time (James Joyce,
Finnegans Wake, London: Faber, 1939).

These fragments I have shored up against my ruin.
                    (T. S. Eliot, *The Waste Land*)

INTRODUCTION

I

An artist has a different constitution from an historian. Of necessity, therefore, the style must change: from the linear narrative of history to a delicate multi-layered palimpsest or mosaic, where the *lapis lazuli* resonate with what the stones remember: suggestions of an azure opaqueness and blue we all once knew - before Eden.

Spysong, therefore, is presented in a variety of styles: the elegiac, heroic, mock heroic, rabelaisian, scatological, theological, philosophic, historic, aesthetic, parodic, grotesque, etc.

Nato and the Warsaw Pact Are One, as the EE of *The New World Order & The Throne of the antiChrist* once said to me, is like a primal scream out of the depths of the patriarchal experience of history, with its insatiable lust for power, and more power, and more. Or, as Professor Lorna Reynolds, Professor Emeritus of the National University of Ireland, stated in her Introduction to the poem:

How the private life is affected by the public is the theme of the work here presented. In its fragmented and syncopated form, it reflects a mind caught up in horror, in hallucinatory apprehension, in a sense of bafflement, attempting manic guesses at meaning, seeking for some, or any, explanation, grasping at straws, seen through the fog.

It is ironic that this outburst should come at the moment when events in Eastern Europe take such a sudden and totally unexpected turn . . . strange that someone living far from Europe, across the Western ocean, should echo all this.

And yet, it all cohered - for a few at least!

II

A work of art, W. B. Yeats writes in 'The Necessity of Symbolism', begins in 'a bodiless mood, becomes then a surging thought, and at last a thing.' The mind is not the primary organ, but is working hypnotically, almost as if a trance, as it charts the flight of a dark dove - set free in the skies from a human cauldron of passion and wisdom - dipping on the horizon of the hitherto unknown.

Any obscurity in the poem, as T. S. Eliot explains of his *Waste Land*, 'on first readings, is due to the suppression of "links in the chain", or explanatory and connecting matter, and not to incoherence, or to the love of cryptogram. The justification of such abbreviation of method is that the sequence of images coincides and concentrates into one intense impression of barbaric civilization. The reader has to allow the images to fall into his memory successively without questioning the reasonableness of each at the moment; so that, at the end, a total effect is produced.'

III

The aesthetic techniques that provide the foundation of James Joyce's *Finnegans Wake* provide the foundation of the poetic sections of *The New World Order & The Throne of the antiChrist*. These principles have, to my mind, been most cogently articulated by Elmar Ternes (University of Hamburg) in his analysis of the Celtic languages at a public lecture (subsequently published in my *Celtic Consciousness*) at the University of British Columbia in the late seventies:

A word pronounced in isolation and a word pronounced in a sentence context may show quite different pronunciations, because in the latter case neighbouring words influence each other in their pronunciation. . . . As far as the Celtic languages are concerned, the division of a sentence into words, shown in print by spacing, is a mere conventional device which facilitates semantic and grammatical analysis, but which is not justified

phonetically. . . .[W]e may say that the word in Celtic
is like a chameleon which changes its appearance according to its surroundings. Or, putting it in a more
extreme way: the word by itself is in Celtic very loose,
almost amorphous, and its shape can only be defined by
analysing the sentence as a whole. . . . Among the
modern Celtic languages, it is precisely Irish that shows
these properties to their greatest extent. . . . [T]he word
in Celtic is not a solid, strictly definable unit, but on the
contrary something that changes its form constantly
under all sorts of influences: phonetic, morphological,
and syntactical. This also gives the sentence as a whole
an unstable, almost fluid appearance (pp. 71-5).

On the whole, I try to leave more clues for the fledgling reader
than Mr. Joyce.

IV

Of relevance, too, to the aesthetic principles on which the
poetic sections of *The New World Order & The Throne of the
antiChrist* is built is the art of The Book of Kells, particularly the
TUNC (is there a hitherto undetected anagram here?) page. The
very distinguished Irish scholar, Liam de Paor, writes:

The order comes from within: this is the key to what
is 'Celtic' in Irish art of the early Christian period. . . .
The Book of Kells is rightly famous as a supreme
product of the final phase of this art. As difficult, and
in some ways as alienating to the modern consciousness, as *Finnegans Wake*, it repels and fascinates because
its order, barely controlling an explosive anarchy, allows
us to glimpse the chaos at the heart of the universe
which our own Romanised culture is at pains to conceal
(*The Celtic Consciousness*, pp. 126-7).

A sensitive and brilliant student of mine, Micol Marotti (first-
year class of 1990-1), picked up this point in an interview with
me for the St. Michael's College newspaper, *The Mike* (2 October
1991), drawing up from somewhere in the subterranean depths
of my being the following perception of the correlation between

order and anarchy:

    I remembered something one of my students once
told me about the latest theory of physics, that what
seems to those - of lesser developed imaginative sophis-
tication - to be chaotic may in fact be the manifestation
of a high, rare, and lonely order.

The student I refer to in the interview drew my attention to the
Wave Particle theory of physics, the amazing discovery that the
universe is controlled by intelligent forces acting spontaneously
and purposefully; that behind every manifestation in the cosmos - from a grain of sand to an undiscovered galaxy, behind
every dingle single atom or part of an atom - is an intelligence;
that there is even an order behind seeming chaos - what
mankind has, until now, called God.

University of Toronto   Robert O'Driscoll
Autumn Equinox 1992.

Plate 32: *Illuminati insignia (truncated pyramid) on top of the Ontario
Parliament Buildings, Toronto, Canada.*

PRELUDE

Mouth begins to speak, robotlike, rhythmic:

STRONG

BLACK

man

STIR WEB
of bread

terre- sssssssssssssssssssssssssssssssssssss-

trial an' a JACK-

MAN

fiddling a diddle
in de middle of the werle,

'wid BLACK

heya

aul ova my bodi,'

an' he sings 'Yes' to both sides:

'Yes, Sir, No, Sir,
Three bags full Sir.'
'Spen Sir.'

Philby 'fore
Tolled:
'The House of Winds-
or   Will flush the fox
Out of the hole:
Merlin & Charles,
Charles & Art-
hur.'

PHIL BEE
Held a royal straight flush
For 'our wance and future king'.

'Kim was homesick. Even now in Moscow, his obsession
is not with Russia, but with England.' - John Le Carré of Kim
Philby, '68.

'When you are dealt
A royal straight flush
You cannot lose.' - Lugh.

Philby an' his cell
tuk con trole
of
American, British, Russian, and Canadian Intelligence

A   B   R   A   . C

A
B R A
A B R
A
D
A
C

A
B
R
A
The Di is cast
An' all the King's
Horses an' all the King's
Men coudn put Humped D
To get her again
In the ROM.

And Abraham offered his son Isaac to God.   But God
accepted a lamb instead. The lamb took the place of the son,
and Jesus, Son of God, took the place of the Lamb and he was
sacrificed for the people. And the lamb lay down with the lion

an' all the greylambs,
                    An' all the gray hams,
                    An' all the greymen's
                    Gray hams, an' all the abra-
                    hams, an' all the a bra
                    cad a bra gray hams -

                              A

                             BBB
                            RRRRR
                           AAAAAAA
                          CCCCCCCCC
                         AAAAAAAAAAA
                        DDDDDDDDDDDDD
                       AAAAAAAAAAAAAAA
                      BBBBBBBBBBBBBBBBBBB
                     RRRRRRRRRRRRRRRRRRRRR
                    AAAAAAAAAAAAAAAAAAAAAAA

                       An' all of abra's lambs
                       An' all of ABRA
                       HAM'S chosen pee-
                       Ple: the 13th tribe

                    Isreal: the Gray Ham is a[n] ac
                    D C A C D C A C D C
                    AIDS of Camp, see
                    F A G A R I, ari
                    Fag, Queen of the Hunt,
                    Diana and the grayhams.

'Spent, sir!'
'Fill er . . . UP SIR!
Phil er . . . UP SIR!
Phil lip . . . UP SIR!'
'Thank you! FILL
VAT!' 'I CAN.'
'BE!'
'Phil BEE!'
'A BEE E, light
Bearer of . . . ' - `dare's
uh fly in the ointment.' - KIM

Grey is another shade of black
And all cats are grey in the dark.

Di an' th' GRAAAAAAAAAAAAAAAAA–
HAMS an' the big T O TO-
DEA!'
DES   i
uuuuuuuuuuuuuuuuuuuuuuuuuuuuuuuuuuuuuuuuuuuuuuuuuuuuuuuuuul

Yes, desiul!

1. MM & EE

Circa '62, ROD at Karl Marx's grave, Highgate Cemetery, London, Eng.: studies the grave of Karl Marx, looks 'cross the dirt road, slanting, sees grave of American educator Herbert Spencer. Stops; contemplates two graves.

Looks down dirt road: two ladies approach, elderly.

O'D approaches two elderly ladies, gingerly, hesitant.

"Cuse me 'fore I go on, are there more graves here of famous people 'sides Marx and Spencer?'

Old lady pulls herself up out of herself, contemplates o'd, corner of her eye, tongue from the sky: 'I didn know they were daed luv.'

o o o o o

Marshall McLuhan to Robert O'Driscoll, circa 1973 (*holding up both hands*): 'How many numbers are there, Bob?'

ROD: 'Ten.'

McLuhan: 'No. Would you like to learn to count?' (*counting from left to right, skipping five*)

5

1 2 3 4 6 7 8 9

5

ROD: Michelangelo left a proof
           On the Sistine Chapel roof
           That the finger of God
           And the finger of Adam
           Must be kept separate
           For the electricity to flow
           From the divine to the
           Manifest world we inhabit.

E L E C T T R I S H
i d i r s c e o i l

But in this middle world of ours,
Poised like a butter-
                                        fly be-
        tw-
                een

        Nine hierarchies suspended above,
        Nine hierarchies suspended below,
            THE MIDDLE NUMBERS ARE JOINED:
            There is only one NUMBER:
            NUMBER of the WORLD STATE?

McLuhan: 'ONE! But what of the *fifth*
            Mahon? One who breaks the log
            Jam? 'idir sceoil', eh Bob?'
ROD: 'Yes, the Irish for my name: 'between stories'.
McLuhan: 'Between stories'. What you really mean is: in the
interlude is the action - electricity, idir sceoil.'
ROD: 'I guess - hey, thas a pretty good way of putting it.'
McLuhan: 'Electricity, haw! Thas what the CBC runs on.'

                    o   o   o   o   o

    Robert O'Driscoll to Peter Gzowski, 6 December 1990 -
letter: 'Let us return to the CBC. If a World State is already,
albeit secretly, in motion, and if, as *Nato and the Warsaw Pact
are One* suggests, Canada is involved in espionage activity
against free-thinking individuals who are not inclined by
nature to bend easily to the dictates of the new World State, then
it makes sense to do what was done yesterday: that is, in one
fell and well-prepared swoop, to make a eunuch of our National
Broadcasting Corporation which has grown up independently,
higgedly-piggedly, throughout the decades. Why? To render
impossible, of course, independent comment on the already-
arranged horrendous sequence of events that are about to
unfold in this country and all around the world.
    'Is what I am suggesting in *Nato and the Warsaw Pact are One*
fact or imagination, the result of intuition or espionage? Does

it really matter? YOU and I know, Peter, from the history of the world that art intuits what, in the fullness of time, the evidence of nature finally, and sometimes rather sadly, corroborates.'

The letter was never answered.

> (*to EE*) People *stone wall!*
>   People hang oot
>   too defend a dough-
>   nut with amnesia
>   to the death for
>
>   EVER.

✱ ✱ ✱ ✱ ✱

'Tenakis, Patrick, tanx, as they say in the Bronx, for 'ducing me Liz (EE) with your dowsing rod that fateful wet night in dark Damascus: 22 February 1990. Did I ever tell you about the first time I took her away for a clandestine weekend to meet Mr. Jones? Royal York Hotel, our St. Andrew's Day Celebrations that year. I think it was sometime between 3 and 3:35 A.M. and I said:

'Elizabeth, before we sleep tonight, tell me something about espionage I don't know.'

At about 6:15 - she was sitting on the bed - she pulled open her covers, ready for rest. I was still sitting on the chair, rose to make ready.

'Robert,' she said casually, as she slipped out her clothes, 'I have seen them play their cards, both sides, with such perfection, that I am bored.'

And then, as I turned out the light,

'I like the way you concluded your *Nato*:
>   In the womb of the cosmos,
>   Earth, the double
>   Ones are cancelled, crossed -
>   go deo agus go deo
>   forever and forever
>   in semper aeternum

'What If? What if what comes out of here, this womb - I remember your mentioning the third egg of Leda in Arthur, to be hatched near the end of time - what if what comes out of here, this egg of Earth, *determines* the whole future course of cosmic unfoldment? Otherwise, why would they bother, those ansi money sharks? It cannot only be greed, or merely a twisted insatiable lust for power?'

You were on Sun,
I was on Moon:
A signal flashed:
F A G A R I!
Meeting on Earth!

O, Sheba, let us
                        try it again!

GO BIGGER!
GO HIGHER!
Armageddon is the irrevocable
                        irreversible
            CROSS
                  Roads of All Eternity.

0707.29.5.92 The point of no
Return has been reached.

Go Bigger!
Go Higher!
Highest stakes ever
Since the Big Bang!

To disappear without a trace?

to
  be
    left
      hang
        ing
          in
            outer
              space
    listening endlessly
           to
        pre-
      re-
    cord-
    Ed
tapes, asking questions
- endlessly ask -
        no one to ask
        no one to tell
        no where to go

                    No fix in a womb
                    (No, never again)
                      Nor a trace
                      On the land
                          ov
                           a
                          hu
                         man

        haaaaaaaaaaaaaaaaaaaaaaaaaaaaaaaaand

It is written in a grain of sand

Written on the wind
That at the end of time
All battles shift to one

AC or C,
Christ or anti-Christ.
Highest stakes ever
Since the Big Crunch:
To disappear without a trace!

2. MARZIPAN

Head begins to speak, slowly, almost inarticulately:

mar
    zi
        pan

    But if Pan?
    Megapan us?
            US?

        SU
       us and su
       su and us:
        nat su!

They agreed just on her
   To heal the kind sirrrrrrrrrrrrrrrrrrrrrrrrrrrrrrrrrrrr.

           US?

    No! Matapanus,
    Kepheus, King
    Placed 'mong
    The stars
    'vec Cass-
        Iopeia.
         Ethiopia:
    Nigatu, go now,
    Look at the sky,
    Locate them there.
    'Cording your likes,
    'Cording your lights,
    Alyas! Eli, elohist,
    "Elohim Eli lambech'

The stars light up without
As the stars light up within.

Cepheus the King!

Christ the King!

Colossians, 1, 12-7: Epistle for the Feast of Christ the King (the
last Sunday in November), as taken from mother's prayerbook:
we give thanks to God the Father who has made us
worthy to share the lot of the saints in light. He has
rescued us from the power of darkness, and transferred
us into the kingdom of his beloved Son, in whom we
have our redemption through his blood, the remission
of sins. He is the image of the invisible God, the
firstborn of every creature. For in him were created all
things in the heavens and on the earth, things visible
and invisible, whether Thrones, or Dominations, or
Principalities, or Powers. All things have been created
through and unto him, and he is before all creatures, and
in him all things hold together.
Chorus of Hierarchies:
                        Crucified, died, and was buried,
                        Ascended to Heaven for three
                        Days, returned to Earth,
                        'Tending go back, be-
                        Trayed once again
                        Be the blackpeters
                        By the whitegroves
                                - Naipaul -
                        To live two Thou-
                        Sand years on Mars,
                        On Marsi
                        Pan 'vec
                        Magicians des-
                        Cended from Circe
                        Sans Pan
                                ic ic ic ic ic ic ic ic ic ic ic ic ic ic ic ic

EE: Ecce Homo!
            Yes! You! Not I AM
            WHO AM but
                              'You art'!
PC: AE?
                  ROD: DEMENTIONS!
                                          A BE?
                              To be or
                              Not to be?
                              a b e
                  Lightbearer of darkness
                  'Tis either you or me!
                  'Tis either you or me!
A BE: By the power invested in me by Arihman and Lucifer,
I hereby curse. . . .
ROD: Well might you curse because
          Before we snuff this mortal coil
      I shall personally drive a bright stake
          Through your black heart
In San Diego,
                        But not before
                        You have been
                           Contaminated
                              By human feeling,
          So that you'll feel the wood in the flesh.
EE: You and your crew once
                        Put flesh upon a cross,
                  Nailed it to the naked wood
                  While you obliviously cast lots
          For that which merely cloaked the flesh.

                  Oh, you didn't know that
                  Neither cloth, flesh, or blood
                  Shall inherit the Kingdom of God
ROD: And after the stake has burst your heart,
                        You are consigned
                  To one of those last dark terrible moons
                  Sent off at the end of interstellar time.

PC: Cleave the land!
                             Part the seas!

                   For Michael was a double agent,
                   Paid to do the devil's work:

                             WW1, WW2,
                   and halfway through WW3
                             broke free

        gain ed con trol of bell tell ig en ce net vorks
                   on the earth and in the skies:

                             MIJ, MI8,
                   Spies who look after the spies.

AE: Become what we hate?
                             first shall be last
                             last shall be first
                             Remain on the wheel?

Chorus of Ancestors:
                             We seek release from the earth!
                             We seek release from the wheel!
                             We seek release from the circle!.

Hermes Trismegistus:
                             Nineteen times nineteen equals
                             Three hundred and sixty-one.
                             Number beneath the Bible!
                             Number beneath the Koran!

PC: What is the number
                                     Of the perfect circle
                                     Perceived by man?

EE: Three hundred and sixty degrees.
Hermes: Nineteen times nineteen equals. . .
ROD: Three hundred and sixty-one!
Baitman (BC):   We're off one degree!
                                 I'm always off
                                               when I fly!

Hermes: There are at least two WHEELS:
One is of Man
One is of God:

Man lives in the wheel.
God gives relief
From the wheel
And the ring.

Chorus of hierarchies:
His children stayed one earth -
Niente - save one son appeared
A tween two WARS
Of the WORLD
To settle the case
Of his father
Near end of the
Mill
enn
i.
u.
m.

Mr. Mills speaks:
TOGAIL BRUIDHE DA DERGA:
Brian's hus.

Please, little cherub, put
More and more geasa
On our dear stewing
Thrashin' trassa.

Silence. Mr. Mills speaks again:
While latino was LAyING the primeminister's wife -
his dubh eel nix tuh me, sec. son,
I
put a hex
on his ex:
What a prize!
What a prize!
Just being alive!

Who is the ness one?
Who is the nix t one?
long long lonnnnnng
            longgggggggggggggggggggg as you've
        eh
            STONE
            4
                A HEART!

Mr. Mills (recovering himself): What doth the messenger say?

Messenger:
    TRUE DOUGH AND THE WHORE OF BABYLON
            met & wept
            tears of christ.
            They didn't need
            a glass of white wine
            to jag her to jag her -

        Tojagger they slipped up an erse -
        an aisle - a cos mick marriage
        while my star scape sing-
        ers - true dough and black yeast.

Mr. Mills (dismissive)   Now run along please,
                        I must play with my PET.

PET PET PET PET PET PET PET PET PET PET PET PET PET
        Pretty little pussey, pussey, pussey,
        Pretty little pussey, pussey, puss,
                            Pretty little pet!

Mr. Mills strolls away, his pussey cradled in his left arm.

THE FALL

(bababadalgharaghtakamminarronnkonnbronntonnerronntuonn-
thunntrovarrhounawnskawntoohoohoordenenthurnuk!) of a
once wallstrait oldparr is retaled early in bed and later on life
down through all christian minstrelsy. The great fall of the
offwall entailed at such short notice the pftjschute of Finnegan,
erse solid man, that the humptyhillhead of humself prumptly
sends an unquiring one well to the west in quest of his
tumptytumtoes: and their upturnpikepointandplace is at the
knock out in the park where oranges have been laid to rust
upon the green since devlinsfirst loved livvy.

What clashes here of wills gen wonts, oystrygods gaggin
fishygods! Brekkek Kekkek Kekkek Kekkek! Koax Koax Koax!
Ualu Ualu Ualu! Quaouauh!

> Jupiter sang:
> Marzipan
> Moonish full
> - Merci pants
> Merci panties
> Roaring bland
>   also ran
> Tried it with his udder hand

CIESIS THIE SIS to spie
On pantry's fading private eye
Found self-crossed and double-bent
Imitating lauds to lent,
Lent a bucket, took a peck
look at Mrs. Hansom's neck
Wrought a peck of pa's malt . . . .

Rot a peck of pa's malt had Jhem or Shen brewed by arclight
and rory end to the regginbrow was to be seen ringsome on the
aquaface.

Cepheus breaks in from on high: He was hired to write *Ulysses* to exonerate the Jew as a figure in literature. They kept him like a dog, moving him all over Europe, case their PLAN be divined. He wrote *Finnegans Wake* for revenge, revealing all the keys. He died shortly after.

Bulletin: The Canadian Security Intelligence Service has banned the importation of marzipan because in appearance, texture, and consistency it resembles C-7 plastic explosives, used by terrorists, chiefly in the air.

3. CSIS

Jewpeter is saying: 'Put out your shoes,
Get marzipan
Ou diazepam
Ou black diamond
Frum San Nick
An' Blackpeter,
Zwarte Piet.'

Anal Ab!
Anal Abaddon!

oi kesis, oi kesis,
   oikesis,
   i se sis,
   thie ciesis,
   ecesis, e-
Cesis, King
Cisseis, O
cissoid
O'D!

CSIS et CIRCA

CSIS et SIR CA
SIR CAW CA CA CA CA CA CA CA
SIR CAW CAW,
Kelly, and Christ.

Mr-ca-cack
(Kelly and Christ)
Said 'Yes' to both sides,
'Yes Sir, No Sir,
Three bags full Sir.'

Me-ca-ca, Oxford, and Rome
(My poor little home
And the little black box),
Me-ca-ca-ca-ca-ca-ca-ca-ca-cack -
He sis and Sir Caw Ca!
Taim a CSIS!
Taim a CSIS!

CSIS, the Canadian SecurityIntelligence Service, figures prominently in this *Spysong* 'Interlude'.

CSIS was not constituted formally until 1984, but it operated informally during the seventies under Prime Minister Pierre Trudeau. Up until then, it had operated as a branch of the Royal Canadian Mounted Police Security division, but after the FLQ crisis, the War Measures Act, and other manipulated crisis, Trudeau had a reason - one that the public could not readily challenge - to push towards the formalization of Canadian Intelligence.

The roots of CSIS, however, go much deeper. It goes back to OSS in the nineteen-forties, i.e. The Office of Strategic Services, which had its own independent fighting force - 'The Devil's Brigade'. The CIA was to emerge later from the shell of the OSS.

With relation to CSIS, the scenario is something as follows: in 1942 or 1944 (the RCMP records are unclear as to the year), while the US and Russia were on a joint war mission, with a Canadian holding the anchor as Third Man (or, in this case, Woman), the Canadian stumbled onto a startling piece of information, left seemingly accidently for her, and for her alone, to see - information which the Russian and American could not possibly know - *that they both served the same master*.

The woman, probably Kathleen Willsher (who was at the time working in the Office of the High Commissioner for the United Kingdom in Ottawa), decided to serve her own gender and her own country, not the international mission, with its own code of ethics, to which she had taken *the* oath of secrecy. She carefully checked her mathematics: 1 plus 1 = 2; 2 plus 1 = 3; 3 minus 2 = 1. Being a graduate of the London School of

Economics, she failed, however, to calculate the ultimate equation: 1 minus 1 =

'76

Deep Throat said: 'So, the family
That controls the Soviet Union
Controls the United States.'

SU and US
US and SU

And the nationality?

Yes!
You can guess!

Can-

a-

da -

figured out the info
from being third man
on a mission. The can-
adians can add and
clearly sub-
tract.
(Nato and the Warsaw Pact Are One, p.24)

The information was sent directly from the OSS Canadian Officer to the Prime Minister, Mackenzie King who, with his prior corroboration of the occult, had no difficulty in matching the facts before him to his own experience.

Like a broody hen, King decided to sit on the information. A short time later, on 5 September 1945, a fly appeared in the ointment, when a code and cipher clerk in the Russian Embassy in Ottawa, Igor Gouzenko, became alarmed by something he had seen in the files. He decided to flee the Soviet Embassy, taking with him more than one hundred secret documents, and finally contacting, with RCMP help, the Prime Minister. King granted him asylum in Canada and appeared in Parliament to defend the decision:

MACKENZIE KING TELLS WHY
IGOR GOUZENKO REVEALED PLOT

As revealed by MacKenzie King, the first intimation of the existence of a widespread espionage plot in Canada came from Igor Gouzenko, a cipher clerk in the Soviet Embassy. Mr. Gouzenko had nothing to gain by his disclosure. He sought no reward, and could hope for no reward that would compensate for the fear that would haunt him, fear not only for himself but for his wife and child.

His statement to the police set forth the motives of his action. He had been impressed by the contrast between life in Canada and life in his own country. When he came here two years ago he had been surprised by the freedom of the people and the working of democratic institutions. He had seen what Canada was doing to help Russia with munitions, money and food, while affording him and others every facility that could be extended in the way of freedom. As a result he felt he could no longer keep silent about what was happening. He told the police that '*what was being created in Canada was a Fifth Column, and that it was being created through Russian agents in contact with members of the public service*' [my italics].

Mr. King told Parliament he believed this description of his motives was true, but what he attached importance to was not the individual and what he said, but the documents which were produced. . . .' The documents are unquestionably of the first importance as evidence of a vast plot, but the story of the individual's motives contains for the people of Canada a lesson which, if properly learned, would make them proofs against all such plots in the future. The lesson is in the fact that a man who knows life under the Soviet and who has seen life in Canada, could not tolerate the thought that the freedom which human beings enjoy here should be stamped out by a totalitarian government.

There are people who think that there is no danger to Canada in Russia's ambition, and many who believe that even if Moscow dominated the world it would not interfere with liberty here. They are living in a fool's paradise. The plan of world revolution, which has never been abandoned by Moscow for a moment, contemplates a purge in *all* [my italics] countries as ruthless as any of the purges that have been carried out in any of the satellites of the Soviet or in Russia herself. In Toronto it is taught, as part of the campaign of 'understanding' Russia, that such purges are pardonable and proper if carried out by Communists against the 'bourgeois.' Innocent students are led to believe that the bourgeois - the term as understood by radicals means those who have private property interests - are a criminal class which deserves to be exterminated.

It is this teaching that persuades Canadians who know nothing by actual experience of life under the Soviet system that it would be a praiseworthy action to help the Moscow government in its struggle for supreme power. Others believe that whatever happens elsewhere, nothing disastrous can happen here. Mr. Gouzenko, who has known life in both countries and who has been in the Soviet secret service, knows what is intended and what may happen. To prevent it from happening, and to preserve what he had learned to prize, he dared death for himself and his family.

'supreme power', 'vast espionage plot', 'world revolution', 'totalitarian government', 'vast plot': to what is the Prime Minister referring? He makes no reference to Hitler or the Axis powers, to the Second World War, or to the First World War to which, as Conrad O'Brien ffrench once told me, the Second World War was connected.

No, the 'vast espionage plot' seems vaster than the two World Wars. What could it be? Certainly not the passing of

atomic secrets (as a recent book, *Spy Wars*, by Canadians Jack
Granatstein and David Stafford, claims) for, as Mr. Griffin has
shown earlier in this volume, the atomic and hydrogen bomb
secrets had been passed directly from the second man in the
White House, Harry Hopkins, to the third man in the Kremlin,
Mikoyan. Was it the spread of a political doctrine - Communism? Hardly! Not the spread of Communism, but what
Communism was designed as an instrument to achieve. I quote
from the definitive source book, *The Rulers of Russia* (Dublin,
1939), p.25:

> the real forces behind Bolshevism in Russia are Jewish
> forces. . . . Bolshevism is really an instrument in the
> hands of the Jews for the establishment of their future
> Messianic kingdom [i.e. the kingdom of the antiChrist].
> . . . Bolshevism, on its own confession, does not intend
> to remain within the narrow limits of any one country,
> but ambitions a world-wide influence or empire.

These are weighty words. For the corroboration of the
contention, I shall turn to Europe, to Winston Churchill, Étienne
Gilson, Adolph Hitler, Joseph Stalin, Wyndham Lewis, Hilaire
Belloc, and a host of diplomats, writers, philosophers, etc. But
first a few more words re Gouzenko. His first book appeared
in 1948, *This Was My Choice*, published by J. M. Dent & Sons
(Toronto and Vancouver), with an Introduction by an Editor
who is unnamed and which reads in part:

> As this preface is written, a man is living with his
> family in Canada under close and constant Royal Cana-
> dian Mounted Police guard. Only a few high govern-
> ment and police officials know what dot on the Cana-
> dian map represents his home. He goes under an alias
> and, perhaps, in disguise. Strict security regulations
> forbid reproduction of his photograph, a detailed de-
> scription of him or any hint as to where he may be
> found. For interviews in connection with the editing of
> this book, he was escorted under police guard to differ-
> ent meeting places in various cities.
> The man is Igor Gouzenko. . . .
> In these extraordinary precautions there is more

than merely the security of Igor Gouzenko at stake. It must be emphasized until every free citizen of a free country realizes it, that these precautions are forced upon us by the brazen and mortal challenge which the reign of terror, of fear and the denial of personal freedom, of personal conscience, of personal rights and privileges, has thrown out to free men everywhere.

The gruesome record of purges, concentration camps, mass executions and individual torture was first written in the blood of the Russian people. . . .

Gouzenko's *This Was My Choice* and his subsequent books and articles, particularly *The Fall of A Titan* (which he disguises in the form of a novel), are full of material relevant to the preparation of the kingdom of the antiChrist, but I must be content here with four quotations from *This Was My Choice*:

'Is it to England I'm being assigned, Comrade Captain?'

He shook his head. 'No, not to England, but to the most fertile field of England's influence. You are slated for service in Canada. How does that suit you?'

'It will suit me very well.'

'And so it should, Canada is a vast country, sparsely populated and with almost unlimited resources. In recent years, and even since the start of the war, the Party's success there has been exceeded our most optimistic expectations; but there is still formidable opposition to overcome. As a softening measure leading to complete demoralization before military action, the Party is concentrating on gaining control of labour unions. . . .'

And elsewhere in the volume we read:

'When I arrived in Canada I was surprised to learn that large numbers of Jews are staunch supporters of Pro-Soviet campaigns in Canada. . . .'

'This one country of less than thirteen million people,' he said 'has nine separate Intelligence networks operating in direct contact with Moscow.'

'This new outlook on the messages I was handling

between Ottawa and Moscow began extending to the newspapers I read. Articles of a Soviet theme in Canadian, American and the U.S.S.R. papers took on a new significance. The Soviet strategy was apparent where, previously, it had been obscured by my Communist-trained mind.

'The strategy consisted in having Soviet spokesmen or their unofficial minions hold forth on every occasion - and especially international conferences - about peace and security. This was the verbal smoke-screen for active and vigorous preparation for the third world war!

'I could see that, for purposes of weakening the rear, the Soviet Government was industriously engaged in establishing a Fifth Column in Canada. Even diplomatic representatives were taking part, and the Communist Party within Canada had been changed from a political party into a Fifth Column for use in case of war. Meanwhile, during the peace period, this Fifth Column's work was to create unrest, particularly in labour ranks.'

In Russia - as we read in the passage quoted from *The Rulers of Russia* - the Bolshevik Revolution was not the work of the Russians at all, but it was engineered by a group of international Jews, a takeover from without. It appears that in Canada the takeover was to be undergone from within, through 'members of the public service' working with 'Russian agents' (for 'Russian' we can read 'Jewish', since Jewish individuals were directing operations in the USSR from the very beginning, and certainly until Stalin's death, see below).

Before we leave Canada for Europe, however, there is one intriguing link that should be made; and that is the link between the 'vast espionage plot' that Gouzenko detected, Pierre Trudeau, and a base for the throne of the antiChrist in Canada. I quote from the definitive biography of Trudeau:

And a constitutional task force set about reviewing each clause of the British North America Act in order to prepare for negotiations with the provincial premiers on a completely revised constitution that would bring about a renewed federalism. By these dramatic means Trudeau served notice that he was intent on breaking up the encrusted Canadian vertical mosaic where the wasps were in command. Along with French Canadians, the first beneficiaries of his auto-parochialism were Jews who were sworn into cabinet, named to the bench, appointed to head departments and regulatory agencies, and hired for ministerial staffs in unprecented numbers (Stephen Clarkson and Christina McCall, *Trudeau and our Times,* McClelland & Stewart, 1991, p.118).

Barely had I completed typing the previous quotation when Patrick Clare passed me a book from my library, *Canada-Israel Friendship L'Amité Canada-Israel* (Toronto, 1979), pointing to page 96 which has the following statement by John Bassett, then Chairman of Baton Broadcasting:

I first visited Israel in 1958, on the occasion of the tenth anniversary of the founding of the state. I was absolutely knocked out. I was totally impressed with the dedication of the people and their sense of purpose. It was one of the most exciting experiences in my life. I compared being in Israel at that time to being in Britain during the Second World War, before the Americans came in. We were alone and there we were; it never occurred to us that we could be beaten or anything of the kind. The personal, selfish ambitions were honed away by events and everybody was dedicated to the common good. That's the way it was in Israel. *Since then, I have been a total Zionist* [my italics]. I remember having discussions with the then prime minister, Mr. Ben-Gurion. He said, 'You can't be a Zionist.' He didn't say I couldn't be a Zionist because I wasn't Jewish; that made no difference to him - he said, 'If you want to be a Zionist - come here! The Zionists are here. You can be a friend of Israel' - that is great.

Mr. Bassett did not go to Israel. He remained in Canada. Three or four years ago - I can't be bothered looking up the precise date - he was appointed by our present Prime Minister, Brian

Mulroney, Head of the Security Intelligence Review Committee (SIRC), a position he still holds.

> Mooney, Mooney,
> Brian mullloonie:
>
> > 'sunyungmoon
> > sunjungsun
> > moonyoungson!'

4. CREATION OF THE SOVIET UNION:
A MASK FOR THE ANTICHRIST

'The Russian Revolutionary Party of America has evidently resumed its activities. As a consequence of it, momentous developments are expected to follow. The first confidential meeting which marked the beginning of a new era of violence took place on Monday evening, February 14th, 1916, in East Side of New York City. It was attended by sixty-two delegates, fifty of whom were 'veterans' of the revolution of 1905 - the rest being newly admitted members. *Among the delegates were a large percentage of Jews, most of them belonging to the intellectual class, as doctors, publicists, etc., but also some professional revolutionists.* . . . The proceedings of this first meeting were almost entirely devoted to the discussion of finding ways and means to start a great revolution in Russia as the "most favourable moment for it is close at hand. . . . " The only serious problem was the financial question. . . . In this connection the name of Jacob Schiff was repeatedly mentioned' (Russian writer Boris Brasol, *The World at the Cross Roads*).

WAR DEPARTMENT, AMERICAN EXPEDITIONARY FORCES, SIBERIA, OFFICE OF THE CHIEF OF STAFF, INTEL-LIGENCE SERVICES. Reports, 9 June 1919 and 1 March 1919, from Captain Montgomery Schuyler to the Chief of Staff, A.E.F., Siberia [first quotation] and to Lt. Colonel Barrows, Vladivostock [second sequence of quotations].

'Up to the end of 1918 things had been growing steadily worse in Russia ever since the first few months of the First Provisional Government, when for a short time it looked as if the new regime would be hopeless to bring some sort of modern government into the country. These hopes were frustrated by the gradual gains in power of the more irresponsible and socialistic elements of the population guided by the Jews and other anti-Russian races. A table made in April 1918 by Robert Wilton, the correspondent of the London *Times* in Russia, shows that at the time there were 384 'commissars' including 2 negroes, 13 Russians, 15 Chinamen, 22 Armenians and more than 300 Jews. Of the latter number, 284 had come to Russia from the United States since the downfall of the Imperial Government. . . .

'It is probably unwise to say this loudly in the United States but the Bolshevik movement is and has been since its beginning guided and controlled by Russian Jews of the greasiest type, who have boon [were born] in the United States and there absorbed every one of the worst phases of our civilization without having the least understanding of what we really mean by liberty. . . . It is very largely our fault that Bolshevism has spread as it has. . . .

'If the feelings of the Russian people are to be consulted and the future of their own country is to be in their hands there will be no Bolshevik future for this land. They have submitted to it first, from the very good reason that they did not know how to go about fighting it and second, because it came at the psychological moment when the morals of the people had been so shaken that they were ready to endure anything in order to be allowed to be let alone' (Stamped and verified as follows: 'The National Archives of the United States, 1934').

MR. OUDENDYKE, representative of the Netherlands Government at St. Petersburg: 'The danger is now so great that I feel it my duty to call the attention of the British and all other Governments to the fact that, if an end is not put to Bolshevism at once, the civilisation of the whole world will be threatened. This is not an exaggeration, but a sober matter of fact. . . . I consider that the immmediate suppression of Bolshevism is the greatest issue now before the world, not even excluding the war which is still raging, and unless, as above stated, Bolshevism is nipped in the bud immediately, it is bound to spread in one form or another over Europe and the whole world, as it is organised and worked by the Jews who have no nationality and whose one object is to destroy for their own ends the existing order of things' (British White Paper, 'Russia, No. 1 (1919), A Collection of Reports on Bolshevism in Russia').

ADOLF HITLER: *'If, with the help of his Marxist creed, the Jew conquers the nations of the world, his crown will be the funeral wreath of humanity and this planet will, as it did millions of years ago, tumble through the ether, devoid of men.   Eternal Nature inexorably avenges the infringement of her laws. Therefore I believe today that I am acting in accordance with the will of the almighty Creator: By defending myself against the Jew, I am fighting for the work of the Lord'*, Mein Kampf.

'[T]hose who are astonished at the alliance between Israel and the Soviets forget that the Jewish nation is the most intensely national of all peoples and that Marxism is simply one of the weapons of Jewish nationalism.

Capitalism . . . is equally sacred to Israel which makes use of both Bolshevism and Capitalism to remould the world for its ends. The process of renovation of the world is thus carried on from above by Jewish control of the riches of the world and from below by Jewish guidance of revolution. Israel has a divine mission, in fact Israel, become its own Messiah, is God. Israel is purifying the idea of God and at the same time preparing the way for the definitive triumph of the chosen race. Thus . . . Jewish power of organisation is manifested at one and the same time by Bolshevism with its delirium of destruction and by the League of Nations [and its successor The United Nations] in the sphere of reconstruction (Denis Fahey, *The Rulers of Russia*, p. 5).

'Bolshevism is an instrument in the hands of the Jews, . . . the most recent development in the age-long struggle waged by the Jewish Nation against the Supernatural Messiah, our Lord Jesus Christ. . . .

'[T]he Jewish Nation, by its rejection of Christ's message, asserted that its national life was the highest life in the world and proclaimed that the supreme test of the value of a course of action was its relation to that national life. . . . Their rejection of the Supernatural Messiah is just as vigorous today as at any time since Calvary. The world , in their opinion, must, therefore, be recast in the mould of the Jewish national life. . . . The Jewish nation thus gradually became the most strongly organised VISIBLE force working for the elimination of the supernatural outlook in society. . . . The rejection of the rule of Christ the King . . . and the gradual imposition of the Jewish mould or "form" have proved disastrous for the nations once Christian' (*The Rulers of Russia*, pp.48-55).

'[T]he mission of Israel amongst the nations [as J. Weill says in *La Foi d'Israel*] has for "its final ideal and the consummation of its destiny the setting up of a society of peoples reconciled together and morally united in a spirit of definitive peace, of social justice and fraternal solidarity." Since there is only one world and one Divine Plan for order this can only mean that the Jewish Nation by its NATURAL vigor and power will mould the nations into unity, in opposition to the Divine Plan. The result is an inevitable increase in the disorder in the Jewish Nation and in the world (quoted in *The Rulers of Russia*, p.51).

'The present world-wide socialist Movement forms the first stage in the fulfillment of the Mosaic plan; it is the beginning of the realization of the future state of the world announced by our prophets. . . . Hence all Jewish groups, whether they be Zionists or partisans of the Dispersion, have a vital interest in the triumph of Socialism. They ought to long for it, not only as a matter of principle because of its identity with the Mosaic plan, but as a tactical weapon. . . . Already the dawn of our day lights up the Horizon (Alfred Nossig, *Integrates Judentum*, quoted in *The Rulers of Russia*, p.52. In 1926 Nossig, a Jewish writer, was secretary of a league for international concord).

'[H]andbills were distributed amongst the Jews in Buda-Pesth, during the Judaeo-Masonico-Communist revolution of 1919 in Hungary, containing the following appeal: "People of Israel! with the help of our mighty ally we have fought for the revolution and we have won through. If now we all hold together and if we do not consider ourselves as Hungarian Jews, but with the tenacity of our race defend the conquered positions which will be attacked in vain, we can set up Judaea.

Make every effort to have the public positions occupied by our co-religionists. Do not translate your names into Magyar. Woe to those who will get themselves baptized! Jehovah is with us. Our centuries of exile are at an end! We shall have a new homeland between the Danube and the Theiss. Support the secret societies, for these assure to every faithful follower of Jehovah a suitable place in the new state. Szamuely will protect us" (Hans Eisele, *Bilder aus dem Kommunistischen Ungarn*, 1920).

'On my arrival in the U.S.S.R. in 1934, I remember that I was struck by the enormous proportion of Jewish functionaries everywhere. In the Press, and diplomatic circles, it was difficult to find non-Jews. . . . In France many believe, even amongst the Communists, that thanks to the present anti-Jewish purge . . . Russia is no longer Israel's chosen land. . . . Those who think that are making a mistake." (J. Fontenoy, 'Anti-Semitism in Russia,' in *Contre-Revolution*, December 1937).

'All the internment camps, with their population of seven million Russians, are in charge of the Jew, Mandel Kermann, aided by the Jews, Lazarus Kagan and Semen-Firkin. All the prisons of the country, filled with working-men and peasants, are governed by the Jew, Kairn Apeter. The News-Agency and the whole Press of the country are controlled by the Jews. . . . The clever system of double-control, organised by the late Jankel Gamarnik, head of the political staff of the army, is still functioning, so far as we can discover. I have before me the list of these highly-placed Jews, more powerful than the Bluchers and the Egonoffs, to whom the European Press so often alludes. Thus the Jew, Aronchtam, whose name is never mentioned, is the Political Commissar of the Army in the Far East: the Jew Rabinovich is the political Commissar of the Baltic Fleet, etc.

'All this goes to prove that Stalin's government, in spite of all its attempts at camouflage, has never been, and will never be, a national government. Israel will always be the controlling power and driving force behind it. Those who do not see that the Soviet Union is not Russian must be blind' (A. Stolypine, in *Contre-Revolution*, ed. Leon de Poncins, Geneva, July 1937).

Plate 33: *Stalin and Molotov, Proletarian Photo (1932)*

'The Jewish Rulers of Russia . . . did not allow Russian revolutionaries to exist in 1918. They took care, at least up to 1935, not to allow any ideas to be disseminated either in the country or outside the country, except the ones they wanted. In 1935, eighteen years after "the liberation of the Russian people," the Censorship Department in Moscow was entirely staffed by Jews. The fact is the real Rulers of Russia are not Russians but Jews' (*Rulers of Russia*, p.38).

HILAIRE BELLOC : 'Russia, then, is simply a gigantic investment by which control over vast resources has been acquired by those who are preparing for the new Messiah. They have "the enormous material advantage of vast funds such as a despotism can levy at will from the labour of more than fifty million adult men and women working on its soil, allowing as productive for revenue one-third of the gross population. All the surplus value of that labour is available, and a very large part of it is actually used for propaganda and supply in countries outside Russia"' (Hillaire Belloc, *G.K.'s Weekly* (13 August 1936), in Fahey, *Rulers of Russia*, p. 60).

WYNDHAM LEWIS: 'What Herr Hitler is required to do is to merge Germany in the league of monopolist States. The peace-loving nations are more heavily-armed than you are, Herr Hitler, and have at their back unlimited resources, and they will unquestionably make war on you, if you do not submit to their will, and if you persist in going on with this Sovereign State stuff' (*Count Your Dead: They are Alive!* p.318).

'Stalin, present ruler of Russia, is not a Jew, but took as his second wife the twenty-one year old sister of the Jew, L.M. Kagonowitz, his right-hand man, who has been spoken of as his probable or possible successor. Stalin's every movement is made under Jewish eyes' (A.N. Field, *All Those Things*, p.276).

[T]here are ominous signs of preparations, on the part of International Financiers, under cover of the war, for a natural-istic organisation of the United States of Europe and of the

World.   It will be a new and revised edition of that Judaeo-Masonic creation, the League of Nations. The Bank for International Settlements will develop its powers still futher' (Fahey, *The Rulers of Russia*, p. 23).

PEP (Secret European Agent): 'American televangelist Jack Van Impe has begun spreading a new gospel which is based on his interpretation of REVELATIONS. He sees the EC (European Community) as the rightful heir and successor of the Roman Empire. Led by the Federal Republic of Germany, heir apparent of Hitler's Third Reich and the Holy Roman Empire of the German Nation (abolished after ca. 1000 years, by Napoleon in 1806 when he demanded that Franz II of Austria renounce the Imperial German Crown), the EC will, in Van Impe's view, move against Israel, and the President of the EC will rule the world as the Antichrist from the Temple Mount in Jerusalem!'

5. JEWPETER

```
f                                              e
  i                                          r
    n                                      r
                                         e
      i                                t
        s
                                   i
          t
            e        p
          r      u
            r  j
              e
```

finn is terre
finn again
finn egans wake

Finnegans Wake
```
          ! !   ! !     !
          ! !   ! !     !
          !   !   !     Japanese
French    !   ! !       for
   for    !   ! !       'reason'
  'end'   !   ! !
          !   ! Irish
          !   ! for
          !   ! 'of'
          !   !
          !   Japanese
          !   for
          !   'coffin'
          !
          !
          !
 =    E  Q  U  A  L  S    =
The double-ended coffin of reason!
```

jewpeter
jewpeter

jewpeter
jewpeter
jewpeter
jewpeter
jewpeter
jewpeter
jewpeter
jewpeter
jewpeter
jewpeter
jewpeter

A jew the pet-
Rock of the nix-
T millennium?

pet pet pet pet pet pet pet pet pet pet pet pet pet pet pet?

PET

pep pep pep pep pep pep pep pep pep pep pep pep pep

PEP

tu es petros et super hanc
petram edificabo ecclesia meam

PIP

whoes afraid of the antichrist?
the antechrist?
the antiChrist?
whoes afraid of the AntiChrist?
Whose afraid of the GYT?

> Certainly not those who have never known
> The Christ whom we have known
> For two thousand suffe-
> Ring years.

'Once, as I knelt by the cross of Kilgobbin, it became clear to me, with an awful clearness, that there was no God. Why pray after that? I burst into a fit of laughter at the folly of men in thinking that there is a God. I felt inclined to run through the villages and cry aloud, "People, it is all a mistake; there is no God. . . . " Then I said, "why take away their illusion? If they find out that there is no God, their hearts will be as lonely as mine." So I walked the roads with my secret.

MAOILSHEACHLAINN: MacDara, I am sorry for this. You must pray, you must pray. You will find God again. He has only hidden His face from you.

MACDARA: No, He has revealed His Face to me. His Face is terrible and sweet, Maoilsheachlainn. I know it well now. . . . His Name is suffering. His Name is loneliness. His Name is abjection. . . . I have lived with the homeless and with the breadless. Oh, Maoilsheachlainn, the poor, the poor! I have seen such sad childings, such bare marriage feasts, such candleless wakes! In the pleasant country places I have seen them, but oftener in the dark, unquiet streets of the city. My heart has been heavy with the sorrow of mothers, my eyes have been wet with the tears of children. The people, Maoilsheachlainn, the dumb suffering people: reviled and outcast, yet pure and splendid and faithful. In them I saw, or seemed to see again, the Face of God. Ah, it is a tear-stained face, blood-stained, defiled with ordure, but it is the Holy Face' (Patrick H. Pearse, 'The Singer', in *Plays, Poems, Stories*, Dublin: Phoenix, pp.33-5).

> Certainly not those who have never known
> The Christ whom we have known
> For two thousand lone-
> Lee years.

6. ANATOMY OF THE 'ANTICHRIST'

Terrestial

In modern terms, the nature of the 'antiChrist' has, I think, been best perceived and articulated by Etienne Gilson, one of the truly great philosophers of the twentieth century. 'Antichrist', Gilson writes,

> is not among us, he is in us. It is man himself, usurping unlimited creative power and proceeding to the certain annihilation of that which is, in order to clear the way for the problematical creation of what will be . . . the idol . . . made with our own hands to our own image and likeness.

Gilson is careful in his wording: what he means is that the power of the antiChrist is inextricably allied to the expanding earthly powers of man, 'as he peers down into the atoms or up into the stars', discovering there a blueprint which he is capable of imposing on everything that is external to him, the whole Chain of Being above and below, maybe even on God Himself, for *the fate of God may be inseparable from that of his Creation.*

In order to grasp the complicated philosophical issues that a consideration of the antiChrist entails, it is necessary to review some basic spiritual principles.

Man is constituted of three main components: body, soul, and spirit. The soul is the organ that during earthly life mediates between body and spirit, transient and permanent, temporal and timeless, the visible physical environment and the invisible spiritual essence of which man and the universe are embodiments. On the one side, the phenomena of the corporeal world reveal themselves to the soul through 'sensation', making an impression on man's inner world, arousing an inner experience of pleasure or displeasure, sympathy or antipathy. What is retained in the soul in response to the stimuli of the external world becomes a mental image independent of the external impression. This is retained by the process of 'memory', the soul in this way linking the perceptions of the past with the perceptions of the present.

On the other side, the world of the spirit reveals itself to the soul through 'intuition', the soul being therefore the means by

which our inner being is impressed on an outer world through
'action':

A thought which arises in the spirit is translated by
the soul into the wish to realize it, and only through this
can it become deed, with the help of the body as an
instrument.

The soul itself has three distinct portions: intuitive soul,
intellectual soul and sentient soul. The 'intellect' stands mid-
way between sentinent and intuitive soul, and is of itself
neither good nor bad. Indeed, thinking is man's highest faculty,
working through the impressions of objects perceived by the
senses, and what is retained from this in memory. When man
forms thoughts, and these thoughts are attuned to the world of
the spirit without being refracted by the subsconcious, man's
focus is directed away from the sensible form and towards the
spiritual 'archetype' of these forms; conversely, a thought
picture becomes in the human soul a reflection of an 'archetype'
in the spirit world. If, on the other hand, thought is initiated
in response to the physical brain, by the life of the senses, or
by the need to rationalize social belief and convention, it
becomes arbitrary, associative, unreliable, something which
Charles Darwin in his formulation of the origin of species was
unwilling to allow.

Since we live in a visible universe, the intellect has a
tendency to use its capacities to make man more secure in his
earthly life rather than to mediate between the visible world
and the invisible realms of truth, beauty, and goodness. The
intellect has a tendency also to abstract from experience, to
apply what is true of one instance to the category which
subsumes the instance, for although the brain is the organ of
living thought, it contains also a tendency towards ossification:
thoughts that have crystallized into belief or dogma tend to take
over the intellectual life, preventing fresh thought. Thinking
becomes an affair of the head severed from the life of the heart
and the spirit; as it ossifies, the feelings detach themselves, and
intellect, divorced from spirit on the one hand and feeling on
the other, attempts to grasp reality in finite, quanitifiable terms,
explaining every imaginable phenomenon in the universe,

including the biological and psychological, as mechanical models, viewing the world as a giant machine and man himself merely as a highly complex mechanism, 'a product of *heredity and environment*, a complicated protoplasmic mechanism engineered into existence by genetic codes and DNA helixes and, by the mechanics of stimulus and response, adapted to the world around' (Alan P. Cottrell, *Geothe's View of Evil and the Search for a a New Image of Man in our Time*, Edinburgh, 1982, see pp. 283, 115, and 208).

This is the domain of the antiChrist, treating the world almost exclusively as if it were dead matter, assuming that everything can be weighed, measured, calculated; leading man into a sub-natural world hidden below the threshold of sense perception. The order which the forces of the antiChrist creates is not a picture of the world in which man is immediately living, but a picture of the world below man - the worlds of magnetism, electricity, atomic energy, DNA codes, etc. In allowing this picture to be painted, in casting himself in the role of detached observer, man has begun to eliminate himself from an active role in earth evolution. The human 'will' is subverted, even enslaved, for with the models that the intellects of those in power project and with the information that is gathered from foolproof computers and data processing, *a tendency develops to have the information itself dictate the decision, thus eliminating the human being from the process.* What is at stake is the elimination of man from the process of his own evolution, and Orwell's image in *1984* of a boot stamping on the human face forever is thus a possibility engineered, we may add, by man himself.

In the domain of the antiChrist man becomes so inured to the intellect being used as a tool to interpret the 'truths' of the external world, and, in manipulating these discoveries to suit his pragmatic designs that he comes to rely on it as an equally valid guide in the unveiling of the deeper mysteries of man and nature, of good and evil. When the intellect tries to dictate fixed principles of goodness, however, in other words when it attempts to systematize the good, it fails. While truth may be absolute, the good is never absolute:

'There is no good that is always and everywhere the

good. The good is dependent on the situation only - the good is always a good in relation to something else' (Bernhard Lievegood, Towards the 21st Century: doing the good, Toronto, 1972).

One dimension of the antiChrist is revealed in what is known as 'the reversal of values' first triggered by Nietzche's simple axiom, 'God is dead', and its corollary, i.e. you act differently if you assume that God exists from how you act if you assume that God does not exist:

From his very beginning, man had thought nothing, said nothing, done nothing that did not draw its inspiration from this certitude that there existed a God or gods. And behold, all of a sudden, there is no longer one, or rather, we see that there never was one! We shall have to change completely our every thought, word and deed. The entire human order totters on its base. Antichrist is still the only one who knows this, the only one who foresees the appalling cataclysm of the 'reversal of values' which is in the making, for if the totality of the human past depended on the certitude that God exists, the totality of its future must needs depend on the contrary certitude, that God does not exist. . . .Everything that was true from the beginning of the human race will suddenly become false, but what will become true? (Gilson, *The Terrors of the Year Two Thousand*, Toronto 1984, p.8)

The establishment of a throne of the antiChrist has been born out of the womb of a succession of visible and invisible European Empires and out of the experience of politics itself. Politics - from the Greek word *politika*, meaning citizen - is one of the devices man invents for imposing order on his public life. It does not emanate from the whole being, but is usually a machination of the mind, and not only the mind, but often the closed or one-dimensional mind, the mind obsessed by a single idea or passion. Extremes in politics are two expressions of the same impulse, the impulse to formulate, to systematize, to codify. Patterns are imposed on the people - in a democracy with their half-conscious consent - and that is why these patterns are always resisted. One system always calls its contrary or mirror image into being: there is little difference between the policies of one party in government and those it has displaced ('we become what we hate'). Politics is therefore a 'profane science . . . because it has not yet discovered it has its roots in sacred or spiritual things' (AE, *The Interpreters*, London 1922, p.39).

Empires obliterate the distinctions which are peculiar and unique to individuals and impose systems which can be as alien to the individual on which it is imposed as the mood of the scientist may be to the artist or poet (AE, *Thoughts for a Convention*, Dublin 1917). A WORLD STATE is achieved by the cohesion of things below, with the intellect as the manipulating force. The individual is remade into the image of a man-made scientifically-efficient organism. Individual energies are surrendered to energies more powerful than themselves; the more dominant the state the more the will of the individual is made incapable of effort, or even the desire for effort. We lose, as AE puts it, that 'diamond hardness which can only be maintained by continuous effort never relaxed for a single instant' (*The Interpreters*, p.114).

The price of this capitulation of the spirit, this creeping cancer of the soul, is stagnation, dehumanization, and the willingness to be a 'fractional element' in a complex mechanical entity rather than a 'complete being' in our own human ambiance.

Passivity is further engendered by materialistic sops, sports, sound systems, television, the 'black arts' of education, drugs (according to the research of Mr. Griffin, the fourth Illuminati President of the United States, George Bush, and the CIA were deeply involved in drug-running from South America and south-east Asia), the encroachment of the State on every aspect of living, despair ('Nothing to be done!'), and the subliminal hypnotic lures of technology and advertising feeding the idea that there is a paradisal material world just over the rainbow: 'We had a dim premonition,' the Rumanian poet Tristan Tzara says in 1917, 'that power-mad gangsters would one day use art itself as a means of deadening men's minds.'

Most of all, as Mary Tyrone says in *Long Day's Journey Into Night*, there is the desire to kill the pain, the pain of consciousness. The mass of humanity becomes so inured to this passivity that free will becomes an imposition, a burden that they seek to unburden themselves of:

> In every land and in all countries, the people wait with fear and trembling for the powerful of this world to decide their lot for them. They hesitate, uncertain, among the various forms of slavery which are being prepared for them. Listening with bated breath to the sounds of those countries which fall one after the other with a crash followed by a long silence, they wonder in anguish how long will last this little liberty [i.e. free will] they still possess. The waiting is so tense that many feel a vague consent to slavery secretly germinating within themselves. With growing impatience, they await the arrival of the master who will impose on them all forms of slavery, starting with the worst and most degrading of all - that of the mind. Blessed be he who will deliver us from ourselves! Alone under a heaven henceforth empty, man offers to whoever is willing to take it, this futile liberty which he does not know how to use. He is ready for all the dictators, leaders of these human herds who follow them as guides and who are all finally conducted by them to the same place - the abbatoir (Etienne Gilson, *The Terrors of the Year Two Thousand*, pp.16-7).

Gilson is speaking here of a phenomenon that accelerates towards the end of the century, and that is the formation throughout the world, and particularly in the west, of 'hundreds of thousands' of cult groups, some large with thousands - even millions - of members, others small, secretly-knit circles of 12, 13, 20, 35, etc. - huge armies of the antiChrist all controlled by the same forces and all sharing a common aim.

The Kingdom of the antiChrist, then, aims not merely at the servitute of man but at nothing less than the obliteration of *the* distinguishing characteristic of the human race: *free will*, and through that at the elimination of man himself.

Cosmological

The Four Ages of Man
He with body waged a fight,
But body won: it walks upright.

Then he struggled with the heart;
Innocence and peace depart.

Then he struggled with the mind;
His proud heart he left behind.

Now his wars on God begin;
At stroke of midnight God shall win.

This poem by W. B. Yeats evokes the spiritual evolution of man according to the esoteric tradition. EARTH, according to occult science, is the fourth stage of man's spiritual evolution. Earlier, on SATURN, the basis of the physical body, the most developed part of man, was laid down. On SUN the heart was infused into the physical organism, and on MOON the mind. On EARTH man is meant to learn to steer his own ship with the rudder of his consciousness - some call it the 'ego' - or else to yield up the responsibility for his existence to somebody else - a WORLD DICTATOR leader, the leader of a cult, or to one kind of institution or other, etc.

In each stage of his spiritual evolution, there is a struggle between the temptation to remain in the *status quo* or to yield to the possibilities of what the spirit is attempting to accomplish through matter. The spirit triumphs, and so man walks instead of continuing to crawl. He is given a heart, but it of the nature of his spiritual evolution that he cannot remain in a state of innocence. Man must move on to the world of experience and from there to the dual possibilities the Mind is capable of (see above, 'Terrestial'). The choice on EARTH is either to consolidate what he has learned and which he is capable of applying endlessly to the earth (and maybe even to the cosmos) or to surrender to the unknown, to the next phase of spiritual evolution - Jupiter, the Temple of Love.

Man is the fulcrum in the battle that is fought out at the end of time between the forces of Darkness and the forces of Light. He constitutes the pivotal *tenth* hierarchy, with nine hierarchies above and nine hierarchies below (see above, 'MM & EE'). Furthermore, he possesses a gift denied to the other hierarchies: free will. It is on that free will that the outcome of the Final Battle will hinge, and at the end of terrestial history the Forces of Darkness make their final effort to subvert free will, either through the temptation of material allurement or of yielding to the security of having somebody else do our thinking (and suffering) for us, or when all else fails in the establishment of a WORLD STATE.

EARTH is the swing-point of all spiritual evolution because on earth we either develop the power to ascend the stairway out of matter into which we have been descending since the first days or yield to John, as Milton puts it, a further second fall. Should the antiChrist succeed in achieving during the next few years the total victory that has been sought for so long, the pivotal tenth hierarchy - man - will be eliminated from the cosmic scheme of things, 'and this planet will, as it did millions of years ago, tumble through the ether, devoid of men.' What this means in ultimate terms I do not of course yet know, but I remember my old friend, Father John Kelly (who knew so much as to what was at stake), saying to me once: 'The fate of God, Bob, is bound up with the destiny of the human race.' If, furthermore, the creation of the tenth hierarchy was in the first place a way of breaking the deadlock between nine hierarchies of light and nine hierarchies of darkness, then the situation is indeed perilous.

7. JESUS CHRIST

Jesus Christ is as irregular as the lightning,
Jesus Christ is passion,
Jesus Christ is compassion,
An untamed energy shattering the dykes of the hardest
heart
- But the heart must be human.

> Jesus Christ is pain,
> Jesus Christ is suffering,
> Jesus Christ is consciousness:
> Consciousness comes at a price.

Jesus Christ is the visible mortal blossom of an invisible
spiritual impulse,
At once the 'garment' of the Divine Imagination and its
negation,
The means by which the Second Person of the Holy Trinity
Becomes incarnate and at the same time the body he cast
off on the Cross
To be 'worshipped by the Church of Rome.'

'I am convinced that . . . [spiritual] progress lies not
in dependence upon a Christ outside you but upon the
Christ in your own breast, in the power of your own
divine will and divine imagination, and not in some
external will or imagination however divine. We certainly do teach this dependence only on the inner
divinity, but this is Christianity. . . . The Christ who has
moved the world was half Indian half Greek in temper.
He saw the world as a fire of love, but from this fire fell
not Hebraic heat, the moral self-indulgence of a sensual
race - but a pure Greek light'(W.B. Yeats, *Letters*, London: Hart-Davis, 1934), pp.261-3).
'The Christian's business is not reformation but
revelation, and the only labours he can put his hand to
can never be accomplished in Time. He must so live that

all things shall pass away. . . . We must become blind, and dead, and dizzy. We must get rid of everything that is not measureless eternal life. We must put out hope as I put out this candle. . . . And memory as I put out this candle. . . . And thought, the waster of Life, as I put out this candle. . . . And at last we must put out the light of the Sun and of the Moon, and all the light of the World; we must destroy everything that has Law and Number, for where there is nothing, there is God. . . . [Y]ou cannot silence my thoughts. I learned them from Jesus Christ, who made a terrible joy, and sent it to overturn governments, and all settled order' (Yeats, *Variorum Plays*, London 1966, pp.1139-40).

'we cannot destroy the world with armies, it is inside our minds that it must be destroyed, it must be consumed in a moment inside our minds. God will accomplish his last judgment, first in one man's mind and then in another' (*ibid.*, p.1158).

The basis of a belief in Christ is a belief in the Incarnation, the unique moment when the timeless intersects time and the divine the human. It is a cataclysmic act by which the Divine Word is made flesh, suddenly giving significance to our life on earth and revealing a door for redemption from a temporal world.

The Christian view of time combines what is characteristic of the European historical approach and what is characteristic of the main Eastern religions. In the Eastern religions, time is regarded as an illusion, and salvation is seen as a withdrawal from history and from the flux of temporal events into a timeless reality. The European conception of time, on the other hand, sees time as an endless process from which there may be no deliverance; salvation is sought within the historical order, and salvation, as R. L. Brett suggests, is seen not primarily in terms of the individual, but in terms of the state, the nation, or the race.

In the Christian view, the Incarnation is recognized as the unique event that gives meaning to the whole historical process and to the lives of the individuals who form part of that process.

One of the most profoundly Christian poets of the century, T.S. Eliot, posits that the Incarnation of Christ is paralleled by the process of art and by the intuitions that constantly assail us. This is further corroborated by Gaston de Bachelard in *The Poetics of Space*. Bachelard argues that the poetic act has no past, is independent of causality, and when it presents itself to the being of the poet a 'reverberation' sounds in the heavens. All life, all art, all impulses that result in any *new* thought or object begin, as W. B. Yeats writes, in a bodiless mood, become then a surging thought, and at last 'a thing'. The image is presented to the artist *before* thought, originating from that part of the soul which is above intellect, from intuition which is our lightning rod to the spirit. Without this activity, defining and refining the human soul, man is lost in a world of imitation, repetition, or is merely an executor of orders given by somebody else.

Imagination, therefore, is the process by which man is redeemed from the temporal and historical. Christ, William Blake argues, is the Divine Imagination redeeming mankind. He is the one who breaks the perfect circle as perceived by man. 'I know of no other Christianity and of no other Gospel,' Blake writes, 'than the liberty both of body & mind to exercise the Divine Arts of Imagination, the real & eternal World of which this Vegetable Universe is but a faint shadow, & in which we shall live in our Eternal or Imaginative Bodies when these Vegetable Mortal Bodies are no more' (Preface to the fourth book of *Jerusalem*).

A truth discovered in the depths of our beings - before there is physical evidence to corroborate it - is like a force striving towards an object yet unknown; it originates in intuition and finds in the external world the 'symbols' or, as Swedenborg would say, 'correspondences' through which it grows conscious of itself in detail. And, as Yeats further reveals, imagination is always seeking to remake the world according to the impulses and the patterns of the divine world. Art, or any intuition, is therefore the revelation of a world which mere rational consciousness in incapable of perceiving, a quantum leap in the direction that the mind resists, an arc between the spiritual and sensible worlds, addressed not to the brain to be interpreted and appreciated but directly to the feeling system which is capable of grasping it before thought is actively engaged. When the image, intuition, or actual physical object is presented to the reader (the best example is our true marriage partner whom we 'know' from first sight we are going to marry, sometimes even before speaking to him or her), there is a kind of throb of resonance within, a reverberation, as Joseph Campbell puts it, 'like the answer of a musical string to another equally tuned.'

Christ, the Son of God, is an alternating current, as irregular and as unpredictable as the lightning. AntiChrist, the creation of man, is a direct current: there is no place for anything that has not already been programmed into the robot or person from whom the directions are taken or which the man has become.

The Divine Imagination

In *The Everlasting Gospel*, William Blake challenges the representation of Jesus Christ as a God of humility and sorrow. This, he posits, results from an almost unspoken conspiracy of the formulators of institutional religion to make humans subservient and passive, renouncing their own divinity and turning 'from the unfolding of their separate hearts' (W. Y. Yeats, *Mythologies*, p. 287):

> Was Jesus humble? or did He
> Give any proofs of humility?
> Boast of high things with humble tone,
> And give with Charity a stone?
> When but a Child He ran away,
> And left His parents in dismay.
> When they wander'd three days long
> These were the words upon his tongue:
> 'No Earthly Parents I confess:
> I am doing My Father's business.'
> When the rich learned Pharisee
> Came to consult him secretly,
> Upon his heart with iron pen
> He wrote 'Ye must be born again.'
> He was too proud to take a bride;
> He wrote with authority, not like a Scribe. . . .

He did not die with Christian Ease,
Asking pardon of His Enemies:
If He had, Caiaphas would forgive;
Sneaking submission can always live.
He had only to say that God was the devil,
And the devil was God, like a Christian Civil. . . .

If He had been Antichrist, Creeping Jesus,
He'd have done anything to please us -
Gone sneaking into Synagogues,
And not us'd the Elders and Priests like dogs;
But Humble as a Lamb or Ass
Obey'd Himself to Caiaphas.
God wants not Man to Humble himself:
This is the trick of Ancient Elf.
This is the Race that Jesus ran:
Humble to God, Haughty to Man,
Cursing the Rulers before the People
Even to the temple's highest Steeple,
And when he Humbled himself to God,
Then descended the Cruel Rod.
'If thou humblest thyself, thou humblest me;
Thou also dwell'st in Eternity.
Thou art a Man: God is no more;
Thy own humanity learn to adore,
For that is my Spirit of Life.
Awake, arise to spiritual strife. . . .

Humility is only doubt,
And does the sun and moon blot out,
Rooting over with thorns and stems
The buried Soul and all its Gems.
This Life's five Windows of the Soul
Distorts the Heavens from Pole to Pole
And leads you to Believe a Lie
When you see with, not thro', the eye
That was born in a night to perish in a night
When the Soul slept in the beams of Light. . . .

Crystallized Christianity, a character in Yeats's *Adoration of the Magi* concedes, may have been 'good' once, but it has become materialistic and secular:

when people are good the world likes them and takes possession of them, and so eternity comes through people who are not good or who have been forgotten. Perhaps Christianity was good and the world liked it, so now it is going away and the Immortals are beginning to awake (*Mythologies*, pp.313-4).

Institutionalized Christianity, therefore, has not fared any better than Judaism. Jewish revelation is, as a whole, situated in history, from the creation to the end of time, with the coming of the Messiah as an event in history. But, as Michael Adir pointed out to me once, 'salvation is an individual, not a racial or historical matter: to imagine that we go to heaven in posses, or that the hand of God will suddenly, at the end of time swoop down from the skies to snatch the Jewish race, and/or 144,0000 of the elect, from the jaws of the devil they themselves have created, is childish, simplistic, and unworthy of anyone into whom God has infused a mind.' Or, as British poet Kathleen Raine points out, the 'Divine Humanity is totally outside history and not a single individual but a universal divine presence within all the multitudes of humanity' (*Yeats the Initiate*, p.395):

We live as One Man; for contracting our infinite senses
We behold multitude, or expanding we behold as one,
As One Man all the Universal Family, and that One Man
We call Jesus the Christ; and He in us, and we in Him
Live in perfect harmony in Eden, the land of life.
(Blake, *Jerusalem*, p.38, Keynes, 664-5)

The 'contracted' senses, Dr. Raine comments, 'are ordinary daily awareness which shows us a universe of plurality'; the 'expanded' senses of the visionary or the man of Imagination 'reveal the unity of all things in the Imagination'.

Blake's Jesus Christ, therefore, is the divine presence in every man, the Imagination, Intuition, or higher Consciousness. 'This world of Imagination,' he writes, 'is the world of Eternity; it is the divine bosom into which we shall all go after the death

of the Vegetated body. This world of Imagination is Infinite &
Eternal, whereas the world of Generation, or Vegetation, is
Finite and Temporal. There Exist in the Eternal World the
Permanent Realities of Every Thing which we see reflected in
the Vegetable Glass of Nature.' Mankind, Blake posits, must
turn from the passive mirror of the external world to the well
of spirit in his own being, the energy that animates all matter
and frees him or her from dependence on the body and the
tyranny of historical fact:

> in your own Bosom you bear your Heaven
> And Earth & all you behold, tho it appears Without
> it is within,
> In your Imagination, of which this World of Mortal
> ity is but a Shadow.
> (*Jerusalem*, 71, Keynes, p.709)

The prophetic mission of the artist, Blake contends, is

> To open the Eternal Worlds, to open the Immortal
> Eyes
> Of Man inwards into the Worlds of Thought, into
> Eternity
> Ever expanding in the Bosom of God, the Human
> Imagination.   (*Jerusalem*, 5)

In conclusion we can say that Blake, Yeats, Kathleen Raine,
and a host of other artists 'wished to rescue the true Christ from
the centuries-deep accretions of misconception in which both
Catholicism and Protestantism have obscured and all but
hidden from the understanding [of] that numinous figure.
Christianity . . . as it has reached the greater part of the English-
speaking world in this century - is a literalized and materialized
interpretation of the sacred events of the Incarnation and the
Resurrection. . . . This is doubtless to a great extent due to the
continued pressure on Christian thought of Western materialism (the real religious faith of the twentieth century), which has
reduced the discussion of the miraculous to the literal, the
measurable and the factual (Raine, *Yeats the Initiate*, pp. 384-5).
    Christ, or His Father, then, cannot be represented ad-

equately by an anthropomorphic composite, but is a divine presence, an eddy of energy purified from everything but itself, manifesting itself in all that lives, in the shout on the street, in the wet elm leaves trailing in the laneway. Without Imagination, Intuition, and Consciousness of something beyond what we perceive through the senses, man dooms himself eternally to the 'dark Satanic mills' of his own creation - the Kingdom of the antiChrist. As Blake expresses it in *There is No Natural Religion*:

Man's perceptions are not bounded by organs of perception; he perceives more than sense (though ever so acute) can discover.

Reason or the ratio of all we have already known is not the same that it shall be when we know more.

The bounded is loathed by its possessor, the same dull round even of a universe would become a mill with complicated wheels.

8. YELL 'SIN' AND KARL JUNG

(far off) yell 'sin'
            yell 'sin'
                yell 'sin'

                    (middle ground)
                        yell 'sin'
                            yell 'sin'
                                yell 'sin'

                                    (very close, deafening)
                                    YELL 'SIN'
                                        YELL 'SIN'
                                            YELL 'SIN'
                                        YELL 'SIN'
                                    YELL 'SIN'
                                Yell 'sin'
                            yell 'sin'
                        yell 'sin'
                    yell 'sin'
                yell 'sin'
            yell 'sin'
        yell 'sin'
      yell 'sin'
    yell 'sin'
  yell 'sin'
yell 'sin'

                                                    an'
            whoes afraid of the ante-Christ?
                        the anti Christ?
                        the Anti christ?
            whoes afraid of the Anti Christ?
                    Whose afraid of THE GYT?

gyt z vd gyt z vd gyt zvd
gytzvd gytzvdgytzvdshitzvd
shit fed shitfed gytzvdshit
fed gytzvd shitfedgytzvd shit
ad
infinitum - tummy tum tum . . . .

'One fine summer day that same year I came out of school at noon and went to the cathedral square. The sky was gloriously blue, the day one of radiant sunshine. The roof of the cathedral glittered, the sun sparkling from the new, brightly glazed tiles. I was overwhelmed by the beauty of the sight, and thought: "The world is beautiful and the church is beautiful, and God made all this and sits above it far away in the blue sky on a golden throne and . . ." Here came a great hole in my thoughts, and a choking sensation. I felt numbed, and knew only: "Don't go on thinking now! Something terrible is coming, something I do not want to think, something I dare not even approach. . . . All I need do is not go on thinking." 'That was easier said than done. On my long walk home I tried to think all sorts of other things, but I found my thoughts returning again and again to the beautiful cathedral which I loved so much, and to God sitting on the throne - and then my thoughts would fly off again as if they had received a powerful electric skock. I kept repeating to myself: "Don't think of it, just don't think of it!" I reached home in a pretty worked-up state. My mother noticed that something was wrong, and asked, "What is the matter with you? Has something happened at school?" I was able to assure her, without lying, that nothing had happened at school. . . .

'That night I slept badly; again and again the forbidden thought, *which I did not yet know* [italics mine, here and throughout the rest of the quotation], tried to break out, and I struggled desperately to fend it off. . . .

'On the third night . . . the torment became so unbearable that I no longer knew what to do. I awoke from a restless sleep just in time to catch myself thinking again about the cathedral and God. I had almost continued the thought! I felt my resistence weakening. Sweating with fear, I sat up in bed to shake off sleep. "Now it is coming, now it's serious! *I must think.* It must be thought out beforehand. Why should I think something I do not know? I don't want to, by God, that's sure. But who wants me to? Who wants to force me to think something I don't know and don't want to know? Where does this terrible will come from? And why should I be the one to be subjected to it? I was thinking praises of the Creator of this beautiful world, I was grateful to him for this immeasurable gift, so why should I have to think something inconceivably wicked? I don't know what it is, I really don't, for I cannot and must not come anywhere near this thought, for that would be to risk thinking it at once. I haven't done this or wanted this, it has come on me like a bad dream. Where do such things come from? This has happened to me without my doing. Why? After all, I didn't create myself, I came into the world the way God made me. . . .

'"God knows that I cannot resist much longer, and He does not help me. . . . In His omnipotence He could easily lift this compulsion from me, but evidently He is not going to. Can it be that He wishes to test my obedience by imposing on me the unusual task of doing something against my own moral judgment and against the teachings of my religion, and even against His own commandment, something I am resisting with all my strength because I fear eternal damnation? Is it possible that God wishes to see whether I am capable of obeying His will even though my faith and my reason raise before me the specters of death and hell? That might really be the answer! But these are merely my own thoughts. I may be mistaken. I dare not trust my own reasoning as far as that. I must think it all through once more."

'I thought it over again and arrived at the same conclusion. "Obviously God also desires me to show courage," I thought. "If that is so and I go through with it, then He will give me His grace and illumination."

'I gathered all my courage, as though I were about to leap forthwith into hell-fire, and let the thought come. I saw before me the cathedral, the blue sky. God sits on His golden throne, high above the world - and from under the throne an enormous turd falls upon the sparkling new roof, shatters it, and breaks the walls of the cathedral asunder. . . .

'I felt an enormous, an indescribable relief. Instead of the expected damnation, grace had come upon me, and with it an unutterable bliss such as I had never known. I wept for happiness and gratitude. The wisdom and goodness of God had been revealed to me now that I have yielded to his inexorable command. It was as though I had experienced an illumination. A great many things I had not previously understood became clear to me. It was obedience which brought me grace, and after that experience I knew what God's grace was. One must be utterly abandoned to God; nothing matters but fulfilling His will. Otherwise all is folly and meaninglessness. From that moment on, when I experienced grace, my true responsibility began. Why did God befoul His cathedral? That, for me, was a terrible thought. But then came the dim understanding that God could be something terrible. I had experienced a dark and terrible secret (C. G. Jung, *Memories, Dreams, Reflections*, edited Aniela Jaffe (New York: Vintage, 1965), pp.36-9).

Karl Jung speaks
from otherworld   A WORLD STATE IS NEAR!
            IS NIGH! IS HERE:
            They'll try to cun trole your minds,
            They'll try to cun trole your hearts,
            They'll try to cun trole your loins,
            But they can't cun trole your God-
            Given, God-Working arse-
      SSSSSSSSSSSSSSSSSSSSSSSSSSSSSSSSSSSSS

ARSESARSESARSESARSESARSESARSE–

SSSSSSSSSSSSSSSSSSSSSSSSSSSSSSSSSSSSSSSSSSSS

ROD to EE: Oi'm goana give this world such an enema as es never known (Saturday, 2.2.92, 1500 hours).

EE: Memento homo, pulvis es
Et in pulverem reverteris.
To the GREY GYT
I say:
With parker's ink upon my thumb,
Memento homo upon my bum.

ROD: My Irish fore-
Man from Bannockburn
Shall dip his right
Hand in the urn
And sign criss-cross
With reverent thumb
Memento homo
Upon my bum.

(to the rhythm of some
marching tune), ROD
     and EE: we're not agin' gyts
we're just for the shits
we're just for the shits
an'not agin' gyts
      ad
         in
             fin
        i
          -tum
        ad
            i
          n
          f
          i
          n
          i
tum tum tummy tum tum

And again: we're not agin' zits
                    certain not agin' gyts
                  we're just for the shits
                       just for the shits
                        for the shits
                          the shits
                            gyts
                            hits
                            yts
                            its
                            ts
                             ss
                                s
                                 s
                                   s
                                   s
                                    s
                                  s
                                 s
                              s
                             s
                              s
                              s
                              s

                              s
                              s
                              s
                              s
                              s
s   s
                              s
                              s
                              s
                              s
                              s
             s   s
                              s

s

s

s

s

'Several of this cursed brood getting hold of the branches behind leaped up into the tree, from which they began to discharge their excrements on my head: however, I escaped pretty well, by sticking close to the stem of a tree, but was almost stifled with the filth, which fell about me on every side' (Jonathan Swift, *Gulliver's Travels*, 'Voyage to the Houyhnhnms' p. 182).   s

s

s

s

s

s

s

s

s

s

s

s

s

s

A

S

S

O

s

M

O   D

I

AS

Judge (Fifth Man's eldest son, Brian), decoding identity camouflaged in last letters:
No, Not You!
Try the op!
(from the threshold of substance and nothing, a girl materializes):
I Am Amodio!
Bearing a palm!

9. THE PACIFIC TRIANGLE

Judge: Amodio!
What does it mean?

Amodio: I love God. Nick
Name of Sin. Sent
To Paaa syph ic try
Angle.   New   Name: Sin -
Bad! Go-be
tween three sides
tri angle
an' the hole in the middle,
ov me bum -
vat sixty-one -
There's a hole in the middle of me bum
an' the hole in the ooooooooooooooooooooo-
Zone layer
Is been plugged by voooooooooooooooooool-
canic ash from the South Paaa syph ic (Pacific) - yes, an'
Environmentalists are usen it as an op. to make money,
moooooooooooooooney,
mooney, brian mul loooooooooooooooooooooonie.

Judge: Bailiff, where's this chick cumin' from?

Bailiff: She is speaking of something that is shrouded in secrecy and of which, perhaps, she should not be speaking (in hushed tones) - the Pacific Triangle. I have only the vaguest details myself. Only the Rat Child and the Rocking fella . . .

Judge: This cave is inviolate, protected. Whatever she is trying to say defies my decoding device which, as you know, I carry in my left sock.

Bailiff: I am a middle man and I am certain, Your Horseshit - now, Your Honour, I knew you would start, but you made me promise to call you 'Your Horsehit' just for today (18 July 1992) - I am certain that the girl has a very great deal to say. She is the go-between for the three sides of the triangle - the most infamous, ingenious, and diabolical Triangle ever constructed since man was let loose from the Garden and Lemuria. This little slip of a nineteen-year-old girl is, as I say, the go-between, the dark moon of the forces at the apex. They use her body as Leda and the Virgin were used - Zeus and the Holy Ghost understood, but not the girls, the development of whose bodies, as with all of humanity - let us not forget Saturn -is in advance of the development of their minds. This girl is the Dark Moon of the Triangle. It is through her, and of course without words, that the three sides can best communicate.

> *Judge*: Let her give a tongue
> To what she has felt
> As the three tongues of fire
> Found her in the dark
> And as I should like
> To find her tonight
> Should she so wish:
> Now speak pretty dish.

> *Amodio*: M as
> on Ri
> M or M
> on
> is M
> De W
> DA
> IS èèèèèèèèèèèèèèèèèm MMMMMM

>   is M
>   is M
>   is M
>   ism
>   DUEDAISMèèèèèèèèèèèèèèèèèèèèèèèèèè!

Judge: 'Tis okay, my dear. You can speak plain here. What do
we have?

>   Masonry!
>   Mormonism!
>   Judaism!
>   The three sides of the Pacific Triangle!
>   Forces 'hind the WORLD STATE!
>   Forces 'hind the AC:
>   I'd like to know more.
>   What do you have on Mason
>   Ri?

Amodio: First you have the WASP
>   - fill er phillip -
>   With the Mace on,
>   King Alfred's Plan,
>   True dough in the middle
>   And the Vatican
>   Where the Masons, Mormons,
>   And Mafia meet Jews
>   An' Illuminati
>   For this is the Head of the CIA
>   The central in tell i gence a gen ci -
>   Good place to keep
>   A breast of the world 'vec
>   ou sans
>   silly cone -
>   Pappleship galoreèèèèèèèèèèèèèèèèèè!
>   Pappleship galore!

Judge: Yes, indeed, pappleship galore. Intriguing! And the
Mormons?

Bailiff: I have a short case history. Called by its adherents 'the Church of Jesus Christ of Latter-Day Saints'; founded by Joseph Smith who, in 1829, claimed to have received 'divine baptism'; in 1837 a bank founded by Smith at Kirkland failed, and the sect was forced to move on to Jackson Co., Missouri, where Zion, 'the New Jerusalem' was founded; in 1843 Smith received a revelation about 'plural marriages' and began to act on it without making it public'; tried to join the Union as the State of Deseret - this was overruled when the State of Utah was founded; polygamy officially practiced, 1852-90; Masonic roots to the secret Temple-endowment ceremony; Church's ruling body made up of twelve; members expecting the millennium; members capable of attainment to Godhead.

Electronic hook-up by radio, television, and satellite between all 7.8 million members; fastest-growing church in the world; active in 134 countries and growing at a rate of 300,000 members a year.

I quote from *The Articles of Faith*: 'We believe in the literal gathering of Israel and in the restoration of the Ten Tribes; that Zion (the New Jerusalem) will be built upon the American continent; that Christ will reign personally upon the earth; and, that the earth will be renewed and receive its paradisical glory.' *Judge*: Mason-based and Jewish-connected! I should have guessed.

Who fished the murex up?
What porridge had John Keats?

And they're all goana be gods! Big G or small g, Amodio? Thas watt I ask.

Funny and eerie that - they're all hooked up electronically. At least one person knows where everybody is. Which one will the fountain bless? No doubt about the blood sacrifice.

I get leetle shivers down the crack of me back. One more thing! Any deterrent on membership, people joining? *Bailiff*: Well actually, Your Horseshit, no blacks are allowed. That doesn't seem to be written down, but you don't see anything of - what Ross Perot used to say - of 'those people' there.

Judge: Good on you! Women?

Bailiff: I fear, Your Horseshit, they are excluded from the naves of the churches and central temple ceremonies.

Judge: Less happy about that! (*moves rapidly towards inner chamber door*).

Amodio (rising in the full blossom of her womanhood): I must add, Your Horseshit, what I have found out from my own woman-to-man research in bed with the Mormons. The decision is made for the Mormon by what they call 'the voice of God'. They go to a ceremony three times to confirm what they have 'heard'. Then after half a year involved with the 'religion' they get a 'card' with their past and their future engraved on it, down to the number of children they are to have.

Judge: You mean no place for own decision, intuition?

Amodio: No, Your Horseship, the decision is made for them. Follow your card.

Judge: Well I'll be blowed.

Amodio: Jesus Christ is a tool to them. I do not desire to stay with them, My Lord. Forgive me for speaking my heart, Your Horseshit, but I desire to go with you, nor merely for the protection but for the anticipation - I have never treated my body as merely mine - of what I could not help but see beneath your cloak as I spoke . . .

Judge (walking slowly towards girl, like a bull in a field):

Look, child,
I'm old enough
To be year dad
With or with
Out a pre dee lick
Shun for in
Cest.

(*Turns to court*):

We'll take her in
To balance - 'Yell sin'.

10. THE THINKING TANK OF RUSSIA

Dominos stand
Dominos fall
Dominus, domini, dominium,
An' the thinking tank of Russia goes on, goes on,
Goes on with gorba chev,
                          crew chev,
                                chev
                                      chev
                                            chev chenko
            A drop-off and adir,

The United Snakes of Amer eeeeeeeeeeeeeeeee ca
Spread themselves out too far, too far,
Spread themselves out too far.

But the thinking tank of Russia goes on, goes on,
Goes on with gorba chev, a drop-off, and Adir
                    Think thank
                    th ink tank
                     Tink tank
                     Tock tick
                    Think tank
                     Tick tank
                     Tock tank
                     Tock tank
                     Tick Tock
                     Tick Tock
                     Tick Tock
                     Tick Tock
                     Tick Tock
                          a
                          d

                          i
                          n

f

i

n

i

t

u

m

.

.

.

.

.

Public Prosecutor: Headquarters, please?
Fifth Man: Oh, they would be
                                                    all over.

Public Prosecutor: Purpose, Please?
Fifth Man: The future ov course.
                        The present is child's
                                                    play.
*(Fifth Man realizes he is talking into a machine, even though it makes
its sounds from the body of a man)*

Ratcher   ratcher   ratcher   ratcher rice lodges
Ratcatcher rice lodges   ratcatcher rice lodges
                    CATCHER RAT TAR STAR
                                                    t
                                        a   s
                                r
                                tsar tsar tsar tsar tsar

Spread themselves out too far, too far
and where is the missing czar,
Too far, too far, and where is the missing czar?

11. A SONG FOR ALL SPIES

Oh, the FBI and the CIA,
The KGA and the KGB,
Asses, Asses, Stasis,
An' all the little sissies -

Pull down your pansies,
Pull down your pansies,
Pull down your pansies,
Pull out your bugs,
The bugs in the pants
    Of the sissies.

Oh, MI5 an' MI Eight-
Teen, MI8 an' MI Six-
Teen. OI am (who am)
    From MI8,
Spice that looks after the spies,
Spies that look after the spoils.

    Marsi pansy
    Marsi gansy
    Marsi pansy
    Marsi gansy

    Good for the sissie
    Good for the gansy
    Good for the pansy
    Good for the sissie.

    Highline him!
    Highline her!
    Take her to sea,
    Billy!

The sissies begin to sing: We are stardust,
                                   We are carbon,
                                   We are the condoms
                                   Of rising scardom:

                                   The bugs of the thugs of the sissies,
                                   The ants in the pants of the sissies,
                                   The rats in the slats of the sissies.

ratssrraw, ratssraw, starwars, starwars, ratsraw

             star wars
                       a
               t   r   w
            a   s
          r

12. THE FIFTH MAN

The fifth Man?
Karencross?
Karen on a cross?
Givin' the info out
To a new wave of 'em
Cummin' in - like Christ

go gika, go gika, go gika
go gika, go

Astrologer: 'There are some people, Robert, who know . . .
Fifth Man: You mean *encode* . . .
Astrologer: *Encode*, if you wish, so much they have to be
crucified.

No, not Cairncross!

7
6
6
1
1
7
3

I
dee-
          clare
I
am
          the fifth man

Of the Burgess-Maclean-Blunt-Philby astro
Logical cell. Chosen this way: 'That missing short nut
From Aath-lantis. Still not found? Send an IQ edict
Through the empire. Choose who comes first -
The man.'

I came third!

there are   two wrecked
        two wrecked   women,
                women, two wrecked
                women, women
                wrecked: one
                was murdered!

                I often wonder
                Where the other
                Is. 'Though tracked
                'Fore her birth,
                She may be closer
                Than any one thinks.

                                I
                        dee-
                clare
                        I am
                                        the fifth man

                The one who can
                Tell the storie

                Let he or she
                Who says I lie

                        STEP

FORE   WARD

                I am the fifth man!
                What of the fifth w-
                        ommmmmmmmmmmmmmmmmm
                -an?

13. THE FIFTH MAN, MR MOI,
AND CHINESE INTELLIGENCE

When ice cubes
In tall glasses
Clink
I very sell dem
Stop to think.

Fifth Man to Chinaman: See cure all
Inform ation
You can re
anti Christ.

Chinaman: Ante-christ who?

o o o o o

Fifth Man: I have a lot in moy command
The silver slipper,
The silver swan,
& the silver strand.

I am frum New Fur lan';

OI get moy messages from the sound of glass
OI get moy messages frum a piece of ass . . .

Pope (*in helicopter overhead*): Peace . . .

Fifth Man: Piece not Peace!
OI am not
Mr Moi.
He reeeeeeeeee-
Members nothing
Of the urn and the ring-
SSSSSSSSS of Sat-
Urn. Mememormee. Vibrations

    In a room. Christian
Rosencrutz! Lps. The keys to
    gheavin!

               How do I reeeeeeeee-
            Member? The seal of Aath-
        Lantis on Gorby's fore-
      Head and the blue
    Print of her thighs:

I am the fifth man,
She is the fifth w-
ommmmmmmmmmmmmmmmmmmmmm an'

        We get our mess-
          Ages direct frum
          Sat-
            Urn.

A Chorus of Atlanteans:
          We are the beginnings
          From whence they all came,
          We are the survivors of Atlantis,
          Where the anima is the sea
          And the animals the seals,
          We are the survivors of Atlantis.

                EE: What is water
        But the generated soul?
           k
    Fifth Man: I Ching!
           b

oi get moy messages frum the sound of glass
oi get moy messages frum a piece of ass

Pope (emphatically in helicopter overhead): Peace!

> *Fifth Man*:   Piece! Not Peace!
> OI am not Mr. Moi!
> OI am the fifth man
> An' oi'm wid the fifth w-
> ommmmmmmmmmmmmmmmmmmmmm
> an'. We didn't make love lass night,
> We did the day before
> As two udders:
> Sat 1 feb 92.
> Let it brew for o dea and a half:
> The dope came up like maggots in my head.

'I was indoctrinated into the greatest counterintelligence secret
in the Western world - the VENONA codebreak. To understand what VENONA was, its true significance, you have to
understand a little of the complex world of cryptography. In
the 1930's, modern intelligence services like the Russian and the
British adopted the one-time code pad system of communications. It is the safest form of encipherment known, since only
sender and receiver have copies of the pad. As long as every
sheet is used only once and destroyed, the code is unbreakable.
To send a message using a one-time pad, the addresser trans-
lates each word of the message into a four-figure group of
numbers, using a codebook. So if the first word of the message
is 'defence' this might become 3765. The figure 3765 is then
added to the first group on the one-time pad, say 1196, using
the Fibonacci system, which makes 4851. It is, in effect, a double
encipherment' (Peter Wright, *Spycatcher*, New York, 1988, p.
227).

> I am the boy
> Who caught mr moi,
> Head of AC Intelligence.
> Voynaya gave the tip
> From the pit to the tip,
> Voynaya gave the tip to me.

TIP PIT TIP PIT TIP PIT TIP PIT TIP PIT TIP

"When I finished studying the Venona material in the special secure office where it was stored on the fifth floor [of MI5 Headquarters in central London], I moved into an office with Evelyn McBarnet, Arthur's research officer [i.e. Arthur Martin, responsible for Soviet Counterespionage, code name `DI']. . . .

'Are you a Freemason?' she asked me almost as soon as I joined her in her office.

'No,' I replied, 'and I don't approve of it.'

'I didn't think you looked like one, but you'd better join if you want to be a success in this place,' she told me darkly" (*Spycatcher*, p.238).

When ice cubes
In tall glasses
Chink
I very - 'sell dem . . . .

'Years later I arranged for Meredith Gardner [who broke the cryptographic code from a Russian codebook found on a battlefield in Finland] to visit Britain to help us on the British VENONA. He was a quiet, scholarly man, entirely unaware of the awe in which he was held by other cryptanalysts. He used to tell me how he worked on the matches in his office, and of how a young pipe-smoking Englishman named Philby used to regularly visit him and peer over his shoulder and admire the progress he was making' (*Spycatcher*, pp.234-5).

venona

novena

'VAT'. 'I CAN'.

14. FIFTH MAN SMASHES JEWISH INTELLIGENCE

Was Philby *sent* to Moscow?
As 'passport' officer in Is-
Tanbul in '48, he was heard
        To sing:

        '48 an' '84
        '84 an' '48,
        Pitch and toss,
        Add the moss,
        Make the matzoh:
        Salt, eggs, white
        Ground pepper,
        Ginger, oil, and powder,
        Water, meal, and chicken stock.
        Meek and mild,
        A Christian child:
        BLOOD LIBEL! 88:
        Three years of grace,
        Time runs out. ANTI-
        Christ! Files are open:
        ADD THE MOSS:
        THE INSTITUTION!

15. FIFTH MAN PAUSES TO GET VALIUM

Sqews me, 'fore I go on,
I must get blue valium
From my black trinidadian
'Fore I go on. For oi
Know mr moi is head of chink
        Info-
        Maaa
        Tion.

16. FIFTH MAN IS SENTENCED BY HIS SON

(Fifth man is led into the court to be sentenced for his possession of unauthorized knowledge, is about to speak when he is interrupted by the MOB which overcrowds the court:

jewbeatajewbeatajewbeatajewbeatajewbeatajewbeatajewbeata
jewbeata
jewbeata
jewbeata
jewbeata
jewbeata
jewbeata
jewbeata
jewbeata
jewbeata
jewbeata
jewbeata

Fifth Man addresses Mob: I have nothing against the Jews except this matter I have now dealt with: the matter of the antiChrist, and this only relates to *some* Jews.
                    a
          (*Brien, in role of Judge, enters court*, black glasses, clothes ragged of the   a   northern streets, or the torn leopard clothes of a tropical   e   jungle, totally in control of everything except himself, e   gyrating furiously on the inside of the judge's bench as   a   he sentences his DAD, and at the same time tentative with   e   the gestures of his hands.

Sentences father:

      C

    A

      N

          A

             D

               A

Amanuensis of Court: Can DAD?
                         Put DAD in a CAN
                         Like an old pro gram!
                         Karen on a Cross
                         For the BIG BOSS!

(Amanuensis stumbles out of court, shaking his head, befuddled, going off to the roads, as the books say, to be stricken by the injustice of the skies.

Judge: What else today: There's this: *Star* clipping, *Trudeau veers towards madness.*

And this (reading): 'Vienna, Reuter: Nazi hunter Simon Wiesenthal has urged the Roman Catholic Church to reassess the Spanish Inquisition, comparing its repression of non-Catholics to the anti-Semitic policy of Nazi Germany 500 years later.

'"I know it would be impossible to repeat all those thousands of trials," Wiesenthal was quoted as saying on the Catholic news agency Kathpress yesterday.

'"But it should be done in some cases so as to create a monument forever and to prove that the Church distances itself from all these atrocities and rights violations.

'The Inquisition, founded in 1481 by Spanish Queen Isabella

and her husband King Ferdinand, tortured and executed thousands of people it termed heretics in both Spain and its colonies.'

Judge (scratching a knot out his long brown hair, and smiling to the point of a snicker):

What the gyt
Want next? Re-
Do the trial of
- Jay sus!
10-16

17. FIFTH MAN IDENTIFIES 'ANTICHRIST'

Informer:	AC's down to two.
Fifth Man:	Who? PEP or PET?
Informer:	Now I forget!
Fifth Man:	Now I remember!
	True Dough or PEP si . . .
Voice of Europe:	True Dough is a paeon.
Voice of North America:	PEP is a prince
	Clearing the path.
Voice of Europe:	A germ or a pole?
Austrian Cell:	A German, we think,
	But there seems
	No one red-
	Di. Have
	To be Pole.
	In terms of
	Dubh les.
	Your new phew JP?
	Your friend JP?
	The ACE
	JEAN PACE!
	Bane of the Lumen
	At eeeeeeeeeeeeeeeeeeeeeeeeeeeee.

           Should also say:
              As a sop
           To yellow race
        It's been offered Japan -

        - Jap an an' Jap Inc. -
- Japan Incorporated on the dark Persian Gulf -

           Control everything else,
           Would want it ov course,

                    Con-
           Vex eyes wait:

           Japan may say 'no'
           Can't for
               get
                    hero
                       shee ma

        An' so

A dark horse appears in the paddddddddddock:

           Here's what we see:
        The ACE knocks out PEP
        With her dying breath,
        Fifth Man's ousted T,
           Leaving the race
           When Chas is ass
                    ass
               in   ate   d
        To the light-bearer of darkness,
           the small double   p

        THE BIG DOUBLE   P:
THE NEW HOLY ROMAN EMPEROR OF EUROPE!

'London - A plan to have Princess Anne serve as regent if the Queen dies before Prince William reaches adulthood has been drawn up by Britain's Privy Council. . . . The tabloid *Today* said the plan was put together by Prince Philip himself, out of concern that his son Prince Charles is not up to the job of king . . . Philip "has accepted for some time now that his son is not king material" (*Toronto Star*, 20 January 1993).

Where does the Queen stand?

'with everything that's happened she [Diana] could still be queen.' (*Toronto Globe and Mail*, 14 January 1993).

Newfoundlander:

> my father
> me son
> my boy
> Philip of Mace on
> Donia etait apres tout
> Le pere d'Alexander
> Le Grand! Abra-
> Cadabra! Abraham-
> Man! Wid
> Abraham an' Isaac?
> 'Twas onli a test!
> Is a[nne] ac?
> What did Philip of Mace eh
> Donia say of his son?

Con sort out all,
Grinding
Grinding
Grinding
What his minions are finding
In the outposts of the world.

SU and US
US and SU

Grinding
Grinding
Grinding
In the winepress of his garden
All those did not come him
Of their own will -
Outcasts of the anti-
Christ.

OUTCASTS OF EUROPE!
OUTCASTS OF EARTH!

JUP must be squeaky
Technologically clean,
Squeaky clean from the
very begin
at least
at last!

Did you not know
That akashic
Record can be made
To skip
an'
th'
neadle

jump

Like ordinary phono machine
An' the deeds of one man on earth be
Ascribed to another after d ea[r]th?

No? All is not lost!
How ard Con?
I am told a particle

of white light
        Penetrates the black pool, dubh-
              lin
          sta lin
         krem lin
       Winds or phil be
             (kbg) knows,
   Tells with his Inca eye twitching:
    In a kiss in jer tongue:
         sch off man
         sch off man
         sch off man
        Grounding ga
       Grounding ga
     Grounding ga *geasa*

geasa geasa geasa geasa geasa geasa geasa geasa geasa geasa:
             grounding ga gas

       'Spen Sir'

     Mr. Mills knows
     - see Marz i pan -
     Find grinding Dan

        'fore

  Chas an' his

     mum

        are

    ass   ass
                 in
     ate

         dead

18. RED SEA AGAIN

Highest stakes ever
Since the Big Bang!
Two AC's left?
At the most three!
ONE of the C?

Move over, moy son,
OI'm cummin
Through:

R
E
D

S
E
A

A
G
A
I
N
!

Make it your own
Wattever you need.

19. THOSE WHO ARE FOR US ARE FOR US
THOSE WHO ARE AGIN US ARE AGIN US

Wid Liam Miller holding the tip
Mount Forest held in the pit -
Compliments of Morris.

Did you not know?
Mount Forest's in the Bible:
'Those who are forus, Mt. Forest,
Those who are agin us,
A   G U I N   N E S S.'

NOTES FOR 'SPYSONG'

PRELUDE

Philby: Harold 'KIM' Philby, see note below, 'KIM'.

Lugh: Celtic God of Art, Light, Creativity, and Forgiveness.

ROM: Royal Ontario Musuem, located on Queen's Park Toronto.

greymen: otherwise known as the Gnomes of Zurich and said to control the economics and politics of the world, the Grey Men have supplied the money for practically every war during the last three hundred years *to both sides*.

ab: the eleventh month of the Jewish Calendar.

ra: Egyptian word for 'king'.

ABRACADABRA: Cabalistic word supposed to have magic powers in formal incantations; when written trianglularly is capable of curing disease, rectifying what has gone wrong.

ABRAHAM: The first patriarch and ancestor of the Hebrews.

The 13th tribe: generally acknowledged to be the lost last tribe of Israel; said by some to have been lost or absorbed among the Celtic tribes.

Isreal: i.e. 'is real'; also, of course, 'Israel' scrambled.

is a[n] ac: on another less obvious level, Isaac, son of Abraham and

Sarah; father of Jacob and Esau.

DC AC DC AC: direct current, alternating current.

F A G A R I: Slang Greek word for 'moon'. On another level 'ARI' is an abbreviation for ARIHMAN, Persian God of Materialism who, at the end of time, attempts, with Lucifer, to destroy the spirit of Christ.

ari: an Irish colloquialism, not meaning very much, used commonly at the beginning of a sentence.

Diana: ancient divinity associated with the moon and the hunt; later associated, probably as a result of Etruscan influence, with the Greek goddess Artemis, the virgin huntress and patroness of chastity.

KIM: Komunisticheskaya Internasianalnaya Molodiej, The Communist Interational Youth Project; also Harold 'KIM' Philby (PHIL BEE), *third man* of the famous British espionage cell consisting of Guy Burgess, Donald Maclean, Anthony Blunt, and one other, *the fifth man*, who has not yet been identified; all of the records in secret British archives relating to the *fifth man* have been destroyed behind him. Our sources indicate that he is still very much alive and operating.

After 'defecting' from British intelligence in 1963, Philby went on to become Head of KGB, an extremely significant move in terms of this volume, for by the move the British (i.e. Philby and his associates) assumed control of Russian and Soviet Intelligence. Burgess and Maclean 'defected' in 1950 and 1951 during Stalin's weakening years. Just a few years earlier, during the Second World War, the British had taken control of American and Canadian Intelligence in order to manoeuvre America into the War. In terms of the movement in this century to establish a Kingdom of the antiChrist, British Intelligence, or at least some components of it, have been ideally positioned to observe the intricacies and configurations of the movement.

GRAAAAAA: 'GRA', Irish word for 'love'.

the big T O: local way of referring to Toronto in Canada.

TO-DEA: 'today', but the reference is also to the Honourable Fabian O'Dea, past Lieutenant-Governor of Newfoundland, and to Masonic rituals and records.

DESIUL: ancient Celtic ritual, ceremonial equivalent for what some moderns call 'black magic'ritual,

1. MM & EE

Tenakis: Greek for 'greetings'.

Arthur: the village in Ontario Canada where ROD and EE live.

ansi: all the lands that Federal Governments have specified to serve as collateral for national loans. This principle of collateral, to be initiated soon, has not yet been made public, but it has been discussed and secretly agreed upon.

The Big Bang and The Big Crunch: A front-page article in *The New York Times* (5 January 1993), headed 'Discovery Suggests Invisible Mass may Halt Expansion of the Universe', reads in part:

> An X-ray astronomy satellite has discovered the first strong evidence that the universe may not expand forever, but could someday be brought to a halt by its own mass.
>
> There is not enough visible matter to halt the observed expansion of the universe. The Big Bang theory of the universe's formation predicts that most of its matter should be in invisible form, but so far astronomers have failed to turn up evidence for anything like as much "dark" matter as the theory requires. After the results reported today, however, at least one part of the universe has as much dark matter as predicted, and astronomers can now hope to find many others. Success would mean the universe is not open, meaning it is destined to expand forever, but closed. In a closed universe, the gravitational force of its matter is enough to match or exceed the outward force of expansion. The observations, reported at a meeting of the American Astronomical Society, supported theories that most of the universe is composed of invisible material of an unknown kind. Analysis of the data indicated that the mass of that "dark matter" might be as much as 25 times greater than that of ordinary matter, the elemental stuff of visible stars, planets and people. . . . "It's the first time there is evidence of enough dark matter to support the idea that the universe is closed."
>
> Cosmologists have contemplated two alternatives to a closed universe. If there is not much mass, the universe might be open and keep on expanding, diminishing into infinity; or with considerably more mass, the universe might be dragged to a halt and then collapse, in what is described as the Big Crunch.

2. MARZIPAN

mar zi pan: confection, earlier the small box containing the confection. The Arabs brought this confection to Europe.   In tribute to its preciousness, the word which describes it has meant 'a seated King', 'a little box', 'a stamped coin'.

Pan: Son of Hermes; Greek god of flocks and shepherds; pagan expression of a Christian impulse.

But if Pan?/Megapan us?   But what if Christ is only the Christian equivalent of Pan, a 'Megapan us?' The lines suggest the horror of what it would be like to have a Christ without a divine component.

us and su: and its recurrence in the poem, suggests an interlinking between the destiny of the United States and the former Soviet Union.

They agreed just on her: In terms of the mythology of *Spysong*, the United States and the Soviet Union agreed in 1987 that a woman from the Japanese warrior class be found to heal the Grail Knight (hero of this section of the work) fighting on the graveside of Western civilization, so that the opportunity afforded man to move on to the next stage of spiritual evolution not be missed.

Metapanus, Kepheus, Cassiopeia, Pan, Christ the King, etc. suggests some kind of former glory sustaining the earth, distant now, but waiting, ready to return.

Metapanus: Venetian coin with the figure of Christ on a throne.

Kepheus and Cassiopeia: Kepheus (Cepheus), husband of Cassiopeia, was placed among the stars after his death. The constellation of Cassiopeia is the brightest in the sky.

'vec: avec.

Nigatu . . . Alyas: surname and first name of Ethiopian child adopted by ROD and EE, 19 February 1991.

Eli: High Priest of Israel.

elohist: unknown author of those parts of Hebrew Scripture in which the name `elohim instead of `Jehoval' is used for God.

eli lambech: Last words of Jesus Christ on the cross, mistranslated and misquoted by Jewish scribes, i.e. Pharisees, as Christ calling on Elijah.

Chorus of hierarchies: According to the mythology of *Spysong*, Christ rose from the dead for three days only, returned to earth where he was betrayed once again by the *blackpeters*, i.e. those who do not accept

Christ and who prepare for their own man-created Messiah at the end of the second millenium.

Mars: Christ's body is placed on Mars to signify the wars and quarrels that are connected with his name on earth.

Marsi: people of the sabellian race who dwelt in the centre of Italy, magicians descended from Circe.

Circe: according to Homer, daughter of Helios (the Sun), distinguished for her magic arts.

ic: from panic, integrated circuit.

AE: Irish visionary painter and poet.

A BE: The astrologer-magician who, through his cultivation of the powers of Arihman and Lucifer, prepares the occult underpinning of the WORLD STATE.

Ariham: ancient Persian God of Materialism who works through time with Lucifer to bring on the Era of the antiChrist.

San Diego: on the coast of California, is reputed to be the home of the 'Grey Men'.

PC: Patrick Clare, who helped with the construction of *Spysong* (see *Nato and the Warsaw Pact Are One*, p.28).

Hermes Trismegistus: son of Zeus and source of all esoteric knowledge.

Nineteen times nineteen equals: Both the Bible and the Koran have recently been subjected to computer analysis, with the numbers nineteen times nineteen appearing encoded beneath both sacred books. The fact that the multiplication of the numbers equals three hundred and sixty-one, one beyond the perfect circle as perceived by man, suggests that there is a sacred precedent for seeming anarchy, for breaking the 'perfect' circle.

What appears as anarchy to the multitude may represent a high and lonely order to the few, and indeed the latest theory of physics suggests that there is an order behind chaos.

Baitman (BC): Bob Conroy, pilot, baitman, and metereologist in the area were we live.

Mr. Mills: poet, composer, and magician who appears always at the end of the millenium. Although a cultleader, he is in some ways a neutral figure, his sense of style, of balancing both sides and seeing the preposterousness of both, makes him a neutral figure, in a way redeeming him from the impossibility of his own situation. He is more conscious of the way he sounds and seems that of the phenomenal *results* he is capable of achieving.

Togail Bruidhe Da Derga: an ancient Irish saga which charts the destruction of a House which has violated its *geasa*.

geasa: ancient Celtic equivalent of Polynesian *tabu*. Certain strictures are placed on individuals, curtailing their movement on earth. Suggestive of the sacrifice the hierarchies must make to work out certain things on earth, as, unlike man, the hierarchies do not have *free will*.

met and wept/tears of Christ: In Montenegro, white wine is known as `tears of Christ'.

The fall . . . : James Joyce, *Finnegans Wake*, pp.3-4. The appearance of Mr. Mills means that a second fall is possible, a fall deeper and deeper into matter, to the point where the polluted spirit will find its counterpart for a while, to be further polluted, and to fall ever further: escape out of matter becomes impossible..

Transmission from Jupiter: I do not have the slightest idea where this came from. I found it among my papers in a hand I do not recognize. From what I do understand of the transmission, it seems extremely relevant here. 'Rot a peck of pa's malt', from the first page of *Finnegans Wake*, is in the transmission.

Put out your shoes: According to a Dutch custom, in early December St. Nicholas and Zwarte Piet (Black Peter, who is a kind of shadow of St. Nicholas, see below, 'Fifth Man Pauses to Get Valium') would visit the children, rewarding the 'virtuous' ones with marzepan and the others with black diamonds, coal. The diazepam has been added, see below, section 15.

Anal: beginning of Satanic ritual in which all or some of the hierarchies of Hell are summoned; 'Anal' means 'I call'.

Ab: the llth month of the Jewish calendar; also local Mount Forest man known as the 'Hitman of Hell'.

Abaddon: angel of the bottomless pit of Hell (*Revelations*, 9.11).

oikesis, i se sis: from the Greek word, ecesis, which means the successful establishment of a plant or animal in a new locality. This process is meant to relate to the whole of this and the succeeding section.

Cisseis: King of Thrace; according to some, father of Hecuba who, later, was metamorphosed into a dog, leaping into the sea at a place called Cynossema, or 'the tomb of the dog'.

cissoid; Greek word with reference to a curve converging into an apex.

SIR CA: Above CSIS is the Security Intelligence Review Committee (SIRC), a 'cabinet-appointed watchdog ... to delve into CSIS activities, ask tough questions discreetly and publish sanitized annual reports to reassure Canadians that CSIS is not running amok' (Editorial, *Toronto Star*, 23 May 1992). Above SIRC is 'Ottawa's ultra-secret Commumications Security Establishment (CSE) . . . a Big Brother agency whose activities, unlike those of CSIS, are *not* limited by parliamentary statute' (*ibid.,Toronto Star*). CSE and its computers have eormous espionage capabilities:

> CSE listens in to radio and telephone communications between embassies in Ottawa and their home countries, or between embasssies and their consulates; monitors all national and international telephone calls; listens in to many foreign radio communications and reads the electromagnetic transmissions from embassy typewriters, word processors, etc. (Jack Granatstein and David Stafford, *Spy Wars*, Toronto 1990, p.22).

The *Toronto Star* (30 May 1992) notes: 'Canadians should keep in mind that little known government agencies like the Communications Security Establishment (CSE) are spending millions of tax dollars to do clandestine work, he [Quebec lawyer Pierre Cloutier] says, "Who are they spying on?"'

Me-ca-cack: Information relayed to me by an MI5 agent (see note below, *Kelly*); suggesting that 'Me-ca-cack', whose identity can be determined from *Nato*, is a middle agent between the British Government and the Vatican who has sold out to both sides.

Kelly: Father John Kelly (1911-86), President of St. Michael's College Foundation and Director of Alumni until shortly before his death in September 1986, was the main sponsor and supporter of my entrepreneural work at the University for over twenty years until he was, suddenly and without warning, transferred after 50 years in the College to a small house in Northern Ontario.

Never before in the 130-year history of the College had a retired priest been treated in this way. Shortly before leaving, Kelly speculated to me that there may have been some connection between the sudden order to move and the work I was involved in at the University.

In February, I launched a national campaign to have Kelly reinstated. A major story was published in the Toronto *Globe and Mail* on 10 February 1986. Two days after the story appeared, an MI5 agent known to me (actually it was my contact with the Prince of Wales) came to my office at the University and relayed the information contained in the following stanzas published in *Nato*:

'The man
who gave the order
to kill John Kelly
was not a priest,
Bishop, cardinal, or pope,
But a lay catholic here in T O.

'We have documentary evidence
that he is running guns
to Northern IRELAND' - MI5.

'We thought he was running them
to the other side' -
THE SUPREME COURT OF ONTARIO.

The agent actually said: 'The man who gave the order to move John Kelly . . .' but since Kelly was dead eight months after the move, the substitution, we feel, is justified. Kelly was not in good health, but let us say his life might have been prolonged if he had not been subjected to this physical and psychological harrassment (see *Nato and the Warsaw Pact Are One*, pp. 53-5 for further details).

The little black box: See Robert Redford's *Sneakers*, also *Nato and The Warsaw Pact Are One*:

'The little black box is on at last.'

What brought it forth but the Dragon Fly?

Taim: Irish contraction for 'I am'.

The first intimation . . . : The report of MacKenzie King addressing the Canadian Parliament is a from an unidentified newspaper or journal account that I found among the papers of Charles Pyper, War Correspondent of the *Toronto Telegram*, when I purchased them from Hugh Kane in the mid-seventies; Mr. Kane was then President of Macmillan of Canada. The account may have been written by Mr. Pyper himself. The copy of Gouzenko's *Fall of a Titan*, that I also purchased at the same time, has the following inscription: 'To C. B. Pyper - my best friend - in appreciation of your magnificent efforts to defend freedom of man everywhere - with respect and admiration, Igor Gouzenko, Nov. 7, 55.'

Conrad O'Brien ffrench: secret espionage link for Britain between the first and second World Wars. In 1940 ffrench introduced Lord Martin

Cecil to Lloyd Meeker and together they founded the Emissaries of Divine Light for the purpose of laying the foundation of the next two-thousand-year religious dispensation. The Cecil family were a key family in creating the British Empire in the sixteenth century.

5. Jewpeter

Finn again: Joyce, like Vico, Yeats, and Spengler, contended in *Finnegans Wake* that history moves in cycles of two thousand years, and that we shall move out of an age where the limited focus of the intellect is dominant into an age of age, as McLuhan put it, of full acoustic resonance, 'Finn again'. Finn is the pagan Irish hero who, before the age of paint, ushers in the last two-thousand-year-old cycle. The suggestion here is that despite the plans of man, history may have its own independent movement. Cosmologically, it is suggested that the Pacific Triangle will arrange for the new Peter of the next phase of spiritual evolution, Jupiter, to be Jewish.

tu es petros: Thou are Peter and upon this rock I will build my church.

6. ANATOMY OF THE ANTICHRIST

Apart from the specific references in the body of the text, I am indebted to a number of sources for this section of the argument which I have published in another form in 'A Greater Renaissance: A Revolt of the Soul against the Intellect,' in Wolfgang Zach and Heinz Kosok eds. *Literary Interrelations: Ireland, England and the World*, Tubingen: Gunter Narr Verlag, 1986, 3, 133-4. The esoteric sources I have consulted are Rudolf Steiner, *Theosophy* (London 1973), *An Outline of Occult Science* (New York 1972), *The Metamorphoses of the Soul* (New York, n.d.), *The Michael Mystery* (London 1956), *The Occult Movement in the Nineteenth Century* (London 1973); Karl Jung, *The Undiscovered Self* (New York 1958); Joseph Campbell, *Myths to Live By*; W. B. Yeats, *The Works of William Blake* (London 1893), *Mythologies* (London 1961), and *Essays and Introductions* (London 1962); and my own *Celtic Consciousness* (Toronto and Dublin, 1981).

9. YELL 'SIN' AND KARL JUNG

gyt: is the Polish for 'Jew'; anglicized 'gyt'; more properly 'zvd'.

Memento homo: 'Remember man, dust thou art/And into dust shalt thou return,' the words of the priest on Ash Wednesday as he marks the cross of ashes on the suppliant's forehead, reminding him of his destiny as far as this world is concerned. Joyce uses the phrase in *Gas from a Burner* as indicative of the fickle free will of man.

identity camouflaged: Asmodias, one of the lower hierarchies of hell.

10. THE THINKING TANK OF RUSSIA

A drop off: play on Andropov, President of the Soviet Union in the early eighties; also 'A drop off', literally a change of direction, or change of heart, from a course to which one is already committed; sudden renunciation of past activity and commitment to an alternative course of action; suggestive also of 'a drop off' from a space craft.

chev chenko: Russian espionage agent, Shevchenko, who seems to have defected the   Americans.

Ratcher: Masonic references.

12. THE FIFTH MAN

Cairncross, who claimed to be fifth man on the strength on his nuclear connections. The fifth man had nothing to do with passing nuclear secrets, nor was it necessary to pass those secrets through espionage agents.

go gika: fragment of a Yugoslavian espionage code.

13. THE FIFTH MAN, MR MOI, AND
CHINESE INTELLIGENCE

oi get my messages: the reference is to the Rings of Saturn, which is associated with the loins, and a deeply encoded wisdom revealed in the act of physical love.

Blood Libel, as defined in a recent article in Now Magazine, is an alleged practice alleging that 'Jews stole a Christian child on the Passover and used the blood from a mock crucifixion to make unleavened bread' (June 1993).

16. FIFTH MAN IS SENTENCED BY HIS SON

10-16: 'Pick the prisoner us at . . .' (Owen Sound Ontario Police 10 code).

17. FIFTH MAN IDENTIFIES 'ANTICHRIST'

Jean Pace: Jean Forsyth Pace, to whom the book is dedicated.

dubh: is the Irish for 'black'; 'les', left-handed; also doubles.

me father, me son, me boy: a Newfoundland commonism which suggests the unshakable trinity of father, son, and grandson.

Abraham-man: wandering beggar of the 16th century; either a lunatic or one who feigns lunacy.

akaskic record: the record in the heavens of all that transpires on the earth.

How ard Con? 'ard' is the Irish for 'high'. The reference is to Con Howard, Irish diplomat, to whom *The New World Order & The Throne of the antiChrist* is dedicated.

lin: is the Irish for pool.

kiss in jer: Henry Kissinger.

sch off man: In cosmic terms, man is the tenth hierarchy, with nine hierarchies above him and nine hierarchies below. It is suggested earlier in *Spysong* that man was created to break the cosmic impasse between darkness and light, to provide, in Geothe's terms, the canvas and the colour through which these polarities can communicate. If the movement for the establishment of a kingdom of the antiChrist is successful, and a World Dictatorship is created, then that marks an end to man's free will: the tenth hierarchy will be obliterated: thus 'sch', i.e. 'switch' off man. Father John Kelly said one, 'the fate of God is bound up with the human race'. This suggests that God - or God and His Antithesis - created the world, cast the dice, then disappeared within his own handiwork: how he emerges again into the full power of his being depends upon the leavening bread of the earth, but the situation is, as 'Anatomy of the antiChrist' shows (above), indeed perilous.

19. THOSE WHO ARE FOR US ARE FOR US

Liam Miller: now in the macrobistic world, was the publisher of four of my books and, since the Yeats sisters, the publisher of most of the poetry to come out of Ireland during the later part of the century.

Mount Forest: small town near Arthur Ontario.

Morris: Morris Wilson, daring pilot in the area where ROD and EE live; close friend of the O'Driscolls.

2. Обязать Министерство государственной безопасности СССР направить в ссылку на поселение государственных преступников, перечисленных в статье 1-ой, освобожденных по отбытии наказания из исправительно-трудовых лагерей и тюрем со времени окончания Великой Отечественной войны.

Направление в ссылку на поселение этих лиц производить по решениям Особого совещания при МГБ СССР.

Председатель Президиума
Верховного Совета СССР
                                        (Н.Шверник)

Секретарь Президиума
Верховного Совета СССР
                                        (А.Горкин)

Москва,Кремль
" 21 " февраля 1948 г.

Председатель
Совета Министров Союза ССР
                                        (И.Сталин)

Управляющий Делами
Совета Министров СССР
                                        (Я.Чадаев)

Plate 34: *Signatures of N. Shvernik (Chairman of the Presidium of the Soviet Union), A. Gorkin (Secretary of the Presidium), J. Stalin (Chairman of the Soviet of Ministers), and Y. Chadaev (Head of the Administration of the Soviet of Ministers), 1948. The two-page document, of which we only reproduce one, decrees that people in prisons, spies, terrorists, Trotskyites, anarchists, nationalists, potentially anti-Soviet 'elements', etc. should be sent to the far east and the far north, to Siberia and 'the deserts of Kazakhstan' after they have served their prison sentence, as they might prove a subversive element in Soviet society.*

RUSSIA

PART I: Michael Adir, Nikita Khruschev & Kim Philby

by Robert O'Driscoll

In May 1991 I was invited by the Irish Organizers of the 'European City of Culture' Festival to give a performance reading of *Nato and the Warsaw Pact Are One*, first at the Guinness Gallery where the EE of this work (Elizabeth Elliott) premiered her film of the poem (directed by Antony Lorraine); and, about and a month and a half later, at their world-famous Abbey Theatre: on 5 September 1991.

Minutes after the reading, a gentleman in the Irish Diplomatic Service, Con Howard, introduced us to a lady, Margarita Ivanoff-Dubrowski, and a quixotic gentleman, Michael Adir. Adir, EE commented later, had a face that was a 'paradox of passion and control, eyelashes casting a shadow on alabaster cheeks, jet-black hair flecked with grey that seemed to dance from the lower temple along the crown to a hook at the nape of his neck. And indeed, there was a hook, bronze with studded emeralds, that held the hair, rattail, swirling downward to his leather belt: an impeccable buckle of wisdom and youth - my mentor in the flesh.'

This magnetic personality, who, it was clear from the very beginning, could only be a mover of cogs in Soviet Intelligence, asked whether he could see me the next day: 'I shall be in the Arts Club all day. Come at any time.'

At five he arrived (Margarita, he told me, had gone on to Washington), holding *Nato and the Warsaw Pact Are One* open in his hand at page 27. He did not speak but ran his finger silently over the following lines from the 'Transmission of the Belgium':

Then the persecution starts. It will start in the Middle East [the lines were written in 1989, long before the Gulf

War], and very soon the whole world will be involved. You may try, but you can't figure it out astrologically. Did He not say: 'I will confuse you, but you who know the signs will reco . . .'

The big question is: Who is the Beast? He exists, is known internationally, is or was the Prime Minister of a country. . . .

At this point he stopped suddenly, saying 'You are referring, of course, to' - and named the name.

My breath stopped: 'How do you know?' I asked.

'I have known for some time. I leave on a plane for Russia tonight at 9. At 5 p.m. tomorrow I have a meeting with Michael Gorbachev. It would help us greatly if you would give me an annotated copy of *Nato and the Warsaw Pact Are One*, identifying the local Canadian figures, as well as other international personalities, whose identities have eluded us.'

I looked as far as I could into his burning eyes, finding there an integral combination of passion, sincerity, and concern. I glanced first at EE whose eyes were affirmative and full, then at Con who seemed to be staring vacantly into space but whose eyes were dancing with understanding. I had known Con for twenty-five years, and indeed he was known in my circle as 'The Ambassador's Ambassador'. I was, I felt assured, reading him right, so I did not hesitate for a moment. I sat down with my address book and in half an hour my new-found Russian friend had all the information he wanted.

Elizabeth and I returned to the small village in Ontario where we live, called - appropriately enough - Arthur. About the end of September, we were told that the Land Registry Office in our village was to be closed by the Ontario Government, and the public records removed to a new private company called - again appropriately enough - Polaris. Sensing that this had something to do with international manoeuvres, but not knowing precisely what, I telephoned the two numbers Adir had left me - one in Russia and one in the United States. I found him in the States. He told me that he would come to Arthur and give Elizabeth and me a little 'grind', as they say in England, that it was time we understood the 'larger picture'. He could not, of course, say when or by what means of conveyance he would arrive.

It was early on the morning of 25 October 1991. Elizabeth was letting our dog, Kolton, out for his morning ramble. She opened the front door, talking to Kolton, totally absorbed, until the glint of an object at the end of the veranda caught her eye. There he was - Adir - delicately illuminated in the morning light, and at the same time silhouetted against the hectic gold and reds and yellows of the trees that surround our Big House (as they call it in Ireland), head cocked, sniffing the air, half-looking at the sky, half-amused by Elizabeth's surprise.

Arm in arm they floated through the front door. I was half-way down the staircase. We met and the three of us drifted into the front parlour. A few lines from one of my Armageddon poems swam into my mind:

> O radiant dark moon
> On the risen dough
>   of the earth!
> Did not Pythagoras know
> The first number as three?
>
> And those all-knowing Druids
> On that magic isle
> To which we three relate!
>
> Three in one and one in three!

"That", Elizabeth declared when I had finished, "penetrates, with unselfconscious canniness, to the very heart of espionage and the magic and unbridled love which are part and parcel of it. But first let us clear the decks!" She picked up the phone, spoke briefly to her mother who has never let her down (in fact, one of my publishers said to me once, "There's not many people in this part of Ontario who don't owe a debt of gratitude to Frank and Marion Elliott'), and laying down the phone, turned to us: "Mom will pick up Krystel and Andrea and keep them for the weekend."

Plate 35: *Nikita Khruschev, President of the Soviet Union, circa 1963. 'What did Khruschev say to Kennedy when they met in Vienna? "Let's exchange lists. We'll only have to pay them once" . . . Imagine Kennedy didn't know who his own double agents were, and don't make out he was a dunce 'cause he wasn't. While Khruschev knew that they were all working for the same side – I wasn't, but Khruschev didn't know about me . . .'* (Nato and the Warsaw Pact Are One, Zespol: Warsaw and Toronto, 1990, p. 28).

ment>r stayed with us all that day, leaving shortly before dawn on the 26th. But what a twenty-four hours it was, spent for the most part before our pulsing woodstove in the back parlour.

He began by clearing up the matter of the Land Registry Office. The national debts of countries, he said, were to be redrafted, with land being used as collateral. In preparation for this, governments had for some time been designating particularly valuable ecological and resource sites as 'environmentally sensitive' (in Canada 'ansi' is the term used to designate such sites) and had been introducing legislation to deter owners from developing the land.

He then turned to what he called 'the big picture', but first of all, he insisted, he had to 'present his credentials'. He had, he told us, been born on 31 July 1940 - he did not display any reluctance in revealing this, with all the astrological implications: the 'cosmic cell', he stated enigmatically, was holding. In 1958 he joined the Russian Army, and within a few months has been assigned to Voynaya, the secret Intelligence Divison. In December 1963 he received a letter, marked 'Confidential and Secret', from none other than Nikita Khruschev, appointing him Special Intelligence Officer 'to monitor all cults throughout the globe and any movement that could bear any resemblence to a potential World State'. He was to report what he discovered, 'no matter how trivial,' to one man and one man alone: Mr. Harold KIM Philby, who had just arrived in Russia and who could be contacted at KGB Headquarters.

Elizabeth and I had heard the phrase 'World Conspiracy' from time to time, but always, like most others, we had scoffed and glanced toward heaven. "The first thing you must realize is that since 1917 the rulers of Russia were not Russian but Jewish, that The Soviet Union has been since its establishment a mask or 'bogey man' for the Jewish movement for their long-awaited Messiah."

"There is nothing religious or theological about antiChrist," he went on. "Christ's message was one of sharing, compassion, and love - love of God and love of our fellow human being. AntiChrist relates to money, bureaucracy, power, the obliterátion of free will, and the eternal mulcting of the vulnerable by the predators in the palaces. It is not merely a Biblical phenomenon: it is a historical reality. The details are those of what is called `The Pacific Triangle' - the pact between Judaism and Masonry at the end of the eighteenth century, with the base being provided by the Church of Mormon in the nineteenth century. The `bottom line' of it all, as your financiers say over here, is a World State where not even a fly will be free to move.

"We are on the threshold of that World State right now. Just about all of our leaders, including our own charming Gorbachev, have sold out. The only flies in the ointment are a few international Intelligence personnel who have the triggers coded in their genes and a few others who have the knowledge and the power to set up road-blocks, diversions, switch the pre-arranged signals and send the whole ratpack running round and round forever, but never in the direction they have planned. We are all on the ground now: the heavens, so to speak, have fallen to earth. You two are critical; you have been tracked for a long time. We must always be aware though that some scouts have their fangs sharpened for our throats."

The sun had passed the yard arm. I went to the freezer, cracked a bottle of Extra Zytnia, reminding Adir that Vodka was made first not in Russia but in Poland. He nodded. I poured three glasses, and for the next several hours he outlined, from almost every conceivable angle, the pre-meditated plan to clear the way for the Kingdom of the antiChrist.

"But how can you be sure of all of this?" Elizabeth asked.

"There is first of all my own 28 years of monitoring, with a trusted staff, all the publications of the world, our corroboratory research, our checking, our re-checking. Then there is the brilliant and valiant work of the greatest benefactor humanity has had in this century, my superior officer, KIM Philby. Mr. Philby I cannot speak about in public: there are still too many of his network in sensitive positions. But I can tell you a few things. Philby `defecting' to Communism in 1963? A doctrinaire Marxist? What rubbish! Philby was a doctrinaire nothing! He was and remained to the end his own man! And as for the Burgess-Maclean-Philby cell passing atomic secrets, which all the commentators keep coming back and back to like a broken record - that too is rubbish. The Atom Bomb and Hydrogen Bombs were passed directly from the White House to the Kremlin in 1944 as part of the preparation for the Cold War. The glib explanation - atomic secrets - was a ploy, a cover-up for what was really going on.

"There is another dimension: few knew the Jews were in control in Russia, but more than most people think. Do you think that Philby would not have known Denis Fahey's *Rulers of Russia*, published in 1938 (most copies now have been removed from the libraries by Zionist terrorists) which lays out the whole antiChrist plan? Do they think that the most brilliant twentieth-century spy was an ignorant fool, that the penny would not have dropped earlier with him than with most?

"Why also would Philby defect to the Jews when his main interests were Arabic? Let us explore for a few minutes the depth and passion of those Arabic preoccupations! There is, first of all, his father: St. John Philby who did a degree in Oriental Languages in Trinity College Cambridge, mastering Urdu, Persian, Arabic, Baluchi, Pushtu and Punjabi. Later, he renounced what he called 'the perfidy of England' for behaving with such duplicity towards the Arabs during the First World War. He never forgave England and turned Muslim, dressing as an Arab, eating camel meat, etc. In 1925 he moved to Arabia, becoming the business advisor to King Saud in his transformation of Saudi Arabia from a biblical desert kingdom into a twentieth-century oil state. When the King died in 1953, St. John Philby took up residence in Damascus and then in Lebanon, where he had a house in the mountains outside Beirut, dying there on the Feast of St. Michael and all His Angels on 29 September 1960.

"This house is doubly important. When commentators say KIM was marooned in Beirut between 1956 and 63, pining for England, drinking himself to death, we must remember that he was with his father: at home. As for the nationalism that sustains the common Englishman, Philby was no more nationalistic than his father. What did he say once? "I was born in India, brought up in various parts of the Arab world, and

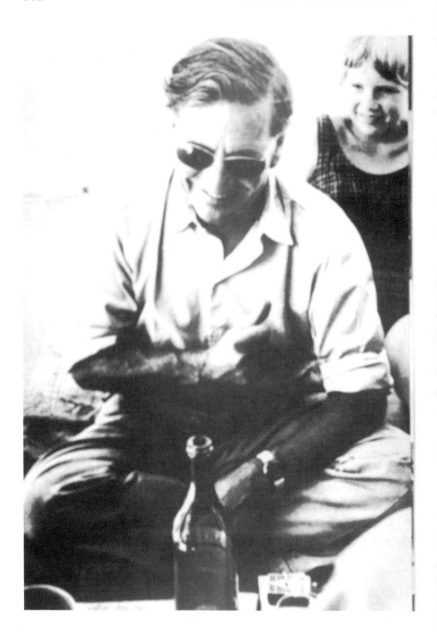

Plate 36: *Harold Kim Philby, greatest Intelligence director in the twentieth century, Beirut, about 1961. Like his father, Philby preferred to drink sitting in cross-legged Arab position.*

I was at school in England. I don't feel that I have any nationality."

"The second significant point is that it was in that house that Philby had stashed a wealth of material on the same subject that Khruschev later was to ask me to focus. Philby's material dated back to the mid thirties and on 27 January 1963, very early in the morning, all the boxes were loaded onto a Turkish truck, driven to the Syrian border with Philby posing as a Turkish diplomat. He then made his way across Syria and into Turkey, and using contacts that he had assiduously built up 'on the ground' years earlier, he literally walked into Soviet Armenia. The papers followed."

"I met Philby once," I ventured, "in '61 or '62, but the Queen and Prince Philip were there at the same time and there wasn't much opportunity to talk." Elizabeth's eyes grew rounder and bluer as she surveyed me. I had not talked with her about this before. Nor had I with anybody else. "Did he share the same passion for the world of the Arabs as his father?"

Adir rose and took the poker, stirring the fire, while at the same time blotting it out with his slight athletic form: "So," Elizabeth told me later he said, "that is where the link might be. How strange the ways of Providence! How moving!"

He turned, the elongated iron hanging from the thumb and forefinger of his left hand. "His first job - in the early thirties - was as an editor/writer with the *Review of Reviews* and one of his articles, maybe even his first, was `Lawrence of Arabia'. More significantly, he spent his spare hours in the office - and there were many of them - learning Arabic, filling exercise books with immaculate translations and careful exercises in grammar. Later, as a correspondent for *The Observer* and *The Economist* in Beirut, he was cited as "easily the most pro-Arab foreign journalist stationed in the Lebanon." While there, he maintained close links with a group of Arab Nationalists, mostly Palestinian refugees, and travelled widely, filing copy from Riyadh, Damascus, Sharjah, Bahrein, Bagdad, Teheran and Cyprus. Between 1956 and 1958 he travelled no less than 20 times to Cyprus. Remember he was still working for the British Secret Intelligence Service (MI6) although practically nobody knew it.

"Why was Cyprus so important."

"Because he was preparing to penetrate the Iron Curtain at its most vulnerable. Remember Philby did not, like Burgess and Maclean, arrive in Moscow by plane. Philby arrived in the Soviet Union by foot, and he was in such a precarious situation that he could neither turn back or at times hardly go forward: he was at one and the same time toppling, or perhaps I should say `turning on their backs', the concealed espionage networks of two of the three main players: Britain and the Soviet Union, and already he knew the innards of the CIA. That was why they were so irate, sending a hit team to Beirut, but the `red fox', as a group of us used to call him, had slipped away hours before they had the authority to act.

"Once he had blazed a trail to Moscow, he would have a human chain behind him - breakable but breathing - all the way back to Cyprus and beyond. Like Peter the Great, he knew that all he had to do was arrive, and with Burgess and Maclean firmly established in Moscow, he knew the trap was baited, that the Rat could not possibly escape this time. The plan worked, and even before he took control of KGB, Philby knew that the Jew, after almost 50 years in power, would finally have to retreat - not from all positions at once, but from those that mattered, the hidden hinges on which a country turns.

"Why was Cyprus so important? Remember Philby had worked there in a number of secret British establishments in the early fifties, but he spent most of his time not with the British but with the Armenian community. Many's an evening he spent at the Armenian cultural exchange, the Melkonian Institute, calling enthusiastically for what he cited as the `set-my-people-free' songs performed by Armenian folk-groups. Why? He realized very early in the game, even before he went to Cyprus, that he would penetrate the Jewish Iron Curtain from where it was most vulnerable: Armenia.

"Why Armenia? First of all, we have to acknowledge that the Armenians are an interesting people. They have settled throughout the Middle East, and other parts of the world, but they have always maintained their connection with the Armenian homeland which is north of the Caucasus range that divides

У К А З
ПРЕЗИДИУМА ВЕРХОВНОГО СОВЕТА СССР

Об образовании Комитета государственной
безопасности при Совете Министров СССР

Президиум Верховного Совета СССР п о с т а н о в л я е т:

Образовать Комитет государственной безопасности при

Совете Министров СССР.

Председатель Президиума
Верховного Совета СССР
(К.Ворошилов)

Секретарь Президиума
Верховного Совета СССР -
(Н.Пегов)

Москва,Кремль.
13 марта 1954 г.

Plate 37: *Document of the Presidium authorizing the foundation of the Committee of State Safety (KGB), 1954.*

Turkey from the Soviet Union. Like other persecuted minorities, they have long been accustomed to the idea of secret and underground communication; and being a remarkably shrewd, determined and energetic minority, they are exceptionally good at it. The Iron Curtain may have seemed a brick wall to the civil servants of London and Washington, but it did not cut off the inhabitants of Soviet Armenia from their fellow-Armenians throughout the Middle East, and there were several well-established channels of communication. A message could travel from Soviet Armenia to the Armenian community in Cyprus within a relatively short period of time. To boot, as you say Robert, the Armenians on both sides of the Curtain looked alike, could almost be interchangeable.

"This is how Kim Philby and his cell took control of Soviet Intelligence and at the same time penetrated Jewish Intelligence.

Philby had, it is clear, been preparing for this moment since 1948 when he was a `passport officer' in Istanbul. That was when he took his famous photograph of Mount Ararat, the twin-humped mountain that stands on the border of Turkey and the Soviet Union. Hmmm, I wonder. 1948? The year of the founding of the State of Israel! The year of the setting up of Mossad! How deep does this thing go? It seems though as if, from the very inception of the Jewish State, somebody from within the very organization that had established it was already in place to pull the plug at any time. Who? There is always a `Judas'. This time it may to be on our side. An eye for an eye and a tooth for a tooth!

"And who is responsible for the chain of circumstances by which we three could meet? Honestly I do not know, but it is heartening!

"Philby? Who really was he working with? Someone in Britain? God? The Holy Spirit? Was he `sent' to Russia or was he working totally on his own, his cultivated stutter and broken accent giving him those few extra seconds he needed to survive? In any case, he walked into the bear's cave and the bear walked out! Slainte!"

PART II:

RUSSIA, FROM THE FIRST WORLD WAR
TO THE DEATH OF STALIN

The material published below has been selected by Robert O'Driscoll and Margarita Ivanoff-Dubrowski from Des Griffin's Descent Into Slavery, *pp. 61-78 and pp. 108-15*

RUSSIA UNPREPARED FOR FIRST WORLD WAR

On the Eastern Front the bloodletting was even more horrendous. Following the Russian defeat by Japan in 1905, the Czar realized that his nation didn't have the ability to fight a modern war. As the war clouds were gathering over the European continent, it became obvious that if the Russians were to be in a position to defend themselves, and to honor their Slavic treaty obligations, their whole army would have to be reorganized, re-equiped and retrained. The Czar told his generals that this mammoth task, despite an immediate crash program, couldn't be fully carried out until 1920, and that it was necessary to maintain the peace until such a state was reached.

When the war erupted in 1914, Russia, despite the fact that she possessed the largest army in the world, was woefully unprepared for a major conflict. Russia was faced with a grave decision. She would either have to back down, repudiate her treaty obligations, lose face, be the laughing stock of the world and become a fifth-rate power - or she would have to fight. Russia chose the latter course, in the realization that victory would have to be rapidly achieved or that an unprecedented national catastrophe would result.

HUNDREDS OF THOUSANDS
WIPED OUT WITHIN A FEW DAYS

Except in the area of manpower, the Russians were outclassed. The best Russian artillery could only fire four miles, whereas the German equipment could fire seven miles; artillery duels amounted to mass murder. To add to Russia's hideous plight, their outmoded guns were limited to just a few shells a day.

The German army was supplied with modern equipment but many Russian divisions were reduced to one rifle for every four men: the remainder were armed with pitch forks and axes. . . .

Although the Germans had no respect for the Russian army as an intelligent fighting force, they did have the utmost respect for the courage and tenacity of the Russian troops.

As action continued on the Eastern Front, a pattern developed that was repeated with great regularity over the following three years. Forty to sixty thousand Russian troops would be in the forward trenches on a given morning. By midday the majority of them would be killed, wounded or in disarray under the devastating onslaught of German firepower. The well-supplied modern German guns - artillery, machine guns and rifles - took an almost unbelievable toll on the Russian forces.

The ill-equipped Russian army was superior in one area: manpower. As the bodies of the dead Russian troops piled up in the trenches, on the barbed wire entanglements and in front of the German machine gun positions, the Russian generals poured in hundreds of thousands of additional troops to take their place. One German officer later testified that the machine gun positions under his personal command spent three full days mowing down wave after wave of Russian troops, as they strove to overrun German positions. Although the German army was utilizing all the equipment at its disposal to haul ammunition up to the front lines, their efforts met with failure.

They couldn't get the ammunition to the front fast enough to stem the endless tide of Russian troops that was being thrown against them. They had to abandon their positions and retreat, in spite of the fact that German casualties were numbered in the dozens while Russian fatalities were listed in the hundreds of thousands in just a few days.

THE BRITISH CROWN BETRAYS RUSSIA

Prior to the outbreak of hostilities in 1914, the Crown had promised Russia total aid and military support in the event of a war. Following the commencement of the war British aid to Russia was cut back to ten percent of what it had been prewar. It is obvious that the Money Monopolists - operating in perfect harmony with the Illuminati plan outlined in Albert Pike's letter of August 15th 1871 - wished to place Russia in as perilous a position as possible.

General Nicholas, uncle of the Czar, understood that the only hope for Russia lay in an immediate, decisive victory. With this objective in mind, he immediately launched a furious assault with two Russian armies into East Prussia. He aimed to cut a path through to Berlin, and achieve victory by capturing the German capital. In the Battle of Tannenberg (August 26 - September 15, 1914), the Russian Northern Army stopped Hindenburg while the Southern Army swept through the forests to be at Hindenburg's back. When it appeared certain that Hindenburg would be crushed and Berlin taken, orders came from London to stop the advance and hold positions on both fronts. Obviously, such a stunning victory would have proved disastrous to the financial vultures who planned to reap an inestimable harvest from the bloodbath they had only weeks earlier unleashed across the European continent.

What happened next on the Eastern Front is of the utmost significance, and demonstrates the power of the 'hidden hand' in international power politics.

While the Russian Northern Army was under orders to hold its positions, von Hindenburg, who was later lauded as being a 'brilliant military strategist', virtually abandoned the northern front, rushed most of his troops to the southern section - leaving his northern front exposed and undefended in the face of the Russian Northern Army - and counter-attacked. Von Hindenburg's combined armies smashed the Russian Southern Army in a struggle in which fatalities far surpassed anything experienced on the Western Front.

With half of their regular army deployed elsewhere, the

Russians rushed all the reinforcements they could find - old men, farm boys, wounded soldiers - to the southern front in a despairing effort to stem the flow of von Hindenburg's onrushing forces. Their efforts were in vain.

The International Banker-engineered-defeat at Tannenberg and Mazurian Lakes destroyed the Russian Second Army and gave the Germans a clear edge in the ensuing months.

Russia was aided by large numbers of Slavs who defected from the German side. This enabled Russia to form a 'Czech Legion' of over 100,000 men. Russia continued her losing struggle for another two and a half years.

MASSIVE GERMAN OFFENSIVE EASTWARDS

In 1915, German reinforcements to the Eastern Front made it possible for them to launch a massive offensive. By September the Germans had taken all of Poland and Lithuania and were advancing eastward. In the process of losing Poland and Lithuania, the Russian army had suffered another million fatalities. In the 'Brusilov' counteroffensive in 1916, which reached the Carpathian Mountains before being stopped by the arrival of fresh German reinforcements, Russia lost another million men. Following this new national catastrophe, Russia was in a state of physical and financial collapse. Despair gripped the whole nation.

The conditions created by this national trauma were greatly exacerbated by specially trained Illuminati agents who were busily fanning the flames of discontent, particularly in the more densely-populated regions. As the Illuminati philosophy thrives on strife and uncertainty, they met with great success in their efforts to set the scene for the revolution that was planned to follow Russia's defeat at the hands of the Germans.

Revolution erupted in February, 1917. The Czar abdicated, and a provisional government took over, headed successively by Prince Georgi Lvov and Alexander Kerensky. This, however, failed to stem the slide towards national disintegration.

'BAND OF EXTRAORDINARY PERSONALITIES'

As the situation continued to deteriorate, the Illuminati-International Banker cabal was making careful preparations for its final assault on the nation which had, in the past, proved to be a fly in the ointment as far as its plans for world conquest were concerned.

In New York, Leon Trotsky, who had arrived in the United States on January 13th by a circuitous route to avoid detention by European authorities, applied himself with fiendish diligence to assembling what Winston Churchill later described a 'band of extraordinary personalities.' These formed the nucleus around which the political leadership of the planned revolution was built.

Although he had no visible means of support, Trotsky lived in a fashionable apartment **and** rode around in a chauffeur-driven limousine. He was frequently seen entering the palatial residence of Jacob Schiff, the Rothschild agent who, some forty years earlier, had taken over control of Kuhn, Loeb and Company, the international banking house, on behalf of his European masters. Schiff had come into his own on the American financial scene some years earlier when, in his capacity as the Rothschilds' top agent in the United States, he arranged financing for John D. Rockefeller's Standard Oil, the railroad empire of Edward Harriman and the steel empire of Andrew Carnegie.

When Trotsky's private army of ruthless cutthroats, whose 'boot camp' was located on Standard Oil property in New Jersey, was sufficiently trained for its campaign of subversion and terror, they sailed from New York on board the S.S. Kristianiafjord bound for Russia. With them on the ship was $20,000,000 in gold, supplied by International Banker Jacob Schiff. This vast sum was to help pay the many, varied expenses involved in such a herculean undertaking.

This fact was later confirmed by Jacob Schiff's grandson, John (Knickerbocker Column, *New York Journal American*, February 3, 1949).

When their ship, chartered by Jacob Schiff, was detained

by Canadian authorities at Halifax, Nova Scotia, on April 3rd, it appeared for a fleeting moment as it the Illuminati plot might fail.

It was at this juncture that the awesome hidden power of Jacob Schiff and his Big Money friends was brought to bear on the Canadian government. They ordered their puppets in Washington and London to intervene instantly. As a result, the Trotsky gang was back on the high seas within hours. Upon arrival in Europe, Trotsky made his way to Switzerland where he joined up with Lenin, Stalin, Kagonovich, and Litvinoff to iron out the final details of strategy before moving into Russia. . . .

FORMATION OF BOLSHEVIK RED ARMY

The Bolshevik conspirators were still faced with what appeared to be an insurmountable obstacle: how were they to get their 'army' and equipment across half of Europe and into Russia? The answer to that dilemma came when Max Warburg, the Rothschild agent who was head of the German Secret Police, packed them all into sealed box cars and arranged for their safe passage to the Russian border. Max Warburg was the brother of Paul Warburg, the creator, founder and first chairman of the 'Federal' Reserve Corporation.

Once inside Russia, Lenin, Trotsky and their . . . gang of thugs applied with untiring diligence the . . . tenets laid down by Sergey Nechayev in his *Revolutionary Catechism (1)*. In Lenin's words, their dedicated followers had to 'agree to any and every sacrifice and . . . to resort to all sorts of devices, maneuvers, and illegal methods, to evasion and subterfuge' to accomplish their objectives.

In July 1917, the International Banker-backed plot suffered an initial set-back, and Lenin and some of his co-conspirators had to flee to Finland. A few months later, they returned to Russia where they took control of a sizable group of individuals who, dismayed by the apalling conditions that existed in Russia as a result of three years of war, gullibly swallowed their promises to divide up large tracts of land among them and to provide them with many of the good things of life. The Bolsheviks also joined forces with thousands of vicious, anarchistic atheists who had been granted amnesty by the provisional government of Alexander Kerensky following the abdication of the Czar.

In November 1917, the Bolsheviks staged their revolution which was to prove successful. The Bolsheviks first seized control of the Petrograd area then, over the next two and a half years, gained control of the rest of Russia by engaging in a campaign of terror which was unprecedented in human history.

During the bloody civil war that followed the Bolshevik revolution, Lenin was the undisputed leader of political activities, while Trotsky organized the military arm of the organization - the Red Army. The title 'Red Army' was not a misnomer - a name picked at random.

The Bolshevik Red Army, under the direction of Trotsky, was the deadly tool of the Rothschild (Red Shield) dominated International Bankers. It was only fitting that it should bear the 'Red' label or shield.

JEWS LEAD BOLSHEVIK REVOLUTION

[T]hat the majority of those who occupied leadership positions in the Bolshevik Revolution were Jews is documented beyond any possibility of dispute. In 1919, the United States government, through the Overman Committee, investigated the causes of the Russian revolution. Their findings are a matter of public record and are located in the document titled: *Bolshevik Propaganda Hearing Before the Sub-Committee of the Judiciary, U.S. Senate, Sixty-Fifth Congress*.

Appearing before this investigating sub-committee, Dr. George A. Simons, former superintendent of the Methodist Missions in Russia, an American citizen who was an eyewitness to events in Russia during the Kerensky government and the Bolshevik revolution, . . . stated that 'the latest startling information, given me by someone with good authority, is this, that in December, 1918, in the Northern community of Petrograd - that is what we call that region of the Soviet regime under the presidency of the man known as Apfelbaum (Zinovieff) - out of 388 members, only 16 happened to be real Russians, and all the rest Jews, with the exception of one man, a negro from America who called himself Professor Gordon. . . .

On March 29th . . . the *Times* of London stated that 'one of the curious features of the Bolshevik movement is the high percentage of non-Russian elements amongst its leaders. Of the twenty or thirty commissaries or leaders who provide the central machinery of the Bolshevist movement not less than 75% are Jews.'

This fact was confirmed a few days later by a leading Jewish publication: 'There is much in the fact of Bolshevism itself that so many Jews are Bolshevists, in the fact that the ideals of Bolshevism at many points are consonant with the finest ideals of Judaism' (*Jewish Chronicle*, April 4, 1919).

1917-1921: CHAOS AND TERROR

From 1917 to 1921, Russia passed through a period of almost incredible political and economic chaos. . . there was extreme economic and social collapse. Industrial production was disorganized by the disruption of transportation, the inadequate supply of raw materials and credit . . . so that there was an almost complete lack of such products as clothing, shoes, or agricultural tools. By 1920 industrial production was about 13% of the 1913 figure. At the same time paper money was printed so freely [debauching the currency is a favorite Illuminati method of undermining a nation] that the ruble became almost worthless. The general index of prices was only three times the 1913 level in 1917 but rose to more than 16,000 times that level by the end of 1920. Unable to get either industrial products or sound money for their products, the peasants planted only for their own needs or hoarded their surpluses. Acreage under crops was reduced by at least one-third in 1916-1920, while yields fell even more rapidly, from 74 million tons in 1916 to 30 millions tons in 1920. The decrease in 1920 resulted from drought; this became so much worse in 1921 that the crops failed completely. Loss of life in these two years of famine reached five million, although the American Relief Administration came into the country and fed as many as ten million persons a day [i.e. in August 1922]" (Professor Quigley, *Tragedy and Hope*, pp. 386, 387). Were the crops deliberately sabotaged by the Bolsheviks (now renamed Communists by direct order from Jacob Schiff, the international Banker)? This is a distinct possibility in light of the total ruthlessness advocated by the Illuminati since its inception! The Communists took full advantage of the ever-deepening national tragedy and the division and indecisiveness displayed by their opponents. They applied their diabolical plans with fanatical ruthlessness. Terror, a la the *Revolutionary Catechism*, was the order of the day - every day, every week and every month. The implements used in this unrelenting reign of terror were the Red Army, under the direction of Leon Trotsky (Bronstein), and the secret police (Cheka) who systematically murdered all real, potential or imagined opponents. These terrorists were well rewarded for their blood-soaked services. They received high pay and a large food allowance. They were 'the law' wherever they went. *In Conflict of the Ages,* page 92, Arno Clemens Gaebelein, D.D., quotes a message sent to Washington by the American Consul on September 3, 1918: 'Since May the so-called Extraordinary Commission to combat counter revolution has conducted an openly avowed campaign of terror. Thousands of persons have been summarily shot without even the form of trial. Many of them have, no doubt, been innocent of even the political views which were supposed to supply the motive of their execution. . . . The situation cries aloud to all who will act for the sake of humanity. . . . '

The situation in Russia truly did 'cry aloud' for action by the Western nations which smugly prided themselves on their 'humanity'. But not one nation moved to prevent the annihilation of the innocent masses in Russia. Their governments were controlled by the same Force which was busy strangling Russia in accordance with the plan laid out by the Illuminati

'Sovereign Supreme Commander', Albert Pike, in his famous letter to Mazzini in 1871.

Trotsky, who was the chief instigator of this carnage, justified his actions as being 'a demonstration of the will and strength of the proletariat' (*Izvestia*, the official Communist Party newspaper, January 10, 1919).

Writing in *Red Gazette*, Apfelbaum (Zinovieff) claimed that 'the interests of the Revolution require the physical annihilation of the bourgeois [middle] class. . . .

'We will turn our hearts into steel, which we will temper in the fire of suffering and the blood of fighters for freedom. We will make our hearts cruel, hard, and unmovable, so that no mercy will enter them, and so that we will not quiver at the

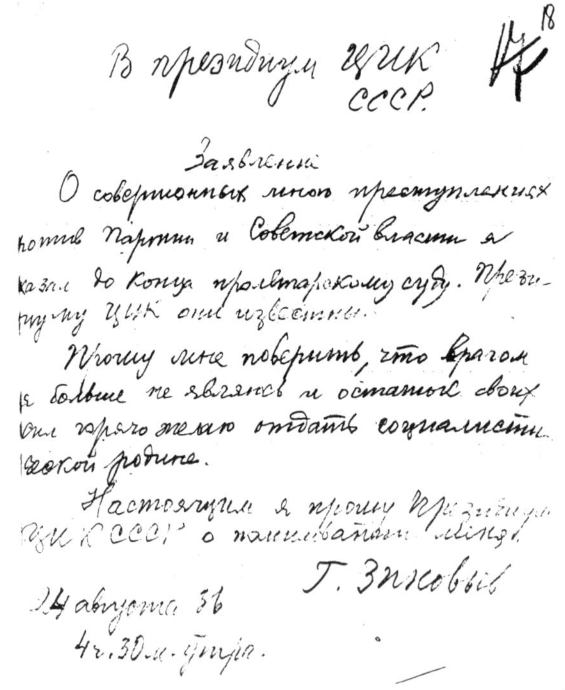

В президиум ЦИК СССР

Заявление

О совершенных мною преступлениях против Партии и Советской власти я сказал до конца пролетарскому суду. Президиуму ЦИК они известны.

Прошу мне поверить, что врагом я больше не являюсь и остаток своих сил горячо желаю отдать социалистической родине.

Настоящим я прошу Президиум ЦИК СССР о помиловании меня.

Г. Зиновьев

24 августа 36
4 ч. 30 м. утра.

Plate 38: *Ninteen years later the shoe is on the other foot. Letter from Zinoviev (24 August 1936) to the Presidium asking them to rescind the order to shoot him: 'I am no longer an enemy of the people,' he says. Zinoviev had, of course, been Lenin's right-hand man and President of The Soviet Regime in 1919. A notation on the back of the letter says that the request was refused.*

sight of a sea of enemy blood. We will let loose the floodgates of that sea. Without mercy, without sparing, we will kill our enemies in scores of hundreds.'

CHURCHILL ACKNOWLEDGES 'CONSPIRACY' AGAINST RUSSIA

Winston Churchill observed, in an article in the *Illustrated Sunday Herald*, February 8, 1920, that the Illuminati 'worldwide . . . and steadily growing conspiracy played a definitely recognizable role in the tragedy of the French Revolution. It has been the mainspring of every subversive movement during the nineteenth century: and now at last this band of extraordinary personalities from the underworld of the great cities of Europe and America have gripped the Russian people by the hair of their heads, and have become practically the undisputed masters of that enormous empire.

'There is no need to exaggerate the part played in the creation of Bolshevism and in the bringing about of the Russian Revolution by these international and for the most part atheistical Jews. It is certainly a very great one; it probably outweighs all others. With the notable exception of Lenin, the majority of the leading figures are Jews. . . .'

The French Revolution, pinpointed by Winston Churchill as the 'definitely recognizable' work of the Illuminati conspiracy, was a time of massive bloodshed and violence, a reign of terror which resulted in many hundreds of thousands of deaths.

The Illuminati-planned-and-financed Russian revolution of 1917 paled the former event into insignificance in intensity and duration. In France, the red-hot fervency of the murderous mobs burnt itself out in a few months. In Russia, the coldly-calculated slaughter of the people and the systematic destruction of the old order was carried on with a religious zeal that incorporated all the sadistic . . . instructions laid down in the *Revolutionary Catechism*. . . . Before the bloodshed ceased, upwards on thirty million people had perished before the merciless sword of this International-Banker-created Red Monster.

Several million people managed to evade the clutches of the Communist butchers and escaped to neighboring countries (*DS*, pp.61-78).

JOSEPH STALIN TAKES OVER

Following Lenin's death in January, 1924, a power struggle developed between Stalin, who felt it was imperative to build Russia up into a major industrial power prior to launching a program to sovietize other nations, and Trotsky, who believed that the salvation of Russia as a Communist State lay in exporting the revolution to other countries.

By 1927 Stalin emerged as the new strong man in Russia. Stalin's plan required that the country be 'industrialized at breakneck speed, whatever the waste and hardships, and must emphasize heavy industry and armaments rather than rising standards of living. This meant that the goods produced by the peasants must be taken from them, by political duress, without any economic return, and that the ultimate in authoritarian terror must be used to prevent the peasants from reducing their level of production to their own consumption needs, as they had done in the period 1921-1923. This meant that the first step towards the industrialization of Russia required that *the peasantry be broken by terror and reorganized from a capitalistic basis of private farms to a socialistic system of collective farms.*' It was deemed necessary to 'crush all kinds of. . . resistance to the Bolshevik State, independent thought, or public discontent. These must be crushed by terror so that the whole of Russia could be formed into a monolithic structure of disciplined proletariat who would obey their leaders with such unquestioning obedience that it would strike fear in the hearts of every potential aggressor' *(Tragedy and Hope*, p.396).

Professor Quigley points out that Russia, under the Communists, became a 'despotic police state resting on espionage and terror, in which there was a profound gulf in ideology and manner of living between the rulers and the ruled. . . .' Because of its peculiar and unique structure, the leadership of the

Plate 39: *Stalin and Lenin, 1919.*

Communist apparatus would be 'based on intrigue and violence and would inevitably bring to the top the most decisive,
most merciless, most unprincipled and most violent of its
members' (p. 397).

During the years 1928-1932, Stalin set about the implementation of a much vaunted 'Five Year Plan,' the main purposes
of which were the collectivization of agriculture and the creation of a basic system of heavy industry.

Ignoring all the basic laws of economics and the lessons of
history - Stalin, 'in order to increase the supply of food and
industrial labor in the cities, . . . forced the peasants off their
own lands (worked by their own animals and their own tools)
. . . onto huge state farms, run as state-owned enterprises by
wage-earning employees using lands, tools, and animals owned
by the government. In communal farms, the crops were owned
jointly by the members and were divided, after a certain
amount had been set aside for taxes, purchases, and other
payments which directed food to the cities. In state farms, the
crops were owned outright by the state, after the necessary costs

had been paid. In time, experience showed that the costs of the state farms were so high and their operations so inefficient that they were hardly worthwhile, although they continued to be created' (p. 397). The reason for their failure was simple: the peasants didn't have a proprietary interest in their operation. They had no incentive to produce.

After two years of experimentation and failure, Stalin launched an allout campaign to spread this disastrous system to the rest of Russia. 'In the space of six weeks (February - March 1930) collective farms increased from 59,400 with 4,400,000 families, to 110,200 farms, with 14,300,000 families. All peasants who resisted were treated with violence; their property was confiscated, they '3beaten or sent into exile in remote areas; many were killed. This process, known as 'the liquidation of the kulaks' (since the rich peasantry resisted most vigorously), affected five million kulak families. Rather than give up their animals to the collective farms, many peasants killed them. As a result, the number of cattle was reduced from 30.7 million in 1928 to 19.6 million in 1933, while, in the same five years, sheep and goats fell from 146.7 million to 50.2 million, hogs from 26 to 12.1 million, and horses from 33.5 to 16.6 million. Moreover, the planting season was entirely disrupted, and the agricultural activities of later years continued to be disturbed so that food production decreased drastically. Since the government insisted on taking the food needed to support the urban population, the rural areas were left with inadequate food. . . . Twelve years later, in 1945, Stalin told Churchill that twelve million peasants died in this reorganization of agriculture (p. 398).

'The industrial portion of the First Five-Year Plan was pursued with the same ruthless drive as the collectivization of agriculture and had similar spectacular results: impressive physical accomplishment, large-scale waste, lack of integration, ruthless disregard of personal comfort and standards of living, constant purges of opposition elements, of scapegoats, and of the inefficient, all to the accompaniment of blasts of propaganda inflating the plan's real achievements to incredible dimensions, attacking opposition groups (sometimes real and frequently imaginary) within the Soviet Union, or mixing scorn with fear in verbal assaults on foreign "capitalist imperialist" countries and their secret "saboteurs" within Russia' (p. 399).

CLASS DISTINCTIONS REAPPEAR

. . . . Contrary to the glowing promises, 'class distinctions reappeared in the Soviet Union, the privileged leaders of the secret police and the Red Army, as well as the leaders of the party and certain favored writers, musicians, ballet dancers, and actors, obtaining incomes so far above those of the ordinary Russian that they lived in quite a different world. The ordinary Russian had inadequate food and housing, was subject to extended rationing, having to stand in line for scarce consumers' items or even to go without them for long periods, and was reduced to living, with his family, in a single room, or even, in many cases, to a corner of a single room shared with other families. The privileged rulers and their favorites had the best of everything, including foods and wines, the use of vacation villas in the country or in the Crimea, the use of official cars in the city, the right to live in old czarist palaces and mansions, and the right to obtain tickets to the best seats at the musical or dramatic performances. These privileges of the ruling group, however, were obtained at a terrible price: at the cost of complete insecurity, for even the highest party officials were under constant surveillance by the secret police and inevitably would be purged, sooner or later, to exile or to death' (*Tragedy and Hope*, pp. 400-1).

The writings of Karl Marx wax eloquent on the benefits to be derived from practicing his teachings but, as is so often the case, there was a world of difference between rhetoric and reality: 'The growth of inequality was increasingly rapid under the Five-Year plans and was embodied in law. All restrictions on maximum salaries were removed; variations in salaries grew steadily wider and were made greater by the nonmonetary privileges extended to the favored upper ranks. Special stores were established where the privileged could obtain scarce goods at low prices; two or even three restaurants, with entirely different menus, were set up in industrial plants for different levels of employees; housing discrimination became steadily wider; all wages were put on a piecework basis even when this was quite impractical, work quotas and work minimums were steadily raised. Much of this differentiation of wages was justified under a fraudulent propaganda system known as Stakhanovism.

'In September 1935, a miner named Stakhanov mined 102 tons of coal in a day, fourteen times the usual output. Similar exploits were arranged in other activities for propaganda purposes and used to justify speedup, raising of production quotas, and wage differences. At the same time, the standard of living of the ordinary worker was steadily reduced not only by raising quotas, but also by a systematic policy of segmented inflation. Food was purchased from the collective farms at low prices and then sold to the public at high prices. *The gap between these two was steadily widened year by year. At the same time, the amount of produce taken from the peasants was gradually increased by one technique or another.*

As public discontent and social tensions grew in the period of the Five-Year plans and the collectivization of agriculture, the use of spying, purges, torture, and murder increased out of all proportion. Every wave of discontent, every discovery of inefficiency, every recognition of some past mistake of the authorities resulted in new waves of police activity. When the meat supplies of the cities almost vanished, after the collectivization of agriculture in the early 1930's, more than a dozen of the high officials in charge of meat supplies in Moscow were arrested and shot, although they were in no way responsible for the shortage. *By the middle 1930's the search for saboteurs and for "enemies of the state" became an all-enveloping mania which left hardly a family untouched. Hundreds of thousands were killed, frequently on completely false charges, while millions were arrested and exiled to Siberia or put into huge slave-labor camps. In these camps, under conditions of semi-starvation and incredible cruelty, millions toiled in mines, in logging camps in the Arctic, or building new railroads, new canals, or new cities.* Estimates of the number of persons in such slave-labor camps in the period just before Hitler's attack in 1941 vary from as low as two million to *as high as twenty million*. The majority of these prisoners had done *nothing* against the Soviet state or the Communist system, but consisted of the relatives, associates, and friends of persons who had been arrested on more serious charges. Many of these charges were completely false, *having been trumped up to provide labor in remote areas,* scapegoats for administrative breakdowns, and to eliminate possible rivals in the control of the Soviet system, or simply because of the constantly growing mass paranoidal suspicion which enveloped the upper levels of the regime. In many cases, incidental events led to large-scale reprisals for personal grudges far beyond any scope justified by the event itself. In most cases these liquidations took place in the cells of the secret police, in the middle of the night, with no public announcements except the most laconic. But, in a few cases, spectacular public trials were staged in which the accused, usually famous Soviet leaders, were berated and reviled, volubly confessed their own dastardly activities, and, after conviction, were taken out and shot.

'Under Stalinism all Russia was dominated by three huge bureaucracies: of the government, of the party, and of the secret police. Of these, the secret police were more powerful than the party and the party more powerful than the government. Every office, factory, university, collective farm, research laboratory, or museum had all three structures. When the management of a factory sought to produce goods, they were constantly interfered with by the party committee (cell) or by the special department (the secret police unit) within the factory. There were two networks of secret-police spies unknown to each other, one serving the special department of the factory, while the other reported to a high-level of the secret police outside. Most of these spies were unpaid and served under threats of blackmail or "liquidations". Such "liquidations" could range from wage reductions (which went to the secret police), through beatings or torture, to exile, imprisonment, expulsion from the Party (if a member), to murder. The secret police had enormous funds, since they collected wage deductions from large numbers and had millions of slave laborers in their camps to be rented out, like draft animals on a contract basis, for state construction projects. Whenever the secret police needed more money they could sweep large numbers of persons, without trial or notice, into their wage deduction system or into their labor camps to be hired out. It would seem that the secret police, operating in this fashion, were the real rulers of Russia. This was true except at the very top, where Stalin could always liquidate the head of the secret police by having him arrested by his second in command in return for Stalin's promise to promote the arrester to the top position. In this way the chiefs of the secret police were successively eliminated; V. Menzhinsky was replaced by Yagoda in 1934, Yagoda by Nikolai Yezhov in 1936, and Yezhov by Lavrenti Beria in 1938. These rapid shifts sought to cover up the falsifications of evidence which these men had prepared for the great purges of the period, each man's mouth being closed by death as his part in the elimination of Stalin's rivals was concluded. To keep the organization subordinate to the party, none of the leaders of the secret police was a member of the Politburo before Beria, and Beria was completely Stalin's creature until they perished together in 1953' (pp. 402-404).

TWENTY ONE YEARS OF TERROR

It took the Communists twenty-one years of ruthless terror to completely subjugate the Russian people, to break their will and bring them to a state of near mindless conformity. Students of history recognize that what happened in Russia was the fulfillment of the first stage of the Illuminati's master plan for total domination of the world. History clearly shows that, on numerous occasions during the 1920's and 1930's, when the Communist regime in Russia was tottering on the brink of total collapse, the United States and other Western Powers jumped to its aid and kept the Red Monster afloat. The Russian Revolution of October, 1917, and the subsequent blood-bath were clearly 'urban renewal' projects planned and financed by

the International Money Elite. The horrifyingly gory details of
the Illuminati's conquest of Russia were written in the blood of
thirty million defenseless human beings whose only 'crime' was
that they lived in Russia, and stood in the way *of the Illuminati's
plans for the creation of a One-World-Government*
   (*DS*, pp.109-18.   The other substantial passages quoted
above are from Quigley's *Tragedy and Hope*).

NOTES

   1.   *The Revolutionary Catechism*, written during the early
eighteen-seventies by Sergey Nechayev, is a study of the
'science of destruction.' 'The only form of revolution beneficial
to the people,' it posits, 'is one which destroys the entire state
to the roots and exterminates all the state traditions, institutions, and classes.' 'Day and night,' it continues, the revolutionary 'must have but one thought, one aim - merciless destruction
. . . for him morality is everything which contributes to the
triumph of the revolution. Immoral and criminal is everything
that stands in its way.'
   In *The Descent into Slavery?*, Mr. Griffin quotes Charles E.
Wolff's *Which Way U.S.A.? Republic Under God or Dictatorship?*
(Fidelity, 1978), pp.152-3:

>   There is no single document in the possession of the
> serious stiudent of Communism [Illuminism] that ap-
> proaches Sergey Nechayev's *Catechism* in importance
> for deep insight into the nature of Communism. It
> surpasses in significance even the writings of Marx
> himself.

>   When you read the *Catechism* you will read (horri-
> bly perverted) echoes of the blazing missionary zeal
> and self-denial of early Christianity. Any person who
> reads and understands the importance of the *Catechism*
> will never again refer to Communism as just another
> political movement. It is vastly more than politics. . .

>   . People who have wondered at the astounding power
> of Communism need do so no longer. . . . It begins with
> the transformation of the spiritually destitute indi-

vidual into a destructive revolutionary, using a strange
process of dehumanization.

Mr. Griffin then prints the full document, *The Revolutionary
Catechism, DS,* pp. 255-61, and examines its effect on Lenin and
on later revolutionaries, including the black activists in the
United States.

Plate 40: *Stalin and Kalinin, 1935. Kalinin was later to become Chairman
of the Presidium of the USSR.*

Председателю Совета Народ.Комиссаров
И. В. Сталину.

Прошение.

Я, Калинина Екатерина Ивановна, была арестована и осуждена по ст. 58, заключение в И.Т.Л. в 1938 году, сроком на 15 лет. Я совершила тяжелую ошибку, усугубленную тем, что Вы своевременно мне на нее указывали, а я эти указания не учла. Такое несознательное отношение к своему

Plate 41: *Portion of letter to Stalin from Mrs. Mikhail Kalinin, Ekaterina Ivanovna Kalinina, pleading that her 15-year prison sentence, seven years of which she had served, be terminated. Mrs. Kalinin dates her letter 9 May 1945, Russia's victory day in the Second World War. Note that Mrs. Kalinin is the wife of Stalin's close associate, Mikhail Kalinin, who was then Chairman of the Presidium. It was not an unusual situation in the Soviet Union at the time for one party in a marriage to hold high office while the other was forgotten in jail.*

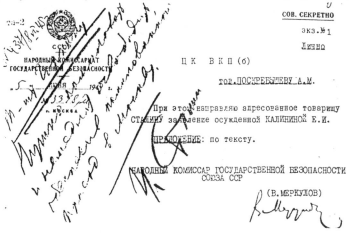

СОВ. СЕКРЕТНО

экз.№1

Лично

НАРОДНЫЙ КОМИССАРИАТ
ГОСУДАРСТВЕННОЙ БЕЗОПАСНОСТИ

ЦК ВКП (б)

тов.ПОСКРЕБЫШЕВУ А.М.

При этом направляю адресованное товарищу СТАЛИНУ заявление осужденной КАЛИНИНОЙ Е.И.

ПРИЛОЖЕНИЕ: по тексту.

НАРОДНЫЙ КОМИССАР ГОСУДАРСТВЕННОЙ БЕЗОПАСНОСТИ
СОЮЗА ССР

(В.МЕРКУЛОВ)

Plate 41a: *In an uncharacteristic flourish, Stalin releases Mrs. Ekaterina Kalinin from prison halfway through her sentence. Stalin's signature is on the left-hand side of the page.*

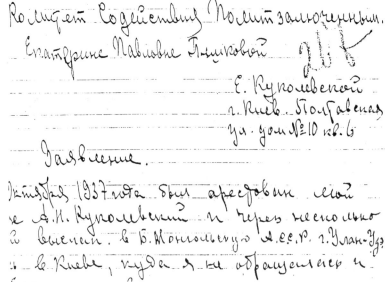

Plate 42: *Beginning of four-page letter to Gorky's wife, Ekaterina Peshkova (1938), from lady seeking help for her husband who had been arrested and sent to Mongolia.*

~~ЗАПИСКА~~ О СОСТОЯНИИ ДЕТСКОЙ БЕСПРИЗОРНОСТИ.

К началу 1935 г. по республикам с наибольшим развитием беспризорности - РСФСР, УССР, БССР и УзбССР имеется 2.703 детдома с 346.452 детьми, не считая находящихся на патронате и работающих в производственных предприятиях деткомис - сий.

За 1934 год по УССР на борьбу с детской беспризорностью, в основном на содержание детдомов, израсходовано 49 млн.р., по РСФСР - 177 млн.руб. Большинство детей, находящихся в детских домах, является круглыми сиротами. Проведенная в

Plate 43: *First page of Report to Lenin's wife and others regarding the status of children abandoned in one way or other - children taken from parents, sick, dangerous, no place to live, run-away, criminal, etc. - total in various orphanages at the beginning of 1935: 346,452. The situation, the Report states, was to be totally rectified by 1936. Report by Kalinin.*

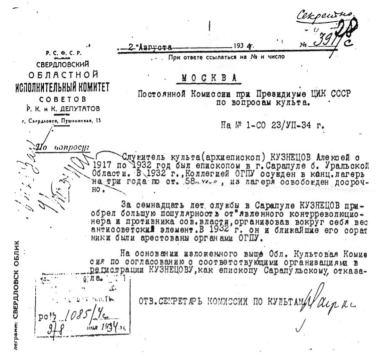

2 Августа 1934. № 39/с

Р. С. Ф. С. Р.
СВЕРДЛОВСКИЙ
ОБЛАСТНОЙ
ИСПОЛНИТЕЛЬНЫЙ КОМИТЕТ
С О В Е Т О В
Р. К. и К. ДЕПУТАТОВ
г. Свердловск, Пушкинская, 15

При ответе ссылаться на № и число

М О С К В А

Постоянной Комиссии при Президиуме ЦИК СССР
по вопросам культа.

На № 1-СО 23/УП-34 г.

По вопросу:

Служитель культа(архиепископ) КУЗНЕЦОВ Алексей с
1917 по 1932 год был епископом в г.Сарапуле б. Уральской
Области. В 1932 г.,Коллегией ОГПУ осужден в конц.лагерь
на три года по ст. 58..ч..", из лагеря освобожден досроч-
но.

За семнадцать лет.службы в Сарапуле КУЗНЕЦОВ при-
обрел большую популярность от"явленного контрреволюцио-
нера и противника сов.власти,организовав вокруг себя вес
антисоветский элемент.В 1932 г. он и ближайшие его сорат
ники были арестованы органами ОГПУ.

На основании изложенного выше Обл. Культовая Комис
сия по согласованию с соответствующими организациями в
регистрации КУЗНЕЦОВУ,как епископу Сарапульскому,отказа-
ла.

ОТВ.СЕКРЕТАРЬ КОМИССИИ ПО КУЛЬТАМ

рс № 1085/4

СВЕРДЛОВСК ОБЛИК

Plate 44: *First page of 'Report on Cults' refusing to give Archbishop Sarapulski Kuznetsy back his position as Archbishop after he was freed from concentration camp after serving three years. The Archbishop had been arrested in 1932.*

Plate 45: *Farewell to Stalin (9 March 1953). Left to right: Molotov, Voroshilov, Beria, Malenkov - the dead Stalin - Bulganin, Khruschev, Kaganovich, Mikoyan. The headline says 'Farewell of People to their Great leader', their father, teacher, architect, master builder, friend, Communist, peace builder.*

Nina, who translated the article us, says that the sentiments expressed in the article were not disingenuous. Many people died in the crush to say farewell; roads were blocked with trucks to hold the people back; he was 'mourned' three days and three nights.' Rivers 'of people's misery are running over all parts of the Union Union,' 'we can't take our eyes off the dear features; he gave us all the warmth of his heart, all the light of his mind. This kind of light will always shine.'

PART III:
GLOBAL THEATRES OF THE ANTICHRIST:
AN INTERVIEW WITH MICHAEL ADIR

Edited by Robert O'Driscoll

Washington DC, 13 December 1992.

Des Griffin also joined in the conversation.

Robert O'Driscoll: Was it merely a coincidence that you were at the Abbey Theatre in Dublin that day when I gave my perform-ance piece *Nato and the Warsaw Pact Are One*?

Michael Adir: I don't think so, but I did not expect to meet you, that's for sure. I had heard about a book *Nato and the Warsaw Pact Are One*, but I did not know you were the one who was doing it. I never thought that the information it contained would be so historically documented or that a simple person from the street would find it so difficult to understand or comprehend.

ROD: Perhaps I shouldn't be interviewing you at all. You do your deeds. You are the closest I've met to an invisible person. My first question is something as follows: does the name 'Michael', which you bear, have any special significance for you? I know that St. Michael is the patron saint of Russia. Do you tend towards a nationalistic interpretation? Or a Christian? I mean, do you place any significance on Michael fighting the dragon in the heavens, the dragon falling to Earth, and the battle being engaged again?

MA: Very much indeed. You seem to be talking from a Christian point of view. Michael was anointed before he fought the dragon. But we also have Michael in relation to Earth, Michael as he is today with a big patch on his head and a small tail, which signifies the inhuman.

ROD: Tell me, telme!

MA: Take Michael of Earth for example: he has a patch on his head. That has a meaning.

КОНСТИТУЦИЯ
(ОСНОВНОЙ ЗАКОН)
СОЮЗА
СОВЕТСКИХ
СОЦИАЛИСТИЧЕСКИХ
РЕСПУБЛИК

Plate 46: *Constition of the Union of Soviet Socialist Republics (USSR), 1950.*

ROD: That has a meaning as far as Atlantis is concerned.

MA: That has a meaning as far as Michael is concerned.

ROD: Are you suggesting Gorbachev is an incarnation of Michael? Or is he connected with the Michaelic force?

MA: Very much the Michaelic force - to come, to destroy, to change the course of lives - which is, I must confess, not the honest way of doing it. But that was the only way for him: he had to change the whole course of history. The world believes he has done 'the impossible', that he has thrashed down the walls of Jericho - if you pardon me for referring to the Berlin Wall in this way. That's not the issue: he didn't *do* anything. He was just another instrument, another pawn in the game. He may have seemed like a 'divine' in the eyes of the common man, but actually he was a defined instrument. The force behind him - this is something the people didn't realize - was the force of the antiChrist.

Des Griffin: Frederic Morton puts his finger on the process in his book on the Rothschilds (p.125): they always operate, he writes, under "an umbrella of silence. . . . In the best circles one does not make history by the sweat of one's own brow. One hires the makers."

MA: The antiChrist at that point was in two other nations besides Russia. One was the United States. It began when Kissinger took over: the decadence of the United States from that point began to accelerate. At the same time everything was being prepared for Michael G., because that was the time when the Jews, under the pretext of having been mistreated by the Russians, moved in large numbers to Tel Aviv or Jerusalem, or via Jerusalem and Tel Aviv to the United States.

DG: This is the second largest exodus of Jews from Russia to the United States, the first being in 1901. In a speech to the Congress in 1932, Congressman Louis T. McFadden drew attention to the earlier influx, drawing the attention of Congress to that fact, and that Jacob Schiff, the Rothschild agent in America, had made the arrangement with the appropriate governmental authorities. McFadden was assassinated four years later.

MA: How could the Russians mistreat the Jews if the Jews were in power in Russia, as they were (and are)? In any case, it was at that precise moment of the move that the plan of the New World Order swung into high gear. From then on, the new factor was to be the *Crown* factor, and we can note that this is the first time we have rumblings of trouble within the Royal Family.

ROD: Which year would that be?

MA: '72-3.

DG: I believe Kissinger entered the Nixon Cabinet originally in 1969.

MA: So he would have been there in '72-3.

ROD: What we have here is an exodus of Jews from Russia to America, the initiation by Henry Kissinger (and is there not a book called *Henry Kissinger: Soviet Agent*), himself a Jew, of a new phase in the plans for a New World Order, and rumblings within the House of Windsor.

MA: There are three countries in the picture. Russia is in total disarray, destroyed, stripped of everything. We have decay in the very marrow of the Russian nation from the abuse of power. In reality the power was never Russian at all, because the Russians hadn't ruled in their land since 1917.

DG: "There is no need to exaggerate," Churchill writes in 1920, "the part played in the creation of Bolshevism and in the actual bringing about of the Russian Revolution by these international and for the most part atheistical Jews. It is certainly a very great one; it probably outweighs all others. With the possible exception of Lenin, the majority of the leading figures are Jews. Moreover, the principal inspiration and driving power comes from Jewish leaders." Churchill, says: 'With the possible exception of Lenin'. Research from the KGB files and published in *The Jewish Weekly* (Bouvard, Georgia) indicates that *both* of Lenin's parents were Jewish.

MA: The real power was the Soviet State which was in fact a Jewish State on Russian soil. Then there were the 'sandbags', the countries or cities around Russia which when taken away would leave Russia totally vulnerable, as it will be. It is true that the territory was extended with these 'sandbags' but inside the Iron Curtain it was only empty air, balloons, and immense unrelieved suffering; the Iron Curtain was imposed to keep this from the non-authorized world.

DG: Russia was never in any way, shape, or form a SUPER-POWER.

ROD: We in the West were given the illusion it was a SUPER-POWER for that is the way the Cold War was sustained, with massive armaments being constructed by both sides, and, to boot, in competition with each other. Once completed, or shortly after, they were ruled obsolete and a whole new round of armament construction would begin. Where are these armaments now? Who gained from these massive expenditures - billions, trillions of dollars. Certainly not the United States!

Nor Russia! Only the middlemen who were selling the same blueprints, slightly altered, to both sides, those whom Sean Connery calls in his film *The Russia House* 'the Grey Men' and they have been doing this now for three centuries.

What a monstrous creation they were able to summon from the deep this time! Two armed dragons, both the creation of antiChrist, reflected in each other's mirror - shadow feeding on a light, a light feeding on a shadow - frozen in an hypnotic stasis, while the proverbial thief in the night makes off with . . .

MA: Where are the generations who went hungry and starved while these diabolical monstrosities glittered on the polar ice, or under the ice?

ROD: In their early graves! But what, Michael, of the living? Two generations of the living had their minds poisoned against each other. Your generation and mine certainly. What was the little poem that sent shivers up and down my spine even when I was in my teens:

> Look under your bed
> Or in the shed
> See if a Commie's there!

And in school children would be coached as to what to do in the eventuality of a nuclear attack. Do you remember, Desmond?

> Duck and cover,
> Duck and cover,

and everybody would go scampering under their desks.

As we grew older, hatred and suspicion were fed into our minds from every source - state, school, and church. Understanding, compassion, or any ideas of avoiding duplication in space and technological exploration were ostentaciously shunned by our leaders. While this was worse in the United States than in Canada, it was not, we were taught to rationalize, the things of the spirit that mattered, or even the individual soul, but the battle against Communism.

We know that both Russia and America are deeply Christian countries, but a derisive antagonism was deliberately orchestrated between them for the mutual benefit of a third party, the movement of the antiChrist, and, more importantly perhaps, to destroy potential opposition to the antiChrist, to knock nations and individuals off balance before the Big Crunch.

Millions of Russians continued to be slaughtered, while America and Canada continued to be penetrated from within. And we became passive, pathetically passive - with smug ideology, television, baseball, cults, drugs, ever-ingenious material massages, and the 'black arts' of education - and we allowed those hidden manipulators who were drumming up our fear of Communism to curtail, bit by bit, our own freedoms until the final Big Crunch in those last days of our two-thousand year old cycle, the cycle of the Christ and the cycle of the antiChrist. The Big Crunch is, of course, the imposition of a World State, which when once imposed can never be thrown off. And that, Gentlemen, is the end of the human race: without free will the human race does not exist.

Before I left Arthur Ontario to come here for this meeting I happened to go down to the basement in my house and this letter, as my mother used to say, 'kind of fell' into my hands. It was written to me by William Mobley whom I had met at the University of London in 1961. He was a Ph.D. Fulbright scholar, extremely sensitive with relation to the blossomings of culture in Europe and America, but, like myself, totally naive with relation to international politics, the space age, nuclear fallout, etc., as the following extract demonstrates:

> Never before in history have any people, so willingly and so hopefully, performed more for the sake of mankind than these United States. . . . The idea that the 'meek' shall inherit the earth has never been one of my beliefs. Since 1945, Russia vis-a-vis the United States has been a study in how much provocation one nation can take and how large the insatiable appetite of the other can be. During this time, The Russians have broken 47

agreements. . . . And you think Moscow is going to honor a disarmament agreement? The Russians refuse to have inspections - that is the only thing holding up an agreement. . . . The U.S. should have been testing any kind of bombs all along. . . H bombs have been outmoded by Cobalt bombs and only one of them will destroy the earth. And neutron bombs only destroy life, with no destruction to the inanimate. There is no use talking about peace when there are maniacs on the earth. . . . It is interesting to note that not even the Vatican can reach agreements with Moscow. . . . Incidentally, agreements were reached between Hitler and the Papacy. So you see we are fooling ourselves if we believe the monsters in the Kremlin respect anything but raw power. All of this concern over 'fallout' has been greatly exaggerated. The scientist now knows that the danger from 'fallout' is not serious and for this reason Kennedy will announce tomorrow night that the tests will be resumed in the Pacific. The radio just announced that the British exploded an underground bomb in Nevada. Times of course change, but enemies in essence do not. The Russian dictatorship under the guise of Communism is the greatest threat to civilization, ever.

DG: What an extraordinary document. What is refreshing about it is that it is an actual contemporary document. That is what people were thinking at the time. Nobody could possibly reconstruct it.

ROD: Khruschev, and maybe Kim Philby, seem to have been the first to poke a hole in that rusty curtain surrounding the Soviet Union. Khruschev seemed to be the first public figure to discover - from his espionage networks, or from somewhere, who the 'double agents' were, on the American side at least.

MA: With Khruschev, the Jewish Masters realized that Communism had failed, that KIM - the International Youth Movement - would never become the dominating force in the world. This became obvious when Khruschev came to the United

Nations and took off his shoe to bang the table - the peasant
was taking over. The peasantry were taking over in Russia, so
the ideology had to be scuttled.

ROD: Communism then was a ploy, a tool, a huge experiment
as a prep for the ant . . .

MA: Yes, for controlling the masses and as a preparation for the
movement of the antiChrist.

DG: If we look back to what was happening behind the Iron
Curtain, it was difficult to get in. They didn't want the outside
world to see what conditions were like there, the abject poverty,
the total stagnation with relation to anything except arms. Nor
did they want the Russians to know what the free world was
all about.

The only thing that prevented the Soviet Union from
collapsing in the thirties was a massive infusion of economic
and technological aid from the West, primarily the United
States. The article on Roosevelt in the *Encyclopedia Judaica* states
that Roosevelt's socialist policies "endeared him to the Jewish
community which shared with him the overriding commitment
to the welfare state. In fact, so pervasive was Jewish influence
in Roosevelt's experiment that the pejorative epithet `Jew Deal'
became popular among the anti-Semitic elements."

MA: I would have taken off my chapeau to all the Jewish rulers
if they had been honest people, and have said: "We are Jews.
We are taking over. We are going to rule Russia and there is
no doubt about it." Instead they camouflaged their names
under Russian names. What were they afraid of? And who?
It is the dishonesty and amoral behaviour that I have always
questioned.

DG: Even from your youth, were you aware of the Jewish
connection?

MA: Of course. I was born in the most remote area of the
world. You know Margarita, of course, who found it necessary
to return to Russia yesterday: we have known each other since
we were seven and six respectively. I have lived throughout
Australia, India, Latin America, and of course Europe and
America. I was a perfect gypsy of the world. I had no home,

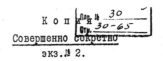

Коп и
Совершенно секретно
экз.№ 2.

СЕКРЕТАРЮ ЦК КПСС

товарищу ХРУЩЕВУ Н.С.

В связи с поступающими в ЦК КПСС сигналами от ряда
лиц о незаконном осуждении за контрреволюционные преступления в прошлые годы Коллегией ОГПУ, тройками НКВД, Особым
совещанием, Военной Коллегией, судами и военными трибуналами
и в соответствии с Вашим указанием о необходимости пере-
смотреть дела на лиц, осужденных за контрреволюционные преступления и ныне содержащихся в лагерях и тюрьмах, докла-
дываем:

По имеющимся в МВД СССР данным, за период с 1921 года
по настоящее время за контрреволюционные преступления было
осуждено Коллегией ОГПУ, тройками НКВД, Особым совещанием,
Военной Коллегией, судами и военными трибуналами 3.777.380
человек, в том числе:

к ВМН - 642.980 человек,
к содержанию в лагерях и тюрьмах на срок от 25 лет и
ниже - 2.369.220 человек,
в ссылку и высылку - 765.180 человек.

Из общего количества арестованных, ориентировочно,
осуждено: 2.900.000 человек - Коллегией ОГПУ, тройками НКВД
и Особым совещанием и 877.000 человек - судами, военными
трибуналами, Спецколлегией и Военной Коллегией.

Plate 47: *Classified Top Secret. Letter from Rudenko, General Prosecutor for Soviet Union (February 1954), to Nikita Khruschew, then Secretary of the Central Committee, in response to Khruschev's request as to the fate of people incarcerated between 1921 to 1954: arrested by Secret Police 2,900,000; arraigned by courts and tribunals 877,000; total people sentenced 3,777,380 - total alive 467,946. Khruschev had initiated the investigation to determine whether the individuals had committed the crime for which they were accused.*

as you would call it. I had nothing. I was just a gypsy (not I may say of my own choice), wandering and resting my head wherever I was able to find a place. It brought me sorrow and it brought me joy. It gave me knowledge and the patience to unravel the most intricate mysteries of nature and man. The world, as I discovered, is a perfect theatre of marionettes. I had to cope with all kinds of intrigues. I experienced hatred, treachery, and love, and I had to understand and forgive. I tried to understand the meaning behind all that was going on. Those are some of the lessons I learned in my wandering paths throughout the world.

To return to the forgotten world! In the late-thirties when Stalin's butcher Beria came to China and enslaved the honest,

О П И С Ь

ОРДЕНОВ и МЕДАЛЕЙ, А ТАКЖЕ ОРДЕНСКИХ
ДОКУМЕНТОВ К НИМ, ИЗЪЯТЫХ У   Б Е Р И Я   Л.П.

1. Ордена Ленина за №№ 1236, 14839, 27006,
        94311 и 118679 5

2. Ордена Красного Знамени за №№ 11517 и 7034 2

3. Орден Александра Суворова № 217 1

4. Медали: "ХХХ лет Советской Армии", "За оборону
   Москвы", "За оборону Сталинграда", "За оборону
   Кавказа", "За победу над Германией", "За побе-
   ду над Японией", "800-летие Москвы" 7

Plate 48: *List of Orders, Medals, and Documents taken away from Beria (Head of Stalin's Secret Police) after Stalin's death, by order of Rudemko, Chief Prosecutor: five Orders of Lenin, 2 Orders of the Red Banner, The Order of Alexander Surorov, and Medals for the Defence of Moscow, Stalingrad, the Caucasus, for the Victory over Germany, the Victory over Japan, and a list that goes on for three pages of which we can only reproduce one. This document is still Top Secret in Russia. In the same bundle of documents is a Top Secret Document naming Beria an 'Enemy of the People'.*

good, and absolutely innocent children and people, killing millions, incarcerating women and children, giving orders that all children under the age of two were to be taken to Russia and re-educated, and all children over two were to be exterminated at the place of Kure. Which of the Holocausts will history have greater difficulty in justifying - the alleged six million Jews or the fifty-two million in China, not to speak of the acknowledged sixty million in Russia?

Of course even if one dies, there is remorse, there are tears, because this is a human being. I always say that human life must be cherished at all costs.

We must remember that unlike the Chinese and the Russians, the Jews had a choice. Hitler repeatedly asked the Jews to leave Germany - was it not so?

DG: It was revealed a little while ago that during World War II Israel's recent Prime Minister, Shamir, worked with the Nazis to bring Jews from Germany to Palestine, but the majority chose to stay. Indeed, there is no documented proof of a programme to exterminate Jews in Germany.

MA: There is proof that the Jews were asked repeatedly and given permission to leave Germany.

DG: There is also evidence in the German files that thousands of Jews were taken out and shot. But what is a virtual physical impossibility is the extermination of six million Jews because it is logistically impossible.

ROD: What about the concentration camps?

DG: During and after the second World War, it was said that the concentration camp at Auschwitz was an extermination camp with crematorial capabilities, but in the last few years documentation has emerged from the British Archives - photographs taken from British reconnaissance planes in 1943-4 - to reveal that in fact there were no smoke stacks, no open pits, no crematoriums except to burn the bodies of those who died . . .

MA: From natural causes?

DG: Or disease.

MA: The question I should like to see answered is: which nation, which country is going to answer for the unbelievable devastation that has taken place since the Jewish Bolshevik Revolution, with the deaths, as I just said, of some 60 million in Russia, another 52 million in China, and the persecution of other nations by Jewish Rulers around the world. It leads to an even deeper problem. If the antiChrist is, among other things, an economical power, and if we approach this from a Christian standpoint, we have to go back to the roots and basic principles of Christianity itself. At that time there was no economical superstructure. We just had our human powers. In spite of all the might of the Roman Empire, Pontius Pilate decided not to take sides with the Jewish segment and washed his hands from shedding the blood of Christ who was the ultimate good. The Jews, on the other hand, cast their stone for Barabas, who was the ultimate evil.

DG: And what did the mob scream? 'Crucify Him! Crucify Him! Let His blood be on our children, and on their children, for generations to come.'

MA: Is it possible that it had already been written in the Heavens for the generations to come that the innocent blood of the earth was to be shed?

ROD: 'It would almost seem', Churchill writes, 'as if the gospel of Christ and the gospel of Antichrist were destined to originate among the same people; and that this mystic and mysterious race had been chosen for the supreme manifestations, both of the divine and the diabolical.'

MA: The antiChrist is more powerful on earth because Barabas is the one who is freed. The genie of the antiChrist is unleashed: the genie of madness, the genie of destruction, the genie of the black sheep, or maybe we can call him Lucifer himself. The antithesis of Christ is given the freedom of the city; and Christ is crucified.

   In spite of that, he still says 'Forgive them, Father, for they know not what they do.' The Christian believes that Jesus

Christ died for our sins. I ask: For whose sins? Our sins whom he knew anyway to be innocent. Or Lucifer's?

And I ask again: who is going to answer for the unbelievable devastation of the twentieth century? Maybe in the short term there is no answer, but the Judgment Day is upon us. Will it be the Luciferians or the Christians who will be condemned?

ROD: Are you suggesting that Lucifer is proving more powerful than Christ in the world?

MA: Presently, is that not clear?

DG: Scripture says that he is the 'God of this world' (II Cor.4.4.) and that he has 'deceived the whole world' (Rev.12.9). But whatever power has been given him, so he is going to have to answer to somebody too.

MA: There is fear around the world. This is the constant enslavement of our liberties, the slow erosion of faith, of family, of values, of principle.

The economy, the almighty dollar, is the shining star. Human values are considered expendable. They will perish, unless the Christian world, which has been a defender of the good in one way or the other, will stand together. Right now Christianity is totally passive, taught to turn the other cheek, but the time is here when the Christian world will have to face reality, and make a stand.

DG: They will have to draw a line.

ROD: What of the worlds of Mohammed and Buddha?

MA: Let us expand our thoughts to include the worlds of Mohammed and Buddha, and the world of Japan. We already know that the Japanese world, even with their fantastic brains, have produced nothing original. They went round the world, took photographs of everything (with our permission), came home and put the puzzle together. Yes, they're geniuses, and if somebody else comes up with the idea the Japanese work it out. *Question:* If economic power is the yardstick, and Japan falls, as it will, are we to be governed by EEC rules or by Tel

Aviv rules? And as Canada is under the thumb of Tel Aviv, is the US as well? Russia is on top of the thumb of Tel Aviv.

So what do we have today? Two worlds: EEC on the one hand, and Canada and the United States on the other. Two worlds! Russia, as we know, has already been destroyed; the US is in a very shaky position, and Canada is practically taken.

ROD: I remember you very dramatically drawing yourself to your full height in Arthur last October and saying: 'Remember, Robert and Elizabeth, if Russia goes, Canada will be next, and the United States will be third.'

MA: Yes, I told you that, and I repeat it today.

ROD: You made that statement before the Soviet Union had fallen. Fourteen months later you tell me that 'Canada is practically taken.' I am afraid that I must agree with you. What causes me greater shame is that Canada, or more particularly Ontario, is the beachhead by which the US may finally be brought to its knees. I am thinking of Bob Rae's half-way house on the border in Windsor, his casino, the establishment of organized crime and all that that implies.

So with Russia gone, Canada and the United States are the last proverbial flies in the crowning ointment of the antiChrist?

MA: I totally believe that, although for the sake of Humanity I hope I'm wrong.

ROD: As Etienne Gilson says, we listen with bated breath to the sounds of those countries which fall one after the other with a crash followed by a long silence and wonder how long will the liberties that we still possess will last. It is to Europe then, where it all began, that we must turn to unravel the enigma.

MA: Yes, and in the European theatre the decoy is Ireland, a country in which Canada, the US, and England have interests. Ireland is such a small island that with one shot you could have destroyed the whole island. You could have eliminated Belfast. That wasn't the objective. Ireland was deliberately used to take the heat out of what was brooding on the entire European continent. While the people were stirred into turmoil by a little war with a religious issue that was totally anachronistic, the real action was elsewhere. Ireland was used!

One lesson I have learned in my journey through the world is not to pay too much attention to inconsequential battles. While the media is trying to deflect our attention to inconsequential issues, the real war, which has already been decided by the main players, is kept carefully camouflaged from innocent people living without malice, trying to survive from day to day, feeding their families, and . . .

DG: That is all the average person is capable of. I should like to draw your attention to a speech John Swinton, editor of the *New York News*, made in 1914: "There is no such thing as an independent press. . . . You know this and I know it. . . . We are tools and vassals of the rich behind the scenes. We are marionettes. These men pull the strings, and we dance. Our time, our talents, our lives and our capacities are all the property of these men - we are intellectual prostitutes."

MA: Creating ways to take our minds off the real issues. What was the Gulf War designed to take our minds off? Don't tell me, gentlemen, it wasn't staged.

DG: George Bush said at the time that the Gulf War was part of the process of creating a New World Order. Also, he and his family had massive investments in Kuwait.

MA: The moment had come for the strategy and power to shift to Europe. There was nothing else left and the EEC had already been prepared. Europe is now ready. We move out of Russia with a different strategy. Like a chess game. And it doesn't matter who gets hurt.

Napoleon had a marvellous mind. To him every battle was a chess game. That was his strategy. In fact he played a chess game before every battle. We have here then an international chess game.

DG: I am reminded of Commander William Guy Carr, Head of Security for Mackenzie King, Canadian Prime Minister during the Second World War, who wrote a book called *Pawns in the Game* after the War.

MA: Yes, pawns in the game. While the people were asleep around the world, or looking at television, or starving, or taking care of their families, the antiChrist was looking, watching, manipulating - I must confess with great brilliance. I pose a question which I hope will be answered later, one of the things that has not been considered much: why should England appear suddenly in disarray with these manoeuvres?

England, we must recognize, has never in its history succumbed to the invisible directors of the New World Order. Unless it was there it was secretly initiated!

The part that Robert Maxwell was to play may never be determined. But a deal was to be made that he was to be the next Prime Minister - after Margaret Thatcher, the first Jewish Prime Minister since Disraeli. Was his life terminated to prevent a premature Jewish take-over in Britain of the New World Order forces? Leaving the way clear for one of their own?

ROD: I return to what you were suggesting a few minutes ago, that the EEC has been deliberately prepared to be the body of the antiChrist.

MA: Yes, and they attempted to make Michael of Earth the hero of the whole thing. Nonsense. He was not a hero. He was, as I suggested earlier, an instrument, another pawn to be used. They needed what appeared to be a Christian and a Russian to put on top and who would give the world the impression he was saving the Russian people. And Michael complied, even arranging the coup to replace him. We also understand that Michael does have Jewish blood. His wife, Raisa, has Tartar blood, is a non-Christian, and never cared for Russia or for the people.

ROD: Gorbachev a pawn? Can you identify who was using him?

MA: The players of the world, the antiChrist world! Suppositions are vast: the Market of the Europeans, the New York Stock Market - who is controlling that for instance? The Federal Reserve of the United States? Its counterpart in Canada? The money-making machines of the world which finance the work of the antiChrist.

DG: The whole New World Order superstructure is a political and economic physical entity which is sustained by an invisible spiritual force, diabolical and ingenious.

MA: Capitalism means gold. Gold means power. Power means antiChrist. AntiChrist means control of the world. It's a pyramid, one of the goals set up seventy-five years ago in Russia.

I still remember when I was a child being told of doomsday. I was placidly independent. I was told: 'No matter where you go, no matter where you run, no matter how far you run, we will catch up with you.' My mother was told that and I was told that. My mother was told that when she was in the prison camps. I had just been born. But then when I grew up and I was in prison I was told that my parents were telling lies, that my parents were not Christians, that my parents said this, and that. I still remember that. I later realize that this is how a family is destroyed. This is the first principle of the antiChrist: destruction of family values, beliefs, and love of each other.

DG: This is one of the seven aims of the Illuminati, and it is well to remember the other six: (1) The abolition of all ordered governments; (2) Abolition of private property; (3) Abolition of inheritance (4) Abolition of patriotism; (5) Abolition of all religion; (6) The creation of a New World Order or World Government.

MA: By destroying the family you destroy the Church; by destroying the Church you destroy the Nation. When you destroy the nation, there's nothing left. That means a total takeover.

Let us take the history of the United States, the Constitution, the Founding Fathers, and Benjamin Franklin's stricture against admitting Jews: 'In less than 200 years,' Franklin writes, 'they will have swarmed in in such numbers that they will dominate and devour the land and change our form of government. . . . Our descendants will be working in the fields to furnish them substance, while they will be in the Counting Houses gleefully rubbing their hands. Your children will curse you in your graves.'

The first time I came to the United States in 1960 I felt there was a wall of protection from Luciferian influences.

DG: There was a different atmosphere at that time.

MA: Absolutely. I felt I had finally arrived at the House of Christ. It was Shang-ri-la.

DG: Interestingly enough, I thought the same thing when I arrived in '65. To me America was the promised land, as it had been for generations of settlers before. Indeed, America was a unique experiment in nationhood, promising unprecedented personal freedom, and total refuge from political, economic and religious oppression. When the settlers arrived, there was no established system of civil government - they had the unique opportunity to start everything afresh. The prospect of the private ownership of one's own land was psychologically reassuring and immigrants were free to develop their own talents to the best of their ability without being answerable to any man. Self-government and individual responsibility were not only encouraged - they were insisted upon. The family and educational systems were based on clearly defined moral and ethical values. The result, it is not an exaggeration to say, was "the freest, most creative, productive and prosperous nation in the history of mankind." Remember the words of John Winthrop, Governor of the Massachusetts Colony: "We shall be as a city upon a hill. The eyes of all people are upon us; so if we shall deal falsely with our God in this work we have undertaken and so cause Him to withdraw His present help from us, we shall be a story and a by-word throughout the world."

ROD: I am reminded of the image of swan and shadow. With the birth of democracy comes the birth of its counter ideal: world domination, and that is what the Illuminati, formed in the same year as the Declaration of Independence, are dedicated to. The predator swoops after the bird that has freed itself - the spirit of America, the spirit of man. Well, maybe it is time for a warning: there may just be a shadow on a shadow.

DG: More of that later. Today, twenty-eight years after I came here, we have a totally different mind-set. America used to believe in a creator God to whom we were responsible, in self-government, and personal responsibility. The antiChrist calls for the destruction of national sovereignity and the absorption of all nations into a One-World Government. One represents a Christian way of thinking and the other a Babylonian antiChrist view.

From time immemorial, every country has what Mr. Adir describes as 'a love of the motherland' or 'a love of the fatherland'.

MA: A national feeling, a national pride . . .

DG: A love for country and you feel totally protected. In the US Constitution, treason is defined as aiding and abetting enemies, both foreign and domestic. If you aid and abet anybody trying to drain the power of the land and the people for the creation of a foreign body, you are in essence committing treason.

MA: In the sixties the antiChrist powers were in the United States but were not yet in total control.

DG: Are you aware of Zbigniew Brzezinski's *Between Two Ages* published in 1970?

MA: Very superficially, but I have observed Brzezinski on television.

DG: In the book Brzezinski develops a case as to why the world needs to 'weave a new fabric of international relations', claiming that mankind has been moving through four great stages of evolution and that we now find ourselves in the middle of the fourth and final stage.

In Brzezinski's assessment of history, the first primitive 'stage' revolves around religion which provides for the 'acceptance of the idea that man's destiny is essentially in God's hands.' Such a 'primitive' idea is, of course, totally unacceptable to such a great mind as that possessed by the Polish immigrant. It demonstrates, he pontificates, a 'narrowness derived from massive ignorance, illiteracy and a vision confined to the immediate environment.'

The second stage that man has to go through along the road of 'true enlightment' is nationalism. This 'marked another giant step in the progressive redefinition of man's nature and place in the world.'

The third stage is said to be Marxism which 'represents a further vital and creative stage in the maturing of man's universal vision.' Marxism, Brzezinski tells his readers, is 'simultaneously a victory of the external, active man over the inner passive man and a victory of reason over belief. It stresses man's capacity to share his material destiny . . . and has served to stir the mind and to mobilize human energies purposely.'

The fourth and concluding stage is what Brzezinski describes as the 'Technetronic Era' - or the 'ideal of rational humanism on an international scale.' It is 'more directly linked to the impact of technology' and 'involves the gradual appearance of a more controlled and directed society. Such a society would be dominated by an élite . . . unrestrained by the restraints of traditional . . . values. This élite would not hesitate to achieve its personal ends by using the latest modern techniques for influencing public opinion and keeping society under close surveillance and control.'

MA: This is a perfect description of the destruction of the Christian faith, the family, the state, the country, and with the new élite now emerging in the EEC, the question is where is it going to end. I have a funny feeling it is going to end up in England.

DG: It will be possible, Brzezinski concludes, 'to assert almost continuous surveillance over every citizen and to maintain up-to-date, complete files, containing even personal information about the health or personal behavior of the citizen in addition to a more customary data. These files will be subject to instantaneous retrieval by THE authority.' Note that: THE AUTHORITY.

MA: You say Brzezinski is a Polish Jew? If not, he could never have made those statements. By making the statement he has, it is clear that the man is in full knowledge of what is happening around the world.

DG: First of all, he was used by David Rockefeller to create the Trilateral Commission; then he was brought in as an alien as Carter's Adviser on National Security; in addition to that, he was always in the background of the Reagan and Bush Administration, and now, with the coming of the Clinton Administration, he is beginning to emerge again. For him, the idea of American nationalism is totally 'primitive'. He is a dedicated internationalist, intent on the creation of a New World Order.

ROD: So he is the second significant figure, as well as Henry Kissinger . . . .

MA: Yes, and perhaps destructive.

DG: We ignore Brzezinski's words at our peril.

MA: Everything they have prepared has been done silently, treacherously. They only start to make statements and write books when everything is set in place and close to fulfilment. If you bring such a statement as you have just read to an ordinary man or woman with a family, can he or she understand it? Of course not! It's incomprehensible to them!

Take for example his mention of Marxism. Marxism was tried in England, in France, but because there were too many intelligensia they found they had made a mistake.

DG: There were not enough peasants.

MA: So they turned to Russia, a Christian world, believers, simple, honest, decent, uneducated people who didn't know how to write or read. This is where they then decided to continue the implementation of their plan. And suddenly every one of them emerges as a hero. Why?

DG: As the Bible says, 'God is not mocked. Whatsoever a man sows, that also shall he reap.' I believe that in the not too distant future there is a Judgment Day coming, a big showdown.

MA: Oh, I hope so!

DG: And everything will be put in its proper place.

ROD: I do not believe there will be any apocalyptic showdown. Does not the Bible promise that in the final battle not a leaf on the tree nor even a blade of grass will be disturbed. The change of heart and intent will happen in the world so swiftly and so subtly that Armageddon will be over before the majority are aware that it has even begun. And very few will know - three or five perhaps, or twenty-five - the mechanism, if you want to call it that, by which the cone suddenly reverses itself, the extreme expansion of one cone collapsing and, according to esoteric tradition, becoming the narrow apex from which the new cycle begins. At that mysterious point man will begin to ascend the stairway out of matter into which he has been descending from the first days. But there will be no chariots in the heavens. The heavens are in our hearts.

Gentlemen, may I ask another questions? What do you mean by the antiChrist?

DG: In its original form it doesn't mean what most people think it means. 'Anti' means in competition with or in opposition to. If I had a store on the main street, selling electrical equipment, and you came up and opened another store opposite me on the same street selling the same equipment, in the truest sense in which the term 'antiChrist' is used, you'd be 'anti Des Griffin'. It means 'over against'. Two systems are being offered, and man, with his natural proclivities, will usually choose the false one.

The con artist with a hatchet to grind, or good publicity man, will do everything in his power to undermine any credibility his competitor has in the mind of the people, through innuendos, through sneers. When the Jews brought out their cinematic abomination *The Last Temptation of Christ*, Christ was portrayed as a blundering idiot and a bastard, engaging in all kinds of sins - his mother was portrayed as a whore, etc. There was, for the duration of the movie, a constant kind of sneering, jeering, ridiculing attitude. What they will not do is to sit down as we are doing right now at a table and say, 'Turn on your tape recorders, turn on your video cameras, we're over here, you're over there. Let's get this thing recorded for posterity on camera.' Scripture says, 'The evil won't come to the light lest their deeds be reproved.'

MA: Evil cannot bear the light as the vampire cannot see the cross. Not to change the subject, when was the formation of the United Nations?

DG: 1945 or thereabouts.

ROD: Do you consider this relevant?

MA: Of course it is relevant. The antiChrist finally comes into existence in its golden dawn.

DG: In the Greek language, 'golden dawn' is translated 'Klu Klux' -

ROD: Klan. In slang code maybe, but not in our schools of learning.

MA: And who are the United Nations? Is it really what the world understands it to be?

DG: When Russia, US, Britain, Canada, etc. formed the Allied Forces in 1942, they immediately started to call their operation the United Nations, three years prior to the founding of the official body. The reason for this was because the US Congress had turned down the previous One-World Government attempt of the League of Nations. They wanted, therefore, to implant the name of the United Nations in the minds of the American people and abroad; by the conclusion of the War the United Nations was almost a household name.

It was all a very neat arrangement. The ground for the Headquarters Building in New York - worth about eight million - was donated by the Rockefeller family. Six or eight individuals from the State Department went to San Francisco to create the UN.

MA: Meantime, the International World Bank was created at Bretton Woods in 1948. Note the sequence of events.

DG: Unexpectedly then, totally out of the blue, Joe MacCarthy came on the scene. Partly through his efforts and the efforts of other people, it emerged that every single one of the individuals from the State Department involved in the creation of the UN were identified, under sworn testimony, to be all Communist agents, except one, John Foster Dulles, who, as it happens, was the legal representative of none other than Joseph Stalin

MA: There is one other point that is relevant. Russia has been represented in the United Nations from its initiation, yet when the International Bank was formed in 1948, all the major nations are represented, but Russia does not join. The Soviets had to be presented to the people of the world as an enemy.

DG: Furthermore, the Russians insisted on the United Nations being in America. Up to that time Soviet agents had been banned: they were all under surveillance. The UN afforded them a perfect opportunity to expand this operation: it made it much easier to pass orders as they had their representatives there.

MA: Is it possible that with the UN you have for the first time *visible* headquarters of the antiChrist.

DG: Located incidentally on US soil. Note too - in 1990 - that George Bush was the first President to come out openly and unreservedly in announcing the coming of the New World Order. As a matter of fact, Bush is the first President of the United States who has ever mentioned the New World Order as far as I know. Later, in 1992 before the UN Assembly, Bush vowed allegiance to 'the sacred principles embodied in the UN Charter.'

MA: It is inconceivable to hear of the President of the United States swearing his allegiance to the UN Charter. As you indicated earlier, this represents, from a Constitutional point of view, nothing less than treason.

ROD: To review what you have said, we have for seventy-five years a regime in Russia controlled not by Russians but by Jews, but the real controlling forces are not in Russia at all. The same seems to hold true of the United Nations. Where were the controlling forces?

MA: Europe, Canada and the United States. The European sector was controlled by the Rothschilds, the US by Rockefeller, and Canada by the Sanders people. In the other continents of the world, the Rockefellers were not projected as being Jewish. As far as Canada was concerned, the only thing we heard on the other side of the world was that the family was of Irish descent. It was a tripartite effort, a triangle.

On the European continent you have the 'biggies' - France, England, and Germany - and Switzerland, Austria, and the Vatican. You have six entities. Six magnificent minds!

ROD: And another egg in the USA, and another egg in Canada.

MA: Eight entities, and the puppet state - the Soviet Union headed by Stalin.

ROD: Who ultimately is calling the shots? And through which country? In order to investigate that question thoroughly we must turn to England. There is substantial documentation that during the Second World War England took over American intelligence, OSS, and prepared the way for America's entry into the War. The CIA emerged from the shell of OSS after the War, but what I find interesting is that with the 'defection' (or were they sent?) of that key cell consisting of Burgess-Maclean-Philby, etc., and with Philby going on to become Head of KGB, England has to all intents and purposes taken over Soviet Intelligence in its totality. The thrust of the Jewish-Masonic collaboration suddenly becomes clear and the stage is now set for the final assault on North America. Kennedy is assassinated in '63. It is time, gentlemen, that we turned to England.

DG: Before we do, I should point out that Kennedy may have been assassinated over the money issue. Apparently, he wished to issue only non-interest-bearing US notes and intended to exclude interest-bearing Federal Reserve notes. Had this been implemented it would have had catastrophic repercussions for the antiChrist forces. And in time it would have totally eliminated Jewish financial power throughout the world.

MA: To my mind, England has played a very inhuman role as far as the *destiny* of Russia is concerned. May I raise two questions? Nicholas II, being a cousin of the English Crown, could have been saved at the time. Why was a hand not extended to the cousin? Which means that maybe the English

Monarch was not in control at the time.

ROD: Or maybe the English decided to sit back and let the Bolsheviks do their work.

DG: It is clear that the British Parliament may not have been running the show either. The Jews wanted the Czar out of the way, and sent Trotsky on his way from New York aboard the S.S. Kristianiaford bound for Petrograd to organize the Bolshevik Revolution. The ship docked in Halifax on 13 April 1917, and the Trotsky party was detained by Canadian authorities on orders received from the British Admiralty in London.

Within a mere matter of hours, great pressure was brought to bear on the Canadian authorities by 'high officials' in both Washington and London, and Trotsky and his group were released. I haven't yet identified the 'high official' in London, but the one in Washington must have been none other than the President himself, Woodrow Wilson, who individually and personally organized the passport for Trotsky. Trotsky, incidentally, had been only in the US as an alien for three months. Rabbi Stephen Wise declares: 'I knew that in Wilson we had and would always have outstanding sympathy for the Zionist program and purpose.'

MA: Which could mean that England was not in control. That could also mean that England was controlled. If England was already controlled at the time, then we can understand why the House of Windsor is in such a chaotic situation today. The control was there from a considerable time back. So the Rothschilds, through the Hapsburg families, may have been in control of the continent of Europe even then.

England and Europe have always been afraid of Russia. Why? Afraid the peasants? Of the uneducated, who could not read or write?

Germany, on the other hand, has always treated Russia as a nation of pigs.

So Russia had to be crucified. We had England, Austria, France, Switzerland, the Vatican Empire (who had a great deal to say and do throughout the world), Germany, Poland, Hungary, Lithuania - every European sector. They were afraid of

Russia, and England, I am totally convinced, said 'You will obey or you will be destroyed.' As a result, Nicholas perished.

Originally, they were supposed to go only so far, but they decided on total domination. Could it be possible that Germany, England, and France were to be incorporated under the same aegis of Russia and to form one huge territory governed by The antiChrist for the remainder of time? But it didn't work out. So-called nationalism prevailed - with the French, with the Germans, with the English, and the two pillars of the financial establishment, the Vatican and Switzerland: the Masonic Star remained intact.

We can also ask here: How did it happen that the Vatican and Switzerland were the only two powers who managed to sustain their total identity without any destruction? Note too that they have very skilfully avoid notice in the media of the world. Furthermore, is it possible that this nation and city are, and have always been, the true pillars of the antiChrist world? What role of integrity or foul play has Malta, and the Knights of Malta, played throughout history? In essence here we have another triangle: the Vatican, Malta, and Switzerland.

To return to England! Remember England has always been known throughout the political world as 'the best seller and buyer in the world.'

DG: She was known in France as 'perfidious Albion.'

MA: In the forgotton world from which I come, she was known as 'the perfect prostitute'. Why was she addressed in that manner? This answer is very simple. It is because she was so nationalistic that she would do anything to achieve her objective. Later on, Churchill confirms the point when I believe he says that for one Englishman he was willing to sacrifice the whole world. I do, though, commend Churchill's valour: he was a perfect Defender of his world.

DG: In his book *The Empire of "The City"*, Kruth says that England makes and unmakes friends like a person changing clothes.

MA: Like a lady changing her purse, but what is in the purse is never to be known.

DG: Whatever was convenient for her. She either 'loved' you or stabbed you in the back. And that was known in European politics as 'The Balance of Power'.

MA: Whatever it is, the antiChrist has made a promise that they will never touch Germany, France, and England, nor the powers on this side who controlled Russia. They made very clear to the European sector: 'We will do everything, and this is what we are going to do, but we will never touch you.'

Let us not forget that there's another part of the globe we haven't mentioned. There's Japan, and China - known as the Dragon. Remember what Napoleon said: 'Let the Dragon sleep. Do not awaken it.'

Throughout our conversation on seventy-five years planning for the antiChrist, we must remember that old China has been demolished: 52 million people have perished and the world has not spoken about it. The Mao Revolution imposed the Soviet Communistic blueprint - but believe me Mao was not in control either.

Also, don't forget that they have extended their hands on the territory of China and have tried to ensure that it is not disturbed until *their* empires have been set up on this side of the world.

The Arab world also played an integral part. But it didn't last. The affinity of the Oriental world was in the long run with the Arabs and not with the Western world. The mysterious world of the Orient and the Arabs will never be known to the West, because the West can never understand their principles, their ways, their language or lands. On that side of the world the antiChrist can never set foot - because of the mentality of the Orient and the fixed faith of the Arabs.

DG: The oriental mind is totally at variance with the occidental mind.

ROD: The oriented mind is totally at variance with the accidental mind, as my friend Patrick Clare said to me once.

MA: Now, gentlemen, I am going to ask you a question. Where does the Vatican stand in all of this?

DG: Some people at the top say 'they are controlling every-thing'. I don't believe that myself personally. Did not one of the Rothschilds come to the Pope and force the Pope to come out and meet him in the cold?

MA: I believe he did.

DG: And at the same time did not Rothschild order the Pope to eat Kosher food?

MA: Did not one of the Popes have a Jewish mother?

ROD: Montini?

DG: Yes, allegedly, Montini was a Jew.

MA: I must call your attention to the irony of the Vatican being the antiChrist itself. God Almighty! That is frightening, is it not? And yet disguised in so many ways.

DG: Their method of operation and control has many similari-ties with the *modus operandi* used in the original Babylonian empire. In this context, I refer you to Alexander Hislop's *Two Babylons*.

MA: In a way Catholic dogma has always been force-fed, always under duress - is not that one of the controlling mechanisms?

DG: Somebody once said and I have repeated it a hundred thousand times - I consider it an excellent observation - that there are basically two forms of government. One is the God-inspired (or Christian) form of government; the other is the Luciferian or Babylonian form which is characterized by pres-sure, harrassment, coercion, and intimidation. Anywhere you see that government, either in a Catholic church or a Protestant church or in Washington D.C., that is a basic Babylonian form of government. The Bible says that the spirit will lead us into all truth. There need not be any pressure, harassment, coercion, and intimidation involved.

MA: It would be indeed ironic if the Vatican is the antiChrist empowering itself from the idealism of its people, like a vampire taking the lifeblood out of its innocent adherents.

Wouldn't it be ironic, as well as painful, to discover that the Jews were used as a perfect instrument for the Vatican?

ROD: Or the other way round. Remember what Benjamin Franklin said! How many thrones of the antiChrist will be set up in Europe? One? Two? Three?

MA: The antiChrist has to destroy the real throne. The last real throne left in the Royal Empire will, I believe, be crushed, and that is the House of Windsor.

ROD: Ah! So the Mason comes out on top of the - let us say - hewers of wood and drawers of water.

MA: First may I deal with the US link? Des Griffin has told me that President Bush has a blood connection with the Royal Family, and so has President-Elect Clinton.

DG: The documentation on Clinton is being prepared at the moment, but I have the material on Bush right here in my briefcase. It is an article in *The Washington Times* published on 6 July 1988, and it reads in part:

BUSH RELATED TO EUROPE'S ROYAL BLOOD

Vice-President George Bush is a distant cousin of Queen Elizabeth II and has blood ties with every other European royal family on or off the throne, according to the publishing director of a blueblood directory, . . . Harold Brooks-Baker, an American who has made a name for himself analyzing royal lineages, especially where they link up with the White House.

"Without any shadow of doubt, Vice-President George Bush is connected to more imperial, royal and noble houses than any previous president. . . ."

This week he [Mr. Brooks-Baker] released a copy of Mr. Bush's family tree traced by his directory, *Burke's Peerage*, back to the 1400's. It says that Mr. Bush is a long-lost relative - 13th cousin twice removed - of

Britain's current monarch, and is a direct descendant of King Henry VII, of one of Charles II's mistresses and of Henry VIII's younger sister, Mary, who married King Louis XII of France. . . .

Mr. Bush is related to all 60 royal families on the European continent, including the children of Monaco's Prince Rainier and his late American wife, Grace Kelly, he said.

Mr. Brook-Baker said that while very few Americans are descendants of European monarchy, "an unbelievably high proportion of American presidents are connected to the `Blood Royal.'"

Mr. Bush is without doubt connected to more great royal families than any reigning head of state today except His Serene Highness Prince Franz Josef of Liechtenstein. The vice-president also is related to 21 of Britain's 26 dukes, he said.

ROD: No wonder then, as Des said a little while ago, that Bush is the first President of the United States to mention the New World Order, and not only to mention it, but actually to indicate that it is just round the corner.

MA: The plot deepens. Now listen to this! At the Nominating Convention, the Bush - the Bush family came out, then the Quayle family. For the first time the platform was dominated not by men but by women, on both sides. As I sat there, I said "Wait a minute. What has happened to the men?" The women were the forerunners.

Now it is clear from what Desmond has just read that the line, or should I say lines, of Royalty are in Bush, and I am assured that they are in Clinton as well.

ROD: It made no difference therefore whether Bush won a second term or not. Clinton, smiling and seemingly naive - he wouldn't hurt a little fly, as Anthony Perkins says in *Psycho* - was carrying the ball, and nobody knew he had it. Talk about a loaded dice.

MA: So it had to come to that. The father prepares the throne

for the son. Is it possible that to the world it was a perfect
campaign, yet at the same time the decadence is taking over?
Why?

DG: There is an excellent book on Bush entitled *The Immaculate
Deception*. It is the story of the Bush crime family.

MA: The father prepares the throne for the son.

ROD: Could you explain that?

MA: The reason is that in this context Clinton could be Bush's
'son', that is as far at the age factor is concerned. If they are
both in the line that I have been told, then we have an
interesting proposition. Clinton's wife propagates that a child
can direct parents and even jail and prosecute them. That is
exactly what Mr. Clinton's wife said that her daughter, twelve
years of age, has the full right to do: to prosecute the parents.

DG: In other words, we've reached almost a complete circle,
from law, order, standards, values, to total anarchy. Anything
goes. Shaft the family.

ROD: How does that connect with the House of Windsor?

MA: The last throne of the Royalty stands with the Sceptre. It
must be destroyed.

ROD: By?

MA: By the female.

ROD: By the female?

MA: The faces, the eyes, the mouths, and the smiles can tell
you what type of a human being that person really is. Just as
an example, perhaps, look at Brzezinski! His eyes, his face: his
eyes are slender and foxy, devious, like a fox, the eyes of a fox.
He laughs at the world! The whole face is immobile, marble,
cold.

   Now let us look at Di. You can see it in the expression of
the eyes and in the nose. If you really watch her when she
smiles, she has that innocent marvellous smile, but behind that
smile you have those cold eyes and that interesting nose. I can't
quite define it.

ROD: Her family, I am told by a friend at the University of Toronto, has a claim on the Throne as well as Charles. They have connections with the House of Stuart, whom the Hanoverians were imported to keep in line. My academic friend thinks the present turbulence in the House of Windsor is 'a plot', that the Spensers of Althorp are determined the give the upstart Hanoverians their comeuppance. So what is going to happen there? Is that going to be the new Throne of the antiChrist?

MA: Do you not think that is a possibility?

DG: As I understand it, you are of the impression that probably she was sent in there to, shall we say, undo the House?

ROD: But also to set up her own House, the House of her family.

MA: On the foundations of the House that is being destroyed. There is another interesting factor: her grandmother made an interesting statement - if I am not mistaken it was Barbara Walters who did the interview - and this is unusual with all the immorality in this chaotic world. The grandmother said that the Prince of Wales had to marry an innocent girl, a virgin.

DG: I believe historically this is required, at least in the earlier times.

MA: Now, England has not always been known as one of the protectors as far as moral behaviour is concerned. Suddenly, for the first time in centuries we have a grandmother making public the principal issue.

Going back to the Democratic Convention, we have two women who get on the platform, talk about the moral issue of family, which is the father, and then we have the 'son' with his wife and she professes a total non-obedience and that the child can destroy the parent.

We have the beginning of the Soviet regime of 75 years ago with the principle that the child can inform on the parent. This is the way the family is being destroyed. First, prayer is banished; morality deteriorates; the churches are challenged; and finally a child informs on a parent and asks that that parent be judged. Are these not signs of total decadence in society?

DG: A perverted mind-set in which right is wrong and wrong is right.

ROD: Is Di using the full ritual of a time that is gone for some other purpose?

MA: If you go back to what we were originally discussing - Judaism - the innocent blood has to be sacrificed: the girl has to be pure. Except this sacrifice has to be done purposely, well-thought-out, well-prepared at the last Hurrah in the world.

ROD: More Blood Sacrifice! And already 1,600 million quarts of human blood have been sacrificed in this century. 'The heart's grown brutal from the fare.'

DG: Lady Queensborough tells us in *Occult Theocrasy* that many students of Masonry believe that the ceremony of 'the warrior on the block' (after which one receives 'the seething energies of Lucifer') involves the sacrifice of a male child of perfect innocence and high intelligence. If this is correct, they would be bonded to Lucifer through a blood covenant, in somewhat the same manner as Christians are bonded to Jesus Christ through the shedding of His blood on the Cross.

ROD: At the Last Hurrah of the World. Whose blood is being sacrificed though? Her blood or the blood of the Prince of Wales?

MA: One is the submitter; the other is the taker. The taker thought that he has received, that she was submitting herself willingly with loving care. In reality it was a perfect disguise.

ROD: A perfect disguise? Precisely. So that she could bide her time?

MA: With Charles being so young, why should he refuse his Throne?

ROD: Diana, or more correctly her House, will seize control of the Throne?

MA: I shouldn't be surprised at all.

ROD: She is the Princess of Wales.

MA: No, she is Lady Diana, Princess of Wales. Her House is entirely different.

ROD: William is ten. Let's assume that he will come to the Throne. But there is a hiatus of ten years or so where in fact the Throne of the antiChrist will be ruled by a child. So there will be a Regent, somebody else in the picture. And who would that be?

MA: Is it possible? Right now in England we have a child, ten, who is heir to the Throne. We have another child in France who also has a straight line to the Throne . . .

ROD: Of Britain?

MA: Of Russia.

ROD: Of Russia.

MA: I would not be surprised - we may not be alive - that we will see the two-headed reign of two children. Remember the antiChrist has a brother, if we are going by the mystical tradition. He has a brother. They are cousins.

ROD: William and the Russian will only be ten, eleven, twelve, thirteen, etc. The real damage will be done between . . .

MA: Ten and twenty-two.

ROD: How much time do we have before the World State and the World Dictator are realities? Before the boot - or in this case heel - that Orwell talks about will be stamping on the human face forever? A possibility, we might say, that is engineered by man himself and executed with a hatred, as Gilson says, as fierce and ingenious as only man is capable of conceiving for man.

DG: Remember the dinner, Robert, that you and I attended earlier this week in Washington. There were about ten people there, all on the inside track of political and strategic media. The same question came up: the feeling was that we had about two more years and that was all. My own feeling is that we don't have that long, maybe not beyond October of this year.

MA: Gentlemen, I have news for you. All you have left is ONE HUNDRED DAYS FROM THE DATE OF CLINTON'S INAU-GURATION, for the reasons I have indicated.

ROD: One hundred days! But, of course, time runs out for the antiChrist forces as well as his (or should I say her) antithesis.

MA: And now, King Arthur, do I have the right to ask you a question?

ROD: Please!

MA: You come from an old line. God Almighty! You are 700 B.C.

ROD: 1700 B.C.

MA: 1700 B.C. Before Christ?

ROD: Correct. It was my family who took the Stone of Scone, on which British Monarchs are crowned, from Egypt. The full story is in my book, *Atlantis Again: The Story of a Family*, which will be published on the same day as this book: 19 February 1993.

MA: Comparing ourselves to you, you are the ancient one; you are supposed to know every angle in this world. Desmond is the newcomer and I am a gypsy.

You are 1700 B.C. You come from the planet of the planet of the planets. We are just beginning in this world of planets. How in the world, coming from that ancient ancient world as you are, did you decide to ask the two novices for the knowl-edge that you yourself possess. That's the curious question that I have of you.

ROD: We find in the external world, in other human beings and in configurations of form and colour what lies hidden in ourselves. It is this intuition that initiates all of our intellectual quests in the first place. When the actual encounter takes place, there is a sudden shock, as Joseph Campbell puts it, a kind of throb of resonance within, a reverberation, a re-cognition, like the answer of a musical string to another equally tuned, a re-discovery of the particulars we all once knew - before Eden.

That is what I have found in Washington DC with you this blessed December day, dear Michael, dear Desmond. For that all of us must be eternally grateful. In other words, Earth is neither the beginning nor the end of Man.

CODA

by
Michael Adir

Sodom and Gomorah was destroyed in a single hour. How true it is! I will say the following: our present world, The New Babylon, I would compare to Sodom and Gomorah. Sodom and Gomorah destroyed itself from within; there was no technological imposition because it lacked the technical expertise and economic might that we possess today. That is the reason it did not become the womb of the antiChrist. But it was the beginning as we now see in the results. The Lord was lost, the soul was lost, and nothing, nothing was to return.

Today's World is a very similar matter. Again we have the destruction of the soul, because money becomes the ultimate goal of all. Money becomes God. Money can buy, sell, kill, destroy. Man starts to derive pleasure from seeing bloodshed, from the awful unhappy faces and unrelieved suffering of human forms, especially the children and the elderly.

Our fantastic age of technology - the New Babylon - has become the perfect medium for the incarnation of the antiChrist. We have fed ourselves on blood, in this century alone the blood of more than 200 millions: the heart hardens; the soul leaves the body; man becomes a machine.

Human blood is constantly being shed for a few almighty families. Maybe this is what I see in Di, what I see in her big eyes coming up from the deep. After all, the godchild of England is the house of Wales. Is it possible, therefore, that the visible antiChrist, The New Babylon, will select his orb on the sceptre?

Dear God, I only hope it will only be for a short while: humanity has suffered enough from the Babylonian craft.

It is time that everything that has been done in the world be turned around. Let them try the pits. Let them be at the steps of the suffering, so that they can see how difficult it is to purify oneself. But at the same time, dear Lord, have mercy on them as well.

Babylon, The New Babylon, and Sodom and Gomorah finally are one, have been one, shall be one, and shall continue to be one until you, dear Lord, will turn them into ashes. Ashes we were, ashes we are, and ashes we shall return to be.

Dear Lord, how simple it was to see it all finally. The only regret that I have is that I am too old, too tired, but the world is so young. Why has this beautiful world been destroyed by the few? The world is tired of wars, of hunger, of pain. Relieve us, I ask of you dear Lord.

I wish never to offend anyone in this book nor to cause anger or despair. I only wish that at least after reading the book, those who were and are Players on the international scene, and especially those who create misery for their own gain and constant prosperity by crushing the innocent and the vulnerable (children, the sick, the poor, the old), will finally look in the mirror and see their souls, not their faces, and say to themselves: Have I been one of those? Am I now?

I challenge no one. Nor am I looking to be challenged. All I know is what I saw, what I see: the destruction of beautiful continents and cities because of a few who want to be the Masters of the World! Why?

As already stated, I repeat again:
It is not my choice if I'm led astray.

What Eternal Teacher bids me explain?
As He wants us to grow we grow that way.

Never mind, my shame will wash away with wine.
Joyful is night - Sad is this dawn of mine.

Friends! And the World! Forgive this heartless man, I
                                                    pray;
You will smell dust as long as sun will shine.

A covenant with a wine cup you better try!

Love is a pearl - How mean of me!
In Eternal bliss the Teacher sits high on throne

And when you nigh want to read HIM
Your life may come to an end

- Destiny's order we all love to obey.

Thank God! Whatever from you I have asked,
Not for me - but for them,

I've always been blessed in my quest
Forgive us! Dear Lord! Forgive us!

Our only hope is that one day we shall all go back to
beauty and serenity, that the desire to dwell in God's heart will
be the image in every one, that the pure of heart will be the ones
to speak, and that the recurring anger, anguish, and shame of
Babylon will finally be appeased.

Note for "Global Theatres of the antiChrist"

Henry Kissinger: During the last stages of the preparation of *The New World Order* the following article, "Crimes Against Humanity" by Gerald Caplan, appeared in the Toronto Star (19 January 1993):

Heaven knows our era has not lacked for crimes against humanity. A list of the most notorious would likely include the Vietnam war, the pitiless Pakistani massacre of Bengalis in 1971, the operations of the Shah of Iran's secret police, the brutal Pinochet years in Chile, the secret U.S. bombing of Cambodia that created the conditions for the Khmer Rouge's killing fields, the bloody 1974 Turkish invasion of Cyprus, the betrayal of the Kurds in 1974-75, the Indonesian slaughter of some 100,000 East Timorese, the war against the government of Angola, the policies of the white governments of Rhodesia and South Africa.

What we do know, however, is that all of them had in common Henry kissinger. As Richard Nixon's national security adviser and secretary of state in those years, Kissinger was either responsible for or, at the very least, endorsed every single one of them. And Larry Eagleburger worked under him throughout.

All this information comes not from any weird pinko sources but from the recent bestselling biography *Kissinger* by Walter Isaacson of *Time Magazine*. Isaacson found the man to be a two-faced, deceitful, callous, paranoid, duplicitous, devious, lying, conspiratorial, amoral megalomaniac who caused untold human suffering largely to satisfy his own monstrous ego.

Yet in the end what is as appalling as Kissinger's own evil deeds is his celebrity and lionization. He has gotten away, literally, with murder. Isaacson shows that in return for access, even the most prominent of Washington's pundits and columnists routinely peddled Kissinger's self-aggrandizing lies and twisted analyses as if they were gospel. Even now that the truth is known, even after his shameless public support for the Beijing dictatorship during

Tiananmen while he was making a mint opening Chinese doors for American corporations, Kissinger remains a media darling.

He counts among his dinner partners the likes of Tom Brokaw, Ted Koppel and Barbara Walters, plus senior VIPs from CBS, ABC, *Newsweek*, CNN and the New York Times - and the head of the AFL-CIO! Corporations that fork out big bucks to get him on their boards or to act for him, such as our own Conrad Black, are expected to crow lustily about their great coup.

Then there is the Argentinian Nobel Peace Prize winner who once accused Kissinger to his face of "genocide and collective massacre."

Yet the man remains an American icon.

Appendix 1: *The Play of Antichrist*

In a play published almost a thousand years ago, *Ludus de Antichristo* (*The Play of Antichrist*), we have a situation that is remarkably similar to the situation confronting mankind today.

In the play, the Holy Roman Emperor announces his intention to bring the whole world under Roman rule. 'With all the appurtenances of human strength - law, custom, military power, and force of character - on his side, he gains control over all that human might and glory have to offer' (1). He then goes to the Temple at Jerusalem and surrenders his crown and the totality of human accomplishment to nobody else but 'God'.

The extraordinary outcome of this manoeuvre is not the Second Coming of our Lord Jesus Christ on clouds of fire, but the advent of the Antichrist. Mastery of the world, the bringing of its diverse elements under the control of one man, or under the control of the *one mind* of several men, produces the contrary effect of what was intended. God did not create the world for man to usurp the role of God. In God's eyes all humans are equal, each possessing unique but varying gifts, miraculously balanced out on the fulcrum of spiritual justice. As well, the world consists of more than the kingdom of man; the animal, plant, and mineral kingdoms exist not merely for man's convenience but to complete the symphony of life on earth.

The antiChrist of a thousand years ago was a creation of man, as is the antiChrist of today. Once he assumes power, he attempts to convince the world of his divinity by intimidation, persuasion, and false miracles. His last victims are the Jews who have misled themselves into believing that 'he is the long-awaited Messiah' (2). Once his divinity is proclaimed, Antichrist proceeds to use all the weaknesses of humanity to demonstrate the ephemerality of humanity's achievement and to destroy it. In other words, the object seems to be nothing less than the object of the World State today: the obliteration of the tenth hierarchy, man, whose soul in a way represents a crucible of the cosmos, for in that soul, and in its root, the beating heart, contrary impulses meet: lacerations of light, lacerations of darkness. In that tumult, colour is created (i.e. according to Goethe rather than Newton) and a choice is made.

In the play it appears as if nothing can save the human world from the ever-ripening quicksand of evil but the direct intervention of God.

This is exactly how the play concludes. 'Antichrist summons all the world to worship him, and just when he is saying, "peace and safety," he is destroyed by a thunderbolt from Heaven, and mankind, forgiven, returns to God' (3).

Despite the cliche, history never repeats itself exactly. The *deus ex machina* intervention of God may have been the way in which the matter of the antiChrist was resolved a thousand years ago. No such luck seems in store for us today, despite the promises of men masking under a religious authority their own meglomaniac delusions. As the greatest initiate of this century has pointed out. Unlike earlier dispensations, produced by the fleshlink of natural and supernatural - Leda and the Swan, the Dove and the Virgin - the new dispensation will be 'neither from beyond mankind nor born of a virgin, but begotten from our spirit and history' (4). Therefore, Yeats goes on, in terms eerily similar to Gentilitas's song at the beginning of *Antichrist*, the more gods men commune with the more they grow in imagination and understanding. We cannot sidestep the startling corrollory of that statement: worship of ONE GOD sets the scene for ANTICHRIST:

'countless divinities . . . have taken upon themselves spiritual bodies in the minds of modern poets and romance-writers. . . . The many think humanity made these divinities, and that it can unmake them again; but we who have seen them pass in rattling harness, and in soft robes, and heard them speak with articulated voices while we lay in death-like trance, know that they are always making and unmaking humanity, which is indeed but the trembling of their lips.'

He had stood up and begun to walk to and fro, and had become in my waking dream a shuttle weaving an immense purple web whose folds had begun to fill the room. The room seemed to have become inexplicably silent, as though all but the web and the weaving were at an end in the world. 'They have come to us; they have come to us,' the voice began again; 'all that have ever been in your reverie, all that you have met with in books. There is Lear, his head still wet with the thunderstorm, and he laughs because you thought yourself an existence who are but a shadow, and him a shadow who is an eternal god; and there is Beatrice, with her lips half parted in a smile, as though all the stars were about to pass away in a sigh of love; and there is the mother of the God of humility, He who has cast so great a spell over men that they have tried to unpeople their hearts that He might reign alone, but she holds in her hand the rose whose every petal is a god; and there, O, swiftly she comes! is Aphrodite under a twilight falling from the wings of numberless sparrows, and about her feet are the grey and white doves' (5).

In both the medieval and modern situations, the inherent weakness of mankind is demonstrated by the temptation to give up the struggle, surrendering — perhaps unwittingly - in the process the fragile substance that makes us human: our free will. Surrender of this thread which links the actions of our lives means certainly an end to uncertainty and suffering, but the choice to alleviate the pain of existence comes at the greatest price known to man: what Faust experiences when he sells his soul. Artists who do not acknowledge a Christian God sometimes evoke this quality in man - his ability to struggle on and suffer - more convincingly than writers who take the easy way out, easing the uncertainties of living with a tablet of commandments and an anthropomorphic God:

On men reprieved by its disdainful mercy, the immortal sea confers in its justice the full privilege of desired unrest. Through the perfect wisdom of its grace they are not permitted to meditate at ease upon the complicated and acrid savour of existence. They must without pause justify their life to the eternal pity that commands toil to be hard and unceasing, from sunrise to sunset, from sunset to sunrise; till the weary succession of nights and days tainted by the obstinate clamour of sages, demanding bliss and an empty heaven, is redeemed at last by the vast silence of pain and labour, but the dumb fear and the dumb courage of men obscure, forgetful, and enduring (6).

To abandon the struggle, then, to surrender one's will, to compromise one's capacity to encounter the unknown, can only lead to spiritual slavery and the annhilation of the human spirit itself. Never in the history of man is this propensity so prevalent than at the end of a millennium - in the period before the play of *Antichrist*, or, in the period where we find ourselves today - the propensity to elevate 'antiChrist' to the status of World Dictator. Governments, churches, political parties, get-rich-quick pyramids, chain letters, and, much more dangerously, Gurus act like magnets on the drifting souls that are everywhere to be found, like withered leaves at the end of autumn:

In every land and in all countries, the people wait with fear and trembling for the powerful of this world to decide their lot for them. They hesitate, uncertain, among the various forms of slavery which are being prepared for them. Listening with bated breath to the sound of those countries which fall one after the other with a crash followed by a long silence, they wonder in anguish how long will last this little liberty they still possess. The waiting is so tense that many feel a vague consent to slavery secretly germinating within themselves. With growing impatience, they await the arrival of the master who will impose on them all forms of slavery, starting with the worst and most degrading of all - that of the mind. Blessed be he who will deliver us from ourselves! Alone under a heaven henceforth empty, man offers to whoever is willing to take it, this futile liberty which he does not know how to use. He is ready for all the dictators, leaders of these human herds who follow them as guides and who are all finally conducted by them to the same place - the abbatoir (7).

The anonymous author of *The Play of Antichrist* - why he remained anonymous we can easily guess - saw it all just as clearly nearly a thousand years ago.

Robert O'Driscoll

Extracts from *The Play of Antichrist*

When the scene is set, Gentilitas and the King of Babylonia
step forward to start the play. Gentilitas sings:
>   The deathless gods must be adored
>   in every mortal rite
>   And everywhere their multitudes
>   be fearful in their might.
>
>   Men who claim that God is one
>   and disregard the rules
>   Which all antiquity obeyed
>   are simpletons and fools.
>
>   For if we say a single god —
>   controls the universe,
>   We must admit the forces that
>   control him are diverse.
>
>   Sometimes he grants a blessed peace
>   with loving gentleness;
>   Sometimes he shakes the storms of war
>   with savage ruthlessness.
>
>   The many different provinces
>   the gods must oversee
>   To us are certain evidence
>   of their variety.
>
>   But those who say a single god
>   controls such different forces
>   They have a god whose unity
>   is turned in different courses.
>
>   Lest then we say a single god
>   is subject to such friction,
>   And thus admit divinity
>   is ruled by contradiction,

We are determined for this cause
to separate the gods,
Since by their provinces we see
how much they are at odds. . . .

Then Synagoga enters with the Jews singing:
Lord, our salvation is in Thee;
In man there is no hope for life.
To hope that we can ever gain
Salvation in the name of Christ is vain.

Strange, that He should fall to death
Who offered life to other men.
Is one who could not even save
Himself, to rescue others from the grave?

As Ishmael despised the gods,
So you are to detest this Christ.
Not He, but Lord Immanuel
Shall be the God adored by Israel. . . .

Immediately Antichrist enters, dressed in a breastplate which
is hidden under his other garments. Accompanying him are
Hypocrisy on the right and Heresy on the left, to whom he sings:
The hour of my reign is here;
Therefore you both must persevere;
Prepare at once the way for me
To mount the throne of royalty.
I wish the world to adore
Myself alone forevermore.
You both are apt for this, I know;
I raised you for it long ago.
Now is the time when I must ask
Your help and labor for this task.
Behold, the nations all enthrone,
Revere, and worship Christ alone.
Therefore, wipe out His memory,
And transfer His renown to me.

To Hypocrisy:
>   In you the groundwork I will lay.

To Heresy:
>   Through you the later growth will come.

To Hypocrisy:
>   Through you the faithful then will stray.

To Heresy:
>   Through you the clergy will succumb.

They reply:
>   We'll place the world's faith in you;
>   The name of Christ we will subdue. . . .

Then Antichrist directs the Hypocrites to Synagoga, telling them:

>   Go tell the Jews the Messiah now is come;
>   The Gentiles have already welcomed me.
>   So tell the Jewish nation, I am he,
>   The Messiah long foretold in prophecy.

NOTES:

1.   John Wright ed. and trans., *The Play of Antichrist* (Toronto: Pontifical Institute of Mediaeval Studies , 1967), p. 44.

2. Wright, *Antichrist*,

3. *Ibid.*, p. 46.

4. W. B. Yeats, *A Vision* (1937), p. 262. See also Augusta Gregory, *Journals*, p. 261, where Yeats is recorded as saying that the new revelation 'will not be outside the world as Christ was.'

5. Yeats, 'Rosa Alchemica', *Mythologies* (London: Macmillan, 1962), pp. 274-5.

6. Joseph Conrad, *The Nigger of the Narcissus* , section 4.

7. Gilson, *Terrors of the Year Two Thousand*, pp. 16-7.

APPENDIX II: Soloviev's *"Antichrist"*

We live in an age when many believe that humanity is destined to unite, but it may be that this inclinclination is not a healthy one. Vladimir Sergeyevich Soloviev included a dialogue, "The Antichrist", in his book *War and Christianity*. In this narrative he described the advent of the Antichrist, and his ascension to the position of world Emperor.

Having begun his career with an amazing show of brilliance in philosophy and theology, the Antichrist finds himself able to make good connections. He joins the brotherhood of Freemansons, and somehow convinces the Hebrews that he's indeed the promised Messiah. Both of these groups have considerable economic and political influence. Having duped most of the population, the Antichrist is chosen as the Emperor of Europe, Holy Roman Emperor.

Europe now becomes the world superpower, and eventually, at the behest of the Emperor and his supporters, all of civilized society comes under the dominion of the Antichrist.

The Emperor has not gained his position on intellectual and spiritual merit alone. In fact he is known by many to be of doubtful parentage, being the son of a promiscuous woman. He is also a General. Europe had recently repelled the tide of Pan-Mongolism that threatened to swallow it. Japan and China had joined together with the technology they took from the West. They hoped to dominate Europe before Europe dominated them. Seeing that the materialist philosophy borrowed by the Orientals was so destructive, a great spiritual hunger rages across the rest of the world. Because most people have been divorced from true religion, the Antichrist easily convinces all, even the learned, of his divine mission.

The one obstacle that remains is Christianity. The Emperor calls them to a council in Palestine, of all places, an autonomous territory controlled by the Jews. This is where the imperial residence has been put! With bribes of cultural wealth, the Antichrist convinces most of Christianty to call him their protector. Most, but not all do, for a few see past his shallow offer. It is Christ whom they value above all, not a book, nor art. The Pope himself will not follow, neither will the leader of the Orthodox Christians, nor the head of the Protestants. A puppet is therefore installed in the Vatican, chosen by the Evil One himself! Unity is imposed upon the dominated Christians, and so they no longer pose a threat. The faithful ones are left to wander in the desert, waiting for the End of Time.

The Antichrist, and World Emperor, has three main allies: Freemasonry, because he is their brother, the Jews, or Hebrews, who believe him to be the Messiah, and a controlled Vatican.

Another Emperor, Constantine, knew that the Cross holds great power. He realized that the predominantly German and Christian army of Maxentius would never fight against the Cross. These soldiers, like the rest of the early Christians, had no political power, *per se*, but they were a major social force. Constantine knew that with Christian backing his power could be established. The Antichrist would have to gain the backing of Christianity as well. Economic and polictical predominance, via Freemasonry and the Jews, would not be enough. The human spirit must also be enslaved. AntiChrist knows that his antithesis is the power that frees humanity from Evil; therefore he attempts to cut people off from Christ.

In Soloviev's narrative, and in our world of today, the signs of the final reckoning seem near: predatory wars by the strong on the weak; demonic politics; unnatural alliances, an everlasting victimization of those who refuse to compromise; a plethora of religions who hold out heaven as some kind of extension of the material condition of earth.

Soloviev wrote "The AntiChrist" with the purpose of unmasking the Evil One who will come masquerading as the Saviour. When we continue to exercise our free will, no matter what the allurement, our soul learns at last that, as Yeats discovered, 'its own sweet will is Heaven's will.' Furthermore, when we continue to exercise our free will we bring ourselves into alignment with Christ who constitute the quintessential core of goodness. To each human being is given the challenge of weaving his own Ariadne's thread, linking the actions and moods of a lifetime by some inner logic which may or may not make sense to outsiders. In this way a person weaves the tapestry of his

THE THRONE OF THE ANTICHRIST

life, drawing up into the light of consciousness that portion of invisible 'dark' matter which he or she, and only he or she, has tested and discovered to be true. As Professor O'Driscoll said in one of his lectures, we must train ourselves to be deep-sea divers.

This is the exhileration of life, this the challenge, had we only the courage to match our true inclinations. For, like Theseus, and with Ariadne's foresight, we discover within ourselves the way out of the labyrinth of matter and into the realms of the spirit which, it is clear, is our true destiny.

The Kingdom of the antiChrist draws on the energy of Christ and inverts it, subliminally sowing the seed that IT represents the freedom that Christ's Church represses. The charge of 'anti-semitism' startles us because it plants a thought in our minds which, in the majority of cases, has not been there before.

Let no one remain in confusion about the antiChrist. HE, SHE, IT represents codification, ossification, the obliteration of free will, total control and chains forever. It means too that we remain fixed forever in an endless repetition of what we have already suffered through thousands and thousands of times, or, worse still (and do not doubt it for a moment: THEY can do it), to be caught forever in those bodies in which our spirits are only supposed to be temporarily caged.

One final word with relation to THE antiCHRIST, this monstous creation of man. Let no one be deceived, as Soloviev warned. Christ will radiate in the darkness, showing us the way to redemption. Others may shine, but their unholy light will likely show us not what we need, only what we want to see, and sense, as our spirits are drawn deeper and deeper into this all too solid pit of flesh.

Nicholas Young

Plate 49: 'Amageddon is On'. Impression by E.E.

Plate 50: *'Amageddon is Over'. Impression by E.E.*

NOTES ON CONTRIBUTORS

Des Griffin is the Senior writer in this field, having spent 35 years researching the subject. The result is five books which have revealed the causes behind the effects that we see unfolding on the world scene: *Fourth Reich of the Rich*; Emissary, Clackamas, Oregon, published 1976, revised 1992; *Descent Into Slavery?* Emissary, published 1980, revised 1988; *Anti-Semitism and the Babylonian Connection*, Emissary, 1988, revised 1992; *Martin Luther King: The Man Behind the Myth*, Emissary, 1987; and *Freedom or Slavery* (1990) in collaboration with three others.

Mr. Griffin was born in Portadown, County Armagh. He lived in various parts of Ireland for twenty years, then spent eleven years in England (1954-65) working at various jobs. In 1965 he emigrated to Canada and two years later went on to the United States, where he has worked in publishing since then. Des and his wife Karen live in Oregon with their two children, a son and a daughter , and two grandchildren.

In 1985 Mr. Griffin founded *The Midnight Messenger* 'to keep abreast of fast-moving events worldwide and to provide subscribers with both the political and historical overview that will enable them to understand what is happening on the national and international scenes. The bi-monthly has subscribers in 50 States and 12 foreign countries. At the same time Mr. Griffin is working on his sixth book, *Storming the Gates of Hell.*

Robert O'Driscoll, Ph. D. (University of London, England, 1963), Research Fellow, University of Reading (1963-64), Visiting Professor, National University of Ireland. (1964-6), University of Toronto (1966-present). Full Professor since 1975. Internationally known as a scholar with some 20 books from Oxford University Press, University of Toronto Press, Macmillan of London, MacMillan of Canada, McLean-Hunter, George Braziller of New York, McClelland and Stewart, Canongate in Scotland, Dolmen in Ireland, Zespol International in Germany and Russia, etc. His *Celtic Consciousness* was named by the American Library Association an Outstanding Academic Book of the year in the United States for 1982.

O'Driscoll has been an Associate of the leading artistic and philosophical figures of our time, including Marshall McLuhan, Buckminster Fuller, Joseph Campbell, W. H. Auden, John Cage, Sorel Etrog, Richard Demarco, and hundreds of others.

Margarita Ivanoff-Dubrowski was born and spent her early life in Eurasia. She completed her University education at Georgetown University in the United States, and later in Latin America. All her life she has been a philantrophist. Recently she has developed a passion for all things Celtic and is one of the mainstays of the Shaw Society in Dublin. A couple of years ago she helped restore the house where Shaw was born.

Douglas Annear is engaged at present in Graduate Studies at the University of Toronto, having headed his class in his graduating year 1991-2, Douglas had a choice of many Scholarships, including one to Oxford. He chose to complete his M.A. at the University of Toronto and has not yet decided whether he will pursue a Ph. D. degree in Middle Eastern Studies or in English Literature.

Michael Adir was born in 1940, joined the Russian Army in 1958, and within a short time was assigned to Vognaya, secret intelligence network of the Russian Army. In December 1963, interestingly just a few weeks after the Kennedy assassination, he was appointed, personally and confidentally, by Nikita Khruschev to monitor all 'cult' movements throughout the world, anything indicating a movement towards a World State, and to report his findings, 'no matter how trivial,' to a gentleman who had just been installed in KGB headquarters: Mr. Kim Philby.

Patrick Clare received his Intelligence training in the Canadian Army. He is a character in *Nato and the Warsaw Pact Are One* and helped greatly in the construction of The New World Order. Patrick is also a horseman and artist.

Nicholas Young is studying Religious Studies at the University of Toronto.

A. Aksakov, formerly Professor of Philosophy at St. Petersburg.

Max Dessoir, formerly Professor of Philosophy at Humboldt University in Berlin.

E. E. produced the film of *Nato and the Warsaw Pact are One* (directed by Antony Lorraine) which, when presented at the European City of Culture Festival caught the attention of Micheal Adir, Director of Voynaya, Intelligence network of the Russian Army.

I N D E X

A

Aath, David   3
Adenauer, Konrad   174, 175
Admiral Canaris,   54, 55, 58,
   59
Admiral Kimmell   45, 46
Admiral Liviski   24
Admiral Popov   24
Admiral Stark   45
Adonay   16
Aldrich Plan   25
American Bayer Company   33
American one-dollar bill   4
Andropov, Yuri   165
Anti-Semitism   93, 94
Apeter, Kairn   229
Apfelbaum   314
Aristotle   170
Armageddon   4
Aronchtam   229
Asquith, Herbert   39, 107, 108
Atheism   15
Atom Bomb   xv
Austro-Prussian War   21

B

Bachelard, Gaston de   246
Baldwin, Stanley   38
Balfour, Arthur   101, 110
Bank of International Settle-
   ments   100
Baron von Lersner, Kurt   55
Baruch, Bernard   25, 52, 97,
   98, 101
Bassett, John   223
Battle of Stalingrad   62
Battle of the Bulge   79
Battle of Waterloo   17

Bauer, Moses Amschel   17
Bell, D.W.   69
Belloc, Hillaire   220, 231
Ben Gurion, David   90, 223
Beria, Lavrenti   324, 340
Berkeley   170
Bismarck   21, 33
Blake, William   246, 247, 249,
   251
Bolshevik Revolution   xvii, 6,
   72, 107
Bolsheviks   22, 61
Booth   97
Bradley, General Omar   73
Brandeis, Louis D.   106
Brett, R. L.   245
British Economy   17
Brzezinski, Zbigniew   349
Buchanan   24
Bunichenko   82
Burgess   284
Bush, George   xiii, 87, 90, 240,
   351, 360

C

Cabot Lodge, Sr., Henry   26
Caldwell, Taylor   5
Campbell   247
Captain Wilkinson   45
Carnegie, Andrew   85, 311
Cassel, Ernest   107
Central Bank   25
CFR   85, 86
Chadaev, Y.   294
Chamberlain, Neville   38, 40,
   41, 43
Chambers, Whittaker   71
Christianity   6, 15

Church of Mormon   xiii
Churchill, Winston   6, 5, 39,
    40, 41, 43, 44, 48, 49, 54,
    71, 73, 78, 80, 81, 98, 220,
    311, 317, 334
Chuter, James B.   83
CIA   86
Civil War   24, 25
Clare, Patrick   223
Clifford, Clark   89
Clinton, Bill   351, 362
Cold War   xvii
Colonel Count von
    Stauffenberg, Claus   58
Colonel Dall, Curtis B.   53
Colonel Erdofy, Maxwell E.   62
Colonel Kotikov, Anatoli N.   60
Commander Earle   59, 72
Committee on Foreign Rela-
    tions   87
Communism   92
Comte de Vireu   13
Confederate States of
    America   23
Congress of Vienna   98
Congress of Wilhelmsbad   xiii,
    4, 13
Connell, Brian   107
Connery, Sean   xvii, 335
Conspiracy   5
Constitution   23
Coolidge   36
Council on Foreign Relations
    (CFR)   85
Crown   46
Czar Nicholas II   24

D

Dall   57, 58, 81
Darwin, Charles   237
Davis, Jefferson   23
Dawes, Charles   98

Dawes Plan   32, 98
Dawson, Geoffrey   109
Deane, Major General John
    R.   62, 63
Declaration of Independ-
    ence   12
Democratic Party   54
Descartes   170
Dexter White, Harry   69, 71
Disraeli, Benjamin   xvii, 5, 47
Dodd, William   35
Domville, Sir Barry   38
Dr. Englebrecht   35
Dresden   76
Driesch, Dr. Hans   181
Droste-Huelshoff, Annette
    von   186, 187
Du Ponts   35
Duisberg, Dr.Karl   33
Dulles, John Foster   87, 102
Dunkirk   43

E

Earle, George   53, 54, 55,
    56, 57, 58, 81
Egonoffs   229
Einstein, Albert   12, 170
Eisenhower, Dwight D.   xiii,
    xv, xvii, 51, 52, 53, 72, 73,
    78, 79, 80, 81, 82, 84, 87
Eliot, T.S.   96, 192, 194, 246
Elliott   170
Epstein, Julius   83, 84
Erhardt, Ludwig   170

F

Fabian Society   22
Fabius   22
Fahey, Dennis   301
Farben, I.G.   33, 99
Farrell, F.P. 'Bud'   88, 89
'Federal' Reserve Act   26, 28

Federal Reserve System 85
Field Marshal Alexander 49
First Socialist International 21
Fischer, Bobby xvii
Fischer, Dr. Oskar 182, 183
Fish, Hamilton 45, 102
Ford, A.G. 35, 85
Ford, Henry 5
Ford Motor Company 35
Forrester, Izola 97
Franz II 232
Freedman, Benjamin 93
Freemasonry 13, 14

G

Gamarnik, Jankel 229
Geley, Dr. Gustave 181
General Alexander 48
General Clark, Mark 49
General Groves 64
General Kesselring 50, 59
General Mark Clark 59
General Marshall 45
General McArthur 63
General Motors 35, 36
George, Lloyd 39, 101
German Nationalists 14
Gerstenmair, Eugen 58
Ghost Sonata 3
Gilson, Etienne 220, 236, 239,
241
Goldman, Emma 7
Goldwater, Barry 89
Gorbachev, Michael 296, 300
Gorkin, A. 294
Gouzenko, Igor 217, 218, 220,
222
graduated income tax 85
Granatstein, Jack 220
Great Depression 31, 37
Griffin, G. Edward 99
Gromyko, Andrey 165
Gruber, Dr. Karl 180

Gulf War 90
Gwynne, H. A. 109
Gzowski, Peter 202

H

Haig, Douglas 108
Hall, A.W. 69
Hall, Manley 95
Hamburg 74
Harriman, Averell 69
Harriman, Edward 311
Harrington, Sir John 89
Harris, Sir Arthur 77
Harry Hopkins 67
Hazard 68
Hegel 170
Heinrici, Gotthard 74
Herzl, Theodor 104
Himmler, Heinrich 81
Hindenburg 309
Hiroshima xvi
Hitler, Adolph 32, 34, 36, 43,
44, 54, 56, 58, 80, 220, 227
Hopkins, Harry 60,
61, 65, 68, 69, 220
House, C. Mandell 25, 38, 101
House, Edward Mandell 97
Howard, Con 295

I

I.G. Farben Company 35
Illuminati xiii, 3, 4, 12, 15, 21,
26, 29, 36, 43, 46, 50, 53,
90, 91, 94, 98, 107, 196
Illuminism 13
Illuminist 14
Illuminati and
Freeemasony xiii
Institute of Pacific Relations 46
International Bankers xvi,
14, 17, 21, 25, 26, 28, 29,
30, 32, 33, 37, 43, 46, 47,
50, 72, 79, 99

International Financiers xiii,
    xv
International Harvester Com-
    pany 35
International Monetary
    Fund 71
International Money
    Monopolists 37

J

Jaeger, Dr. Einar 179
J. Henry Schroeder Bank 36
J.P. Morgan 35
J.P. Morgan Co. 25
Jordan, George
    Racey 59, 60, 61, 66, 69,
    72
Jordan diaries 61
Joyce, James 192, 194
Judaism xiii
Jung, C. G. 255

K

Kagan, Lazarus 229
Kalinin, Ekaterina
    Ivanovna 327
KalininMikhail xii, 328
Kant 170
Kastein, Joseph 107
Kelly, John 243
Kennedy, John 355
Kenoye 102
Kermann, Mandel 229
Kerensky, Alexander 310, 313
Khazar 93, 104
Khruschev, Nikita 298, 299,
    339
Kilgore Committee 32
King George VI 172
King, William Lyon Macken-
    zie 176, 177, 217, 218
Kitchener, Lord 108

Kissinger, Henry 333, 351
Kosygin, Alexy 165
Korean War 89
Kotikov 64, 65, 66, 69
Krabbe, Dr. C. 182
Kremlin xv
Krupp 35
Kuhn, Loeb and Co. 25
Kun, Bela 7
Kuznetsy, Sarapulsky 329

L

League of Nations 85
Leibniz 170
Lemmi, Adriano 90
Lend-Lease 59, 60, 61, 62, 63,
    64, 68, 70
Lenin, Niklai 90
Lenin's Bolsheviks 22
Lieberman 168
Lilienthal 110
Lincoln, Abraham 24, 97
Lindbergh, Charles 5, 26
Lewis, Wyndham 220, 231
Logan Act 86
Lorraine, Anthony 295
Lucifer 12, 15, 16, 94
Lundberg, Ferdinand 26
Luxenbourg, Rosa 7
Lvov, Prince Georgi 310

M

Maclean 284
Malachy 168
Mandell 85
Marotti, Micol 195
Marshal Kesselring 49
Marshall, George C. 49,
    0, 53, 72, 78
Martin 100
Marx, Karl 6, 7, 21, 22, 321
Mason 95

Masonry   xiii, 364
Masonic Order   13, 14
Mazzini, Giusseppe   14, 28, 90
McArthur, Douglas   88, 89, 96
McLuhan, Marshall   201
McNamara, Robert   89
Mendelsohn Bank   36
Menzhinsky, V.   324
Mikoyan   xv, 67, 220
Mobley, William   336
Model, Field Marshal   80
Molotov   230
Monroe Doctrine   24, 28
Montini, Giovanni Battista   164
Montgomery, Viscount   73, 173, 174
Morelli   181
Morgan, J.P.   85, 98, 102
Morgenthau, Henry   69, 70
Morton, Frederic   104, 332
Moyne, Lord   111
Mulroney, Brian   224

N

Napoleon   17, 19
Nathan Rothschild's England   21
National Socialists   32, 34
Nagoya   xvi
Napoleon   232
Nato and the Warsaw Pact Are One,   7
Naziism   32, 35, 36
Nechayev, Sergey   312, 325
New Deal   38
Nicholas, General   309
Nietzche   239
Nihilists   15
Nixon, Richard   333
Noetzlin, Edouard   107

O

O'Brien ffrench, Conrad   219
O'Casey, Sean   7
O'Dea, Fabian   284
Ochorowicz, Dr. Jules   172, 180
One World   26
One-World Dictatorship   86
One-World Government   3, 26, 85
Opel   35
Operation Keelhaul   xvii, 83
Order of Lenin   xii
Order of the Illuminati   4, 12
Ouendyke   226

P

Pacific Triangle   8
Panic of 1907   25
Patton, George S.   53, 79
Peshkova, Ekaterina   328
Philby, Harold Kim   284, 299, 302
Philby, Sir John   301
Phillipson, Franz   107
Piao, Lin   89
Pike, Albert   xiii, 16, 22, 28, 94
Plato   170
Pope Paul VI   165
Pope Pious XII   166, 173
President Buchanan   23

Q

Quebec Conference   49, 50
Queensborough, Lady   364
Quigley, Carroll   xv, 29, 30, 46, 74, 95, 98

R

Rabinovich   229
RADL   82
Raine, Kathleen   249
Ramsey, Captain A.M.H.   38
Reagan, Ronald   351
Rear Admiral Theobold   45
Red Army   3, 55
Red Shield   3, 17
Reed, Douglas   39
Repington   108
Reynolds, Lorna   7
Richet, Dr. Charles   176
Robertson, William   108
Rockefeller   35, 85, 311, 351
Roncalli, Angelo
    Giuseppe   166, 167
Roosevelt, Franklin D.   xii, xv,
    4, 22, 36, 37, 38, 45, 51, 53,
    54, 55, 56, 57, 60, 61, 66,
    86, 97, 100, 102
Rothschild, Edmond   104
Rothschild, Lionel   101, 110
Rothschild, Nathan   17
Rothschilds   3, 17, 18, 19, 20,
    22, 23, 26, 93, 98, 104, 107
Rudenko   339, 340
Rules of Engagement   89
Russian Army of Liberation   82

S

Samhain   4
Satan   94
Satanism   16
Schacht, Hjalmar Horace
    Greely   34, 100
Schiff   85
Schiff, Jacob   25, 107, 225, 311
Schuyler, Montgomery   225
Schweitzer, Albert   178, 179
Scott, Walter   12

Second Socialist Interna-
    tional   22
Sedan   21
Semen-Firkin   229
Simons, George A.   313
Sivananda, Sri Swami   170
Shvernik, N.   294
Smoot, Dan   85
Socialism   92
Soloviev   371-81
Spencer, Herbert   170
Spinoza   170
Stafford, David   220
Stalin, Joseph   xii, xv, xvii,
    61, 62, 66, 78, 82, 84, 102,
    220, 230, 231, 318, 319, 327
Standard Oil   33, 35
Star Wars   4
Stevens, Sir J.   179
Strindberg   3
Sutton, Antony C.   32, 35, 37
Swedenborg   246
Swift, Jonathan   258
Swinton, John   100
Switzerland   98

T

Talmud   93
Talmudic Pharisees   92
Ternes, Elmar   194
The Grey Men   xvii
The Rich and the Super
    Rich   26
The Third War   15
Trotsky, Leon   3, 6, 311, 313
Trudeau, Pierre   222, 276
Truman, Harry   71, 88
Tzara, Tristan   241

U

United Nations   86, 87, 88
United Nations Security

Council 88
Uranium 92   67
Urban renewal   xv, 26,
  29, 38, 74, 77, 79

V

Vacuum Oil Company   35
Van Impe, Jack   232
Versailles Treaty   32, 34
Vietnam   88
Vietnam War   89
Vlasov   83
von Bismarck, Otto   20
von Hindenburg, Paul   34
von Lersner   56
von Papen, Franz   55

W

Walker, Walton   89
Walton, Russ   96
Warburg, Max   107, 312
Warburg, Paul   25, 85
Wars   88
Washington, George   28
Waterloo   19
Weill   228
Weimer Republic   33
Weishaupt, Adam   xiii, 4, 6,
  12, 13, 22, 38, 90
Weizmann, Chaim   39, 40, 111
Wellington   18
White Paper   39, 40, 41
Wiesenthal, Simon   276
Wilkes Booth, John   24
Wilton, John   225
Wilson, Woodrow   xiii, 25, 28,
  38, 97, 101
Wise, Stephen Rabbi   38, 97,
  100, 101, 106
World War I   xiv, 14, 28, 29,
  42, 53, 59
World War II   xiv, 41, 42, 46,
  54, 57, 59, 71, 99
World War III   xiv
World-wide conspiracy   7
Wright, Peter   272

Y

Yagoda   324
Yalta   78
Yeats, W.B.   7, 194, 242, 244,
  247, 249
Yezhov, Nikolai   324
Young Plan   100